The Course of Landscape Architecture

A History of our Designs on the Natural World, from Prehistory to the Present

THE COURSE OF LAND SCAPE ARCHI TECTURE

Christophe Girot

Thames & Hudson

In memory of Michel Corajoud, master of the clearing in the clearing

Cover image: Atelier Girot, Ilmar Hurkxkens.

First published in the United Kingdom in 2016 by Thames & Hudson Ltd,
181a High Holborn, London WC1V 7QX

The Course of Landscape Architecture © 2016 Christophe Girot

Designed by Praline (Al Rodger, David Tanguy)

British Library Cataloguing-in-Publication Data
A catalogue record for this book is available from the British Library

ISBN 978-0-500-34297-8

Printed and bound in China by Toppan Leefung Printing Limited

To find out about all our publications, please visit
www.thamesandhudson.com

There you can subscribe to our e-newsletter, browse or download
our current catalogue, and buy any titles that are in print.

Contents

Foreword 6
Between the Human and the Non-Human

Introduction 8
Imagine Landscape

1. Roots 14
On the Origins of Landscapes
Avebury, England
Bagh-i Fin, Iran

2. Hydraulic Civilizations 44
The Geometry of Water in Landscapes
Faiyum Oasis, Egypt

3. From Temenos to Physis 68
Sacred Landscapes in Greece
Delphi, Greece

4. Of Villas and Woods 92
Roman and Barbarian Landscapes
Hadrian's Villa, Italy

5. The Rule of Faith 114
Santa María de Poblet, Spain

6. Gardens of Perspective 144
Architectural Landscapes in the Renaissance
Villa Lante, Italy

7. The Measure of Reason 172
Vaux-le-Vicomte, France

8. Gravity 200
The Constant of Nature
Rousham, England

9. Combustion 232
Escape into the Exotic
Parc des Buttes-Chaumont, France

10. Acceleration 256
Landscapes of the 20th Century
Parc de la Villette, France

11. Terrain Vague 282
Prospect Cottage, England

12. Topology 304
Rediscovering Meaning in the Landscape
Sigirino Mound, Ticino, Switzerland

Afterword 334
Towards a Cultural Revolution of Nature

Notes 340
Bibliography 346
Acknowledgments 347
Sources of Illustrations 348
Index 349

Foreword
Between the Human and the Non-Human

In his poem 'To Posterity', published in 1939, shortly before the beginning of World War II, Bertolt Brecht wrote: 'Ah, what an age it is / When to speak of trees is almost a crime / For it is a kind of silence about injustice!'. Brecht's poem was a call for writers, artists and intellectuals to address the scandalous political change happening in front of their eyes. It was a critique of an artistic tradition that romanticizes nature and evades political controversies. But it was also a sorrow-filled acknowledgment that under the rising pressure of the Nazi regime, art could no longer refer to one of its oldest and dearest subject matters – landscape. Today, the situation is different. Today, it is almost a crime not to speak of trees when addressing political issues. I remember when I first encountered as a teenager the phenomenon of the forest dieback, the *Waldsterben*. Suddenly trees started to lose their leaves and die. Spectacular scenery such as in the forests of the Swiss Alps or the Black Forest in southern Germany were freckled with brown spots as if the entire landscape had been hit by a mysterious plague. The effects of the environmental pollution predicted in books such as Rachel Carson's *Silent Spring* (1962) or *The Limits to Growth* (1972) commissioned by the Club of Rome were now evident. The vanishing trees in Europe triggered a heated debate about the causes and consequences. After a couple of years, the forests recovered, but something had changed. To speak of trees was no longer a sign of escapism, but of activism.

When Brecht wrote his poem, nature was considered as fundamentally different from civilization. Brecht stood in a tradition that conceived nature and culture as binary poles opposing one another. With the forest dieback, however, this view began to alter. It became difficult to distinguish clearly between the natural and the man-made, in other words between the human and the non-human. And it became more and more evident that man was shaping nature through the large-scale interventions of industrialization, and most obviously in the treatment of forests. The 'Forest Principles' published by the United Nations at the Earth Summit in Rio, in 1992, considers 'all types of forests, both natural and planted' as 'essential to economic development and the maintenance of all forms of life'.[1] One generation after the Earth Summit in Rio we have certainty that the Earth's climate is changing as a result of industrialization. We know for sure that the rise in temperature, the increasing number of floods, droughts and storms are ultimately man-made. Nobody derided as romantics the delegates of the United Nations Framework Convention on Climate Change in Paris in December 2015 who wore pins made of dried coconut fronds as a sign of solidarity with the Marshall Islands threatened by the rising sea level. And there is little doubt that the change in climate that brought several years without rain and also famine to Syria was one of the causes for the civil war and thus for one of the biggest refugee crises in history.[2]

On the level of theoretical discourse, the supposition that nature is not a given but that it is formed by humans finds its expression in the concept of the 'Anthropocene', in other words the hypothesis that mankind has inscribed itself into the history of the Earth.[3] The Anthropocene has proved to be a fruitful concept because it provides a common ground between artists and scientists, architects and writers, specialists and laymen. It might be too early to decide if the Anthropocene, or the more general notion of 'climate change', is a new paradigm of contemporary societies, a conceptual horizon, so to speak. It is still uncertain if this horizon will have the same impact on our thinking and acting as the concept of the Cold War and 'mutually assured destruction', which prevailed from the 1950s to the 1980s. But already it is evident that the experience of the strange behaviour of the weather and the encounter with the tragedy of people forced to leave their homes because of the changing climate obliges us to think beyond our immediate environment, in larger dimensions, both temporally and spatially.

The acknowledgment that man shapes nature has not only heightened our concern about nature turning itself against us, it has also moved us closer to nature. On the one hand this is in the guise of a growing appetite for domesticated natural beauty, for retreat and recreation, for the life outdoors. On the other hand it is in the guise of the desire to involve the natural in city centres, be it by transforming wastelands into new parks, by making cities green or by introducing urban gardening. Interestingly, it is rarely the 'untouched' landscapes that are popular today. Most attractive are sites where the man-made and the non-human meet and interact, where the present and the past interact, be it an industrial ruin or a former religious centre.

The shift in perspective is the reason, I would argue, why landscape architecture has moved centre stage. Long considered an appendix to architecture and urban planning, a rather futile specialization at the margins of 'serious' design and planning, it is currently finding its place at the intersection of various disciplines. Christophe Girot's book is thus a timely and a much needed contribution to the current debate. It unfolds a vast panorama of landscape architecture in the widest sense and makes accessible examples from different geographic areas and different historic periods. And it presents landscape architecture as a practice of synthesis and connection, where the tiny scale of a plant and the huge scale of the climate relate to each other. Landscapes, Girot argues, are interesting namely because of their hybridity, their internal contradictions, their anachronisms and complexities. They are shaped by geological transformations, the weather, vegetation, but also by hydraulic constructions in the form of irrigation or flood control, by agriculture, by infrastructure of commerce and trade.

Unlike many other publications on landscape architecture, the focus of this book lies not primarily in works by specific landscape architects, nor primarily on authors. In analogy to Bernard Rudofsky's legendary book *Architecture without Architects: A Short Introduction to Non-Pedigreed Architecture* (1964), Girot shows connections between various artefacts from prehistoric times to the present, which are traditionally not considered within the genealogy of landscape architecture. His book is not a survey of canonical landscape architecture. On the contrary it suggests that such a canon does not exist, or that if it did then it ought to be revised. The book demonstrates that the scope of landscape architecture is broader in space than the scope of architecture, which concentrates on individual buildings and their immediate surroundings. Landscape architecture has a wider horizon and takes into consideration the flow of waters, the shape of topography, but also the movement of people and the exchange of commodities. The book further demonstrates that landscape architecture is broader in time than urban planning, with its notorious lack of memory and its chronological horizon of no more than one to two generations. Landscape architecture deals with the different hours of the day, the different seasons of the year, but also with the history of civilization and the history of the Earth.

A crucial element for landscape architecture is the aesthetic experience. The time it takes to walk through a garden or over a defunct field, with the smell of the grass, or rusty metal, the sensation of humidity, the sound of animals or cars, but also the tactile sensation of the ground under one's feet, the unforeseen incidents, the mixture of remembered images and actual perception, all blending into an experience which is different from that of the *flâneur* in the city centre or the visitor to an individual building. Girot has travelled a great deal over the years and shares his discoveries with the reader. The result is an immensely rich source of inspirations, which outlines the terrain of landscape architecture. The narrative and images of the book imply that landscape architecture is not so much located at the margins of the categories of architecture and urban planning, but rather moves dynamically among these categories and sets them in motion. It shows landscape architecture as a practice that opens up the field for the unexpected, for the experimental and the playful.

Philip Ursprung
Professor for the History of Art and Architecture,
Department of Architecture, ETH Zurich

Introduction
Imagine Landscape

'This is the place where we act with imagination, not so much by modifying the world, but rather by preparing it.'
J. M. G. Le Clézio[1]

Over the course of time, landscapes have been transformed through the extraordinary workings of the imagination. Places have been converted from their original, natural state via a gradual process of abstraction. Our manipulation of space and settled exploitation of the land have created a range of artefacts, each with their own atmosphere: fields, dams, ditches, groves, avenues, sanctuaries, parks, gardens and terraces like those of the Villa Noailles in Grasse (1950), to give but a few examples [0.2].[2] Taken as a whole, these artefacts reveal how nature has been reshaped by human culture throughout history. Landscape architecture has profoundly influenced the way in which society experiences and appreciates its natural surroundings, as in the case of Albert Park (1885) in Auckland, where an imported Victorian landscape style meets local trees like the Moreton Bay Fig [0.1]. Our reception of landscapes has changed radically over time; and one might argue that we have now reached the point where we can no longer rely on the models of the past and must question their relevance to the present. It goes without saying that climate change, the depletion of the environment and demographic trends will dramatically affect our future lives, having a direct impact on the way landscapes are shaped, used and regarded. Today, the empirical approach to environmental problem-solving has in many instances superseded aesthetic concerns, with far-reaching consequences for our general understanding and conception of nature.

This paradigm shift towards a more quantitative and scientifically guided approach to the design of nature is intrinsically ahistorical, and spells the end of a millennia-old intricate – not to say intimate – relationship between humankind and landscape. This development is worrying for, if landscape architecture can no longer rise to the challenge

0.1 (opposite) Albert Park, Auckland, New Zealand.
The native tree (Moreton Bay Fig) is used here with strong cultural connotations. This late 19th-century park is a good example of the way in which an established northern landscape tradition has been transposed to the Antipodes, while using local vegetation to suit the environment.

0.2 The Villa Noailles, Grasse, France.
Some old olive groves set in lawn on stepped terraces frame a cistern and topiary below. The garden by Charles de Noailles is a construct of the 1950s, where productive minimalism meets the beautiful intentionally.

0.2

0.3

of imagining the next significant bond between humankind and its natural environment, it will simply disappear as an art, to the benefit of science and engineered sustainability. The aim of this book is to present a long-due assessment of this radical shift in knowledge and values. It places the reader in both an introspective and retrospective mode with regard to the fundamentals of our landscape imagination.

Landscapes have undergone various stages of development through history, as human hands changed the wilderness and cultivated the desert into more structured and sacred environments. The Cedron Valley and Mount of Olives in Jerusalem is the sublime expression of such a convergence [0.3].[3] As landscapes evolved, they unmistakably reflected an extraordinary power of transformation and charted a changing relationship with the world around us. They have always mirrored the religious and political forces in society, and each transition demonstrates a response to the sacred beliefs and the technical progress of a given period. This is still true today, and the present book will draw little distinction between the powerful influence of oracles in ancient Mesopotamia and the blind faith we currently place in scientific predictions. Transformations in the landscape are part of an ingenious process of transmission from generation to generation, but with each step forward these attitudes become increasingly distanced from their original bond with nature and the early archetypes. Despite their great age, these

early landscape structures, such as the paradise garden and palace in Pasargadae, have proven extremely resilient and are still identifiable on the ground today [0.4].[4] Although some doubts prevail as to the proper way to record and depict these archetypes – owing to the absence of living traces of the earliest walled gardens and forest clearings, the scarcity of remains and the lack of reliable written records – this does not necessarily diminish their importance. More often than not, uncovering layers of meaning in a landscape is a task best left to the imagination, which can help decipher the beliefs and attitudes behind the making of each place.

Like so many pieces of a secular puzzle, landscapes are tied into their historical, environmental and cultural contexts. Even the alpine meadows in Davos are structured and drained for the purpose of cattle herding [0.5]. Thus each transformation not only contributes to a better understanding of the genesis of a landscape, but also reveals the deep economic forces at work, as seen in a fenced-in chalet garden [0.7]. The impact of successive epochs is an indelible part of our landscape legacy in all parts of the world, substantially affecting the way we perceive, experience and shape our environment. These many different periods put together form a landscape reality, a complex mosaic of intentions and events that have shaped the world we occupy. Intricate societal mechanisms have transformed and instrumentalized nature over time, making any direct relationship with it less tangible.[5]

0.3 The Cedron Valley and Mount of Olives, Jerusalem.
This sacred landscape, with its old gnarled olive and cypress trees, its cemeteries of stone and rock-hewn tombs, is one of unfathomable symbolic significance for three monotheistic religions. Believed to be the place of the coming of the Messiah and the resurrection of the dead, it is a holy site – a place of passage and absolute natural reduction. It is our appreciation of a landscape as a cultural artefact and religious symbol that is represented here.

0.4 Ruins of King Cyrus's palace and gardens, Pasargadae, Iran.
Water from the Pasargadae River, visible on the left, was fed into the rectilinear rills and channels of the ancient Achaemenid palace and its luxuriant pleasure gardens enclosed within thick adobe walls. This offered pleasing shade in strong contrast to the parched landscape of the desert beyond.

0.5 Drainage rill across a meadow in Davos, Switzerland.
Specific drainage structures, such as this rill, and ancient pastoral practices in the Swiss Alps create the image of nature that we confer on these mountains today. Landscape in this sense is always an artefact that expresses a balance between the needs of society, seasonal customs and natural conditions. The Swiss Alps are heavily grazed, but still contribute to our understanding of nature.

0.4

0.5

It is almost impossible to imagine a return to a state of natural innocence today, even though we are being asked to promote the 'renaturalization' of devastated areas for the wellbeing of society [0.6]. Exactly which society is being considered here, and on what symbols and values is its appreciation of nature ultimately based?

0.6

0.7

0.6 Schöneberger Südgelände Park, Berlin, Germany.
Spontaneous vegetation growing undisturbed for decades in the bombed-out rubble of this rail yard in Berlin has paradoxically served as a model for a new kind of landscape aesthetic, which can also be seen in some of the most prestigious projects including the High Line in New York. It is ironic that contemporary landscape architecture finds more inspiration in the ruins of past civilizations than in their purposefully constructed achievements.

0.7 High altitude alpine garden, Switzerland.
The word garden derives from *garto* in Old German, which literally means 'fenced-in'. This high altitude alpine garden shows clearly how a landscape needs to be fenced in for the requirements of cultivation. Evidence for such a response to ambient factors has led to a specific genealogy of landscape types found across the world from the earliest times on.

0.8 Oerliker Park, Zurich, Switzerland, 2001.
This new park of the early 21st century is made on heavily contaminated industrial ground, with new housing built around it. Designed by the office of Zulauf, Seippel, Schweingruber with the artist Christoph Haerle, the park trees planted in a tight grid are meant to cleanse the ground naturally over several decades. It is a place in transition, imbued with hopes of a better landscape in the future.

0.9 Mauerpark, Berlin, Germany, 1994.
Built on the ruins of a no-man's-land between East and West Berlin, the park plays with a reduced landscape palette akin to the numerous *terrains vagues* that were once strewn across the city before the fall of the Berlin Wall. The park's success is owed in part to its relative isolation, and also to a subdued design statement by Gustav Lange, consisting of a large area of grass which emphasizes the void. It is a void that recalls the past, but also invites large crowds on hot summer nights for memories in the future.

0.8

0.9

This book will reflect on different stages of landscape transformation in light of their contemporary relevance and will pave the way towards a more critical approach to nature and the way we shape it. It is not meant as a nostalgic glance at artefacts from the past; rather, my hope is that the examples from across the centuries will nourish a stronger sense of continuity and purpose. It will stress the importance and significance of cultural specificity and identity over systemic thinking. And, perhaps most importantly, it will bring valuable insight into the mechanisms that lie behind the poetics of space and creative invention.

The realities of current climatic and demographic change have undeniably brought us to the threshold of a new period that some scientists have labelled the 'Anthropocene'. Landscape architects are being asked to produce 'responsible' design and to accept their role as 'preparators' in buffering environmental degradation. Still, we ought to question the dominant moralistic posture behind the ecological and the sustainable, and allow ourselves to demystify this vision of nature critically, while acknowledging the reality of new necessities. Oerliker Park in Zurich (2001), by the office of Zulauf, Seippel, Schweingruber, planted on a highly contaminated site, promises a return to a better environment through the remedial action of trees over the next three decades [0.8].[6] Nature is thus being re-created on severely disturbed terrains. The same could be said of the abandoned

rail yards of Schöneberger Südgelände in Berlin – literally, as well as in a broader ecological sense [0.6].[7] However, this conceptual inversion where design is no longer considered as significant is something of a contradiction, for landscapes have always resulted from strong formal acts upon nature and not just environmental modalities. Landscape architecture must continue to serve as a cultural beacon despite the current moral imperatives of 'biopolitics' that contradict it.[8] But even as designated 'preparators', it is precisely our ability to cultivate a strong poetic response to human needs and beliefs that will help us find better expressions of nature. Mauerpark in Berlin (1994) is the direct expression of such a societal conjunction; its success relies not so much on elaborate aesthetic constructs, as on the possibility of freedom of assembly through informal social organizations [0.9].[9]

Through a critical understanding of this genealogy, landscape architecture can serve as a major force in the definition of our future environment. The aim is to decrypt an intelligence of nature that has prevailed for millennia, deeply marking our collective appreciation of landscapes. It promotes a belief in our capacity to reinvent, with confidence, a constructive imagination. People have always needed a clear symbolic expression of nature. May this book be a plea for a return to the fundamentals of a culture of landscape true to the values of human balance and meaning that have nurtured and enriched countless generations.

1. Roots
On the Origins of Landscape

'The bird of gardens sang unto the rose,
New blown in the clear dawn: "Bow down thy head!
As fair as thou within this garden close,
Many have bloomed and died." She laughed and said,
"That I am born to fade grieves not my heart
But never was it a true lover's part
To vex with bitter words his love's repose."'

Hafez of Shiraz[1]

Everywhere we look, we see nature only through the lens of the man-made. Intervention in the landscape has become a reference point by which we distinguish and experience the natural world. Landscape architecture is concerned with places and environments that are continuously under the influence of human control. Whereas geological factors and the forces of weather, water and topography shaped the Earth over the course of millions of years, humans have had a significant impact on the environment only over the last ten millennia. Yet in terms of human culture this duration is almost an eternity, extending back into the farthest regions of sedentary prehistory, at the confines of our collective memory. The roots of an old beech tree growing on top of an artificial chalk bank at Avebury are a testimony to a powerful image of nature forged by culture [1.0].

The poetic and religious meanings of early landscapes conferred a sense of sacredness on individual places, each uniquely crafted for a particular purpose. Whether these environments were used for providing sustenance, as dwelling places or to mark the rites of life and death, the art of landscape has symbolically set them apart. The depiction of the walled garden of Nebamun in Thebes, Egypt (1350 BCE), is a paradise full of fruits, fish, birds and tree spirits and the promise of a better afterlife [1.1].[2] These beliefs are still an intrinsic part of our religious culture and continue to evolve through time. Landscape is evidence of an accrued intelligence of place through topological transformation and

1.0 (opposite) Ancient beech tree at the east entrance of Avebury henge, England.
The tree's position on the outer bank above the internal ditch coincides with the original edge of the Neolithic forest clearing. The beautifully contorted roots result from the stress of growing on the dry substrate of the artificial chalk bank.

1.1 Wall painting from the tomb of Nebamun, Thebes, Egypt.
This 18th Dynasty painting depicts a walled garden. Taken together, the central lotus pond with fish and ducks surrounded by neat rows of date palms, sycamores, pomegranates and other fruit trees, symbolize fertility and order.

1.1

an exchange of techniques, beliefs and actions. The location of a particular terrain, its specific arrangement within borders and the manner in which permanent and seasonal vegetation is handled touch not only on the constructed materiality and pragmatism of an individual culture, but also on the aesthetic and symbolic level as a source that nourishes beauty and reverence for nature.

Landscape results from repeated spatial interventions that bring about meaningful changes on the land. Each period in Western history reveals particular stages of development through a range of artefacts and transformations that interact with, and gradually uproot, older lore. We can well imagine that forms of tribal belief led to the creation of the first artificial forest clearings, when ritual ring dances holding hands were staged around a fire. Likewise, we can easily picture the earliest gardens where, alongside the necessity of basic food production, rites of love and fertility – as well as those of life and death – were staged within its four walls. This idealized form of nature would have helped forge strong symbols and a sense of common destiny. An ancient hillside in Gortyn in Crete reveals a topology that speaks of a sacred past over 4,000 years ago of which we have little clue [1.4]. In essence, landscape is nothing more than a chosen form of topography responding to cultural demands, and gives an accurate portrait of a society's sensitivity to the sacred meaning and the features of the natural environment.

To look for the origins of landscape is hazardous. In fact, both architecture and landscape began to appear with the first sedentary settlements at a moment of climatic change towards the end of the last ice age. The low-lying landlocked lake that later became the Black Sea was the only important source of fresh water for a large region. It seems that most Indo-European and Semitic languages stem precisely from this area where people gathered around the water. This was perhaps the closest humankind ever got to Eden; the bountiful harvests allowed for the development of various crafts such as metallurgy, pottery, weaving, house-building and boat-building.

According to this theory, debated in terms of scale and date ever since, original settlements around the lake were severely disrupted. A massive glacial melt in Greenland, caused a sudden rise in sea levels around the world, leading to the last major cataclysm to affect our planet [1.2]. The Black Sea is thought to have risen more than 50 metres (164 feet) within a year, until it was level with the Mediterranean, dramatically changing the local landscape and prompting a massive population exodus [1.3]. The latest established date for this event is c. 7400 BCE.[3] This same flood would also have cut off the British Isles from the European continent, forming the English Channel.[4]

The cataclysm was sudden and provoked massive upheaval, drowning forests and villages and forcing

The Deluge myth was first transmitted by oral tradition over centuries through the folklore of the region of the Middle East, appearing subsequently in the earliest texts such as the Epic of Gilgamesh. In those days, a physical phenomenon of such magnitude, caused by climate change, could only be explained by some divine act of punishment or providence [1.2].

1.2

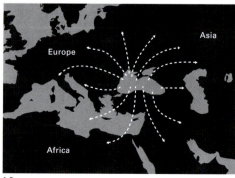

1.3

1.4

1.2 The Deluge.
'The Deluge' refers to a dramatic event that occurred at a time of major climate change. Not only must have it generated genuine heavenly fear in the peoples living in the region, it also forced them to flee and settle elsewhere, and to adapt. This moment coincides with the birth of both landscape and architecture.

1.3 Map showing hypothetical movement of Indo-European, Semitic and Turkic tribes caused by the Black Sea Deluge.
Before the flood occurred, the lake that became the Black Sea was an important and reliable fresh-water source, and cultural landscape practices may have originated here before being disseminated elsewhere.

1.4 Ancient landscape, Gortyn, Crete.
After the flooding of the Black Sea there was a long process of acclimatization and acculturation in neighbouring regions. This ancient landscape above Gortyn in Crete is a good example of such cultural influences in Europe resulting from practices originating in Anatolia.

Societies such as the Minoan civilization, which first brought agricultural practices to the island of Crete along with the adoption of early female fertility cults, achieved a much closer bond with nature than others that followed in Greece and in Rome. Although little is known about life in these early palatial cultures of Crete, the extraordinary sense of sacredness, beauty and proportion emanating from the cultivated sites of Gortyn, Phaistos, Knossos and Zakros leave no doubt as to the deeper faith in a goddess of nature that drove them to reach this level of refinement [1.4].

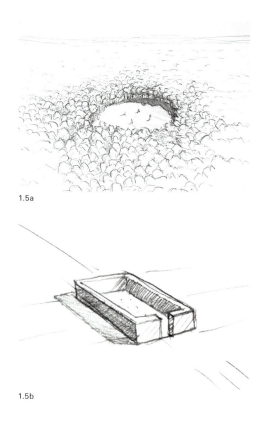

1.5a

1.5b

1.5a, 1.5b Two archetypes.
The forest clearing and the walled garden form the basis of a genealogy of Western landscape architecture. The differences between the two stem essentially from distinct climatic and topological conditions, but it is precisely the cultural juxtaposition, the mixing and hybridization of these two 'chromosomes' over time, that is of particular interest.

1.6 Walled gardens and fields, Yazd, Iran.
Adobe walled 'paradise' gardens containing fruit orchards stand among irrigated fields in the desert region of Yazd in Iran. The grid of main water lines is etched by a hoe into a consistent agricultural topology, with the short side of each garden, like the furrows, running perpendicular to the incline of the terrain.

1.7 Hambledon Hill, England.
This hill fort was originally a Neolithic clearing in the form of a causewayed enclosure on top of a chalk hill, formed by the intentional removal of material from the outcrop at a time when the surrounding landscape was still densely forested. A continuous ditch and wooden palisade, built with the help of antler picks, offered protection. The clearing was used for ritual and mortuary purposes.

1.8 Stonehenge, England.
The ring of stones at Stonehenge, intended for ritual and funerary purposes, was built on an older forest clearing consisting of a circular outer ditch and an inner bank. The Neolithic stone uprights with mortised lintels are ordered concentrically on a flattened circular plane and aligned with the solstices.

1.6

1.7

1.8

populations to flee. Faced with the need to find sustenance, these forced migrants resettled by inscribing simple spatial forms upon a given piece of forest or land. We can discern two early types of spaces: the forest clearing and the walled garden – the original 'chromosomes' in the long genealogy of Western landscape architecture [1.5a, 1.5b]. Both archetypes reflect a strong transformative attitude towards nature, as humans began to distinguish themselves from their natural surroundings.

In temperate forests, on sites like Hambledon Hill in England, trees were felled to create a patch of open sky in the dense canopy, bringing light to the forest floor [1.7].[5] In arid regions walled gardens were built on foothills overlooking expanses of desert. Water was channelled along the terrain or underground; every drop was then distributed to plants, which were tended to provide sustenance and shade in a scorching environment, as can be seen in Yazd, Iran, today [1.6]. Sacred landscapes gradually evolved around these two archetypes: artificial forest clearings were circled by deep ditches studded with impressive rings of stones, and walled desert sanctuaries came to harbour exquisite shade gardens or chapels at their heart. These enabled the appearance of ritual constructs specific to each culture that mirrored the celestial movements and their seasonal occurrences. At Stonehenge for instance, the land was shaped and completed with huge blue stones standing on end brought in from Wales

[1.8]. The stone ring became not only an instrument for keeping track of the seasons, but also a soundscape where the stones were struck to sound on ritual occasions.[6] Landscape was about making sense of the world and providing a fundamental model for cultural transformation.

The forest clearing

The clearing marks a break from the surrounding wilderness. Some were dedicated to hunting, and others to early farming. Sacred clearings created an inner sanctuary, consisting of a vast circular space surrounded by a ditch separating it from the forest. Totems and palisades enclosed these open areas, transforming them into spaces for polytheistic rites. The tree was understood as a symbol of life, light and regeneration, as we can see in the figure of Brigit and the birch tree sacred to early Celtic and Nordic cultures.[7] Much later, once the sacred tree had died and totems weathered away, henges, introducing stone circles, replaced them. The stones first embodied the defunct sacred trees, and only gradually became instruments to trace celestial movements.[8] These sacred spaces were soon linked by a network of paths – the first large-scale landscape structures to see the light in Europe.

1.9

Avebury, England

The best surviving example of the early type of clearing is the ring at Avebury, located 30 km (19 miles) north of Stonehenge, in England. It stands in the gently rolling chalk hills of Wiltshire, where a clearing was made using primitive tools in a dense forest of English oak, beech and lime trees almost 5,000 years ago. Compared with Stonehenge, the landscape of Avebury provides a more complete glimpse into the surrounding network of avenues, rings and artificial hills that was constructed during that period.

During the Mesolithic period, Britain had still formed part of the greater European landmass. This connection ended in the 8th millennium BCE, during roughly the same period as the Black Sea flood.[9] It is was not until the beginning of the 4th millennium BCE, in the early Neolithic period, that older, nomadic tribes of hunter-gatherers were superseded by new peoples arriving by boat from the continent with domesticated animals and crops. In time, as this advanced civilization of tribes formed into sizeable communities, it began to create alliances along established thoroughfares. This is the context in which the Avebury henge first appeared [1.10].[10] It must be understood as one of the first cultural endeavours in the region on such a scale, and would have allowed for large gatherings within the expanse of the forest. Such places quite naturally became nexuses of human interaction, propagating innovation that in turn fostered further cultural change.

Rings appeared in the Neolithic throughout Europe, from Spain to Scandinavia, such as that at Ismantorp, Sweden [1.9]. Clearly the largest and mightiest megalithic complex to be have been constructed in Britain, Avebury was systematically altered over the course of 600 years as successive generations built on the work of their forefathers. The ditch, which is 10 metres (33 feet) deep and 20 metres (66 feet) wide, has been carbon-dated to between 3300 BCE and 2630 BCE, whereas the ring of sarsen stones was raised somewhat later, between 2900 BCE and 2600 BCE (the neighbouring structure at Silbury Hill was recently dated to around 2600 BCE, thus making the West Kennet Long Barrow, built around 3650 BCE by far the oldest structure by several centuries).[11]

We can imagine long ropes produced from the bark of linden trees being used as radius cords to trace the ring's arc, over 420 metres (460 yards) in diameter, from a central pivotal point, such as a single totem or tree [1.11a, 1.11b]. What matters most at Avebury is that the change in landscape practice and the introduction of pastoral agriculture allowed

1.9 Ismantorp ringfort, Öland, Sweden.
This ringfort was built on the island of Öland almost two millennia ago. It is interesting to note how the forest clearing archetype, which appeared in the Neolithic, subsequently spread across the whole of Europe from Spain to Scandinavia.

1.10 Plan of Avebury, England.
Avebury is the largest henge monument in England, a Neolithic clearing defined by an outer bank and an inner ditch constructed within an original oak forest. Four ceremonial entrances lead to a central levelled area, with a great outer circle of sarsen stones and two smaller inner ones.

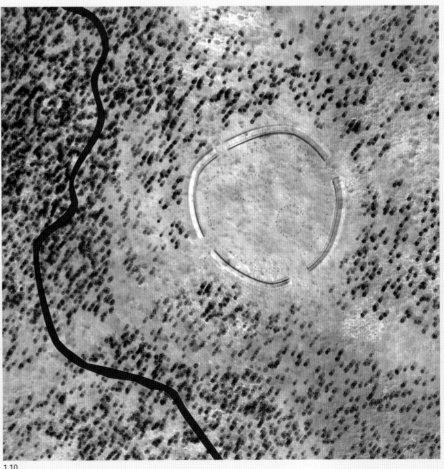

1.10

1.11a

1.11b

1.11a, 1.11b Avebury before and after.
Views of Avebury before and after the creation of the henge in Neolithic times. The dense oak forest had already been partially cleared for early scattered pastoral and agricultural practices. Then, later in the Neolithic period – in the mid-3rd millennium BCE – the Avebury henge appears as a vast clearing. The West Kennet Avenue leads to the horizon, connecting with the Ridgeway. On the upper right Silbury Hill looms over the Swallowhead Spring of the River Kennet.

1.12 Aerial view of Avebury.
Today a hamlet occupies the centre of the henge, with roads crossing the circle. The bank and ditch are mostly intact, but many stones have disappeared, quarried to build the houses and church. Instead of a dense forest, open fields and grazing meadows now surround the monument. The sharp differentiation between the inner clearing and outer forest has gone, leaving the strong, flat topology of the circle.

1.12

local inhabitants the freedom, the time and enough food to support the construction of such a monument.

By their very nature, such strategic sites provided an opportunity for local groups to control communication lines by secular and / or religious means, which thus in turn allowed them to garner social prestige, power and wealth. In the case of Avebury, the surrounding area probably housed the Neolithic equivalent of a city; it is situated where the Ridgeway thoroughfare, which stretches for 400 km (250 miles) and links Dorset in southern England with the Norfolk coast in eastern England, intersects with the source of the River Kennet, a main tributary of the River Thames, connecting the site to the North Sea. In its grandness of scale, time and space, as well as the symbolic vocabulary that separates off and encloses the inner part of the ring, Avebury reveals itself an important ritual site.

There is much speculation about the rituals that would have taken place in the wider landscape of Avebury, comprising the ring, West Kennet Avenue, Swallowhead Spring (source of the River Kennet), West Kennet Long Barrow and Silbury Hill [1.17]. But what interests us more are the principles that led to its precise topology and the way in which existing paths and natural features, such as the thoroughfare and Swallowhead Spring, were integrated into the overall design. It is particularly interesting to note the early attention to topography at Avebury and how the site's

rolling, chalky surface was effectively scraped and flattened into a vast circular table intended for ritual gatherings [1.18].

The henge is equally intriguing, consisting of a large circular bank and a deep ditch just inside, dug using antler picks [1.14] and filled over time with skulls, amulets and offerings. No one can explain why the ditch is on the inner side of the circle, for this arrangement runs contrary to the most elementary principles of defence – unless, that is, we imagine ourselves inhabiting the ancestral forest and looking out, in which case the clearing itself becomes the 'outside' world [1.21]. There is an extraordinary sense of scale and purpose at Avebury; it marks a transition from an ancestral forest culture to a more open pastoral society, secured and framed by a ring of megalithic emblems [1.19].

1.13 Engraving of Avebury by William Stukeley.
This engraving records a section of what
remained of the original stone circle at the
beginning of the 18th century, with a sheep
pen on the bank ridge. The Diamond Stone still
stands at the edge of the road today; weighing
50 tons, it is the largest stone to remain
undisturbed in its original position at Avebury.

1.14 Antler pick.
The antler pick, the stone hoe and axe
were the basic tools used in early landscape
transformations for breaking ground and
purposefully adding or removing natural
material from a particular place.

1.15 View of the north-eastern bank, Avebury.
Originally this bank would have been twice as
high and appeared as a stark white chalk slope,
with a dense forest canopy as backdrop. The
inner area with its sacred rings of sarsen stones
would have been hidden from outside view. The
centre was artificially levelled, the entire chalk
surface scraped flat to provide a vast flat area
for ritual gatherings.

1.13

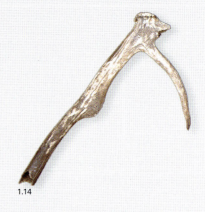

1.14

1.15

1.16

1.16 **Reconstruction of the Avebury region.**
Silbury Hill rises in the foreground, with the Avebury henge in the background. Both sites stand on flattened areas that have been cleared of trees. The relationship between these separate clearings and their avenues remains a complete enigma. Nonetheless, Avebury introduced an approach to landscape clearing that was to be replicated countless times again.

1.17 **Silbury Hill today.**
The Swallowhead Spring, just visible in the background, probably provided the water for a circular ditch around Silbury Hill. Material to create the cone came from scraping the surrounding clearing and ditch. It probably took decades, if not centuries, of work to raise the mound to its original height. No one knows what was staged here, but it is clearly the expression of a powerful society.

1.17

1.18

1.19

1.18 Inner edge of the Avebury ditch.
The remnants of the large outer ring of stones stand above the edge of the ditch. It is thought that the stones could have had an acoustic function, involving reverberation or echo, while the flat inner circular area provided a vast space for ritual gatherings; it is probably the closest ancestor of the fair ground and village green.

1.19 Reconstruction of a section of the bank and ditch.
The bank was almost 10 metres (33 feet) high and the ditch over 10 metres (33 feet) deep and twice as wide. The exposed white chalk surface must have created a dramatic contrast with the dark native forest beyond.

1.20

1.20 Section across the centre of the Avebury henge.
This section reveals how the bank and ditch worked together to create an enclosure. The small southern ring of stones in the foreground was roughly 100 metres (328 feet) in diameter. The man-made flattened surface of the clearing, with its intentional architecture and geometry, and set in the natural wooded hills of Wiltshire, stands out strongly.

1.21 Avebury ditch.
Originally deeper and steeper than it is today, the ditch protected and controlled entry to the ritual ground, while leaving it open visually to the forest beyond.

1.21

The development of the forest clearing

Early forest clearings, whether sacred or profane, gradually evolved out of the dense temperate and boreal forests of Europe and Asia. Stone rings can be found from the Solovki archipelago in the Arctic Circle to the tip of the Iberian peninsula. The clearing became the standard landscape system for most temperate forest regions of the globe, as can be seen in a clearing in Davos [1.22]. Early forest clearings developed gradually into permanent settlements and maintained their original form well into the early Middle Ages, when Christian monasteries spread northwards through the European wilderness all the way to Scandinavia, repeating the practice of clearing the forest for the purposes of settlement. At that time the forest was host to countless ancestral demons and polytheistic beliefs; indeed, the English word 'forest' derives from the Latin *foris*, meaning the world 'outside' or 'beyond'.

During the Renaissance the concept of the forest clearing reappeared within the context of courtly gardens. By that time the countryside had undergone significant cultivation, and there remained but few original stands of forest. In the Renaissance gardens at the Villa Medici at Castello, near Florence, and at the Villa Lante and Villa Orsini, both near Viterbo, the forest was replanted around a clearing to re-create a *sacro bosco*, or 'sacred wood'. This marks the moment when, instead of resulting from the removal of trees in an existing forest, the clearing in fact becomes a construct: trees are planted around a void to reproduce an 'original' forest setting. This practice of replanting forest anew continued throughout the Baroque period (Vaux-le-Vicomte provided the first example) and into the English landscape movement of the 18th century, with an early example being the circular ring clearing drawn according to proportion around the Ionic temple at Chiswick House [1.24]. The earliest example of a larger landscaped forest to be found in England is Ray Wood at Castle Howard, Yorkshire [1.23]. The same trend spread farther to inform the design of urban parks, such as the Englischer Garten in Munich, Central Park in New York and the Buttes-Chaumont in Paris, and reappeared in more abstract form in 20th-century schemes such as Montjuïc in Barcelona, the Stadtpark in Hamburg and Aarhus University campus in Denmark [1.25].

The walled garden

In comparison to the humid reaches of north-western Europe, the arid regions of Eurasia and North Africa witnessed the development of an entirely different kind of landscape archetype. The walled garden enclosure is probably as old as the first settled home. Its four walls resemble those of a large house, but this patch of land is open to the sky, waiting for the rare and providential seed to be sown, watered and cared for.

1.22

1.23

1.22 Clearing above Davos, Switerzland.
If this meadow in the Swiss Alps was not hand mown or grazed each year, the forest would return in the space of a decade and the clearing would be gone. This familiar scene that has forged our understanding and appreciation of nature is therefore the result of a repeated cultural practice.

1.23 Clearing at Castle Howard, England.
Ray Wood to the left was planted artificially at the end of the 17th century to recreate the impression of a forest. The Mausoleum in the far distance, with its mortuary symbolism, is a reminder of one aspect and intrinsic meaning of the landscape and its sacred narrative.

1.24 Chiswick House, England.
The carefully crafted incline of the Orange Grove lawn framing the round pond at Chiswick House is meant to be sat upon, underlining the care that has been placed in the topology of clearings since Avebury. The clearing is recognized here as a strong cultural act that shapes our environment according to a certain idea of nature in which humankind finds its place.

1.25 Aarhus, Denmark.
The amphitheatre at the campus in Aarhus in Denmark was planted with oak trees in the 1930s by Carl Theodor Sørensen in the early phase of construction; they are now grown to their full size. The harmonious play of strong cultural artefacts like this amphitheatre in a rolling natural topography typical of the area makes this one of the most successful man-made landscapes in Denmark. The heritage of ancient gatherings in forest clearings is inherent in this project.

1.24

1.25

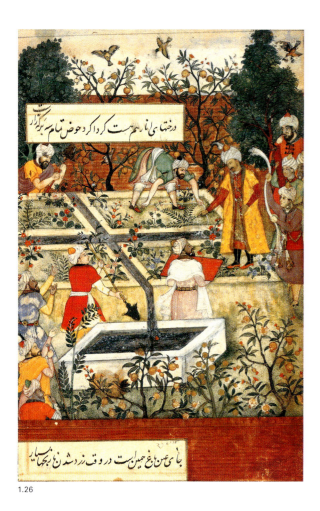

درختها ی انار هم هست کرداد که دوض تمام بر گرفتار

جای عین باغ همین است در وقت زرد شدن نان بجای انار

1.26

Our image of Eden, most famous of all gardens, most likely derives from the rich, cultivated lower plains of Mesopotamia, and the many gardens that grew there, thousands of years ago, remain vivid cultural symbols.[12] We can assume that the archetype of the walled garden – a re-creation of the paradise evoked in the biblical books of Genesis and the Song of Songs, and in the Epic of Gilgamesh – spread across the Fertile Crescent of the Middle East shortly after the Deluge.

Here, the understanding of nature extends to the selection, collection and propagation of appropriate specimens imported from elsewhere. Each plant acquires a particular place, meaning and purpose, as in the Garden of Fidelity built later in Kabul by the Mughal emperor Babur [1.26].

This second archetype, the walled garden, is square or rectangular in form and constructed with a careful sense of proportion. It is the product of close attention to local topography, consisting of a carefully levelled area of soil, and plants and trees spaced according to an overall geometry derived from the first irrigation patterns, which ran parallel to the contour lines of the terrain to facilitate even watering and to limit the effects of erosion. This layout allows for an elaborate, symmetrical arrangement of water rills, pools, rows of trees and plant beds. Very much like the woven carpets of the Islamic world, the original walled gardens reflect a stylized version of nature, based on an organized collection of cultivated plants brought through various trade routes from far away. A 4,000-year-old wooden model of a walled enclosure from the tomb of Meketre in Thebes, Egypt, replicates an archetype of a paradise in the afterlife [1.29].[13]

In essence, the walled garden is not merely a productive food patch: it can also be a secluded world of beauty, intimacy and delight. Since it required intensive maintenance, it was linked to the social elite early on. Compared to the communal nature of the forest clearing,

the walled garden was exclusive and introverted, providing shade and privacy for the privileged few. It was a paradise yielding exquisite fruit such as the pomegranate, the sweetest scents and the most beautiful flowers, including roses, for the pleasure of a discerning caste [1.30].

At ancient sites such as the royal gardens of Cyrus the Great at Pasargadae, modern Iran, founded in the middle of the 6th century BCE, it is easy to imagine the powerful scent of roses and cypress trees casting shade over gurgling water troughs. The walled garden is not only the living metaphor of a heavenly promise: it embodies the sensual reality of a terrestrial paradise, a place of pleasure conceived for a ruler's comfort (indeed, the English 'paradise' derives from an old Persian word for an enclosed pleasure ground). From the smallest vegetable patch behind mud walls to palatial gardens hidden by masonry bastions, the archetype of the walled garden offered a huge range of possibilities. The remains of the earliest walled garden at Pasargadae have almost vanished into the semi-arid steppe. All that is left is the ancient garden rill, which encloses an area of grassy land where the garden would once have stood [1.28]. As a type, the walled garden is vulnerable to change, since it represents a conception of nature entirely shaped by its historical context. On the arid plateau next to the garden at Pasargadae the tomb of Cyrus the Great stands on an abstract square plinth, calling for the walled garden to return [1.27].

1.26 Miniature painting of Babur in a garden.
Babur, the first Mughal emperor, oversees
the making of his Garden of Fidelity, or Bagh-i
Wafa, in Kabul, in the arid desert of Afghanistan,
which he designed himself. The garden follows
the secular archetype of the *chahar bagh*
or four-quartered garden born in Persia two
thousand years earlier.

1.27 Tomb of Cyrus the Great, Pasargadae, Iran.
The modesty of this monument dedicated to
the great king and his wife has perhaps helped
it to resist the assaults of time. The simplicity
and clarity of the architecture are reflected
in the adjacent garden.

1.28 Rill and decanting tank, Pasargadae, Iran.
This limestone water rill and decanting tank are
remains of the earliest known Persian paradise
garden at Cyrus's palace at Pasargadae (529 BCE),
on the high desert plateau of Iran. The four-
quartered garden, inspired by earlier Babylonian
and Assyrian gardens, was filled with fruit and
cypress trees as well as flowers. Nothing now
survives of the adobe walls that once framed
this vast enclosure, nor of the plants and trees
that offered solace to the king.

**1.29 Wooden tomb model of a garden from
Thebes, Egypt, 11th Dynasty,** *c.* **2000 BCE.**
The walled enclosure contains a fish pond
shaded by rows of sycamore fig trees. The
archetype of the paradise garden as a place
to rest in the afterlife was later common to
most cultures of the Levant in antiquity.

1.30 Pomegranate tree.
A ripe pomegranate in a walled paradise garden
splits open, ready to be picked and eaten.
Because of its plentiful red seeds, it is seen as
the fruit of life and a symbol of prosperity and
immortality. It is also one of several plants that
have been regarded as the forbidden fruit of the
Garden of Eden.

1.27

1.28

1.29

1.30

Bagh-i Fin, Iran

One of the oldest surviving examples of a walled garden in Iran is the Bagh-i Fin, near Tepe Sialk in Kashan, which dates as far back as 6000 BCE [1.32]. Although the present garden is more recent, dating to the reign of Shah Abbas in the late 16th century CE, it probably sits on some of the oldest garden foundations known to humankind. Cradled in the foothills of the Zagros mountain range at an altitude of 1,600 metres (5,740 feet), and served by a permanent spring linked to an underground irrigation system, the garden faces the vast, wind-swept expanses of the Dasht-e Kavir, the Great Salt Desert [1.33a, 1.33b]. The Bagh-i Fin follows the archetype of a paradise garden perfectly in both its location and its form, as is the case with countless other paradise gardens, illustrated here by the one located outside the city of Yazd on the fringes of the Dasht-e Lut [1.31]. The highly structured space embodies the archaic geometry of the *chahar bagh* or 'four-plot' garden, whose four rivers of life converge at a pool at its centre [1.34].

The numerous exquisite water channels of the Bagh-i Fin are fed by gravity from a bountiful source called the Suleyman Spring [1.35, 1.37]. Surging from the hillside behind the garden, the water has been channelled and stored in a pool ever since Tepe Sialk was settled more than 7,000 years ago.[14] The entire water supply is brought via an underground network of ventilated channels called *qanats* running for several kilometres underground [1.36, 1.44]. The *qanat* system, with its deep, well-like shafts, is ingeniously contrived so as to bring a plentiful water supply from an aquifer located in the distant mountains, thus sustaining the entire garden and human settlement. Without the presence of water at the Bagh-i Fin, the garden could not have existed, situated as it is at the edge of the desert.

The garden appears at the threshold of the eastern gate, where the haggard traveller, having crossed an arid expanse of desert, would have entered the massive adobe walls into what must have seemed a mirage [1.45]. It then unfolds repeatedly in all four directions into a refreshing shaded paradise comprising running waters, scented flowers and intimate shaded groves with a pavilion at its centre [1.42, 1.43].[15] Viewed from the surrounding arid landscape, the garden resembles a miraculous oasis full of evergreen cypresses pointing to the blue Persian sky. It is carefully proportioned and rectangular, positioned with its shortest side facing the foothills. Following the rules of gravitational flow, the watercourse continues through the garden, the natural direction and artificial deflection of the flow dictating

1.31 Walled garden, Yazd, Iran.
An archetypical four-quartered *chahar bagh* near Yazd in Iran: this vernacular example is enclosed by tall adobe walls, adjacent to a line of underground *qanats* supplying water. A central fountain stands at the intersection of the four paths.

1.32 Plan of the Bagh-i Fin garden, Iran.
The Bagh-i Fin garden is located at the edge of the Great Salt Desert near Kashan in Iran. The present garden dates back to Shah Abbas in the late 16th century in the Safavid period, but it stands on the remains of one of the oldest *chahar bagh* gardens in Iran. The Suleyman Spring has provided abundant water from the Karkas mountains from the times of the Tepe Sialk settlement around 6000 BCE.

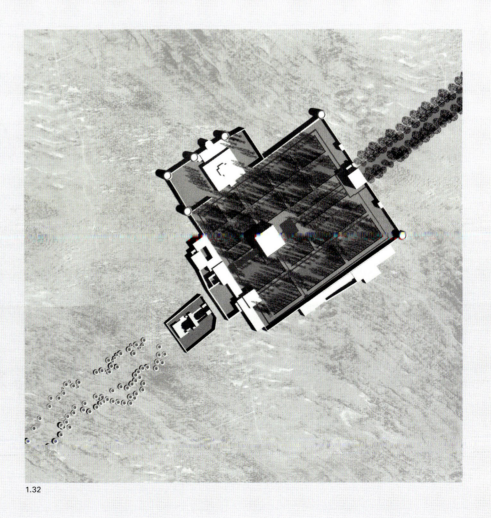

1.32

1.33a

1.33b

1.34

the garden's entire layout. Four channels in the form of
a cross converge at a pool at the garden's centre, marked
by an elegant pavilion. The main pavilion stands where
water channels meet. The covered space takes advantage
of a cooling basin, where the ruler's bed was placed during
hot nights. During the day, shade is provided by the many
oriental plane trees and Persian cypresses planted in dense
alignments [1.41].

    The art of water direction and distribution constitutes
the heart of the garden scheme. Although it steps just a few
metres down along its entire length, the carefully gauged
incline is sufficient to make the water sing and gurgle as
it runs through the rills and channels [1.40]. The water
then continues to run well beyond the garden's walls,
and lines the route to Kashan with gardens in a thousand
shades of green, before losing its way in the salt flats of
the desert and evaporating [1.38]. It is said that it was so
bountiful that it once powered many mills, irrigated the
ruler's fields and supplied year-round water to the masses
living in the Kashan.[16]

    The Bagh-i Fin's proportions make it perhaps one
of the finest examples of the walled garden genre still in
existence today. It stands as an archetypal *hortus conclusus*
('enclosed garden') – an adaptation of nature that went
on to inspire many gardens in history, from the Roman
and Renaissance periods to the Alun-alun of Java, the
Mughal palaces of India and the Baroque parks of France.
The precision with which the garden is traced and made
to unfold represents a mastery of geometric composition
and topography inherent to Persian culture. It recreates
the symbolic microcosm of the four rivers of life, as in a
17th-century Persian rug from Kerman [1.39], and achieves
a conceptual construct representing a higher order of
mathematical and proportional thinking. The Bagh-i Fin
moves the art of landscape design into the realm of pure
arithmetic and the mathematics of water [1.47].

    In the three monotheistic cultures of Judaism, Islam
and Christianity, 'paradise' has come to signify a garden as
a peaceful, harmonious space reflecting the glory of heaven.
Without its walls, artificial water ducts and daily rounds of
maintenance, the Bagh-i Fin simply would not exist nor resist
the harshness of the dusty and wind-swept desert. It is a
powerful construct where nature, set in a careful arrangement,
is protected by thick adobe walls to convey a measure of
timelessness from within [1.46]. The Bagh-i Fin is one of the
most striking examples of constructed landscape on earth,
a walled garden archetype that has prevailed at this very
location since the earliest civilization.

1.35

1.37

1.36

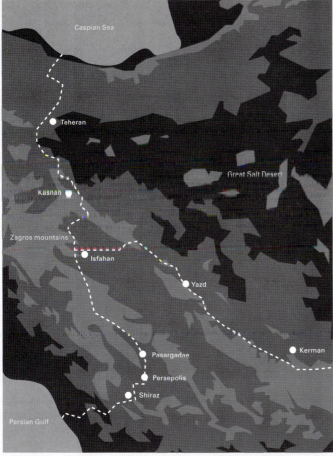

1.38

1.39

1.35, 1.36, 1.37 The Suleyman Spring, Bagh-i Fin.
The waters of the Suleyman Spring, essential for the walled garden, are brought from the Karkas mountains by underground brick-lined *qanat*s. When the water reaches the upper garden it surges up through the perforated base of a pool.

1.38 Map of gardens of the Iranian Plateau.
The high Iranian Plateau was dotted with ancient gardens on the edge of the Dasht-e Kavir and Dasht-e Lut deserts.

1.39 Persian garden carpet.
A four-quartered garden is evoked in this early 17th-century Persian garden carpet from Kerman, Iran, as a place of dreams, with myriad fantastic animals and flowers.

1.40 Rill and basin, Bagh-i Fin.
The arrangement of rill and basin at the Bagh-i Fin is similar in essence to those found at the ancient Persian garden at Pasargadae [1.28].

1.40

1.41

1.41 Qajar pavilion, with pool and central rill, Bagh-i Fin.
The elegant refinement of the ornament in the vaults echoes the fine texture of the garden trees, including the chenar (*Platanus orientalis*) and the cypress (*Cupressus sempervirens*). Different depths of the crystal-clear water appear as shifting shades of blue.

1.42 View to the west of the Bagh-i Fin.
The protected garden landscape with tall cypress trees surrounding the pavilion is clearly evident as an artificial construct in the desert, with the Karkas mountains in the background.

1.43 Overhead view of the central pavilion, Bagh-i Fin.
It is said that Shah Abbas would have his bed installed above the pool on hot summer nights to refresh his dreams. Together with the shade from the grove of trees, the water would help keep the central pavilion cool on hot days by means of convection.

1.42

1.43

1.44

1.45

1.16

1.44 Longitudinal section through the garden and spring.
On the left the water is brought to the Suleyman Spring through the underground *qanat*, with its vertical shafts reaching up to the surface. The entire system steps down through the garden and then runs out to the right, towards ancient Sialk and the city of Kashan. The topology of the garden is precise and regular, and with each quadrant arranged for flood irrigation, the gardeners could control the allocation of every drop of water.

1.45 Eastern gate of the Bagh-i Fin.
The gate faces towards the Great Salt Desert and the city of Kashan. The line of water through the garden runs out along the avenue and continues to irrigate gardens further away.

1.46 Walls and tower, Bagh-i Fin.
The tall adobe walls with their corner towers give a strong sense of the enclosure of the paradise garden.

1.47 The Qajar pool pavilion.
Water is handled here like a liquid jewel set in stone. Beyond, the massive adobe walls and old cypress trees offer shade and comfort from the harsh sun and wind.

1.47

The evolution of the walled garden

Soon after its inception, the garden developed from its most minimal state – a single walled cultivated space within a domestic settlement – to the more expansive systematic deployment of agricultural fields. With the planted court of the temple dedicated to Marduk in ancient Babylon and the early Minoan garden devoted to a goddess at Phaistos, the walled garden became a highly ritualized symbol of exclusivity, faith and power, open only to the privileged few. The archetype continued to spread through the Fertile Crescent of the Middle East, eastwards to India and China, and to the tip of Western Europe via ancient trade routes. It became part of the colonial war machine of Rome in Africa and Europe, always remaining true to its initial productive purpose while varying greatly in scale, style and proportion. In other words, thanks to the Silk Road the *Siheyuan* courtyard gardens of the Ming Dynasty in China have the same common ancestor as the earlier courtyard gardens at Pompeii [1.49]. The luxurious Roman walled gardens that reached their apex in the imperial period have scarcely been surpassed in refinement and exuberance. The Romans borrowed much of their design ideas and techniques from Ptolemaic, Babylonian and Persian sources, and managed, unlike the Greeks, to incorporate their gardens into larger urban patterns. Throughout the Middle Ages the gardens found within monastery cloisters and castle walls remained austere, minimal and protected.

It was only with the appearance of Renaissance villas that such gardens broke out of their defensive bounds and developed into a series of remarkable terraced spaces. The pinnacle of this geometric approach to landscape design was the Baroque park, a hybrid concept of forest and walled garden rolled into one and contained within a vast enclosed domain as at Vaux-le-Vicomte [1.48]. Albeit from the 19th century, Central Park in New York offers an excellent example: a 'walled' space vast enough to contain reservoirs, meadow clearings and forests within the bounds of the city [1.51]. The same model went on to colonize the great agricultural expanses of America, Brazil and Australia, its geometric nature allowing it to be easily replicated on a territorial scale along lines of irrigation and ownership [1.50].

Nature transformed

Successive stages of landscape development occurred throughout history, inexorably changing the face of the wilderness into a more cultivated and civilized environment. The archetypes of the forest clearing and the walled garden have remained distinct, but they have also mingled and merged. As they converge and evolve, they remain relevant and useful. Landscapes are not conceived from scratch: they have an ancestry and share common fundamental features. It is this essence of invention and transformation that has accompanied us since the dawn of sedentary existence.

1.48 Vaux-le-Vicomte, France.
The view looks towards geometric parterres and terraces against an artificially planted forest backdrop. Despite a tremendous leap in scale, this garden remains true to the *chahar bagh* tradition established by King Cyrus at Pasargadae over two millennia earlier.

1.49 Traditional courtyard gardens, Ming period, Suzhou, China.
The walled garden archetype gradually reached China along the desert caravan routes, albeit with substantial modifications in both pattern and style.

1.48

1.49

1.50

The Jeffersonian grid, which divided the land of the United States into uniform square plots as part of the 1785 Land Ordinance, is probably the most striking example of the walled garden's development into a continental landscape typology [1.50].

1.50 Grid layout, South Dakota, USA.
Thomas Jefferson created a grid across the entire United States in the Land Ordinance of 1785. Here, in the upper reaches of the Missouri watershed in South Dakota, the geometric principles appear analogous to the early archetype at Yazd, Iran; but a grid set at a continental scale rarely conforms to the slope of a terrain or the natural direction of its waters.

1.51 Central Park, New York, USA.
Central Park is the ultimate enclosed garden, so vast it contains a series of forested clearings. The hybridization of both archetypes has produced one of the most remarkable projects in modern landscape architecture. The majority of visitors would like to think that this is original nature, when in fact it results from a long process of cultural transformations.

1.51

2. Hydraulic Civilizations
The Geometry of Water in Landscapes

'From the terrace, see the planted and the fallow fields, the ponds and orchards. One league is the inner city, another league is orchards, another league is fields ... and the precinct of the temple of Ishtar. Measure Uruk, the city of Gilgamesh.'
    Epic of Gilgamesh[1]

The origins of landscape settlements
Imagine the very first settlements in the Neolithic villages of Jarmo and Jericho, where nomadic tribes gradually evolved into larger sedentary communities framed by new landscapes comprising terraces, gardens, orchards, fields and pasture. The success of these settlements was based on an understanding and mastery of water, which allowed crops and trees to thrive independently of rainfall, and resulted in the irrigated terraces of Judaea we still see around Jericho.[2] This led to further developments during the urban periods of Sumeria and later Assyria, where water-elevating methods reached a pinnacle to provide for the extravagant hanging gardens of rulers like that for Ashurbanipal's palace in Nineveh [2.1].

Landscape came to embody the cultural expression of a people, but also that of political power, creating a strong sense of identity, and setting the stage for entirely new scales of landscapes like the Faiyum irrigation project of Twelfth Dynasty Egypt [2.0]. How did this occur? Scholars suggest that, after the Black Sea Deluge, fleeing tribes drew on their knowledge of irrigation and cultivation to enable agriculture in subsequent locations. Whether we should speak of 'inheritance' or 'invention' when addressing the birth of agriculture in the Fertile Crescent remains a matter of dispute.

One thing is clear: the efficient use of water resources was a decisive factor in the survival of each of these settlements, hence their description as 'hydraulic civilizations'. Before irrigation could be set in motion at a given location, several preparatory steps were necessary: the landscape around a potential water source needed to be cleared of trees

2.0 (opposite) Irrigated fields in the Faiyum Oasis, Egypt.
Desert sand was transformed here into fertile land through human intervention. The daily care brought to each patch of earth characterizes this landscape.

2.1 Assyrian relief from Ashurbanipal's palace, Nineveh, Iraq.
In this relief, dating to around 650 BCE and thought to show the hanging gardens at Nineveh, alignments of trees replicate the rhythm of the building's columns, while, below, abundant fruit trees are irrigated by channels fed with water from a vaulted aqueduct.

2.1

2.2

2.3

2.2 Olive grove, Marrakesh Oasis, Morocco.
The precise topology of the ground here is a result of the agricultural practice of tilling the earth with a hoe to direct water into a series of squares. The terrain is ordered according to a constant – water is fed, drained and chanelled from quadrant to quadrant by the pull of gravitational flow following the natural slope of the land.

2.3 Pomegranate trees, Marrakesh Oasis, Morocco.
Over the course of a day, water is redirected from one quadrant to another each hour, here a quadrant of pomegranates. Without this shared provision of water, all plants would perish within days.

and scrub; stones were gathered and constructed into a series of walls or terraces; and the plots of land thus created were levelled off, ploughed and sown. It was only once the terrain had undergone years of tedious preparation that it was ready for flood irrigation as in this oasis outside Marrakesh [2.2, 2.3]. Plots were watered regularly by adduction, producing bountiful crops via a system of troughs that could connect differing levels of fields and terraces with great precision.

These early landscapes bore the fruit of careful maintenance and were the result of a direct but gradual interaction between city, terrain, labour and water, creating as in Shibam, Yemen, a fragile balance between sedentary ownership and environment [2.4]. Orchards bloomed in spring, and crops of apricots, peaches, plums, figs and grapes ripened throughout the summer. Most fruit trees grown in these early cities of the Fertile Crescent and the Arabian Peninsula were not local species, but had arrived along the trade routes from India and China. They were carefully selected and sorted according to their quality, suitability, colour, scent and taste. Some rare fruiting and flowering plants – roses, tulips, peonies, lotus, myrtle, citrus, pomegranate, apples and pears – were kept within walled gardens, where they grew into countless symbols of nature's beauty. Cereal and date crops grew among olive and almond trees in open agricultural plots, as in Yemen, where a water divider would provide adequate irrigation for each family to prosper [2.5].

A good harvest meant not merely adequate food supplies, but also the promise of successful commerce in the form of exchange. As crops became more bountiful, landscapes were established and cities grew and diversified in their trades. As stocks and wealth increased, wars and inequalities ensued.

Early agricultural landscapes appeared along river courses and around wells at the desert's edge, as in the Hadhramaut mountains of Yemen [2.6]. They used an extensive irrigation system derived from the orthogonal principles of the walled garden, but also demonstrated a mastery of topography and a general understanding of the effects of gravity in water flow when applied to a particular terrain. The extensive framework of irrigation not only gave structure to the overall landscape, but also facilitated the transport and exchange of goods. Agricultural land thus became a strong binding element between city-states.

From the southern ranges of the Hadhramaut mountains in Yemen, through Egypt to northern Anatolia and the Taurus mountains, from the Persian Gulf to the Indus Valley, along the trade routes that skirted the torrid Dasht-e Lut stretching to the Zagros mountain range of Media and Mesopotamia, early hydraulic city-states established an agricultural system whose landscapes prevail to this day. Inhabitants of early villages such as Jarmo, located in the foothills of the Zagros mountains in upper Mesopotamia, probably used the most rudimentary form of hand-controlled

2.4 Shibam, Yemen.

The organic relationship between the adobe walls of the coastal town of Shibam in Yemen and those of the surrounding gardens is striking. There is here a balance both in form and scale between a settlement and its productive landscape. Water brought through underground *qanat*s is distributed sparingly to the gardens before it supplies the houses.

2.5 Stone water divider in Yemen.

The different widths of the rivulets indicate a different share of water allotted to a particular villager or clan. This marks the birth of distinctions and growing inequalities between people – someone who receives more water, harvests more and tends to accumulate more wealth.

2.6 Irrigated valley in the Hadhramaut mountains, Yemen.

Each patch of cultivated land becomes precious and reliant on the attentive care of man. Countless dams in the foothills of Yemen retain the waters of rivers like the Wadi Dana, which would otherwise vanish in the Arabian Desert.

2.4

2.5

2.6

2.7

Karl Wittfogel's theory of 'Oriental despotism' asserts that oppressive forms of government, from Egypt and Mesopotamia to China, were a feature of many early hydraulic civilizations. Most major irrigation works were built by either prisoners or slaves, implying a hierarchic society with a proprietary caste of priests and rulers and a significant functioning bureaucracy. It is no surprise that Egypt, which benefited from the regular and predictable flood of the Nile, developed into one of the most advanced hydraulic civilizations of the time, producing an extraordinary set of agricultural landscapes along the course of the dry desert valley. Yet this form of landscape, beautiful though it may be, was obtained at considerable social expense, as is shown in the example of the Faiyum (p. 59).

2.7 Remains of the Harbaqa Dam on the upper Euphrates, Syria.
Built in the heart of the Syrian Desert in 132 CE under the Roman emperor Hadrian, the dam's impressive structure held back water to irrigate an oasis located at a major crossroads connecting the eastern and southern regions of the Fertile Crescent.

2.8 Plan of part of the early settlement of Çatalhöyük, Turkey.
Dating to around 7500 BCE, this substantial and long-lived settlement marks the passage from a nomadic to a sedentary mode of life in the region. Its architecture was collective and non-hierarchical.

2.9 Female figurine from Çatalhöyük.
This imposing seated female figurine, flanked by felines, probably attests to the presence of an ancient fertility cult reaching far back into prehistoric times.

irrigation to water their fields, cultivating the land by hand with a hoe. The city of Jericho, located north-west of the Dead Sea on the banks of the River Jordan, was permanently settled nearly 9,000 years ago, in *c*. 6800 BCE,[3] and its people cultivated crops on irrigated terraces now common to Judaea.

The surface area of a field for arable land was dictated by the amount of time it would take to water. Crops were planted in furrows and spaced according to their size, level of water consumption and expected yield. The resulting geometric layout of water rills and furrows subsequently provided a basis for the plotting of new landscape districts.

Agriculture appeared in many regions of Europe, the Levant, Anatolia, Media, Mesopotamia, Egypt and India almost simultaneously, during the 7th millennium BCE. It reached a point of advancement where the growing of emmer, wheat and barley provided sufficient food and reserves for societies to diversify in trade, political and economic alliances, and religion. Mastery of water resources was the single most important development, ultimately deciding which civilizations would be dominant and which subservient. The Harbaqa Dam on the Euphrates in Syria, although built much later, is a good example of an act of empowerment by the Romans; placed at the crossroads of major trade routes it acts both as an agricultural irrigation dam and bridge [2.7]. Whether through the use of wells and cisterns, as in the case of Çatalhöyük and Jericho, or with underground *qanat*

systems, as in Yemen and Media, or through the controlled tapping of rivers via dams, levees and canals as in Syria, the Indus Valley, Egypt, Mesopotamia and China, early societies' mastery of water was a significant motor in the evolution of landscapes. Increasing social stratification among denser urban populations sparked the birth of an elite class of priests and warring chieftains, who either oversaw temple shrines and their granaries or were in charge of justice and government, settling water conflicts and maintaining social order.[4]

Early settlements

Large-scale landscape thinking gradually marked the territory of the Fertile Crescent and Anatolia from the onset of sedentary cultivation. A highly productive initial period, in the 7th and 6th millennia BCE, saw rapid developments in agriculture, urbanism and architecture. The case of Çatalhöyük in Anatolia shows a very early form of collective architecture, where dwellings were reached by ladders from the roofs [2.8].[5] A well irrigation system filled cisterns, which then distributed water to the neighbouring fields. It appears that mismanagement of this stagnant cistern water led to severe outbreaks of malaria that subsequently decimated this early civilization. The religion at Çatalhöyük was based on an imposing female goddess of fertility, who can be seen flanked by two feline figures [2.9]. Throughout the region, the gain in agricultural productivity was the result of a combination

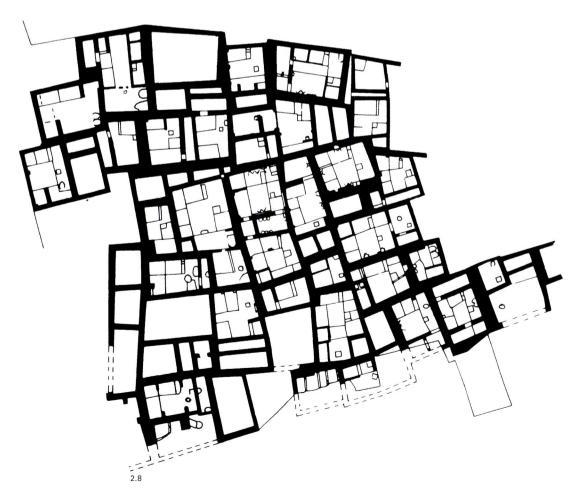

2.8

2.9

2.10

2.11

2.12

Later agricultural civilizations appeared around 7000 BCE; these include settlements in Anatolia, such as Hacilar and Çayönü, and in Mesopotamia and Media. Similar patterns are found in the Mehrgarh Period of the 7th millennium BCE which subsequently led to the Harappan civilization of the Indus Valley four thousand years later. The theory of a Black Sea Deluge (see p.16) is compelling, if we accept a modified date of *c.* 7400 BCE. It would account for the spread of agriculture, irrigation and handicrafts to all adjacent regions.[6] The recent discovery of a city called Hamoukar on the upper Euphrates in northern Syria, dating back to 6000 BCE, adds weight to this hypothesis. The earliest European settlements also spread around 7000 BCE, such as Sesklo in Thessaly and Lepenski Vir on the Danube in Serbia [2.11]. The connection between the earlier Black Sea cultures and the Balkan peninsula via the Danube seems quite plausible. Another settlement in Iraq called Hassuna (6000 BCE) located in the Taurus mountains, communicates directly with the Black Sea. The coincidence of these sites developing agriculture at around the same time calls for an original landscape that inspired them, on the lake shores of the Black Sea depression [2.12].

2.10 Cuneiform tablet with the Epic of Gilgamesh.
From King Ashurbanipal's library at Nineveh, this tablet tells the story of the Epic of Gilgamesh, in which Utnapishtim builds a boat to save humanity and animals from the flood. The story dates back into Sumerian times and is identical to the Deluge in the Bible, though written two millennia earlier.

2.11 Lepinski Vir on the Danube in Serbia.
Lepinski Vir is one of the oldest agricultural settlements in Europe (*c.* 7000 BCE). The shift towards a sedentary way of life coincides with the same transition in other places in Anatolia, Media and the Middle East.

2.12 Babylonian seal impression showing an agricultural scene.
Three men tend an ox-drawn plough (two are repeated): one guides the plough, the next feeds in the seed and the third drives the ox with a whip. A depiction of a commonplace agricultural practice is elevated into the sacred, religious realm, but also relates to the human condition on earth.

2.13

2.14

2.13 Statue of a goddess, possibly Ishtar, holding a vase from which water flows.
This powerful goddess controlled the precious waters of the Tigris and Euphrates and was both feared and unpredictable in her actions. She is the Semitic goddess of fertility, love and war and is the counterpart of the Sumerian goddess Inanna described in the legend of Gilgamesh.

2.14 Aerial view of Sialk in Kashan, Iran.
The site of Tepe Sialk (6000 BCE) shows traces of the first irrigated fields in the region. Sialk is thought to have been the seat of an important harvest cult dedicated to the goddess Anahita, the equivalent of Ishtar.

New cults dedicated to Ishtar in Mesopotamia developed into a state religion. Ishtar, the goddess of fertility and harvest, was depicted holding an urn from which water flows upwards towards the sky [2.13]. She symbolized time, life and abundance and was conflated with the goddess Anahita in the later Zoroastrian religion of Media. She shared similarities with the mother goddess of the Minoan culture. The city of Sialk, built around 6000 BCE, was probably an early religious centre of Iran [2.14]. Temple ruins indicate that it was a society centred on harvest cults. One is tempted to link all these developments with what occurred on the Black Sea a millennium before.

of factors, including favourable climate change (warming) and a high degree of cultural convergence between Indo-European and Semitic peoples. It was the economic success enjoyed by larger Mesopotamian cities that prompted a definitive break with older, nomadic tribal lore and pushed towards an entirely new kind of social hierarchy.

The first known dominant hydraulic societies appeared over 7,000 years ago, and were significantly larger and more productive than the previous Neolithic settlements of Jarmo, Jericho and Çatalhöyük. They were built at the southern tip of the Fertile Crescent, in the Euphrates Delta, at the crossroads of three continents. Eridu was founded during the Ubaid period, around 5400 BCE, where the lower Euphrates empties into the Persian Gulf. It was followed by the city of Ur, whose inhabitants dug an elaborate network of canals linking their fields to the river, through numerous levees and troughs perpendicular to the Euphrates's course.[7] This system worked successfully and was replicated in cities further upstream, including Uruk: here the Euphrates was slightly higher, and less saline, than the Tigris, so its water could drain across a mosaic of fertile fields towards the other river.

The Sumerians mapped the course of celestial bodies to produce a precise astrological calendar that would guide the harvest and other seasonal events throughout the year.[8] In remote times religious calendars served a double purpose, giving a young but thriving agricultural society a strong,

unifying culture, and backing its religious beliefs with elaborate rituals to mark the cycle of seasons. The priestly caste enriched itself with the offerings it received and, newly empowered, the founding dynasty coalesced around the figure of a supreme leader, half-god, half-man, perhaps even tyrant.

The towering ziggurat of Ur was built c. 2100 BCE for the worship of the moon goddess; it still stands today, a symbol of the strongly hierarchical society of the Sumerians. It was this level of organization that enabled the Sumerians to fabricate the bountiful landscape of canals, fields, orchards and gardens that served Ur and other Sumerian cities over the centuries.[9] The plough, the wheel and the mill became vital instruments for development. The earliest known wheels appear simultaneously in various regions of the Caucasus, Central Europe and Mesopotamia during the 4th millennium BCE.[10] In Mesopotamia potters' wheels were used at Ur as early as 3500 BCE, whereas cartwheels first appeared in around 3000 BCE [2.16]. The need for vessels to store grain, oil and wine pre-dated any kind of heavy hauling. Remains of monumental structures dating back to the early 4th millennium BCE mark the birthplace of some of the most refined landscape systems Mesopotamia ever saw, accompanied by a culture that was able to benefit from plentiful livestock, grain, fruit and wine, all of which could be carried on the canals. Yet in time this crucible of early agriculture was deserted, on account of ignorance about correct irrigation practices.

2.15 Babylonian clay tablet with a plan of canals.
This clay tablet (c. 1684–1647 BCE) is inscribed with a precise plan of Babylonian canals and irrigation system. By the 2nd millennium BCE accurate surveying of the landscape through triangulation, calculation and notation is evident.

2.16 Detail of the Standard of Ur.
A Sumerian soldier wearing armour drives a four-wheeled chariot drawn by asses in this detail from the Standard of Ur (2550 BCE). Such a technological leap in metallurgy and transportation was made possible by flourishing irrigation agriculture.

2.17 Assyrian relief from Nimrud, Iraq, depicting an attack on a city.
Trees are being felled during an assault on a walled city. The legend of Gilgamesh describes the destruction of trees as a common practice in the region.

2.18 The remains of the Tower of Babel, Babylon, near Hillah, Iraq.
Built around 3000 BCE, the stepped ziggurat surrounded by a moat once stood out prominently in the landscape as a place of worship. It now sits within a palimpsest of foundations and fields that unfold along the same orientation.

2.15

2.16

2.17

Water, power and measurement

In Sumerian times, the landscape was irrigated by an intricate network of canals and rivulets. Water was distributed to the fields on a double hourly basis according to the seasonal needs of crops. Stocks of grain from successive harvests (sometimes up to three per year) were kept in jars and silos, hidden behind strong fortifications that were defended by armies. This level of complexity led to the invention of writing, geometry and accounting [2.21].[11] These fortifications in turn became palaces and temples, complete with lavish gardens enclosed behind walls, for that select portion of the population who could afford not to work. The walled garden thus became an expression of differentiated wealth in society. Furthermore, rivalry between rich city-states became a matter of life and death for their rulers. Social inequality and a division of labour led to acerbic feuds between siblings and rival tribes, provoking death and destruction. The Epic of Gilgamesh, one of the oldest known works of Sumerian literature, describes these early wars. It relates how the first sanctions imposed on a conquered city were to ransack the palace, behead its ruler and fell all the trees in his garden as a symbol of disempowerment [2.10, 2.17].

The landscape around Ur and Uruk was marked with countless irrigation channels and small levees, in a pattern that mostly ran perpendicular to the contour lines of the terrain. These irrigation rills, and the furrows that branched off at right angles, were flooded at regular intervals during the growing season and divided fields into smaller plots. For the first time, the fields' geometric framework allowed the productive landscape to be perceived and measured, with the surface area of each plot dictating the amount of time it would take to be watered [2.15]. Because water needed to be allocated parsimoniously in this drought-prone region, time and surface area were carefully studied and mathematically correlated. To this end the early Sumerians invented the sexagesimal system, founded on a base of 60, as the most practical method for dividing time and for the establishment of surface geometry on the basis of 360° triangulation and the square root of two – a system we have kept to this day [2.19, 2.20].

Advances in irrigation techniques affected not only agriculture; in time, they also allowed the dry desert to bloom in the form of pleasure gardens. Some of the earliest tiered paradise gardens appeared in locations including the palace at Mari [2.22] (18th century BCE), Nineveh (late 8th century BCE) and, possibly, Babylon (9th or 6th century BCE) – places that entered into legend only subsequently. Even the Garden of Eden itself is thought to have some basis in fact, and is possibly related to the fertile area between the Tigris and the Euphrates rivers known to the Sumerians as 'Edin'. The hanging gardens at Nineveh, constructed by the Assyrian king Sennacherib in 703 BCE, are known to have utilized an extensive system of aqueducts and hydraulic devices

2.18

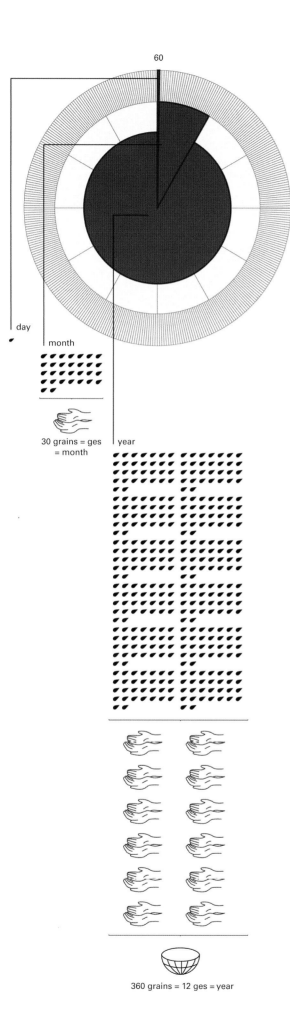

60

day

month

30 grains = ges
= month

year

360 grains = 12 ges = year

Sumerians used base 60 for time because it allowed for many multiples and dividers. Time was conceived in order to monitor water distribution, and as the basis of a 360-day calendar [2.19]. We still use their numeric base for geometry and time today. The development of writing and counting also helped codify and quantify laws relating to irrigation and supported a more productive landscape. Cuneiform surveying records on clay tablets reproduce by analogy the lines of furrows defining the plots of land they were initially measuring [2.15]. Sumerian priests charted the celestial vault with extreme accuracy; the heavens were divided into the twelve houses corresponding each to a 30° segment of the sky. From the smallest garden to vast constellations, Sumerians and Babylonians mapped, calculated and predicted the fundamental physical, spatial and temporal elements of our world. Their legacy resides in precisely managed landscapes, and a notational system that helped develop time, geometry, mathematics and literature in modern society.[12]

2.19 Diagram of the Sumerian calendar.
The Sumerian calendar had 360 days, with each day divided into 12 double hours. The use of base 60 in Sumerian calculation allowed for an extremely precise measurement of time and surfaces. We still measure time in 12 hours, 60 minutes and 60 seconds today, and also calculate using triangulated surfaces that add up to 360°.

2.20 Sumerian mathematical tablet with calculations for the square root of two.
Fitting in the hand, this small tablet concentrates all the knowledge that was developed during this period of rapid urban and agricultural change.

2.21 Sumerian cuneiform tablet.
This clay tablet from Tello (2350 BCE) in Mesopotamia records a tally of sheep and goats in cuneiform script. The layout of the tablet is reminiscent of small plots of agricultural land.

2.22 Aerial view of Mari, Syria.
The ancient city of Mari, modern Tell Hariri, stood on the upper Euphrates. On the left are traces of old agricultural fields that once fed the city. There is a striking resemblance between the cuneiform graphics of a Babylonian clay tablet and the layout of the fields. It is almost as if the first writing was made on the ground before being transferred to clay.

2.19

2.20

2.21

2.22

resembling Archimedes screws to irrigate extensive patios and terraces.[13] The result of recent research, these findings have made the historical existence of complex gardens at Babylon more likely [2.18].[14] All these schemes were meant to function as a metaphor for nature, pregnant with sensual symbolism. In their degree of refinement, they were undoubtedly a match for the later Roman, Renaissance and Baroque gardens of Europe, as well as the Mughal gardens of India. Babylonian garden technology was derived from the earlier Ubaid culture, whose influence gradually spread to Egypt, Susa in Media, Mohenjo-daro in the Indus Valley and Pataliputra in the Mauryan Empire of India. In Europe, it first appeared with the construction of Minoan palaces on Crete.

Bitter salt

Why, after such success, did the early hydraulic civilizations of Mesopotamia collapse one after the other? And why did the surrounding fields return to desert so quickly thereafter? First, one needs to understand the basis of agricultural success in Mesopotamia. The Ubaid and early Sumerian civilizations invented the rudiments of surveying and could calculate the gradual declivity of water runoff fairly well, but they had not developed the system sufficiently to permit fields to leach their briny water back into the river system again. The Sumerians usually allowed the less saline waters of the Euphrates to drain slowly away towards the Tigris – a system that worked

successfully for centuries. In the case of Uruk, the choice of location – in the Mesopotamian Plain, on what was once a branch of the Euphrates – was risky, since both major rivers behaved unpredictably and were prone to impetuous flooding.

The city of Uruk succeeded the settlements at Eridu and Ur; it grew to over 50,000 inhabitants. Its sumptuous palaces and gardens required solid protection from repeated floods of cataclysmic proportions; indeed, the floods and subsequent displacement of the Tigris River to the north-east was one of the causes of agricultural decline in the region. An unspoken rule in Uruk was that water for irrigation was drawn from canals from the Euphrates. The river's water supply, as with the Tigris, was sporadic, affecting crop yields from one year to the next. But the single most important cause of decline in the agriculture of Mesopotamia was the presence of salt in this water supply – a fact that had long been recognized since fields were kept fallow over long periods to help metabolize the salt.[15] Peasants took their daily share of water in accordance with the written law, but none of them properly leached the irrigation water away from their flooded fields. A crust of salt gradually formed in the soil and on the surface of the fields where standing water evaporated, leading to the rapid, man-made desertification of the lower Mesopotamian Plain. Sumer vanished as a power essentially because of agricultural mismanagement, and the landscape of Ur that had once delivered great prosperity in turn was rendered desolate [2.23].

The *qanat* channels of Media

Other hydraulic civilizations arose along similar agricultural patterns, but they handled the salinity problem differently. Sialk near Kashan in Iran was built over 7,000 years ago; it occupied the foot of a mountainous region where fresh water was channelled through *qanat*s down to the desert of the high plateau [2.14]. Traces of proto-agriculture and irrigation lines can still be seen around this early fortified settlement. With the arrival of the Medes – an ancient Iranian tribe – at the end of the 2nd millennium BCE, the region developed a better irrigation system than that of ancient Sumer. It was not so much the plain as the slopes of the foothills that were cultivated; the local inhabitants made use of the *qanat* system, employing underground channels that irrigated towns, gardens and fields. The foothills of ancient Media were a complex mosaic of walled gardens and open fields located where the *qanat*s emerged, producing a unique landscape of desert and contrasting gardens. Media showed that it had learned lessons about salinity from the demise of its Babylonian neighbours. Persian gardens kept both irrigation and drainage troughs side by side, to flush salt out of the fields and gardens and into the desert flats.

The miracle of the Nile

By good fortune, the Egyptian god Osiris would order the annual flooding of the Nile Plain in late summer to fertilize the soil naturally. The silt deposited during the floods was a heavenly gift to agricultural crops, following the belief that Osiris's phallus had been thrown into the river after he was murdered and cut up by his brother Seth, and that a Nile fish called *medjed* swallowed it. This led to a specific cult of fertility, which subsequently developed into the Greek and Roman rites of Priapus.[16] Egypt obtained high yields on small plots of land. Rectilinear and compact fields along the river edge were set on stepped terraces; at the top of each row were cisterns filled with Nile overflow [2.24]. The stored water provided irrigation for the growing season and received regular additions of Nile water using a *shaduf*. The *shaduf*, a kind of pail hanging at the end of a levered pole, was the common watering tool used by peasants during the dry season to extract water directly from the river [2.26]. Water was poured into irrigation troughs flowing through cultivated patches, allowing its distribution to fields downstream [2.25]. The absolute predictability of the Nile's annual cycle meant that Egyptian civilization relied on it as a god-given gift from Osiris. This marked difference between the regular flooding of the Nile and the erratic behaviour of the Tigris and Euphrates rivers gave rise to a different form of agriculture and civilization. Ancient Egyptian tombs are rich with depictions of harvest, complete with exquisitely detailed scenery that clearly shows the highly refined landscapes and gardens that flourished in Egypt at that time.

2.23

2.24

2.25

2.23 Ziggurat of the Moon Goddess, Ur.
Early agricultural practices ignored the elementary principles of drainage and leaching in irrigating fields. This resulted in the inexorable desertification of the lower Mesopotamian Plain through salt deposits, revealed here as white patches on the ground.

2.24 Aerial view of the upper Nile in Nubia (Somalia).
Desert agriculture still thrives here today because irrigation water from the fields is returned to the river, thus preventing the build up of salt. The pattern of the fields corresponds to the topography of the river banks and to the lines of irrigation and drainage that imprint a web-like structure on the landscape.

2.25 Date palms, Saqqara, Egypt.
Tall date palms line the irrigation rills in this garden patch along the Nile at Saqqara in Egypt; the plot at the centre remains clear and is used for cereal and vegetable crops.

2.26 Wall painting showing a *shaduf*.
The *shaduf* was used to lift water from the Nile or a pool into an irrigation channel, as shown in this Egyptian wall painting. The beauty of the Egyptian agricultural landscape, with its intensively cultivated patches, comes down to this simple device consisting of a bucket attached to the end of a rudimentary lever.

The Egyptians used a different calendar from the Mesopotamians, and a counting system in base 10 rather than base 60.[17] They developed a complex geometry based on cardinal points, in which notions of bilateral symmetry and balance were of the essence. Nile river water was considered the divine embodiment of time, and a measuring device, later known as a 'nilometer', allowed early Egyptians to track and to anticipate fluctuations in the river's flow. Despite its divine origin, however, the storage and allotment of water during the dry season became a major problem as the population grew. Egypt needed to produce at least two crops a year in order to survive.

2.26

2.27

Faiyum Oasis, Egypt

The establishment of a functional landscape typology in Egyptian agriculture – in the form of cisterns redistributing floodwater in the dry season to terraced fields – was an intelligent response to seasonal variations in the Nile's flow. It was a net improvement on previous systems such as the ones developed in Shibam, Yemen, where agriculture was either fed by *qanats* or simply occupied the main bed of a dry river or wadi waiting for a storm to come [2.27]. Further developments, however, pushed the idea of Nile water storage to a higher level. These were the irrigation works carried out at the Faiyum, which demonstrate an advanced knowledge of hydraulic engineering and surveying, carried out with great precision and efficiency. The irrigation system was created four millennia ago and continues to function remarkably well to this day. The Faiyum region occupies a natural depression approximately 50 metres (160 feet) below sea level, about 80 km (50 miles) south-west of Cairo in the Libyan Desert [2.30]. The project transformed an arid bowl of drifting sand dunes into an immense and fertile fresh-water oasis measuring almost 100 km by 60 km (62 miles by 37 miles).

In order to avoid famine in Egypt, Pharaoh Senusret II initiated the construction of an artificial canal and of a dyke at El Lahun in 1895 BCE [2.29a, 2.29b].[18] This initial canal was 15 km (9 miles) long, 5 metres (16 feet) deep and flowed on a slight incline towards the Faiyum; it was controlled by a system of dams at both ends. It enabled water to be distributed through an extensive network of canals that came to determine the contours of Lake Moeris [2.28]. Known as the Bahr Yusuf ('Joseph Canal'), it brought the rising waters from further up the Nile at Assiut, charged with fertile silt, into the depression, helping change desert sand into fertile gold [2.32]. Most of the water was distributed within the landscape of the Faiyum itself, irrigating new tracts of land and countless gardens, palm groves, orchards and fields [2.33]. The scheme, completed around 1800 BCE, was conceived on a vast scale; and the Egyptians' mastery of irrigation techniques achieved a balance and perfection seldom attained thereafter. The closest comparable achievements from the same period are the dams and drainage canals of the Copaic basin in Boeotia, Greece, constructed by the Mycenaeans c. 1900–1600 BCE,[19] and the Great Northern Canal that runs alongside the Yangtze River in China, built roughly a thousand years later.

The Bahr Yusuf took the form of a broad aqueduct conveying Nile floodwaters from Assiut into the Faiyum depression [2.31]. Farmers working in the irrigated fields on either side of the canal today still till the soil with hoes,

2.27 Shibam, Yemen.
The old city of Shibam, with its bountiful gardens, represents the prototype of the earliest hydraulic civilizations. An elaborate underground system of *qanats* was built with immense care and effort to irrigate this productive landscape.

2.28 The Faiyum Oasis and Lake Moeris, Egypt.
A plan showing Lake Moeris in its original dimensions; the artificial oasis derives its waters from the Nile, which floods regularly into the depression. Irrigation of what was previously desert was made possible by the pharaoh Senusret II, who began work on the construction of the Bahr Yusuf (Joseph Canal), probably the first hydraulic work to have been undertaken on such a scale. Four millennia later, the agricultural system of the Faiyum still provides food for the region.

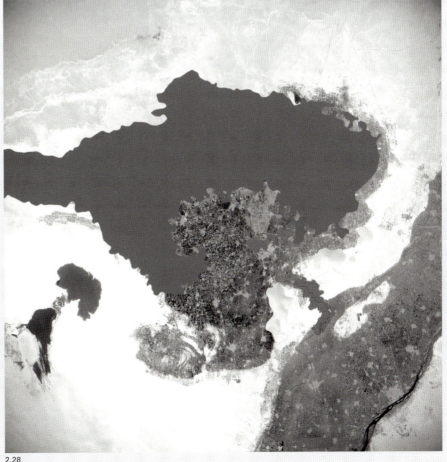

2.28

2.29a

2.29b

2.29a, 2.29b The Faiyum Oasis and the village of El Lahun before and after.
Before the construction of the Bahr Yusuf, irrigated fields were confined to the Nile Valley. But with the construction of the waterway the entire Faiyum became a lake surrounded by luxuriant gardens, thanks to the waters flowing in each year with the annual Nile flood.

2.30 Satellite view of Lower Egypt
The Delta can clearly be seen at the top of the image, with the Nile Valley snaking back from it. The scale of the Faiyum Oasis, clearly visible on one side of the valley, is immense. It measures a little under 100 km (62 miles) in length and 55 km (37 miles) in breadth. The stark contrast with the Libyan Desert is very clear.

2.30

and they are followed by flocks of white egrets in scenes reminiscent of remote antiquity [2.37a, 2.37b]. Engineers have often wondered at the extraordinary balance of nature achieved in this vast work, which still nurtures fields, villages and gardens in the midst of a scorching desert. Water was brought into the depression through a natural gorge located north of the village of Moeris, then flowed down to the basin's lowest point through branching locks and sluices, forming a fresh-water lake later known as Lake Moeris [2.35]. Nile floods had reached the depression before, but irregularly, whereas the annual flow of Nile water along the Bahr Yusuf now provided a regular, dependable supply, thus helping to create the largest artificial breadbasket of its time. The redistribution of water from this huge reservoir to the surrounding fields resulted in some of the most beautiful and productive of all agricultural landscapes. Thanks to the large quantities of Nile silt brought in by the canal, the Faiyum soil became more fertile each year. As well as irrigating the entire depression and transforming a piece of dry desert, the lake was well stocked with fish, birds and crocodiles [2.38, 2.39].

What made the unique landscape at the Faiyum possible was the advanced surveying of the surrounding topography combined with the Egyptians' efficient geometry and construction techniques. Water could be channelled, stored and shared out along the eastern rim of the entire depression, similar to the way the upper cisterns watered the terraced fields of the Nile Valley. Redistribution was via an elaborate system of dams, steps and locks, backed up by batteries of *shaduf*s [2.34]. The landscape that developed was a patchwork of highly productive fields and orchards, small towns, private estates with fine walled gardens, and wild reed and papyrus beds that grew around the lake's edge [2.36].

Lake Moeris offered luxurious hunting and fishing grounds, reserved for the sole pleasure of the pharaohs. The town of Shedyet, later known by the Greeks as Crocodilopolis, became a centre of the cult of the crocodile god Sobek during the 12th Dynasty. Sobek gradually came to symbolize the fertility of the Nile, as well as being viewed as its protector. The 12th Dynasty was the Faiyum's most important political period: the nearby city of El Lisht had briefly taken over as the country's capital, and the area's monumental building projects included pyramids and a labyrinthine mortuary temple. In the Ptolemaic period, the Karanis promontory (modern Kom Ushim) at the north-eastern edge of the Faiyum was irrigated via a canal that originated near the town of Moeris, at the foot of the Hawara pyramid [2.40]. The water was subsequently elevated a further 15 metres (49 feet) through clay pipes, similar to those used in the hanging gardens at Nineveh. Having reached the top of the promontory, it fed a series of palatial gardens and Roman-style baths. The Faiyum Oasis is thus ripe with symbolism, and serves as an extraordinary example of sustainable desert reclamation.

2.31

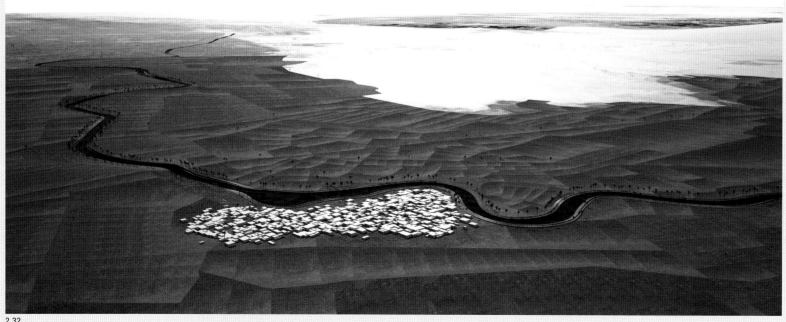

2.32

2.33

2.31 The Bahr Yusuf (Joseph Canal).
Meandering into the Faiyum depression west of El Lahun, the canal is built in such a way as to minimize velocity while preventing the build up of silt. The outlying fields are mostly lower than the channel, thus facilitating gravitational irrigation.

2.32 El Lahun and the Bahr Yusuf.
The Bahr Yusuf at El Lahun branches out further up the Nile Valley at Assiut. The scale of the 4,000-year-old project is astonishing.

2.33 Irrigated fields in the Faiyum.
The Faiyum fields have been worked on with dedicated attention over the millennia, in a landscape of extraordinary flatness and regularity.

2.34 Section through the Bahr Yusuf.
At El Faiyum the canal branches into various irrigation canals – the distribution of water to different sectors of the oasis is carefully controlled.

2.35 Distribution channels from the Bahr Yusuf.
Desert sand mixed with silt deposits from the Nile resulted in very fertile soil and the artificial agricultural landscape of the Faiyum became the new breadbasket of Egypt.

2.34

2.35

2.36

2.37a

2.37b

2.38

2.39

As the name suggests, the Bahr Yusuf is traditionally believed to have been built by the biblical Joseph, acting as vizier under the Egyptian pharaoh. Some historians have even proposed the theory that the 'sea of reeds' of the Faiyum, rather than the Red Sea, is the original site of the Israelites' famous flight out of Egypt.[20] Whatever the case, the extraordinary, antique landscape structure of the Faiyum, with its overlay of legends and cultures, retains an ability to inspire wonder.

2.36 Aerial view of the Faiyum Oasis today.
Over the centuries, Lake Moeris has shrunk and its salinity has increased: today it can no longer be used for irrigation directly and few edible fish thrive in its briny waters. Water for agricultural purposes comes exclusively from the Nile via the Bahr Yusuf.

2.37a, 2.37b A farmer in the Faiyum Oasis.
The hoe is a simple tool but can be used with precision for both moving earth and directing the flow of irrigation. This timeless image would have been familiar 4,000 years ago, when the canal was first built.

2.38 Verdant landscape of the Bahr Yusuf.
Today the Joseph Canal is framed by a prosperous landscape of date palms and fields. An artificial landscape created specifically for cultivation, it was all once just sand.

2.39 The birds of the Faiyum.
The Bahr Yusuf has become host to an ecology of its own, one in which white egrets have replaced the crocodiles and sacred ibis.

2.40 Pyramid of Amenemhet III, Hawara.
The pyramid of Amenemhet III was built at Hawara at the entrance of the Faiyum depression, thought to have been one of the oldest and most important burial sites of the oasis.

2.40

Distant echoes of the Faiyum

What remains of the Faiyum lake today is a brackish body of water supporting a couple of varieties of edible fish, but the fields around it still produce crops thanks to a modern canal rebuilt by the English precisely where the ancient Bahr Yusuf once ran. Like other such projects in history, the success of the Faiyum is closely connected to a politically strong regime. Most early hydraulic civilizations had similar kinds of political systems, from Mesoamerica to China, and from Egypt to Mesopotamia. The most successful waterworks required huge amounts of effort and discipline, both in construction and maintenance. The invention of mathematical calculation and writing in Sumer coincided with a will to inscribe water rights into laws – laws that defined the social hierarchy and could, in turn, make people accountable. The same hierarchy pertained later in Egypt, though with better knowledge of the problem of salinity. Egypt, perhaps, had a 'better' form of tyranny over its people, since it cared for the land, prevented famine and delivered precious water to all.

The Canal du Midi built by the French absolutist king Louis XIV in the 17th century to connect the Atlantic Ocean to the Mediterranean was not so much for irrigation as for the transportation of goods, but it is a strong and unambiguous political statement of power over nature [2.41]. Now more than ever, fresh, channelled water is a critical commodity around the world. The great South–North water transfer project in China illustrates this perfectly: currently the world's largest water diversion project, it will displace half a million inhabitants and be almost 1500 km (930 miles) long [2.42]. It will bring water to the parched regions of the north, including Beijing, at a rate of 15 million megalitres per year. The cost of the construction is estimated at $40 billion, plus an additional $5 billion for water treatment plants. Some 34 pumping stations will manoeuvre the water north to the latitude of the Yellow River, at which point it will continue by means of gravitational flow. The Bahr Yusuf barely compares in scale, but the principle is the same: to bring water to cities and parched lands. Whether the great South–North water transfer will be as sustainable as the Faiyum remains to be seen.

In California, the plan for the Peripheral Canal – designed to pump 425 cubic metres (15,000 cubic feet) of water per second from the San Joaquin and Sacramento river deltas to the arid Los Angeles Basin – has triggered a heated debate [2.43]. It will convey water in one direction only; water that will never return. In both scale and ambition, these 21st-century projects are derived from the same nurturing spirit as the Faiyum, but how long can such an immense hydrological imbalance be sustained? There is a need to recover a sense of balance and parsimony in modern metropolises such as Los Angeles, where native scrub should be encouraged to return, reinstating a much-needed sense of balance between the city, its history and its immediate environment.

2.41

2.42

2.42 **South–North water transfer project, China.**
In this massive project, a significant part of a watershed originating to the south of the Yellow River is being transferred to the north. When completed, this system will deliver 15 million megalitres a year, cost over $40 billion to build and should help maintain cities and their landscapes.

2.43 **The Peripheral Canal, California, USA.**
The main water supply to Los Angeles, the Peripheral Canal, here in Bakersfield California, derives from an important part of the Sacramento and San Joaquin watershed. Without this water pumped at a rate of 425 cubic metres (15,000 cubic feet) per second, Los Angeles and its landscape would simply not survive.

2.41 **The Canal du Midi, France.**
Built for transportation rather than irrigation, the Canal du Midi linking the Mediterranean to the Atlantic Ocean was a feat of engineering by the French engineer Pierre-Paul Riquet in the late 17th century. It reached a high point of 189 metres (620 feet) above sea level through a series of locks and tunnels, and produced a landscape of extraordinary beauty, which is now a UNESCO World Heritage Site.

2.43

3. From Temenos to Physis
Sacred Landscapes in Greece

*'Persephone was picking flowers – roses, crocus, violets –
up and down the soft meadow … And the narcissus, which
was grown as a lure for the flower-faced girl by Gaia …
a wonderful thing in its splendour … Persephone was filled
with a sense of awe, and she reached out with both hands to
take hold of the pretty plaything. And the earth, full of roads
leading every which way, opened up beneath her.'*
Homeric Hymn to Demeter[1]

Both myth and the belief in sacred places inform our
understanding of ancient landscapes. Natural sites that are
breathtaking or otherwise unusual are imbued with special
meaning: they instil awe and respect, or are deemed to be
holy. At the dawn of sedentary civilization, even amid the
early trappings of clans and settlements, humankind was
united in worshipping these powerful, magic places, brought
together by fear of the unknown. Natural phenomena were
attributed to gods. The intertwining of nature and myth as
the cornerstones of an ancient civilization is perhaps nowhere
more clearly visible than in the landscapes of Greece and more
particularly the sanctuary of Apollo at Delphi [3.0]. Historical
records and archaeological artefacts, as well as a landscape
almost unchanged since ancient times, reveal how earlier
chthonic cults and shamanistic rituals – such as the worship of
a fertility goddess in Crete[2] [3.1] – were gradually supplanted
by Olympian male deities like Apollo, encompassing all gods
and prompting humankind to become aware of its own
condition and to take control of its own destiny.[3]

The Minoan civilization

When the forest cultures of northern Europe in the Neolithic
created settlements and practised early forms of agriculture,
the old merchant routes of the Mediterranean coast and the
Danube became more vital. The Minoan civilization that
arose on the island of Crete around 3500 BCE provides an
interesting example of the arrival and gradual transformation

3.0 (opposite) Delphi, Greece.
The amphitheatre within the sacred precinct
of the sanctuary of Apollo at Delphi sits beneath
the Phaedriades cliffs of Mount Parnassus.

**3.1 Minoan figurine of a goddess or priestess,
holding two live snakes, Crete.**
Minoan religion seems to have been strongly
matriarchal, with a central goddess figure
perhaps related to fertility, as with the cult
of Ishtar in Mesopotamia.

3.1

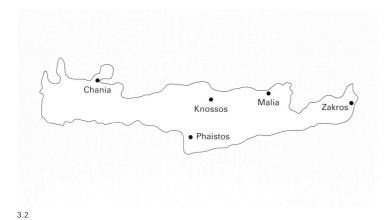

3.2 Map of Crete, showing the principal palace sites.
The palaces of Minoan Crete are found in all parts of the island. They were associated with sacred peaks and caves.

3.3 View of the Mesara Plain from Phaistos, south central Crete.
This fertile plain was an early site of agriculture in Europe; the structure of the irrigated fields today follows the general slope of the plain down towards the sea.

3.4 The snow-covered peak of Mount Ida viewed from the courtyard of Hagia Triada, Crete.
In legend, the infant Zeus was hidden in a cave on Mount Ida by his mother Rhea to escape being swallowed by his father, the Titan Kronos. This landscape marks the birth of time in Greek mythology.

3.5 The Idaean Cave, Crete.
While hidden in the Idaean Cave, Zeus was fed either milk by a goat or honey by a priestess named Melissa. After safely reaching adulthood, Zeus set out to accomplish the founding myth of Europe.

3.4

3.5

of Anatolian, Mesopotamian and Egyptian influences in south-eastern Europe. The fertile Mesara Plain, in the south centre of the island, is probably one of the earliest sites of organized irrigated agriculture in Europe, thanks to techniques learned from the Levant; the landscape that developed has remained almost unscathed for 5,000 years [3.3]. It is also the birthplace of European mythology, as it was at Matala nearby that Zeus, in the form of a white bull, came ashore carrying Europa from Tyre (Phoenicia); he then took her to Gortyn and raped her under a plane tree. From this violent union Minos, the first king of Crete, was born [3.6, 3.7, 3.8].[4]

Minoan religion appears strongly matriarchal and focused on a fertility goddess bearing some resemblance to the goddess Ishtar of Mesopotamia. With time, this figure became conflated with Rhea, known to the Greeks as the 'mother of the gods', who gave birth to Zeus following a union with the Titan Kronos. To prevent the infant from being devoured by his father, she hid him inside a cave on the northern slopes of Mount Ida, where – according to different versions of the myth – the young god was either fed milk by a goat or given honey by a priestess named Melissa [3.5].

The ruins of Minoan palaces, such as at Phaistos [3.15], to the west of the Mesara Plain, and Knossos in the north centre of the island, are somewhat reminiscent of the mythical labyrinth built to house the Minotaur [3.13].

The palace at Knossos has an incredible density of rooms, similar to Babylonian palaces, including grain storehouses and workshops organized around vast courtyards, indicating that the palace was also used for produce storage and distribution [3.11]. Archaeological evidence reveals that Minoan society was decentralized, consisting of communities with palace-like structures at their heart, and funerary practices point to a relative lack of social hierarchy. Beehive or 'tholos' tombs, often found at prominent spots in the landscape and particularly in the island's south, represent the most significant type of funerary architecture; they first appeared in the 4th millennium BCE and continued into the late Bronze Age. Similar conical stone structures can be found throughout the Mediterranean, from the tholos tombs of Mycenae (not directly related) to the tower-like *nuraghi* of Sardinia.

Around 3500 BCE, the first agriculture on Crete marked the beginnings of a more organized society.[5] Although many peoples around the Mediterranean had shared fertility cults, symbolized by the figure of a mother goddess, since prehistoric times, it was their shift from nomadic hunting to a sedentary form of agriculture that brought about a significant change in emphasis. The shamanistic magic of the hunt in all its unpredictability was replaced by agricultural rituals recognizing the importance of the seasonal regularity. Although we are only able in part to decipher the earliest Minoan inscriptions on the Phaistos Disc, artefacts such as

3.6 Matala, south-western Crete.
It was to the beach at Matala, at the edge of the Mesara Plain, that Europa was brought by Zeus in the form of a white bull. She had been carried off by him from the Phoenician city of Tyre, and was never to return. The Mesara Plain can thus be seen as the cradle of European civilizations.

3.7 Plane tree at Gortyn, Crete.
In the myth of Europa, Zeus raped her beneath a plane tree at the site of Gortyn. She then gave birth to three sons, one of whom, Minos, became the first king of Crete. An old plane tree at Gortyn with strong feminine traits still stands today next to the ruins of a temple dedicated to Isis.

3.8 Minoan stone bull's-head vessel.
The bull is a significant symbol in Minoan culture. King Minos's wife, Pasiphae, fell in love with a bull. She then hid inside a hollow wooden cow, was thus mounted, conceived and gave birth to a monster, half-man and half-bull – the Minotaur. In order to hide the beast King Minos and the architect Daedalus built a huge labyrinth at the palace of Knossos.

3.9 Still from *Medea*, by Pier Paolo Pasolini, 1969.
A priestess (played by Maria Callas) performs a sacrificial harvest ritual. The setting in Cappadocia, Turkey, recalls the archaic roots of agricultural rituals revolving around death and rebirth that originated in Asia Minor.

3.10 Relief of Demeter and Persephone, Eleusis.
Demeter, goddess of fertility, and her daughter Persephone stand either side of the young Triptolemos who receives the first grains of wheat. In her grief at the abduction of Persephone by Hades, god of the underworld, Demeter allowed all vegetation to die. New seasonal growth coincided with Persephone's return each year.

3.6

3.7

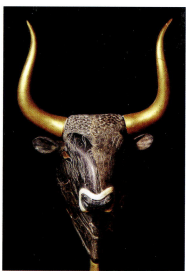

3.8

statuettes and jewels show that the great mother goddess played a prominent role in guaranteeing cyclical fertility [3.18].[6] She had her own attributes, and was not simply a forerunner of Demeter, the Olympian deity who eventually supplanted her. Nonetheless, over the course of centuries the two figures became conflated. One of the oldest Greek deities, Demeter looked after the fertility of the earth, agriculture and farming. She can be seen as a reincarnation of the mother/earth goddesses worshipped all over the Mediterranean from the earliest of times [3.9]. Flowers feature prominently in Minoan art and culture, and one can well imagine this early agricultural society still bonded closely with nature [3.14].

Phaistos

The remains of Phaistos (*c.* 1900 BCE) and Hagia Triada are located on an outcrop facing the southern foot of Mount Ida [3.4]. To the north lies the Mesara Plain, where Cretans began to farm the land. Indeed, the labyrinthine plan of Phaistos – and, to a greater extent, that of Knossos – bears a similarity to the layout of Babylonian palaces, perhaps revealing more about the reality of Minoan life than was previously thought.[7] What is striking here is the maze-like architecture: the palace functions as an elaborate, self-contained beehive protecting a ruling queen. The setting of Phaistos, with its view over the plain below, is breathtaking [3.15].

Around 2000 BCE, settlements were organized around royal palaces such as those at Knossos, Phaistos, Zakros and Malia – buildings that functioned as both real and symbolic centres [3.12]. These great complexes, with their prominent processional courts, were carefully sited so as to make the most of the surroundings. A network of roads linked most palaces and facilitated trade, on Crete and beyond [3.2]. Minoan merchants, who dominated the Aegean, gradually penetrated the southern Peloponnese. This is a period of administrative and economic unity throughout the central and eastern Greek islands, with signs that Minoan Crete was at its zenith.[8] The gold artefacts and luxury items suggest a very affluent upper class. The frescoes found at Knossos attest to a peaceful society, in which women held positions of power, and young men are portrayed gathering flowers as ritual offerings [3.16, 3.17]. Likewise, the motif of a pair of queen bees holding a honeycomb that often appears in Minoan art and jewellery is also strongly matriarchal in its symbolism [3.19].

The rise of Mycenae

During the middle of the 2nd millennium BCE the Minoan civilization began to show signs of decline, perhaps weakened by a series of natural and man-made catastrophes. There is some evidence that the large volcanic eruption on the island of Thera (modern Santorini), located in the Aegean Sea north of Crete, provoked a violent tidal wave and huge ash deposits.

3.9

3.10

The story of Demeter and Persephone appears in some form throughout the Minoan, Mycenaean and Classical Greek periods [3.10]. These two goddesses explain and personify the relationship between the seasons and the cycle of growing – the dying of vegetation in the scorching heat of summer and regrowth with the return of rains. The Mycenaeans established the cult of Demeter at Eleusis, in the middle of the 2nd millennium BCE, which gave birth to the Eleusinian Mysteries.[9] In the Classical period, this chthonic cult was seen as the counterpart of the cult of Apollo. Demeter personified agricultural fertility and Persephone, abducted by Hades, god-king of the underworld, was forced to spend one-third of the year underground [3.20]. She personified the hidden mysteries of soil fertility, death and rebirth. The cult of Demeter, which began in Crete in the 3rd millennium BCE, stemmed from earlier fertility cults in Anatolia and the Levant.

3.11

3.13

3.14

3.12

3.11 Palace of Knossos, Crete.
The sheer monumentality of the Minoan palace at Knossos and its deliberate insertion into the steep topography create a strong contrast with the olive groves surrounding it.

3.12 Throne room of Knossos.
In the throne room at Knossos a wall painting depicts a landscape with plants and mythical creatures. Minoan art frequently conveys the impression of a culture living in close harmony with the natural environment.

3.13 The labyrinth.
The labyrinth has recurred in landscape architecture ever since its invention by Daedalus, as recounted by Homer. This 18th-century example is in the Parc del Laberint d'Horta in Barcelona, Catalonia. The form relates to the taming of nature, but also to the taming of the bestial within ourselves. Its complex folds warp our understanding of space and time and offer a metaphor of our own destiny on Earth.

3.14 Blue bird fresco, Knossos.
This wall painting from the palace at Knossos (1550 BCE), depicting a blue bird perched amid wild roses and irises growing in a rocky landscape, once again reveals the Minoan love of nature.

3.15 The palace of Phaistos, Crete.
The dominant position of the Minoan palace at Phaistos on a promontory in the Mesara Plain, close to Mount Ida, Matala and Gortyn, ties it into ancient mythology. Its impressive processional court and stairs have the acoustic qualities of an early amphitheatre or odeon.

3.16 Prince of the Lilies fresco, Knossos.
In this wall painting from Knossos, a young prince wearing an elaborate crown strides across a field with lilies and butterflies.

3.17 Wild flowers in a field near Phaistos.
Our reverence for the mystery of flowers and nature has been lost, replaced at best by scientific explication. It is this inexorable distancing between ourselves and the natural world that is at stake in any act of landscape intervention today.

3.18 The Phaistos Disc (reverse side).
Dating to 1700 BCE, the inscribed text, with some symbols perhaps related to Linear A, reads in a spiral towards the centre. The disc has for a long time defied complete decipherment, but one theory is that it is a prayer to a Minoan goddess.

3.19 Minoan gold pendant.
Two golden bees hold a drop of honey: this pendant discovered at the palace of Malia attests to the strong matriarchal symbolism of cult in Minoan society. Honey was frequently used in ancient rituals to anoint sacred figures.

3.15

3.18

3.16

3.17

3.19

3.20

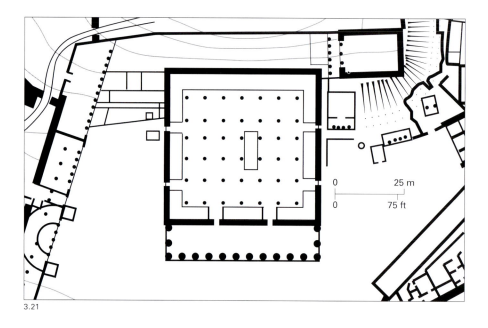

3.21

These decimated coastal settlements and hampered plant growth in Crete for several years.[10] This event, which took place around 1500 BCE, disrupted the local civilization, and put the Minoans' seafaring trade to a disadvantage, making the island more vulnerable to invasion. The Mycenaean occupation of Crete that followed shortly thereafter marks the moment when the Greek language was introduced to the island.[11]

It seems that Crete was already suffering from significant deforestation and overgrazing at the time, which caused severe soil erosion and changes in its river systems, which in turn affected the proper irrigation and maintenance of fields.[12] By the time the Mycenaeans had completely overtaken Crete, it is unlikely that the island bore much resemblance to the extraordinary agricultural civilization that once existed. (Unfortunately, deforestation and overgrazing would subsequently become widespread around the Mediterranean basin.) The Mycenaeans pursued a policy of colonization on the Greek mainland, borrowing some of the harvest rituals from Crete, and were probably responsible for establishing some of the earliest agricultural practices there.[13] They brought the existing vegetation cult over from Crete and chose to establish Demeter's principal shrine at Eleusis in the agricultural Thriasian Plain – the area that would later serve as Athens's main breadbasket [3.21]. The contrast between this sanctuary, set amid the fertile fields of Eleusis, and the stark rocky outcrop of the Phaedriades later consecrated to Apollo at Delphi could not have been more striking. This marks also a transitional period in Greek history, one in which female deities and more generally the role of women in society were considerably revised. A later bas relief showing the Amazon Queen Myrine and her troops being defeated by male soldiers is perhaps quite telling [3.22].[14]

Unlike Crete, with its strong Levantine heritage, Mycenae did not boast a culture of gardens, meadows and advanced agriculture. The Mycenaeans were primarily a warring and defensive civilization, their compact, fortress-like cities circled by huge cyclopean walls [3.23]. While Minoan palaces maintained a connection with the surrounding landscape, Mycenaean cities became much more introverted. In contrast to the Minoans' carefully tended fields, the Mycenaeans recognized the forested wilderness of Arcadia as a place worthy of veneration. Here, a pristine, natural region recalled the divine, rather than the walled paradise gardens of the Orient. It is possible that this fundamental difference in outlook was inherited from the northern tribes of Doria and Scythia; whatever the case, the Greeks paid little attention thereafter to the model of the enclosed garden and focused instead on sites that would incorporate the contemplation of nature from within a sacred precinct or *temenos*.

3.22

3.20 Terracotta plaque from southern Italy.
Persephone is seated on a throne next to Hades, god of the underworld. As Persephone was gathering flowers in a meadow, the ground opened beneath her feet and she was abducted by Hades, who took her back to his kingdom. He then tricked her into eating some pomegranate seeds, obliging her to return to the underworld each year.

3.21 Plan of the Telesterion at Eleusis, Greece.
The Eleusinian Mysteries, staged in this shrine, were the most secret religious rites of ancient Greece. Initiates who revealed them would be sentenced to death, as would any trespasser entering the shrine. Remains of a Mycenaean shrine have been found beneath.

3.22 Relief from the Mausoleum of Halicarnassus, Turkey.
The relief depicts a battle between Greek soldiers and Amazons. Queen Myrine led the Amazon armies on military expeditions to found a matriarchal empire. The myth may reflect a shift in religion from a matriarchal to a patriarchal focus; this in turn had a considerable impact on our apprehension of nature.

3.23 Citadel of Mycenae, Greece.
Mycenae was encircled by a massive fortification wall, creating a clear demarcation between the architecture and its surrounding environment. This is in contrast to Minoan culture, which cultivated an open relationship between palace and landscape.

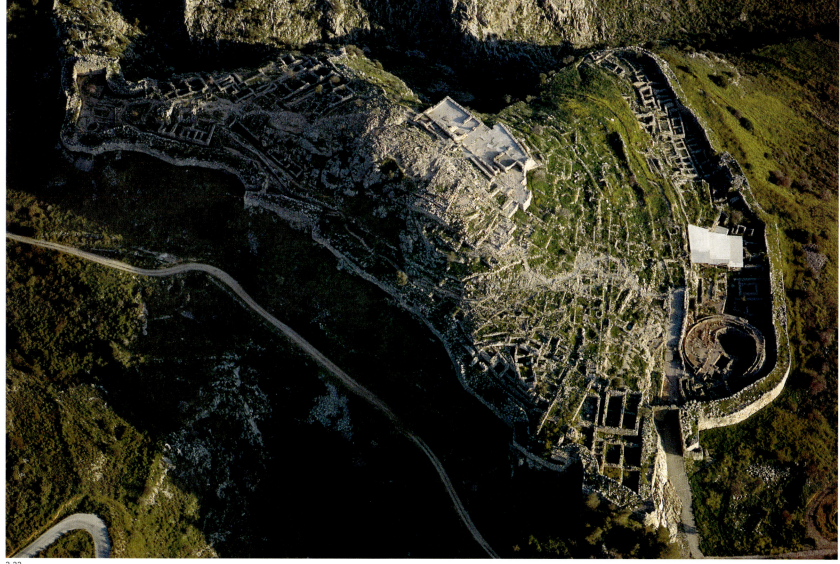
3.23

3.24

Delphi, Greece

The setting of the sanctuary complex at Delphi, under the semicircular spur of the Phaedriades mountains at the foot of Mount Parnassus in Greece, is both ominous and breathtaking [3.25, 3.27]. Its recognition as the principal sanctuary dedicated to Apollo, enclosed in the walls of its sacred *temenos*, is a further demonstration of the Greeks' fascination for a divine natural order wrapped up in the exquisite beauty of a site. Temples in Greek colonies elsewhere, such as the Elymian shrine at Segesta in Sicily, tended to be set in similar striking locations [3.24].

The name, Delphoi, comes from the same root as the Greek word for 'womb', and possibly refers to a more ancient worship of Gaia, or Mother Earth, on this site.[15] There are Mycenaean remains at the site and by the 1st millennium BCE the cult of Apollo at Delphi was home to a symbolic stone navel, or *omphalos*, marking the spot where direct communication with the gods was possible [3.30, 3.31].[16] Visiting the site, at high altitude in a rocky terrain, involved a strenuous trek from Athens, thus enhancing a sense of purity and 'otherness' [3.26a, 3.26b]; this removal from everyday urban life was clearly intentional. In a wider religious context, the story of Apollo defeating the dragon Python, who previously presided over the sacred Castalian Spring,

represents the ascendance of the Olympian gods over their more ancient chthonic counterparts.[17] Through its setting, the sanctuary of Apollo at Delphi distinguishes itself from the sanctuary of Demeter at Eleusis, the second most important cult centre in the Greek world and a place of chthonic worship, as a gendered male space that is assertive and dominating.

The Castalian Spring, nestled in a ravine between two rock faces of the Phaedriades cliffs, is probably the oldest site of worship at Delphi [3.37, 3.38, 3.41]. Its lustral waters, originating in the white snowy caps of Mount Parnassus, flowed year round and fed into an ablution pool that marked a sacred threshold for those wishing to enter the sanctuary [3.40]. The waters used by the Delphic Oracle (also known as the Pythia), on the other hand, flowed under the Apollo temple from a smaller source called the Kerna Spring, situated above [3.39]. It was said the vapours from these waters helped the Oracle enter a trance, in which she uttered powerful, unintelligible sayings that were then entrusted to priests for interpretation.[18] A significant physical effort was demanded of pilgrims on their ascent up the Sacred Way past the Treasury of the Athenians to the Oracle and temple plinth [3.29].

The landscape at Delphi is less archetypal than conceptual in spirit and marks an important moment and

3.24 The Elymian sanctuary at Calatafimi near Segesta, Sicily.
This early Doric temple (5th century BCE) built by the Elymians on the southern foot of Mount Barbaro in Sicily, shows clearly the importance attached to site in sacred settings.

3.25 Reconstructed view of Delphi, Greece.
The Castalian ravine on the upper right and that of the Kerna in the upper centre frame the topography of the site. The Sacred Way winds up to the sanctuary; beyond it, on the far left is the stadium.

3.25

3.26a

3.27

3.26a, 3.26b Reconstructed views of Delphi, before and after.
The Amphissa Valley slopes down to the Gulf of Corinth on the right and the Phaedriades cliffs rise to Mount Parnassus on the left. Before the sanctuary was built, the site was an ancient place of worship to Gaia, Mother Earth. Below, the stadium for the Pythian games and the sanctuary of Apollo are visible.

3.27 Aerial view of Delphi.
The sanctuary at Delphi is tucked into the foot of the Phaedriades cliffs beneath Mount Parnassus, between the Castalian Spring flowing down a ravine to the right, and the stadium perched on a promontory to the left. Within the sacred precinct of the *temenos* are the theatre, the Oracle, the temple of Apollo and the Sacred Way.

3.28

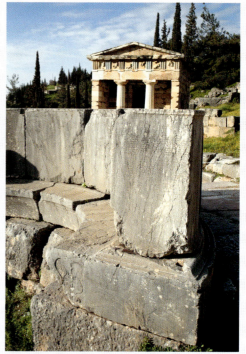

3.29

3.30

3.31

3.28 View from the amphitheatre.
Beyond the amphitheatre is the Sacred Way, with the Treasury of the Athenians celebrating the battle of Marathon, and the valley falling away below. The theatre was an integral part of the rites of the sanctuary and the Oracle.

3.29 Bench near the Treasury of the Athenians.
The Sacred Way was lined with numerous monuments, statues and commemorations set up by individuals and cities.

3.30 *Omphalos*, Delphi.
The *omphalos* at the end of the Sacred Way designates the navel of the Earth. Legend has it that Zeus sent out two eagles from Mount Olympus in opposite directions – the *omphalos* marks the location where the birds crossed.

3.31 Original *omphalos*, Delphi.
The original *omphalos* is carved with a knotted mesh. It possibly pre-dates the cult of Apollo at Delphi and may have served in an ancient cult of Gaia; it is thus an important symbol of the intrinsic sacredness of Delphi.

3.32 Columns of the temple of Apollo.
As viewed from the *omphalos*, the temple's columns shoot up towards the sky. The Pythian Oracle was located within the temple's massive base in a small, closed chamber or *adyton*.

shift towards a strong symbolic correspondence between man and nature [3.32]. After the visitor has passed the temple and reaches the top of the theatre dedicated to Dionysus at the highest point of the *temenos*, a breathtaking view across the Amphissa Valley, carpeted with countless olive groves, opens out [3.28, 3.45]. The relative asymmetry in the site's layout within the sacred precinct, its long, narrow pathways and its terraces on different levels are a response to the particularities of the Pythian rites with respect to setting and topography. Moreover, the manner in which the adjacent cliffs framed the sky above the temple of Apollo mattered as much to the Pythia as the waters of the Kerna Spring. Although the reasons for siting the Oracle at Delphi are not yet fully understood, the writings of Herodotus, Pausanias and others confirm a strong belief in the natural powers of this landscape, which resonated with the beauty of man – an effect so grand that no garden aesthetic could ever replicate it.

The first structure the pilgrim arriving from Athens would encounter is the Tholos of Athena [3.33]. Its *temenos* marks the upper limit of the 'profane' olive groves that drape the Amphissa Valley down to the Gulf of Corinth with a vast expanse of silvery-blue foliage [3.35]. Although native to Greece, the olive tree – sacred symbol of Athena, the warrior goddess of Athens – was introduced into this valley. The Tholos of Athena is the only temple at Delphi devoted to a female divinity; its location on the lowest terrace, at the entrance of the sanctuary, affords it the role of a threshold between the sacred and the profane.[19] It designates the point at which the chthonic fertility cults found on the plains of Attica around Eleusis cease to have any relevance. Here, the more rugged mountainous terrain dedicated to Apollo has precedence. The achievement of Delphi is to enforce on the pilgrim the realization that sublime reason and natural order exist in the world, this not an earth-bound, domestic fertility cult, like that of Demeter, but a phenomenally powerful cult in celebration of a virile god of the heavens [3.42, 3.46, 3.47].

Next to the *temenos* of the Tholos of Athena, on the profane side of the Castalian chasm, stood the men's gymnasium with its open-air exercise ground overlooking the verdant Amphissa Valley [3.34, 3.36]. This was a place of physical, spiritual and mental preparation for young men who took part in the Pythian Games, which were staged every four years in the stadium above the Apollo sanctuary [3.44]. These games were Panhellenic, meaning that the fittest athletes would converge from all over Greece to take part; and it was during such competitions that the male body was glorified to almost divine proportions [3.43]. Once the young men had been initiated into the rites of the Pythian Apollo in the gymnasium, they were invited to stop at the Castalian Spring for ablutions and rise then towards the stadium through the inner sanctuary, where they would compete naked, and in full communion with nature.

3.32

3.33

3.34

3.35

3.36

3.33 Tholos of Athena.
The Tholos marks the entrance to Delphi on the road from Eleusis and Athens. Athena, the warring goddess of wisdom, became the virgin protector of Athens by offering the city the domesticated olive tree, which cannot be grown naturally from seed but only from cuttings.

3.34 The gymnasium.
Used by the youth of Delphi to train for the Pythian games, the gymnasium consisted of a *palaestra* garden on an upper level and a stoa with pools on a lower one. The pools were said to have magical properties that allowed the young athletes to communicate with Apollo.

3.35 *Temenos* wall.
The *temenos* wall separates the sacred Tholos of Athena from the profane olive groves on the slopes of the Amphissa Valley. Crowds of pilgrims from Athens would have streamed into the sanctuary, with the olive trees, symbol of their city goddess, framing the entire backdrop.

3.36 Reconstructed view of the lower sanctuary.
The Castalian Spring flowed from the foot of the deep gorge that cut through the Phaedriades cliffs towering over the site.

3.37 Reconstructed view of Delphi.
The great cleft of the Castalian Spring between the lower sanctuary to the right and the inner sanctum of Apollo to the left formed a tangible physical threshold where both athletes and pilgrims were required to stop for ablutions and purification rites. One of the most notable aspects of the site of Delphi is the integration of strong natural features.

3.38 Section across Delphi from the temple of Apollo and the Pythian Oracle to the Castalian Spring.
The interplay of downward slopes and physical ascent is fundamental to the experience of the sacred at Delphi. The physical effort required of pilgrims walking along the Sacred Way, particularly on hot summer days, was very demanding.

3.39 Water basin for the Kerna Spring.
The Kerna Spring was located just above the Pythian or Delphic Oracle. One theory is that its waters, which were also carried to the Oracle chamber beneath the temple of Apollo, contained high levels of ethylene – enough to produce euphoria and trances.

3.40 Water basin for the Castalian Spring.
The Castalian Spring flows down from Mount Parnassus and its waters were collected here for ablutions and purification before worshippers entered the precinct of the sanctuary.

3.41 The Castalian cleft above Delphi.
The Phaedriades cliffs split open above Delphi on the north, where the Castalian Spring is born. It is a humbling and powerful site, full of natural hazards and challenges.

3.39

3.40

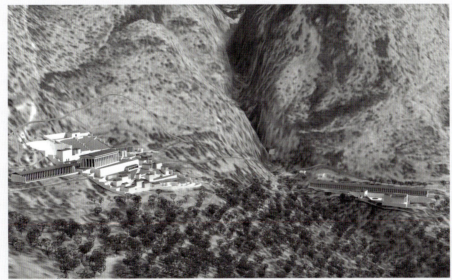
3.37

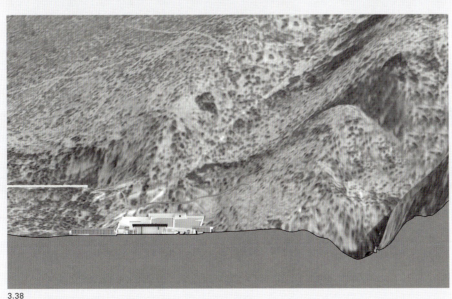
3.38

3.41

3.42

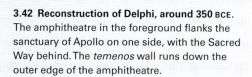

3.42 Reconstruction of Delphi, around 350 BCE.
The amphitheatre in the foreground flanks the
sanctuary of Apollo on one side, with the Sacred
Way behind. The *temenos* wall runs down the
outer edge of the amphitheatre.

3.43 Statue of a naked youth, or *kouros*.
Statues of young men were frequently found
in sanctuaries to Apollo. We have inherited the
notion that a perfect male body can be divine
even today. Delphi, together with other shrines
of Apollo such as on Delos, represented a shift
from the worship of female deities towards
male gods, a change brought about through
a complete conceptual, philosophical and
aesthetic revolution.

3.44 The stadium, Delphi.
Located in the upper part of Delphi, this artificial
platform built on a steep slope marks a striking
contrast and balance between the man-made
and nature. Here landscape architecture defines
the levelled arena of civilization against a natural
vertiginous backdrop.

3.43

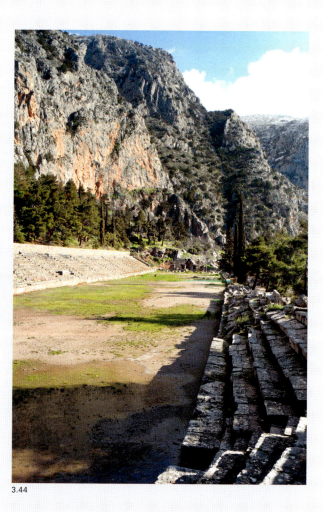

3.44

3.45

3.46

3.45 View down to the Amphissa Valley.
The *temenos* wall defining the sacred sphere
is visible in the foreground. The cypress tree
was first brought back from Persia by Alexander
the Great. Its unchanging evergreen properties
made it a symbol of eternity and of the dead.

3.46 The sanctuary of Apollo, Delphi.
The temple sits on top of the Pythian Oracle
chamber, with a view stretching all the way
down the Amphissa Valley to the Gulf of Corinth.

3.47 Plan of the sanctuary of Apollo.
Contained within its roughly quadrangular
enclosure or *temenos*, the sanctuary and its
Oracle exerted considerable political and social
influence on Greek society over a long period.
The Oracle could be consulted on just one day
in the month, and only when Apollo was
believed to reside at the site.

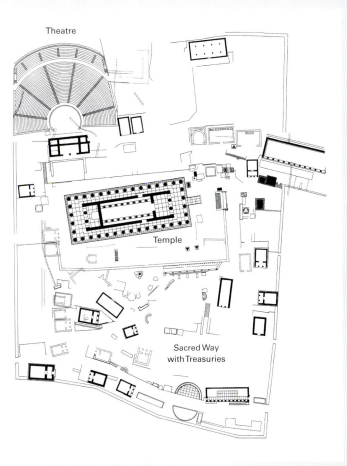

Theatre

Temple

Sacred Way
with Treasuries

3.47

Greek civilization and new concepts of nature

Delphi marked not only a period of religious transition, but also a change in environmental perception. This is the moment when Western civilization began to turn its back on superstitions of Mother Earth in favour of a future guided solely by human intention. In this context Delphi stands for the new ideals of democracy and the birth of natural philosophy, as well as the definitive establishment of a male-dominated society. The pre-Socratic thinkers who emerged in the 6th century BCE in the Greek cities of Miletus and Ephesus represent a milestone in abstract thought and a fundamental break from traditional explanations of the universe [3.50]. Their willingness to question older religious and superstitious accounts of the world was simply astounding, and the influence that their principles had on the landscape was not only immediate but also lasting.[20]

In this early flowering of Greek philosophy, thinkers attempting to explain the world around them arrived at various conclusions. Heraclitus, for instance, proposed that phenomena were animated by an unceasing 'flux' of material. This view subsequently influenced the works of Democritus of Abdera, with his doctrine of atoms, which in time led to the *Metaphysics* of Aristotle and eventually to Lucretius's *De Rerum Natura*, a Latin work on natural physics written in the 1st century BCE. Heraclitus's rival Parmenides speculated on the existence of a single immutable substance that constituted the stuff of the world – a view that led ultimately to Plato's Theory of Forms. Philosophers such as Thales of Miletus and his pupil Pythagoras developed axiomatic thinking in mathematics and geometry that led ultimately to Euclid's elemental theorems. Much of the mathematics and trigonometry were inherited from Babylon, but their transformation into a tool of rational perception was quite new.[21] What all the pre-Socratic thinkers had in common was that they abandoned a long-established worldview to formulate aspects of a new, all-encompassing notion of *physis*, which instead described the world in complex spatial and temporal materiality. As Anaximander wrote: 'The origin of things is in the illimitable. It is the source of their existence, to which in the end they return, as ordained by the law of necessity: for they are answerable to, and must atone for offending against, the just decrees of time.'[22] Furthermore, through the principle of open discussion, Greek society allowed a paradigm shift to occur, leading to a new culture of thought and debate. New public gathering spaces such as the agora and stoa were created.

The rational perception of the world instigated by pre-Socratic thinkers is not only a founding block of Western thinking: it also marks a departure from the ancient fertility cults and a deliberate change in attitude towards nature and landscape at large. Having ignored the Oriental model of the walled garden, which they would have associated with their

3.48

3.49

3.50

arch-enemies the Persians, the Greeks concentrated their thoughts on their natural surroundings instead. From the 6th century BCE, their ideals also influenced the development of the urban environment. Greek cities were non-palatial and democratic, and thereby conducive to the exchange of ideas. The grid plan of Miletus, for instance, was non-hierarchical and clearly expressed an environment in which citizens (those who were not slaves, that is) were treated and housed equally. There were no exclusive gardens in this city, simply a set of public, open spaces such as the agora, the stoa and the gymnasium, which were conducive to democratic interaction between men. After its rebuilding in the early 5th century, Miletus never really grew in size, although it could have developed into a much larger commercial centre. This seems to have been the result of a conscious decision: a desire to limit the size of the population in order for democratic society to function well.

Greek cities that had expanded to their limit were obliged to establish colonies elsewhere, including Italy and Sicily [3.48], which led to the spread of Greek ideas, culture and art throughout the Mediterranean and beyond, especially following the conquests of Alexander the Great [3.48]. During his campaigns of the 330s and 320s BCE, reports of the Orient – more particularly from Bactria, Ctesiphon and Pasargadae in the eastern reaches of Alexander's new empire – reached Greece [3.49, 3.51, 3.52]. They mentioned extraordinary

pleasure gardens full of fantastic plants, and introduced an exotic note to garden culture that lasted well into the Roman period.

During the Hellenistic period, Greece seemed to wake up to the wider world. In earlier times, civilizations scarcely looked farther than their nearest geographical borders, but in the Hellenistic period the Greeks began to perceive cultural and philosophical relationships with the world beyond. The exodus of the Pythagorian school of Alexandria to Syracuse, Sicily, marks a significant shift in the perception and use of landscape. We are far from Aristotle's assertion, made only a few generations before, that man, as a social animal, prefers life in the *polis*, the city, as the most natural for him. With experience gained from foreign landscapes, the concept of nature acquired a new cultural dimension and was observed objectively, independent of any religious considerations. The Pythagorian school went so far as to transfer some papyrus stands from their native Nile Delta to the banks of the Ciane River near Syracuse, where they still thrive today [3.54].

Documented experiences of travel and exploration led to the comparison of landscapes for the first time. Faced with cultures such as those of ancient Egypt and Persia, so strikingly different from their own, the Greeks not only were forced to acknowledge their existence, but also acquired a critical distance when considering their own understanding of nature. This interest in nature, emboldened and inspired

3.48 Cave of Archimedes, Sicily.
Lost amid a garden of wild flowers, bitter oranges and lemon trees in the Neapolis area of Syracuse, Sicily, this cave is said to be the tomb of Archimedes, the great mathematician and philosopher. Syracuse was founded by Greek settlers from Corinth, and became the flourishing cultural capital of Magna Graecia.

3.49 The Arch of Ctesiphon, Iraq.
Alexander the Great conquered Ctesiphon on the banks of the Tigris River in 330 BCE, initiating a long period of Greek rule in the region. The large free-standing arch was built much later, during the Sassanid era of Persia. The Persians conquered Ctesiphon in the 6th century and made the city their capital.

3.50 Aerial view of the ancient city of Miletus, Turkey.
For democracy to function well, Greek cities like Miletus set clear limits to their growth. After a certain point new colonies had to be founded elsewhere, leading to the spread of Greek culture across the entire Mediterranean.

3.51 Gandharan relief.
The art of Gandhara, as seen in this intricate relief, represents an extraordinary mix of Greek and Buddhist cultures, which developed into this very particular style after the passage of Alexander the Great. Indo-Corinthian capitals with the Buddha at their centre are also found in Gandhara.

3.52 Tomb of King Darius the Great, Naqsh-e Rustam, Iran.
Darius the Great died in 486 BCE; Alexander the Great visited his tomb, near Persepolis, 150 years later, on his victorious return from defeating the Persians.

3.51

3.52

3.53

3.55

3.53 Doric Greek temple, Segesta, Sicily.
The well-preserved temple of Segesta, was
built in the 5th century BCE. The surrounding city
was subsequently completely destroyed by the
Vandals and what remains today is an idyllic
pastoral landscape that vividly recalls ancient
Greece. It is one that could have been described
by Virgil in the *Aeneid*.

3.54 A papyrus stand on the Ciane River, Sicily.
When the Pythagorean school fled to Sicily, it
brought with it papyrus plants from Alexandria
that were planted in the Ciane River near
Syracuse, where they still grow today.

3.55 Pan and a goat.
This sculpture from Herculaneum shows the god
Pan having sex with a goat; its striking realism
demonstrates how integrated Greek mythology
was in Roman culture.

3.56 El Capitan, Yosemite National Park, USA.
The rock face of El Capitan in Yosemite National
Park is reminiscent of the Phaedriades cliffs
at Delphi. It is interesting to note how the
American National Park movement drew its
inspiration from the Greeks to domesticate
the American wilderness.

3.54

3.56

by eastern influences, and heightened by the urbanization of new colonies such as the Doric temple site in Segesta in north-western Sicily, engendered distinctions between nature and art, the wild, the rural and the cultivated [3.53]. It was these latter stages of Hellenistic civilization that profoundly influenced the Romans and instigated a notion of 'landscape' within urban culture.

The birth of Arcadia

The notion of idealized landscapes lying outside the realm of the sacred figured prominently in Hellenistic literature. One genre of poetry took as its theme the pastoral landscapes of Sicily – a sensual setting free from external danger. Poets who wrote about these idyllic places, beginning with Theocritus in the 3rd century BCE, drew on the earlier writings of Hesiod and Homer to evoke an idealized view of the life of Arcadian shepherds, who spent their time exchanging poems, making love and playing the flute to their god Pan. The landscapes, too, were idealized, but also devoid of any specific religious character. Theocritus was the first to confirm the significance of the pastoral Arcadian aesthetic in Hellenistic culture. A tinge of nostalgia haunts his *Idylls*, which evoke a time when the world was simpler, more immediate and innocent. The Roman poet Virgil, deeply influenced by Theocritus, later gave full voice to a poetic vision in which pastoral landscapes served the sensual yet nostalgic purpose of man. A sculpture

from Herculaneum showing Pan making love to a goat indicates how deeply Roman culture was moved and influenced by the Arcadian ideals [3.55].

Virgil's literary landscapes correspond more closely to those of his native northern Italy than Arcadia. But dialogue and interaction between Arcadian shepherds, and their communion with nature, remain at the heart of his *Eclogues*, published *c*. 39 BCE, which ensured that the concept of the idyllic landscape remained of the utmost importance in the development of Western landscape aesthetics.[23] One might argue that our 'original' closeness to nature was lost a long time ago, when the landscape ceased to be viewed as the home of gods and spirits, and instead became a secular place of learning, scientific reasoning and pleasure. The melancholy embodied in the concept of the idyll may still be found in the sense of 'holiness' that surrounds national parks and conservation areas such as Yosemite National Park in California that have been set apart [3.56]. Now that environments are created according to concepts rather than being rooted in place, our curiosity regarding what is foreign in a landscape, as well as our objective, distant appraisal of it, are direct consequences of this remote Hellenistic heritage.

4. Of Villas and Woods
Roman and Barbarian Landscapes

'Tityrus, you lying there beneath the shade
of a spreading beech,
Practising your woodland music on a slender pipe,
we are leaving
The boundaries of our country and our sweet fields.
We are being
Exiled from our country, while you, Tityrus, at your
ease in the shade,
Teach the woods to re-echo the name of beautiful Amaryllis.'
　　　Virgil, *Eclogue* 1[1]

The Roman fresco depicting Flora from a villa near Pompeii reminds us of the distant Minoans and their heightened appreciation of flowers [4.1]. The origins of the ancient Etruscan civilization, which flourished in the area north of Rome between the 7th and the 4th centuries BCE, has long been debated, though modern DNA testing now suggests strong Italic and Anatolian roots.[2] The Etruscans contributed to the spread of agriculture, including the planting of olive groves on terraced fields where cereals were grown. Like their Semitic rivals the Phoenicians of Carthage, the Etruscans also aided the dissemination of fruit and nut trees, chickpeas, the grapevine and wheat, among other crops. Unlike the military-minded Romans, however, they did not promote their agriculture systematically. Their primary intent was to provide reliable sustenance for their commercial outposts around the Tyrrhenian Sea. Little is known about their exact farming practices, but the Etruscans' supposed origins would point to a common pool of techniques inherited from early times.[3]

Etruria suffered from the expansion of Roman interests and was eventually conquered during the 3rd century BCE. The rise of the Roman Republic marks an unprecedented change in the European landscape. The subsequent success of the Roman Empire, epitomized at Hadrian's Villa in Tivoli, was shrouded in myth and legend [4.0]. It attests to

4.0 (opposite) Hadrian's Villa, Tivoli, Italy.
A statue of Hermes (Mercury) stands under an architrave in a colonnade around the Canopus canal at Hadrian's Villa in Tivoli.

4.1 Roman fresco of Flora.
A young woman depicted as Flora gathers wild flowers in a fresco from the Villa Arianna in Stabiae, near Pompeii, Italy.

4.1

4.2

4.3

4.4

a superior strategy based on an efficient social hierarchy and the assimilation of conquered cultures and lands. The rigour of its political and social organization matched the systematic manner in which outlying lands were bound back to Rome. Colonies, in turn, provided the resources and military might for further expansion. The establishment of an efficient system of paved roads planted with trees for shade, the building of border defences and aqueducts, the clearing of forests for farming land and the creation of new urban centres with civic spaces left an indelible mark on three continents.[4] Last but not least, the Romans prized sensuality in garden design – a trait that has influenced the aesthetics of landscape to this day.[5]

The myth of the founding of Rome – the adoption of Romulus and Remus by a she-wolf – says much about the Roman attitude towards nature: it was to be tamed of all wildness in the service of humankind [4.2]. According to tradition, Romulus and Remus became shepherds, the former subsequently founding Rome on what would become the Palatine Hill.[6] Virgil's texts touching on the making of the Roman landscape highlight the tilling of the soil and pastoral activity as the two fundamental acts of civilization on the land. The Romans' understanding of geography, civic planning, hydrology and construction, based on simple surveying methods and geometric calculation, formed the basis of an expertise gradually refined over time.

Claiming the territory

The Roman land management system was not a Western invention. Rather, it should be understood as the careful selection and distillation of earlier, Eastern agricultural models. The importation of productive technology, such as the plough, had a huge impact on the natural environment [4.3]. As Rome became an empire, extensive forests were cleared to meet agricultural needs and to facilitate military and political control. Retiring centurions were rewarded with tracts of land that were readily surveyed and subdivided into sectors based, like the Roman cities, on a grid layout.[7]

Having fought wars to further the empire, retired veteran soldiers took on the task of battling against nature, employing various farming techniques and, for the richest, using slaves and local peasants as labour. The organization of Roman society thus contributed greatly to the transformation of the land, as legions of productive farmers defined a new kind of landscape in striking contrast to the continent's forested past [4.4]. This applies as much to the north coast of Africa, from Egypt to Carthage and beyond, as to mainland Italy; along with Sicily, Africa was considered the breadbasket of the Roman Empire.

The conquest and control of land on a territorial scale were made possible only through the empire's impressive network of roads and aqueducts [4.6]. In terms of road construction, the Romans were efficient and pragmatic, using

4.2 *The Capitoline Wolf*.
This bronze sculpture, probably medieval in date, depicts the suckling of Remus and Romulus by a she-wolf, the symbol of the founding of Rome.

4.3 Reconstructed Roman plough.
Legend has it that Romulus traced a furrow known as the *urbis pomerium* around Rome, defining a precise boundary between city and countryside. The plough thus became an instrument of city planning, tracing the intangible limit between a settlement and its hinterland.

4.4 Landscape around Segesta, Sicily.
A tract of agricultural landscape at Segesta, in Sicily, reveals a clear distinction between the cultivated land, the forest and the wild scrub vegetation.

4.5 Reconstructed Roman *groma*.
Throughout the Roman empire, the *groma* was used in laying out urban settlements and roads. This simple surveying instrument was set up to trace precise alignments and establish the standard grid that radiated from the Cardo, the main north–south road, and the Decumanus, the main east–west road.

4.6 View along the Appian Way.
The Appian Way was begun by the Roman Censor Appius Claudius Caecus in the early 4th century BCE, initially for military purposes. Together with aqueducts such as the Aqua Appia, the road became a vital element in the strategic infrastructure of the Roman Republic.

4.5

4.6

4.7

4.8

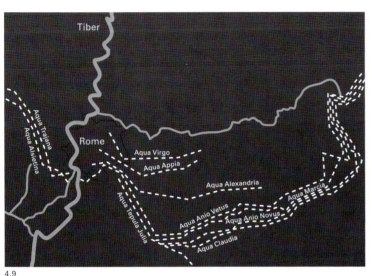

4.9

4.10

4.7 The thermal pool, Bath, England.
While not comparable in scale to the Baths of Caracalla in Rome, the thermal pool at Bath certainly provides a sense of the standard of luxury that prevailed in the late empire, and is one of the best-preserved examples of Roman thermal architecture.

4.8 Remains of aqueducts outside Rome, Italy.
In the reign of the emperor Augustus the population of Rome had grown to more than a million. Sufficient provision of food and water for the inhabitants had to be met on a daily basis, which translated into massive infrastructure being built in the surrounding landscape. These remains of aqueducts run parallel with the Appian Way, south of Rome.

4.9 Map of aqueducts supplying Rome under the Empire.
Some of these aqueducts are still in use today, supplying the city with water, and are now a fixed part of the topology of the city's landscape.

4.10 The Roman Forum.
The Via Sacra crosses the Forum in Rome. This once marshy area was completely drained to make way for the most important civic site in the city, where triumphs were held and important religious processions came down from the Capitoline Hill.

4.11 The Arethusa Spring, Syracuse, Sicily.
The miracle of the Arethusa Spring on the island of Ortygia in Syracuse remains intact to this day: the spring mysteriously delivers its sweet waters within a few steps of the Ionian Sea. Thick stands of papyrus provide shade for its wildlife.

4.12 Detail of the Nile Mosaic.
This mosaic dating from the 1st century BCE is from the Sanctuary of Fortuna Primigenia in Praeneste (Palestrina). The scene is teeming with life, with temples and crowds of worshippers, boats, hunters and a variety of exotic animals. These pygmy landscapes, as they are known, were probably made by artists from Alexandria, and show the influence of Hellenistic culture and the exotic on Rome at the time.

tools such as the *groma* [4.5]. Roman roads were established according to a thorough understanding of geography, hydrology and topography, and always followed a given contour line above a valley and, where possible, stuck to the ridges of hills for maximum visibility. River crossings, be they bridges or fords, took advantage of surrounding topography. For their first stone roads the Romans borrowed much of their technical knowledge from the ancient processional routes that they encountered during their campaigns in Egypt, Asia Minor and the Middle East. The difference, though, was that the Romans went on to develop their roads into an extensive network that connected some of the most remote regions of the empire with its capital.[8] The extraordinary location of some of these roads, which have permanently influenced the layout of entire territories, still surprises.

Aside from their road systems, the Romans' other great technological breakthrough was their planning and regulation of urban water systems, which improved the efficiency and hygiene of cities throughout the empire [4.8]. The Romans' understanding of the way water behaves was apparent in their aqueducts, which all functioned in Rome according to a principle of the smallest possible degree of declivity [4.9].[9] The high degree of expertise visible in Roman baths gave birth to a new culture of bathing for pleasure; from Bath to Alexandria via Baden-Baden, it was now possible to enjoy the same facilities throughout the empire [4.7].[10] Roman building practices were consistent, in line with the rigour of the entire system. The circular arch formed the basic element of construction; from aqueducts to palaces and thermal baths, it was replicated systematically throughout Roman times, despite the inherent limitations that it imposed on architects. The civic building types to be found in all important Roman towns, such as the exercise ground and the amphitheatre, were inspired by their Greek predecessors but given greater prominence and scale. The Romans did not invent new models of civic space, but the sheer monumentality of their urban architecture and of their territories' infrastructure was a significant change in the urban landscape – one that would characterize and unite an empire [4.10].[11]

Between the idyll and the pleasure garden: the courtyards of Roman villas

The Romans' pragmatic and structural approach towards the landscape required a balance: something that would satisfy the basic human need for focus and comfort amid rapid expansion and assimilation. This longing for a simpler past, which led to a cult of idealized landscapes in the form of gardens rich in symbolic meaning, is a direct inheritance from the Hellenistic period and cities such as Alexandria and Syracuse [4.11]. Although the Greeks were not especially known for their gardens, the Hellenistic world bequeathed a significant part of its mythological substance

4.11

4.12

4.13

to the Roman landscape ideal, such as the 'pygmy landscape' mosaic depicting the Nile in Palestrina (Praeneste) [4.12].[12] As we have seen, the Roman poet Virgil played an important role in this cultural transfer, transcribing – and adapting – an older tradition in his *Eclogues* and *Georgics*. The image of the singing shepherd familiar from the *Eclogues* set in idealized pastoral scenery reminiscent of ancient Sicily – at a time when the city of Rome had between 1 million and 2 million inhabitants – was already but a dream.[13]

This distance between fantasy and reality is a fundamental characteristic of Roman landscape architecture, and provided the inspiration for countless frescoes in sumptuous Roman villas depicting natural, Greek-inspired idylls [4.14]. These paintings provided windows into landscape mythology – a world where the gardens were inhabited by birds, fruit trees, fauns and nymphs. In *Les jardins romains* (1943), the historian Pierre Grimal even developed a thesis that these works were not only a painted representation of the idyllic texts of Virgil and his predecessors, but that they also served as a source of inspiration for a particular kind of garden art with trimmed hedges called *topiaria*.[14] In any case, this cultural inheritance of a pastoral golden age is far more substantive than it is formal. For the most part these scenes are remnants of older beliefs and lore, which have little to do with the constructive and expansive pragmatism of the Romans. The distinction

between art, literature and garden design came only later, with the complex gardens of Hadrian's Villa at Tivoli, built from 118 CE.

Our perception of the Roman garden is often dominated by the rectilinear peristyle, which derived from the Oriental walled garden. But the Romans' understanding of nature was animated far more by archaic beliefs in the pastoral landscape that had little, if anything, to do with the patterns of formal geometry. The notion of the land itself was sacred and rich with myth through the ancient cult of the Lares.[15] These guardian spirits, who presided over fields, borders and local neighbourhoods, watched over particular locations from small shrines in the form of temples that could be found in homes and by the side of country roads, marking each place with strong religious symbolism.

The contradiction between the rich, Oriental style of garden imported into Rome by its rulers and the archaic, pastoral ideal, understood as a last refuge from the excesses of civilization, was brought into sharp focus during the Social Wars of the late Roman Republic (90–88 BCE). Through a mix of religious belief and political conviction, the impoverished native tribes of the peninsula strove to defend the 'true' values of the earlier agrarian model against the Roman rulers, with their migrant slaves and merchants, streaming in from the East. The pre-existing cult of the Lares, with its rituals and offerings to nature, reached back to the Etruscans and Sabines

4.14

4.15

4.16

and cannot be ignored. It explains, in part, why it took so long for the Oriental style, as well as the Christian religion, to take hold and be fully assimilated by the Romans.

The region of Campania became the experimental laboratory of new forms of garden design during the late empire. This was due to the fact that Naples, with its Greek origins, had strong ties to the cities and trade routes of the East, and had continuously imported plants that would gradually become part of the Italian landscape. Exotic species such as the citron, which originated in Asia, arrived in Naples via Media around the time of Christ; the same can be said of the peach and plane trees, which also came from Media. Frescoes in Pompeii depict these exotic plants, suggesting that by the middle of the 1st century CE they were common sights in the suburban gardens of Naples and the Campania region [4.15]. The Phoenicians and the Greeks had brought other plants, such as the olive (from Greece), the grapevine (from Egypt) and the cypress (from Media), into Italy in earlier times; the Etruscans had cultivated them or planted them as windbreaks alongside cereal crops. The collection of such plants, for food, medicine or textile dyes, shows to what extent the 'original' landscape of the Italian peninsula had been transformed by the time of Christ [4.13].

One of the most famous early examples of an Oriental-style park is the garden of Lucullus, built and planted in the late Roman Republic. Lucullus, upon his triumphant return

from his conquests, chose to import the idea of a luxurious garden like the ones that he had seen in distant Mesopotamia. The vast garden was constructed on the outskirts of Rome, on the Pincian Hill, overlooking the Campus Martius.[16] A walled garden was placed within a larger park on the southern slope, at the place where the gardens of the Villa Medici currently stand. There was a great public outcry when Lucullus built this 'foreign' garden for himself, for it had little to do with the strongly naturalistic aesthetic of the pastoral landscape inherited from early Italic peoples. Although Lucullus's garden, modelled on the four-tiered examples of the Sassanian Empire, was short-lived and controversial because of its overt display of luxury, the fashion caught on in Rome and among the landed elite elsewhere.

During the early empire, the Roman nobility started to build their villas around larger courtyards, which thus became private spaces of repose. In fact, such villas played a vital role in the genesis of the Roman landscape. Their concept was radically different from the row-house urban fabric of the Greeks. These spaces were more ample, and the intricate play between indoor and outdoor, through the open-roofed atrium and the garden peristyle, meant that the architecture was more articulated and capable of variation. In the extraordinary gardens and villas of Pompeii, we can clearly see that of the art of the *hortus conclusus*, the enclosed garden, had reached its peak [4.16].

4.17

4.19 Cistern at the House of Julia Felix, Pompeii.
Water from this long rainwater cistern spanned by bridges was used for both domestic and gardening purposes. The evergreen box hedges recall the trimmed topiary seen in frescoes.

4.20 Garden peristyle, House of Julia Felix, Pompeii.
A drain running along the foot of the line of rectangular columns collected rainwater from the roofs and channelled it into the cistern.

4.21 Fresco depicting a figure of Priapus in an idyllic setting.
Like Dionysus, Priapus was a sacred figure of fertility and good luck with Eastern origins. With his grotesquely inflated phallus he was often found in Roman gardens as an object of amusement; his introduction there helped to accelerate the shift from a symbol of the sacred to an icon of the profane.

4.22 Roman bronze basin supported by ithyphallic fauns, from Pompeii.
Phallic symbols found in the Roman house and garden were thought to bring fertility and good luck.

4.17 The garden of the House of Julia Felix, Pompeii, Italy.
This 'suburban' garden with clipped hedges and fountains is asymmetrical – one side works as 'peristyle' facing the wall of the property on the other.

4.18 Aerial view of Pompeii.
The Cardo runs diagonally through the photograph, with the Decumanus at right angles to it leading to the Forum left of centre. The countless luxurious gardens, and the generous structure of streets and open spaces, confer an extraordinary landscape quality on the city.

4.18

The gardens of Pompeii

The houses and gardens uncovered in the excavations at Pompeii are excellent examples of Roman urban and suburban development in the 1st century CE. Since the Romans considered horticulture to be a minor art form (it did not call for the same level of skill as architecture, painting, sculpture or literature), there is scant written information about how gardens were actually created, maintained and used. This should in no way detract from their intrinsic value, but simply indicates, as with the House of Juia Felix, that the gardens preserved at Pompeii and in the surrounding area represent an average trend in landscape design at a given point in time, rather than pieces of exceptional design and quality [4.17].

The urban density of Pompeii can in no way be compared with that of Rome, a city of between 1 million and 2 million inhabitants during the 1st century CE [4.18]. But its largely homogeneous urban fabric contains many examples of the generously sized courtyard house, with gardens, large pergolas and extensive plant beds, which would suggest an increasing 'Orientalization' and secularization of the idea of nature in the private gardens of the period [4.19]. At their heart, these gardens boasted horticultural and decorative schemes that referred to mythology and to bucolic poetry, as if to compensate for the abstraction of the Roman garden *per se*. Each garden came to display a complex mix of the sacred and the profane, which in practice often meant depictions of

Venus, goddess of love and fertility, and Priapus (derived from the ancient Egyptian god Osiris), symbolizing prosperity and protection [4.21]. Particularly in the later imperial period, the garden came to be associated with lust and seduction, as several artefacts like the ithyphallic bronze basin from the Secret Cabinet of the Archaeological Museum, Naples, would seem to show [4.22].

In the gardens of Pompeii, the natural, bucolic aesthetic inherited from the early Romans had been reduced and replaced by a formal geometry replete with abstract symbolism. Even though the gardens, in all their exoticism and refinement, had never before harmonized so successfully with domestic architecture, they nonetheless represented a 'foreign' idea of nature, imported from the Orient [4.20]. Venus and an accompanying plethora of gods and mythological figures – Bacchus, Silenus, Cupid, fauns, goats and birds – played an important part in this cultural transposition. As it abandoned its links with the sacred and assumed an erotic, and sometimes exotic, symbolism devoid of serious religious significance, the domestic Roman garden of the 1st century CE grew far removed from the productive model of the vegetable patch that had prevailed just two centuries earlier.[17]

The same can be said of the exercise grounds (*palaestrae*) of Pompeii, which can be understood as deriving from the groves where Greek pupils learned how to wrestle.

4.19

4.20

4.21

4.22

4.23

4.23 House of the Beautiful Impluvium, Pompeii, Italy.
Rainwater was collected in pools and stored in underground cisterns in most villas in Pompeii. Water also was brought via aqueducts to public places in Roman towns. The elaborate mosaic around the well shows a reverence towards water that is very Oriental.

4.24 The *Palaestra*, Pompeii.
The *Palaestra* stood next to the amphitheatre: these leisure facilities were derived from the Greek academia and gymnasium, but the open green lawn of the *palaestra* is a Roman invention. A variety of events and gatherings could be staged in this public space.

4.24

The Greek themselves had been inspired by the paradise gardens of the Persians to create their first gymnasia. What is clear in this typological evolution is a transition from the private function of the earlier walled garden to the public sport function of the Roman *palaestra* [4.24]. On the one hand it expresses a necessary transformation of the urban landscape owing to acute demographic pressure. Roman cities needed public spaces to allow their citizens some kind of breathing space. Obviously Pompeii did not have the same problems as Rome, but the presence of such urban structures there attests to the importance attached to wellbeing throughout the empire. On the other hand it also expresses an unusually high degree of civic tradition, like that of the Greeks, in which the internal landscape of a city was actually thought to be sufficient for its citizens. In other words, the Roman architecture of civic spaces and landscapes had grown to replace any kind of lingering nostalgia for an idyllic form of nature. By the 1st century CE, when Pompeii was at its height, one could say that the Roman city in general had acquired a sufficient degree of autonomy to be able to detach itself from the landscape aesthetic of its rural hinterland [4.18]. As often, the Greeks provide a model here: Socrates is said to have left the walls of his city only three times in his life, and against his will at that.[18] He was the very model of a civic individual detached from toiling in the wider landscape – something that all the Romans subsequently strived for.

A new era, a new narrative

Roman gardens of the 2nd century CE were mostly the product of their owners' creative imagination. To be acceptable, everything had to be grandiose, beautiful and rare, as in the House of the Beautiful Impluvium. In this sense, one can say that the late Romans' sense of exuberance created a new approach to landscape architecture, one that broke loose from the pastoral idyllic tradition. This very particular form of Oriental and Hellenistic syncretism became a hallmark of late Roman imperial culture [4.23]. At Hadrian's Villa, the inventive combination of influences from the eastern Mediterranean and beyond meant that the pastoral symbolism of early Roman times was relegated to the background, in the form of extensive olive groves surrounding the palace. All references to Rome's pastoral past were gradually submerged in the prevailing cultural relativism of the period. But it is the scale of the transformation at Hadrian's Villa that marks it out as an important moment in the history of landscape architecture. The site, in the western foothills of the Apennines, was completely removed from its surrounding context and made to embody the choices and taste of one individual ruler. Behind its walls, palace buildings, temples and peristyles, the villa became an extraordinary playground of subjective and cultural eclecticism that would be copied by other rulers in centuries to come. It is the first true example of an invented landscape narrative in Europe.

4.25

Hadrian's Villa, Italy

Roman culture freely assimilated the cultural relics and rituals of conquered lands into a garden resembling a collage, much like the 'Nilotic' peristyle reconstituted at the Getty Villa in Los Angeles today [4.25].[19] Although much older and larger, Hadrian's Villa, built in 118–38 CE near Tivoli, outside Rome, represents an extensive assemblage of landscapes that came together from various origins [4.26]. The fact that this complex appeared in later Roman times can be explained by the profound change that took place in the Romans' attitude towards nature [4.40]. The villa shows how Hellenistic and Oriental influences were finally appropriated into what we call the Western tradition. This shift perhaps reflects a gradual loss of faith in nature and humans' growing importance. The transformation of this series of walled gardens into landscapes that were both urban and horticultural in form, as for instance the immense Poecile garden, is also something particular to the Villa [4.28, 4.29, 4.30].[20] The circular Maritime Theatre, the Cistern Peristyle, the Thermal Baths and the Piazza d'Oro all served the distinct purpose of the emperor [4.36, 4.37, 4.38, 4.39, 4.41]. Renaissance Humanism could not have existed without this transformation from Eastern to Western tradition. It is therefore the conception of the villa's garden as a kind of meta-world entirely detached from its natural surroundings that is of particular interest [4.27a, 4.27b].

The glory of Hadrian's Villa is apparent when the visitor enters the garden's southern gate and is suddenly transported into the world of the porticoed Canopus canal leading to the Serapeum, a temple devoted to the cult of Serapis [4.33]. The original city of Canopus is located on the western arm of the Nile near Alexandria. So why do we find this diminutive reproduction of the Nile on a scrubby hillside of the Latium? Hadrian vowed to build this garden in memory of his young Bithynian lover Antinous, who had drowned at Canopus in the emperor's presence [4.35]. The long canal is flanked by a series of leaping arcades and Egyptian-style statues as it leads to the Serapeum [4.34]. The temple is housed under an impressive suspended half-shell strongly reminiscent of a Persian *iwan* [4.32]. It is said that Hadrian attempted to re-create a place of genuine cult initiation under this vault. The canal evokes the power of subjective memory and the exotic lure of distant places, somewhat reminiscent of the 'pygmy landscapes' found at the Temple of Fortuna in Praeneste [4.31].[21] Through this complete change of scenery, the visitor is transposed into a fantastical landscape that reflects its creator's most intimate dreams.

4.25 The Getty Villa, Los Angeles, USA.
In an exact replica of a Roman villa, the main peristyle includes the topiary hedges in vogue at the beginning of the Empire, along with strong Egyptian influences, including a central 'Nilotic' basin. Later Renaissance and Baroque periods would borrow much from this style.

4.26 Plan of Hadrian's Villa, Tivoli, Italy.
Built between 118 and 138 CE, the villa's buildings and landscape were modelled around numerous references to the emperor Hadrian's travels in Greece, Egypt and the Orient. The strong and clearly differentiated juxtaposition of pools, buildings, orchards and gardens was deliberately planned, and creates a grand assemblage of landscape memories.

4.26

4.27a

4.27b

4.28

4.27a, 4.27b Hadrian's Villa, before and after.
Above is the original pastoral landscape before
Hadrian's Villa was built, with a modest late
Republican villa surrounded by fields and
orchards. Below is the imposing structure of
the Villa. The estate covered over 120 hectares
(296 acres) and employed 3,000 servants and
guards, all at the emperor's service.

4.28 Aerial view of Hadrian's Villa today.
The villa spreads over a very large area,
with the Poecile at top left, the Thermal Baths
at the bottom and the circular Maritime Theatre
top right.

4.29 The Poecile.
The long rectangular basin of the Poecile is the
size of two Olympic swimming pools. Its north
wall was made higher to protect the complex
from cold winds and increase comfort in the
peristyle garden around the pool.

4.30 Reconstruction of the Poecile.
Orientated east–west, the entire Poecile was
over 200 metres (656 feet) long and 100 metres
(328 feet) wide. Because of its vast proportions,
it is thought that horse races may have been
staged there.

4.29

4.30

4.31

4.32

4.31 Reconstruction of Hadrian's Villa.
In the bottom right the Serapeum stands in front of the Canopus. The Poecile is visible in the distance, beyond the thermal baths.

4.32 Section through the Canopus and the Serapeum.
The Serapeum, resembling an Oriental *iwan*, housed statues of Antinous and Egyptian divinities. Because of the natural topography of the site, its underground ritual rooms are set into the hillside.

4.33 View along the Canopus canal from the Serapeum.
Canopus was a city in the Nile Delta of Egypt where Hadrian's favourite lover, Antinous, drowned. Hadrian designed this impressive landscape to immortalize Antinous, consecrating him in the cult of Isis as the figure of Osiris.

4.34 The Canopus.
View down the Canopus (123 CE), lined by 'Egyptian' caryatids, looking towards the Serapeum and its *iwan*. This was where the cult devoted to Antinous took place.

4.35 The Canopus colonnade.
The Canopus colonnade is flanked on both sides by statues of Amazons. In the centre, beneath the architraves, are statues of Ares, Athena and Hermes. The thermal baths are visible in the background.

4.33

4.34

4.35

4.36

4.36 The Maritime Theatre.
Located in front of the Court of the Libraries, the Maritime Theatre was intended as a place for meditation and retreat. Set concentrically within a circular colonnade was a central island, on which stood a ritual building where the emperor would retire each noon to perform his *otium* (ease or relaxation).

4.37 Rectangular pool with peristyle.
A smaller pool surrounded by a peristyle is located on the south-east corner of the Poecile, framing a magnificent view of the Abruzzo mountains to the east.

4.38 Entrance to the thermal baths.
From the direction of the Poecile, the visitor then reaches the remains of the *palaestra* that once fronted the thermal baths. The Canopus colonnade is visible in the far distance.

4.39 Reconstruction of the Piazza d'Oro.
The Piazza d'Oro garden surrounded by a peristyle was close to the imperial palace. Built in the vicinity of the earlier Republican villa, this was where the emperor stayed when in residence here.

4.40 An old olive tree at Hadrian's Villa.
The olive grove dates back to the creation of Hadrian's Villa. Whether this ancient tree has actually withstood two millennia of history is uncertain, but it represents the spirit of continuity that prevails in this exceptional landscape near Rome.

4.41 The Piazza d'Oro garden, with remains of the palace.
Traces of the original structure of an elaborate garden with water features recall the palace garden of King Cyrus at Pasargadae.

4.37

4.38

4.39

4.40

4.41

Beyond the borders

Just as the garden once served to distinguish cultivated land from uncultivated, Roman garden architecture came to express the experience and knowledge that distinguished the cultured Romans from their 'barbarian' counterparts. The Roman landscape was highly structured, especially compared with the wilderness across the Rhine in the barbarian territory of Germania. Tacitus's *Germania*, written in 98 CE, highlights the perceived differences between the Roman Empire and the rest of northern Europe at that time [4.44].[22] It is particularly interesting to note how the philosophies underlying the two landscape archetypes of the forest clearing and the walled garden come up against each other in the battle of the Teutoburg Forest. This famous battle that took place in 9 CE between the Germanic Cherusci tribe and three Roman legions led by Publius Quinctilius Varus freed a greater part of Germany from Roman occupation, thereby changing the course of history by enabling another type of landscape culture to thrive, north and east of the Rhine, well into the Middle Ages, as can be seen at the memorial to this battle erected in Kalkriese [4.43].

In other regions, a feeble attempt to secure boundaries in a territorial sense drove Hadrian's decision to build a fortified wall in the far northern reaches of Britannia [4.42]. This structure erected in the 120s CE was designed to keep the barbaric Picts at bay, but also to distinguish the landscape shaped by imperial rule from the rustic, forested wilderness beyond.[23] And yet this simple decision, affecting the landscape of Northumberland, would play a significant role in history, as if each gesture and each mark made on the landscape by the Romans really did become geographically significant.

In comparison to, say, the Great Wall of China, built during the Qin dynasty three centuries earlier, Hadrian's Wall looks ridiculously diminutive [4.46].[24] But it has been highly effective in defining the boundary between two worlds and two distinct cultures to this day. And it was precisely because of an ill-defined forested frontier in Germany that the entire Western Roman Empire was defeated by the barbarians in the early 5th century CE [4.45]. Moralists might describe Rome's fall as the legitimate triumph of a people who belong to an authentic landscape wilderness over a decadent, eclectic army that preferred lust and gain to a genuine respect for god-given nature. As civilized as it seemed, because of its extraordinary cultural and religious eclecticism the Roman Empire arguably provoked the complete collapse of an established belief in nature – a belief that we have attempted to reinvent time and time again, to no avail.

4.42

4.43

4.42 Aerial view of Hadrian's Wall, England.
Hadrian's Wall, with its series of forts such as this one at Housesteads, was built to secure the northern frontier of Roman Britain against the Picts, in a relentless battle akin the one fought against the barbarians in Germany. At the time, this border was thickly forested and difficult to defend. The Wall has impressed a distinct border on the landscape between two cultures to this day.

4.43 The site of the battle of the Teutoburg Forest, Kalkriese, Germany.
This design by Gigon Guyer architects reveals the site of a decisive battle in 9 CE, when Germanic tribes led by Arminius completely crushed three Roman legions. The Romans thereafter never conquered territory beyond the Limes east of the Rhine.

4.44 Germanic warriors dressed for battle.
An illustration of 'Goth Germaniae', following the description of Germanic warriors by Tacitus: two men dressed in short cloaks and animal pelts wield a club and a spear to confront an enemy.

4.45 The original forest.
The German oak forest was charged with strong beliefs and symbolic meaning which resisted Roman influence. These beliefs were gradually assimilated during the Middle Ages, becoming absorbed into the prevailing Christian doctrine.

4.46 The Great Wall of China.
A wonder of defensive architecture, the Great Wall of China, initially built before 200 BCE and later augmented during the Ming period, stretches over many thousands of kilometres. Like Hadrian's Wall, which it dwarfs, it effectively defines a boundary in the landscape, in this case between China and the desert culture of Mongolia.

4.44

4.45

4.46

5. The Rule of Faith

'My brothers, birds, you should praise your Creator very much and always love him; he gave you feathers to clothe you, wings so that you can fly and whatever else was necessary for you.'
    St Francis of Assisi[1]

The medieval period stretches from the decline and dissolution of the Western Roman Empire in the early 5th century CE to the fall of Byzantium over a thousand years later. The ravages perpetrated by the barbarians shortly after the fall of Rome did not, contrary to belief, herald a return to Gothic and Nordic forest cults in Europe. Instead, church doctrine laid down by St Augustine in the late 4th century gradually became the prevalent dogma, establishing a doctrinal rule that remained resilient to fundamental change for almost a millennium.[2] It was a time when Europe was undergoing great transformation, suffering social, religious and environmental upheaval interspersed with countless wars, famines and plagues. But there were also positive aspects

to the great cultural brawl of the Middle Ages: during this period Christian religion established a firm foothold, and landscape later came to represent a microcosm of its dogma, as in the 12th-century Cistercian example of Poblet [5.0].[3] This implied a resolute belief in the reduction and adaptation of nature in the service of meditation and an immutable geocentric concept of life. The countryside came under the sway of human hours and days, and the pilgrim's path showed the way across the landscape. Giotto's painting of *St Francis Preaching to the Birds* (1299) mirrors a rule of faith that cast its net across an increasingly Christianized continent [5.1].

The apparatus employed by the church to perform this transformation was, significantly, the same as that used by the Romans. What wilderness remained was duly tamed, cleared and turned into productive land. Following the Rule of St Benedict, who died in 547, missions were founded on sites of great natural beauty that were gradually cleared for agricultural purposes between the 6th and 10th centuries, like

5.0 (opposite) An almond orchard at the Cistercian abbey of Santa María de Poblet, Catalonia, Spain.
The crenellated wall defines the inner sanctuary, separating the monastery, founded in 1151, from the outside world. In the background, the forest-covered Prades mountains are a reminder of the wilderness that once stood here.

5.1 *St Francis Preaching to the Birds* by Giotto, late 13th century, the Basilica of St Francis, Assisi, Italy.
The scene epitomizes the medieval Christian relationship towards nature, with animals, plants and people all seen as in the eternal custody of the Lord.

5.1

5.2

5.3

5.4

5.2 The abbey-church of Conques, France.
Nestled in a small valley on the pilgrim route to Santiago de Compostela, the abbey was founded in the late 8th century by a hermit seeking a place of contemplation.

5.3, 5.4 The monastery of Ittingen, Switzerland.
On the left, a vineyard is framed by tall hornbeam hedges on a slope that was once forested. On the right a quadrangular garden with box hedges and standard roses follows the model of the *chahar bagh*, but its stark cruciform Christian motif is evident.

5.5 *The Lady and the Unicorn*, French tapestry, late 15th century.
In a mythical courting scene, a unicorn chastely places its hooves on a lady's lap and gazes at itself in a mirror. With its idyllic setting of a 'thousand flowers' and a holly tree, the scene emanates a sense of docile innocence.

5.6 Medieval manuscript depicting a walled medicinal garden within a city.
The garden, with ornamentals and edibles as well as medicinal plants, is organized with rudimentary simplicity and regularity, harking back to previous periods of garden history.

5.5

5.6

the abbey of Conques founded by the Benedictine hermit Dadon in the 8th century [5.2]. The first wave of monastic settlement by the Benedictines was followed by the construction of large numbers of Franciscan, Augustinian and Cistercian abbeys during the 12th and 13th centuries. The Franciscan, Augustinian and Carthusian orders also built numerous monasteries, like the one in Ittingen (1150) [5.3, 5.4]. This second wave completed the spread of Christianity across Europe, from Spain to Scandinavia. The most emblematic image of this conversion of Europe to Christianity is the tale of St Francis of Assisi taming the wolf of Gubbio around 1220, in which symbols of nature, both good and bad, came to embrace the message of the Christian faith.[4] With seemingly inexorable force, medieval morality converted older societal beliefs and rituals into a new dogma, as shown emblematically in *The Lady and the Unicorn* tapestries, woven in Flanders in the early 16th century, where the mythical wild horned animal is tamed by a lady [5.5].[5]

The organization of the church in the Middle Ages was instrumental in forging strong landscape governance that has left a mark on the land to this day. Agrarian and pastoral practices flourished at every new settlement, radically transforming the features of each place.[6] The dioceses and monastic orders followed patterns established by the Romans in their administration of land and played an essential role in advancing and shaping this transformation. Cardinals gathered income at the regional level under the pope's direct authority. At the local level the parish priest or the chapter, abbot and communities of religious houses kept a close watch on daily affairs. Each village came under feudal protection and was expected to follow Christian doctrine. The church erected chapels and shrines like so many sacred seals across the land. Peasants and serfs living in misery worked long, tedious hours with the sole promise of eternal salvation, a goal far removed from the daily toil they had to endure.

Clearing the land

Before settling, monks would have done reconnaissance work to choose the exact location of their next monastery.[7] They then prepared the land for agricultural production by stripping a patch of forest and clearing it of roots and lumber, piling stones at the edge of the clearing. Swamps were drained or dug into fishponds. Once the land was free of all stones and vegetation, it was tilled until it was suitable for agriculture; seasonal crops were sown and harvested. Depending on the quality of the earth and the local topography, monks undertook other tasks, ranging from extensive herding to the planting and tending of orchards, walled gardens and vineyards [5.6]. During the Middle Ages the notion of 'earth' was all-encompassing and sacred, describing land that was cultivated, the place where a church was founded and the sacred ground where one was laid to rest.[8]

5.7

The way in which the church organized its land was linked to existing feudal structures, which thus also played a part in shaping the medieval countryside. The local church, with its bells resounding across the land at regular intervals, was the timeless epicentre of medieval life. The land was now managed on a human scale, and by the year 1300 most of the original European forest had disappeared with the spread of monasteries, to be replaced by a landscape of fields, hedgerows and terraces that we recognize today [5.8a–c]. Each village, town or monastery was located roughly at the heart of a vast, open forest clearing [5.9]. In the vicinity of the settlement were vegetable patches, orchards and, climate permitting, vineyards. Beyond these gardens, the village was surrounded by extensive fields of rye, barley or wheat, flanked by pastures that separated the clearing from the forest edge and provided shade and foliage for cattle.

Under feudal law we find not only the division of land between the nobility, the church and tenant farmers, but also a precise division of labour inherited from much earlier agricultural systems, including the Romans'. This is evidenced by the Domesday Book (1086). Composed in the 11th century, it was designed as an inventory, for taxation purposes, of England's entire societal pyramid. Here and elsewhere, the different levels of society were clearly demarcated. The poorest worker, the serf, was not free to move, owing his labour to just one individual. Next came the boor, the lowest class of peasant, and just above him was the cottager, who owned a little land. The smallholder owned more land than a cottager, but less than a villager, who of all the peasants owned the most. Then there came the freeman and the burgher, who were the most prosperous commoners except for those in the army. Beyond questions of class and land ownership patterns, the Domesday Book also paid attention to specific agricultural units as the 'plough' – a team of eight oxen – which allowed the amount of land such a team could plough in one day to be calculated.[9] One can extrapolate the situation described in the Domesday Book to most feudal countries in Europe at that time, excluding Scandinavia, where laws regarding peasant labour seemed to be somewhat more lenient.

The forest

The people of the Middle Ages derived moral strength from contrasting the sacred universe of the town and church from the dark forest. The word 'forest' is derived from the Latin word *foris*, literally meaning 'beyond', as is the English 'foreign'. The forest represented ancient beliefs often believed to be malevolent; it never became part of the Christian sphere and continued to form a pagan backdrop to every village, as well as a hiding place for brigands, lepers and whores [5.10].[10]

The landscape surrounding Chartres, with its imposing Gothic cathedral towering over plentiful wheat fields, was imposed on a vast stretch of ancient forest [5.7]. The

5.8a

5.8b

5.8c

5.7 Chartres Cathedral seen in the distance.

The twin spires of Chartres Cathedral, built in the 12th century, could be seen by pilgrims approaching from a great distance. Located on an ancient Celtic shrine, Chartres houses a statue of a Black Madonna, to which a cult is dedicated each summer at harvest time.

5.8a–c The spread of monasteries across Europe.

From the early Benedictines in the 5th century though the 10th century to the spread of the Franciscans and Cistercians in the late 12th century, over 5,000 monastic sites were founded across Europe. The model of the walled mission subsequently spread through the Americas.

5.9 Nuremberg forest plan.

A parchment plan by Erhard Etzlaub shows a forest around Nuremberg (1516). Wood was a precious commodity during the late Middle Ages, and was managed by the city's council. Like a green belt, the forest protectively encircles the city, which stands in a large clearing.

5.10 The medieval forest, *Les Très Riches Heures du Duc de Berry*, mid-15th century.

A peasant watches over his pigs gleaning acorns on a common, but anyone caught stealing wood could face death. Lepers, whores and brigands banned from the city lived in the forest, amid the pagan creatures of folk beliefs who could cause great mischief by casting spells.

5.9

5.10

cathedral's twin spires dominate the entire area.[11] Chartres is a remarkable example of a medieval landscape, with the pilgrim routes of the region all converging on the cathedral. This sanctuary was built on top of an ancient crypt that harboured a Celtic well, whose square base was turned towards the four cardinal points. In time, this place devoted to ancient pagan cults was rededicated to the Christian faith, as were so many other such Celtic sites throughout France [5.12]. A cathedral was raised, pierced with stained-glass windows that celebrate light. It shelters a paved, circular labyrinth at the entrance of the nave, through which every pilgrim is meant to pass as he enters the house of God. The cathedral at Chartres is a symbol of Christian unity that embodies an extraordinarily static medieval worldview; villages in the region still celebrate old traditions, such as lighting bonfires to St John in midsummer to reiterate the power of light over darkness.

The sacred tree

As Christianity progressed, it clashed with older forest cultures in Europe that still followed ancient animist beliefs. These cults reached far back to nomadic times, spanning vast territories of Europe and Asia. Specific types of trees were strongly symbolic. For instance, the ash, the linden (lime) and the oak featured prominently in old Germanic and Celtic forest lore. The ash played a central role in religious rituals, for it was considered to be the most heavenly of trees, growing only in the presence of underground water sources. According to Norse cosmology, an ash tree named Yggdrasil connected heaven and earth.[12] It grew symbiotically with the hazel, whose branches were used as divining rods, associated with the god Thor. Ash wood was both supple and strong, making it a perfect material for the handles of tools and weapons; and its sap was used to make balsam [5.11].[13] Linden trees were also venerated for their bark, known to make exceptionally strong ropes. The tree's blossom, with its heady scent in spring, was used for medicinal potions. It attracted bees and became a symbol of healing and fertility. Romans witnessing ancient ritual offerings made to healing trees then established the cult of Isis there. The linden became associated with the Virgin, with people nailing amulets or prayers to its branches.

The prayer tree is common to cultures worldwide; in the desert ranges of Iran an ancient cypress tree in the city of Abarkuh (legend has it that Alexander the Great visited it) is still venerated [5.15]. Statues of the Madonna, like that in Chartres Cathedral, are made of linden wood.[14] Hermit monks would sometimes inhabit sacred linden trees to proselytize, particularly in remote areas where such cults had been spotted [5.14].[15] The oak was revered for its strength, resilience and longevity. It came to represent royalty dispensing justice and reason: both kings and druids sat beneath oak trees to preach, teach or confer judgment – a usage inherited also from the ancient Greeks [5.13].

Norse mythology tells about the world's creation, when three gods – Vili, Vé and Odin – came across two trees. They took the wood and, breathing life into it, created a man (Ask) and a woman (Embla). The couple lived in an original, Eden-like forest. Trees of wisdom were singled out in the forest and venerated, with shamans carrying out sacred rites under them. In medieval times, trees were marked out for healing properties – in the belief that the tree embodied a spirit capable of healing and salvation. In the north the bark of the birch was used for writing, and the hollowed-out trunk was used to bury the dead. The word for a hollow trunk in old Scandinavian, *ludr*, refers to the cradle, the skiff, the bed and the coffin. The birch was the symbol of light and rebirth. To honour their goddess Brigit, the Celts heralded the return of light by making blazing bonfires out of birch faggots in the middle of winter.[16]

5.11

5.12

5.13

5.14

5.15

5.11 Extracting balsam from a young ash tree in spring.
In the Middle Ages the ash was considered one of the most useful trees, employed for medicinal purposes as well as for making tools and weapons.

5.12 Standing stone of Celtic origins at Espeyrac, south-central France.
Located on the pilgrim route to Conques and Santiago de Compostela, the rock is crowned with a small cross of wrought iron to Christianize it. Christian symbols were often attached to pagan features encountered on pilgrim paths.

5.13 Miniature painting depicting a king on a throne in a clearing with oak trees.
The oak was sacred in earlier Celtic cultures and regarded as a symbol of both power and justice.

5.14 A hermit monk in a linden tree.
Celtic healing and prayer trees, often linden, were widespread in Europe. In an attempt to Christianize the trees, religious statues were subsequently carved from their wood, as in the case of the Black Madonna in Chartres.

5.15 An ancient cypress tree in Abarkuh, Iran.
This cypress tree, over 4,000 years old, is still revered as a focus of prayers. It is said that Alexander the Great paid his respects to it on his way to Bactria in 330 BCE.

5.16

The cathedral

Gothic architecture embodied a form of syncretism, including elements from the heathen faiths even as it attempted to challenge them. On the exterior of Gothic buildings, mythical monsters and demons of pagan origin demonstrated the savage cults to be found in the woods [5.16]. Alchemical symbols carved onto cathedrals walls were meant to offer protection against their spells.[17] The placement of chimerical creatures and gargoyles, which represented the dark old forces of nature on church roofs, exposed the stone beasts to the wrath and fury of the ancient Germanic gods Woden and Thor, gods of thunder and lightning; this was in strong contrast with the serene, almost womb-like haven inside the nave, devoid of any such monsters.[18] This conscious play between inside and outside, between the sacred and the profane, between the monstrous and the divine became the driving force of the Middle Ages, which in turn shaped the face of the entire territory.

The notion of a sacred, enclosed space that contrasted with older beliefs was further developed in many Gothic cathedral sites across Europe. Begun in 1079 on the site of an older 7th-century church founded by a pagan king who had converted to Christianity, Winchester Cathedral has the longest nave of any cathedral in Europe. It is an example of the way Christian buildings took account of barbarian beliefs and transformed them. Here, as in the other great Gothic

cathedrals of Europe, slender stone columns line the nave and give the impression of a deep forest of trunks and branches reaching for the heavens and spreading out to show the way [5.17]. In mimicking a grove of trees, the Gothic cathedral represents not only the gradual conversion of barbarian tribes to Christianity, but also a changing attitude towards nature, as people's long-standing beliefs regarding the darkest recesses of the forest were exorcized. This exorcized forest thus became desacralized, and was suddenly a mere wilderness to be cleared and cultivated in the name of God [5.18].

The medieval garden

During the Middle Ages, the archetype of the walled garden lost all the refinement and sensual extravagance it had inherited from the Romans to become a reduced – albeit still symbolic – sacred space for the clergy. Many of the older symbols of the geometric garden were Christianized and transformed into a rather austere place for meditation. Although just shadows of their luxuriant ancestors, the enclosed gardens drawn for the foundation of the abbey of St Gall in Switzerland were used to grow plants for medicinal purposes. Early records from the plan of the Benedictine abbey (which was never built) show the medieval way of ordering space and more particularly the garden where a methodological selection and arrangement of medicinal species can be seen within regular geometric rectangular

5.16 Gargoyles on the main portal of the 13th-century Church of Notre Dame in Dijon, France. Symbolizing the dark spirits, chimera and monsters of the pagan world outside the church, and braving the elements such as thunder, lightning and hail, the gargoyles exorcized the malevolent forces from the quiet inner sanctum of the church, where a Romanesque Madonna made of wood still stands.

5.17 The nave of Winchester Cathedral, England. The analogy to an orderly forest of stone columns is clear. Gothic architecture sought to rival the original forest in splendour and glory, in order to Christianize the Goths and barbarians.

5.18 The Forest of Tronçais, central France. Managed by the French crown for centuries, the forest became a cathedral of sorts with its rows of living trees defining a natural nave.

5.17

5.18

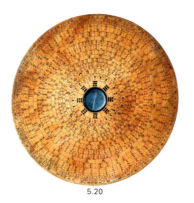

5.19

5.20

5.21

5.19 Early Qibla chart, with the sacred Ka'ba at its centre.
Using an astrolabe and compass it was possible to ascertain the precise direction of prayer towards Mecca from cities named around the circumference of this chart. Advances in the science of navigation were here put towards a higher religious purpose.

5.20 A Chinese Luopan.
Luopans have existed for over 2,000 years, and were used extensively in geomancy to detect hidden forces in the landscape. With a magnetic compass in the middle, the dial has 40 concentric rings with markings to determine up to 24 different directions.

5.21 Cosmographical diagram from the Catalan Atlas, the Majorcan cartographic school, attributed to Cresques Abraham, 14th century, Spain.
The diagram emphasizes a spherical earth at the centre of the universe surrounded by concentric rings symbolizing the four elements, the seven planets, the zodiac and the phases of the moon framed by the four seasons.

5.22 A French copy of the late 8th-century *Mappa Mundi* by Beatus de Liébana.
Jerusalem is shown at the centre, on the Mediterranean, Europe is to the left, with the Bosporus on top, and Africa with the Nile to the right; above is Arabia with the Euphrates and Tigris. There is no scale to this map, which converges on the Eternal City. Surrounding all is the oceanic abyss.

5.23 Plan of St Gall, dedicated to Abbot Gozbert, Switzerland.
The minimalist layout of the medicinal gardens within the architectural complex is both striking and in keeping with the Benedictines' ascetic way of life. Drawn on parchment in the early 9th century, the plan was never fully realized.

5.22

Throughout the Middle Ages, God was understood as a beacon of light cutting through darkness, revealing himself only through spiritual enlightenment and meditation. During this period meditation was considered a type of inwardly directed prayer, its effectiveness heightened by the scents, sounds and incantations reverberating within the church. The public observation of Christian rites was accompanied by colourful works of art and sculpture, while private devotion took place in front of icons or illuminations that served to enhance the act of prayer. Highly orchestrated processions would pass through the countryside, during which people would stop at sacred spots and even throw offerings in rivers and wells. Asceticism was encouraged, since it was believed self-denial would bring the sinner closer to heaven. God was at the centre of all things – a belief reinforced by medieval atlases like the *Mappa Mundi* by Beatus de Liébana that place Jerusalem, at the centre of the cosmos [5.22]. Islam developed a similar concentric conception of the universe during this period, producing Qibla maps designed to point the way to the Ka'ba in the sacred city of Mecca [5.19]. This form of world chart probably arrived from distant China, where the first Luopan compasses were used on fortune-telling boards. These showed the flow of magnetic energy from a centrally located heaven to the world around it [5.20].

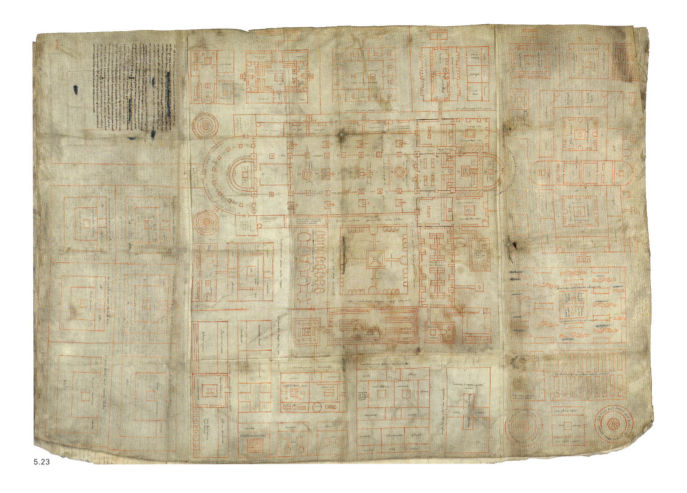

5.23

plots [5.23]. Such gardens were also used to grow crops during sieges and periods of upheaval.

The ascetic walled gardens of Christian Europe contrasted strongly with their luxurious Islamic counterparts, to be found throughout the Muslim world during the same period, most particularly in Cordoba, Seville and Granada in Spain. Historians often explain the cultural regression of medieval gardening, and the patent loss of aesthetic and technical know-how, as a consequence of successive waves of invasion and tumultuous unrest.[19] But this explanation fails to take account of the deep societal and cultural shifts that occurred shortly after the fall of the Roman Empire. Many barbarian rulers came from archaic tribal forest cultures that had little understanding of, or patience for, delicate pleasure gardens.[20] Instead, the absolute typological reduction of the medieval walled garden carried a deliberate cultural and moral message: no garden on earth could, or should, even begin to imitate the promise of heavenly paradise. The austere cloister garden was a *hortus conclusus*, sealed from the outside world and often reduced to its simplest possible expression: a tree surrounded by four squares of low, trimmed box hedges framing a meagre choice of emblematic plants. Human presence was tolerated only as long as behaviour complied with the strict precepts of Christian morality. It was no longer a place of decadence and lust, as it had been in the late Roman period. Delights,

if any could be found, were spiritually coded, and the senses were harnessed solely for the purpose of eternal salvation.[21]

The typology of the monastery thus provides an excellent example of the convergence of the two landscape archetypes we have studied: the large forest clearing surrounding a settlement and the cloister garden within four walls at its centre. The first act, the stripping of the forest, was a prelude to agriculture and devoid of any sacred connotations. The cloister garden, representing the second ancient archetype, was characterized by a Spartan appearance, in which vegetation was often limited to a few evergreen trees symbolizing the promise of eternity. This juxtaposition of the walled garden, full of religious connotations, with the larger but profane farmed strip in the clearing surreptitiously degraded the ancient forest land to a lower, more profane level of symbolism than previously. The church's inclination towards denigrating the forest was neither innocent nor neutral, especially in regions peopled by Celts and Goths, who stemmed from the oldest forest cultures of Europe. The expansion of Christianity through such focused spaces opened the way for broader transformations in the European landscape. In abbeys all over Europe, monks tended the fields, vineyards and orchards, harvested fruit and grain, collected honey, raised cattle and kept fisheries, and made bread and wine, both of which – in addition to being everyday foodstuffs – played fundamental roles in Christian ritual.

5.24

Santa María de Poblet, Spain

It was the Cistercian monks who laid claim to the furthest reaches of the European wilderness. With their advanced agricultural practices – including a sophisticated knowledge of irrigation – and a will to transform the wild and untamed, they were able to conquer formerly untouched lands, bringing productivity and prosperity to them. The Clos de Vougeot vineyard in Burgundy, first worked by Cistercian monks from the abbey of Cîteaux in the 12th century, is an excellent example: with their remarkable understanding of the land, the monks transformed a rough woodland slope into something far more valuable. This model of landscape organization, perfected by the Cistercians and the Franciscans, had already been put in place earlier by the Benedictines as at the Abbey of St Foy in Conques (1041) [5.24] and it became instrumental in establishing medieval Christianity across the whole European continent.

The most emblematic example is the fortified Cistercian abbey of Santa María de Poblet (1151). It was founded by monks from France on land reconquered from the Moors at the foot of the Prades mountains in Catalonia [5.25], and constructed shortly after the Second Crusade as a bulwark against Islamic Spain. The choice of location, at the foot of the Prades mountains, is remarkable: here, all the elements for a sustainable settlement – a good supply of water, forest, fertile land, limestone outcrops and sun – come together like a gift of divine providence.[22] The site confirms the Cistercians' understanding of site reconnaissance, a skill most likely inherited from the Romans. Water from the Francolí River and its tributary was channelled into and stored in two vast cisterns inside the abbey grounds for the purpose of cultivation and ablutions [5.30, 5.32, 5.33, 5.37]. The monks at Poblet treated the lustral waters with the utmost respect, as a precious liquid that symbolized purity; its presence in the abbey gardens was considered a blessing and a guarantee of livelihood. At Poblet, older beliefs in pagan deities of the forests and streams ceased to exist: instead, the abbey expressed a single faith under one Christian God, without deviation. Here, God held sway over the surrounding natural world and transformed it into a powerful manifestation of divine order. The wild poplar tree expressing the last shadows of forest shamanism in the local Visigoth population was enthroned by the monks in a determined faith capable of conquering entire regions of Spain through pious cultivation [5.28, 5.38].[23]

Before the monastery was built, the densely forested site would have been stripped of trees to make way for an

5.24 The village of Conques in France, with the Romanesque abbey of St Foy.
Nestled in the valley of the Ouche River, the contrast between this Christian haven on the pilgrim route to Santiago de Compostela and the surrounding 'wilderness' is typical of the period.

5.25 Reconstruction of the Cistercian Abbey of Santa María de Poblet, Catalonia.
At the heart of a walled bastion stands the abbey and cloister, built in the middle of the 12th century. Outside the walls, a vast clearing was made in the forest for agricultural terraces, vineyards and fields. Water from Francolí River was captured in cisterns serving the compound.

5.25

5.26a

5.26b

5.26a, 5.26b Reconstructed before and after views of Poblet.
Above is a view of the wild Prades mountains as they were in early Visigothic times before the abbey was built; below is the abbey and the site as cleared by Cistercian monks for agriculture. The vast walled enclosure around the abbey was intended to form a self-sustaining stronghold in case of siege. Nature has been controlled for the purpose of God.

5.27 The monastery bastion with a rectangular cloister at its core.
The main entrance yard can be seen to the right, with the stables. Two cisterns in the upper fields provide irrigation for all the cultivated allotments within the enclosure of the abbey. To the left of the river and beyond the abbey wall, stepped terraces with orchards stretch down the slope.

5.27

open, gently sloping clearing, in which vineyards and orchards would be planted [5.26a, 5.26b]. Orchards and crops were planted on a series of wide terraces outside the monastery walls that stepped down from the mountain along the Francolí River, and whose retaining walls were made of loose stones cleared from the fields [5.29]. The sustenance provided by its agriculture enabled the monastery to thrive and expand into an extraordinary bastion of Christianity [5.27]. In time, Poblet became the most prominent religious foundation in Spain, attracting royal patronage and housing the dynastic tombs of the house of Aragon.

Above all, Poblet presents an austere contrast between the reduced, elemental sacredness of the cloister garden and the blossoming fields and orchard terraces outside its walls. The combination of the walled garden archetype with that of the forest clearing turned agricultural is striking here. The inner cloister garden remains minimal in essence, and represents nothing more than a patch of earth planted with a few tall cypresses embodying eternity played against a piece of sky, light, air and water [5.31, 5.36]. Although the cloister's architectural elements have different origins – the colonnade derives from a Roman peristyle, the quadratic garden and its cypress trees from the ancient Persian *chahar bagh* – the fusion of these two elements into a single archetype, protected by tall defensive walls, marks a definitive break from nature [5.35]. This powerful combination of landscape

and architecture was subsequently duplicated across the rest of Spain and Europe, before being transferred to the American missions. The cloister garden approximates an abstract metaphysical space, a reflection of the divine, and the transitory embodiment of a future promise of paradise. The lavabo fountain – where monks performed their ablutions – protrudes into the garden from one corner of the cloister. It fills the courtyard with the timeless rhythmic melody of trickling drops and casts a shimmer of light as the ripples on the water's surface are reflected [5.40, 5.41].

With a sobriety that is typical of the Cistercian brotherhood, the monastery's proportions and elementary architectural style served a divine purpose: to help discipline the minds of the faithful. The minimalist but powerfully introverted architecture is particularly well suited to control spiritual meditation [5.39]. But when the bells of Poblet toll, they override the surrounding landscape and signal the presence of the abbey as the centre of Christian faith for the entire valley. Bells resound across vast areas like few sounds found in nature [5.34].

5.28

5.28 A thicket of poplar trees on the Francolí River upstream from Poblet.
The name 'poblet' comes from a Catalan word for a species of poplar endemic to the region.

5.29 Almond trees in bloom in an orchard on an artificial terrace at Poblet.
It was the vision, determination and labour of the Cistercian monks who created the monastery and its agricultural terraces and orchards that made the entire enterprise possible.

5.30 Upper water cistern.
Like their Roman forefathers, a complete mastery of water by the monks at Poblet was essential to achieving their goals.

5.31 The inner cloister.
The bell tower can just be glimpsed beyond the eroded, trunk-like colonnade of the inner cloister and old cypress trees. The Catalan architect Gaudí grew up in the vicinity of Poblet, and was deeply impressed by the timeless beauty of such sights.

5.32 Section showing the route of water through the upper cistern and cloister at Poblet.
Note the careful stepping of the entire architectural ensemble against a backdrop of cultivated terraces.

5.29

5.30

5.31

5.32

5.33

5.34

5.35

5.33 Reconstructed view of the circular cistern on a small tributary of the river above the abbey.
A meandering channel runs perpendicular to the slope and regulates a constant flow of water to the monastery.

5.34 View of the abbey across vineyards from the foothills of the Prades mountains.
The trees in the centre mark the path of the tributary water channel that feeds into the upper cistern.

5.35 A grove of hazel trees in front of the eastern wall at Poblet.
As with a Greek *temenos*, the crenellated wall separates the inner sanctuary of the monastery from the profane landscape of orchards and forests.

5.36 Reconstructed view of the abbey and its cloister with lavabo.
The strong defensive walls facing the main entrance yard protecting the cloister are clearly visible to the right.

5.37 Reconstructed view from the upper river valley into the monastery.
The monastery sits securely within its enclosure wall. The main cistern is in the foreground, with the crenellated wall following the watercourse down into the plain.

5.36

5.37

5.38 The main entrance yard at Poblet.
The red flowers of the single poplar tree that
appear around Easter each year are revered
as they are said to incarnate the blood of Christ.
The transfer of an ancient tree cult into the
Christian faith is quite clear.

5.39 The inner cloister.
With its Gothic arcade bathed in sunlight, it is
easy to imagine the hours of quiet meditation
spent within the haven of this sacred peristyle.

5.40 The central lavabo of the cloister.
This was where ritual ablutions were performed
before meditation and prayer. The timeless,
abstract framework of this inner realm,
completely separated from the outside world,
creates a tranquil space.

5.41 Close-up view of the lavabo.
Water was distributed drop-by-drop from
the basin, like some elixir of life. The delicate
acoustics of trickling water resonates throughout
the cloister.

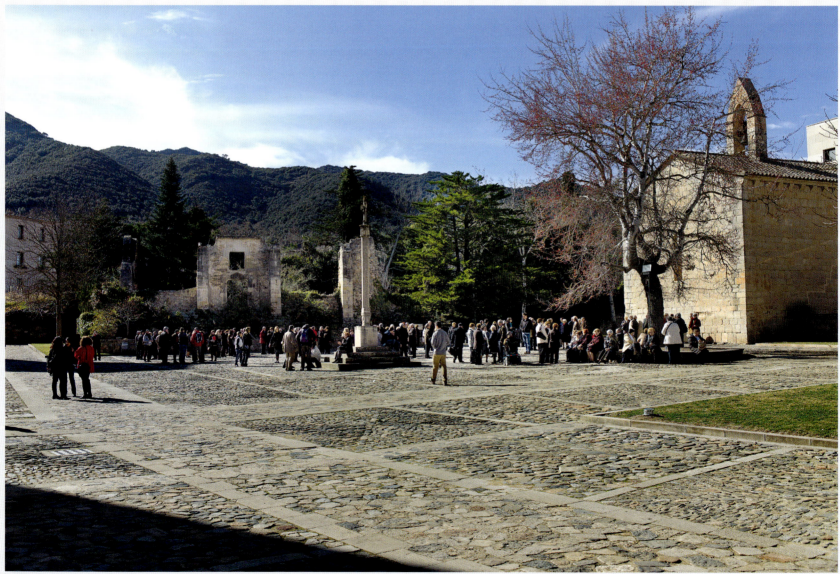

5.38

5.39

5.40

5.41

Islam

From the mid-7th to the early 8th centuries, a series of Umayyad Muslim invasions swept through the Mediterranean basin, effecting cultural change and ultimately bringing stability and continuity to an ethnically disparate region.[24] The arts of irrigation and cultivation imported from the Middle East reached a high degree of sophistication in North Africa and Andalucia, transforming what were arid landscapes into bountiful oases [5.46]. This agricultural legacy remains visible to this day in Spain, where an impressive network of channels and devices such the Albolafia water wheel in Cordoba marks an entire region [5.44, 5.45]. The windmill was another technology introduced from the East, around the time of the First Crusade, when improvements in farming and a period of climatic warming resulted in more regular and abundant harvests.[25]

Advanced geometry and mathematics developed by the Arabs allowed Islamic art and architecture to attain a high degree of abstraction and structural precision from the outset [5.42, 5.43]. The principal reason for the Muslims' perfection of abstract decoration was a religious proscription against figurative art; instead, the Islamic faith strove to express harmony and unity through abstract geometric designs and constructed voids [5.47]. In the Christian world, the Arabs' mastery of mathematics, geometry and algebra was seen as a key to the mysteries of vision and optics.[26] Thus manuscripts from Cairo, Baghdad and Damascus were tentatively copied by bishops and monks such as Robert Grosseteste, Roger Bacon and Leonardo Fibonacci. Fibonacci's *Liber Abaci* (1202) was the first to describe Arabic numerals, which were gradually adopted by mathematicians and entered mainstream usage during the 15th century.[27]

The impact of Islam on the Eurasian continent during the Middle Ages was immense. It is important to make a chronological distinction between early Islamic expansion, which took place during the 7th and the early 8th centuries, spreading through Arabia, Persia, Syria, Egypt, North Africa and Spain, and the subsequent golden age of Islamic civilization. Covering over 400 years, between the 8th and 12th centuries, this is the period when art, architecture and literature flourished brilliantly. During this time of cultural bloom and exchange, Islamic scholars were highly practised in the fields of mathematics, philosophy and science. Both architecture and landscape design profited tremendously from this pool of knowledge, as some of the most exquisite gardens known to humankind that were produced at this period demonstrate.

5.42

5.43

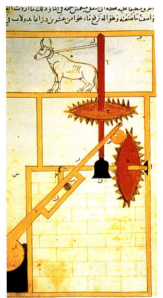

5.45

5.42 Pool in the Court of the Myrtles, the Alhambra, Granada, Spain.
Reflecting the women's quarters of the Comares Palace, this tranquil pool in the Court of the Myrtles is a masterpiece of Islamic garden architecture.

5.43 Detail of a 14th-century Islamic fountain, Alhambra, Granada.
The treatment of water as a precious resource is evident in this single scalloped fountain at the entrance of the Comares Palace.

5.44 The Albolafia water wheel on the Guadalquivir River, Cordoba, Spain.
Originally built in the 12th century, the wheel, called a *noria*, lifted water for the emir's palace in the Alcázar.

5.45 Detail from an al-Andalus manuscript showing an Archimedes screw for lifting water driven by an ox.
The transfer of knowledge about irrigation from Baghdad to the Caliphate of Cordoba left its mark on the entire landscape of Andalucia.

5.46 Stepped pool in the Garden of the Partal in the Alhambra, Granada.
Framed by orange trees and clipped hedges, this replicates the Egyptian style of garden seen in Chapter 1. The heady perfume of orange blossom contributed to an overwhelming sensory experience, with the sounds of water, music and birds blending with the scent of innumerable flowers.

5.47 The archetype of an Islamic courtyard.
The void is a dominant feature of Islamic patio design and relates back to the open desert as a place of meditation and revelation.

5.44

5.46

5.47

5.48

5.49

Thriving trade routes from the East brought in silk, spices, exotic plants, seeds, precious metals and gemstones, among other things. The irrigation of agricultural land attained an impressive degree of precision and efficiency under Islamic rule. From the eastern reaches of the Great Salt Desert in Iran to the western borders of the Sahara in Morocco, the underground channels called *qanat*s fed entire cities and their surrounding fields. The walled gardens of palaces and mosques reached a level of refinement that has hardly been matched at any other time in history. In the walled paradise gardens of Shiraz in southern Iran, the Medina Azahara near Cordoba and the Alhambra of Granada, both in Spain, the poetry of nature was chiselled into exquisite designs for a privileged few [5.52, 5.53].

With foundations such as the House of Wisdom in Baghdad (786–1258), the Abbasid caliphs and their successors promoted the diffusion of philosophical and scientific texts throughout learned Islamic society.[28] But it was the widespread use of Arabic in poetry that allowed for an extraordinary register of authors to exchange their thoughts and dreams. Figures such as Hafez of Shiraz, Omar Khayyam and Saadi were known and appreciated during their lifetimes by readers all over the Muslim world. Their romantic poetry, often set against a backdrop of luxurious gardens, illustrated the perfect balance between man and nature. These works, some of which are almost a thousand years old, are just as refreshing and restorative today as when they were first written. When one walks through the gardens of Granada [5.48, 5.49, 5.60], one cannot help but think of the achievements of Islamic culture, which – far removed from the austerity of medieval Christian monasticism – was able to convert the dream of an earthly paradise into reality. Spain's golden age, in Toledo and the cities of al-Andalus, was the result of a religious culture so developed, so different from what pertained in the rest of Europe, that all three monotheistic religions embraced tolerance in their common thirst for truth and knowledge [5.51]. The level of commerce, cultural exchange and erudition thus attained was extraordinary. Philosophers such as Maimonides showed an advanced awareness of the societal and ethical concerns shared by all faiths.[29]

The Medina Azahara, built by the Umayyads in Cordoba during the 10th century, and the Alhambra complex, completed by the Nasrid dynasty in the mid-14th century, demonstrate clearly how the Islamic gardens of Spain were the continuation of an art form pioneered in early Sumeria and perfected over the course of millennia [5.58]. The tradition of combining high garden art with architecture would be perpetuated with other medieval examples, such as the Arab–Norman cloister of Monreale Cathedral, Sicily, begun by William II in 1174 [5.50]. A couple of decades earlier, al-Idrisi had produced his world atlas map for King Roger II here [5.56]. Complementing the Byzantine biblical mosaics inside

5.50

5.48 The Court of the Myrtles in the Comares Palace, the Alhambra, Granada, Spain.
Built under Nasrid rule, this court at the Alhambra differs significantly from a Roman peristyle in that two porticoes are juxtaposed at either end of a large open space.

5.49 One of two fountains under the porticoes of the Court of the Myrtles, the Alhambra.
Water flowed very gently into the pool in order not to disturb the mirror-like surface. There were no water jets in early Islamic gardens since they would have disrupted the reflective qualities.

5.50 The lavatorium fountain in the cloister at Monreale, Sicily.
The fountain was created for the Christian cathedral by Muslim sculptors in the late 12th century. In the background, the ornate architecture of the peristyle with its slender double columns inlaid in gold and coloured tesserae frames a garden of clipped hedges. It is a fine example of Islamo-Norman architecture.

5.51 Horseshoe-shaped arches of the 12th-century Ibn Shushan or Congregational Synagogue in Toledo, Spain.
The arcades catch the light from a typical round window. The synagogue had a courtyard where people could congregate in a context in which religious communities shared much of their knowledge.

5.52 An elaborate stucco canopy in the Court of Lions at the Alhambra.
Slender marble columns support square capitals and abacuses in stylized vegetal forms with sacred arabesque inscriptions. The metaphor of the oasis as a built paradise is clear.

5.53 An inverted tree from an 18th-century Turkish prayer book, now in the Chester Beatty Library, Dublin, Ireland.
The symbol of an upturned tree as a cosmic pillar reaching down from heaven to earth by which souls can descend reaches far back in time; it is common to Islamic, Jewish and Vedic traditions.

5.51

5.52

5.53

5.54

By the 9th century, Islamic architecture reached a peak. The Great Mosque of Samarra (851 CE) [5.54, 5.55] with its peristyle and *Malwiya* minaret, built by the Abbasid caliph al-Mutawakkil, reflected the wealth of the land.[30] The success was due to improved agriculture and trade routes that carried up to 100,000 camels at a time. The saffron route linking Cordoba with Baghdad and Samarra, via Morocco, continued through Samarkand and Tashkent reaching Xinjiang in China. Arabic culture spread widely, following the introduction of paper from China. This had a unifying influence on the *Umma*, which extended from the Himalayas to the Atlas [5.59]. Caliph Harun al-Rashid established the 'House of Wisdom', which functioned as library and observatory, in 8th-century Baghdad. Watermills and windmills were developed, improving the quality of milling considerably. These inventions originated in Persia and China, but technological progress spread rapidly through the Islamic world, contributing without question to the development of European culture thereafter.

5.55

5.54 The Great Mosque of Samarra, Iraq.
Built in the middle of the 9th century by the Abbasid Caliph al-Mutawakkil, this was thought to be the largest mosque in the Islamic world at the time. Its spiralling minaret stands outside the walls of the inner sanctuary.

5.55 Aerial view of Samarra today.
The mosque, which can be seen in the upper left corner, was destroyed by a Mongol invasion in the second half of the 13th century, when the entire city of Samarra was also razed, as was the library of the House of Wisdom in Baghdad. This marked the end of the golden age of Islam.

5.56

5.57

5.58

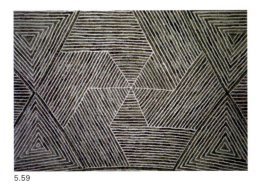

5.59

5.60

5.56 Map from Muhammad al-Idrisi's world atlas, made for the Norman king Roger II of Sicily, 12th century.
South is at the top, Africa is shown too large and largely consists of *terra incognita* beyond the Sahara Desert, but Eurasia is remarkably accurate, ranging from Spain and Scandinavia through Arabia to India, China and Sumatra.

5.57 An astrolabe.
The astrolabe originated in Hellenistic times but was developed further by the Arabs as an aid for navigation and to help find the direction of Mecca for prayers.

5.58 The patio of oranges at the Great Mosque in Cordoba, Spain.
A regular system of channels provides irrigation to each tree. It is evidence of an inherited landscape model originating in the Middle East transferred to Western Europe.

5.59 The brick vault of the mihrab in the 10th-century Ustadh Iwan (Teacher's Iwan) of the Friday Mosque, Isfahan, Iran.
The relationship between early Islamic brick architecture in Persia and the Moorish Mudéjar architecture of Morocco and Spain attests to the broad cultural exchanges that were taking place between different regions of Islam.

5.60 Gardens of the Alhambra, Granada, Spain.
The Alhambra is a relatively late addition to Islamic garden culture in Andalucia. It was converted into a sumptuous garden by the Nasrid ruler Yusuf I of Granada in the early 14th century. At night the garden is filled with the song of nightingales and the scent of oranges and roses. Nowhere else in medieval Europe was a garden of such outstanding quality, beauty and refinement achieved.

Many branches of science and academic study originated in the golden age of Islamic culture. We owe our understanding of trigonometry and modern algebra – including the complete solution of quadratic equations – to the Arabs. Instruments such as the astrolabe, developed in order to locate any place in relation to Mecca, were subsequently used for navigation [5.57]. Averroes, who lived in 12th-century Cordoba, was a mathematician, lawyer, physician, astronomer and theologian. He influenced European philosophy with his commentaries on the works of Aristotle, thus preparing it for a definitive break from medieval dogmatism at the onset of the Renaissance.

5.61

5.62

5.63

the cathedral, this beautiful garden, full of citrus trees, myrtle and roses, stands today as a unique testimony to cultural and religious cross-fertilization in Christian Europe: an early but rather limited example of a northern people meeting and mixing with an African–Moorish culture. And yet Monreale reminds the visitor of divine salvation in a way that is dramatically different from the stark austerity of Poblet.

The legacy of the Middle Ages

The most interesting aspect of the Middle Ages that remains in the landscape is the precise scale of human settlement. Villages were separated by the physical distance that could be travelled in a single day; and although similar patterns are found elsewhere, European settlements showed something different in their attitude towards nature – one that has left an indelible mark [5.61]. These landscapes represent genuine artefacts, in which regularly spaced villages are interspersed with woods, rivers and fields, exuding the charm of carefully crafted settlements [5.62]. Although forests disappeared as monasteries were built, the transformation was undertaken with care, and given meaning within a Christian context. We now look at these landscapes in a way that would have been impossible at the time, for we are unable to detect the sense of divine purpose that prevailed. To work within these landscapes today requires not only great environmental knowledge, but also cultural intelligence. Study of the area

surrounding the village of Ensérune in southern France shows this precisely. The finely tended, wedge-shaped fields that radiate out of a central point – the remains of a medieval marsh-drainage – complement a promenade that winds its way through this timeless landscape [5.63].

The Italian painter Giotto began his experiments in perspective at the end of the 13th century. He paid particular attention to landscapes in his paintings, so as to make his figures stand out. Metaphysical vision thus gradually turned into empirical laws governing perspective; and in time the expression of these rules resulted in a form of beauty produced not by God, but by humankind. It was in the late Middle Ages that people began to undertake the climbing of mountains for the pleasure of the view. In April 1336 Petrarch, who is considered the 'father of humanism', produced an account of his ascent of Mont Ventoux in Provence [5.64].[31] During the climb he looked out upon the broader landscape with a new, humanist gaze; and acknowledged the existence of a vast, open world, worthy of consideration in its own right. The ascent of Mont Ventoux thus marked a turning-point of sorts: when notions of gazing at and travelling through the landscape for pleasure took over from the introspective Christian attitude that had prevailed before. Though difficult to imagine, it appears that the humanist march of the Western world was set in motion by a singular walk up a mountain, above the tree line, far removed from the sound of bells.

5.61 Aerial view of 'Hochäcker' fields in Thurgau, Switzerland.
A palimpsest of parallel drainage and ploughing patterns from the Middle Ages still stands out in the typical Hochäcker landscapes of Thurgau. The topography of the fields was intended to improve harvests in the Middle Ages, when the climate reverted to colder periods.

5.62 The village of Vichères in the Perche region of France.
The village sits comfortably in a small vale amid fields, meadows and thickets on a pilgrim path to Chartres. It remains close to the medieval landscape structure of its origins.

5.63 Medieval fields arranged radially near the Oppidum of Ensérune, southern France.
The former wetland of the Étang de Montady was drained in the 13th century, with ditches directing water to the centre from where it flowed away in underground channels. The gravitational system still works today.

5.64 The snow-capped slopes of Mont Ventoux, Provence, southern France.
Petrarch made his famous ascent of the mountain in 1336 and viewed the world from far above the dogmas of his time.

5.64

6. Gardens of Perspective
Architectural Landscapes in the Renaissance

'How many times, do you think, did I turn back that day, to glance at the summit of the mountain that seemed scarcely a cubit high compared with the range of human contemplation?'

Petrarch, 'The Ascent of Mount Ventoux'[1]

Traditionally, historians have pinpointed the beginning of the Renaissance as the sudden appearance of humanism in late 14th-century Italy, with subsequent beautiful gardens, like the Villa Lante [6.0]. But in fact this development was preceded by visual and conceptual revolutions all over the civilized world. Much of our understanding of navigation, for instance, comes from China and arrived in Italy via the Arabic world. Our knowledge of algebra stemmed from India, was translated in Cairo and then spread via Italy to the rest of Europe. The fact is that some of the most important inventions of the period – paper, printing, map-making and mathematical calculation – were known in the East long

before they reached Europe, as seen in the General Chart of the Integrated World [6.3].[2] This is also the time when the magnificent landscapes of the Ming tombs were created in China [6.4]. It is probably only oil painting and the *sfumato* technique of painterly representation and storytelling, culminating in the 16th-century school of Titian, that stand out as something particularly original to Europe [6.1].

The most significant changes of the Renaissance were the reduction in the number of feudal wars, the opening up of fortified cities to the countryside, and the establishment of the 'three-field' crop-rotation system, which rendered the soil more productive. From the 12th century, the wider use of the horse-drawn plough and the shoulder harness enabled farmers to work a greater stretch of field, which in turn brought higher yields. Advances in agricultural technology changed the entire scale and appearance of the landscape. Few stands of original forest remained and overgrazing became a serious problem from the Mediterranean to the

6.0 (opposite) View from the third terrace of the garden of the Villa Lante, Italy.
A stone table with a trough of still, reflective water stands on perspectival axis with the cascade of the river gods, which leads up to the water chain and then to the Deluge grotto far beyond.

6.1 *The Death of Actaeon* by Titian, *c.*1559–75.
The subject is from Ovid's *Metamorphoses*: while hunting, Actaeon accidentally catches a glimpse of Diana bathing naked. The outraged goddess sprays him with water that transforms him into a stag. His dogs suddenly turn on him and kill him. It is a story about the fate of man when his instincts go astray.

6.1

6.2

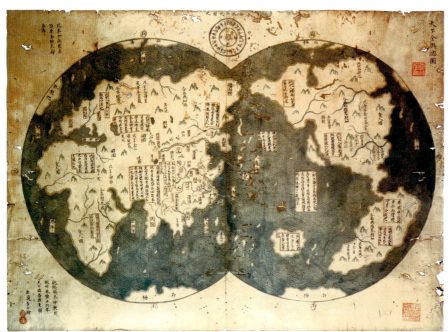

6.3

6.4

6.2 *Allegory of Good Government*, by Ambrogio Lorenzetti, 1338–39.
This fresco in the Palazzo Pubblico of Siena shows a peaceful and prosperous Tuscan landscape in the mid-14th century, one where any form of original nature has been replaced by productive agriculture and civic space.

6.3 **Chinese 'General Chart of the Integrated World'.**
An 18th-century copy of an original thought to be dated 1418, the chart shows all the continents though it precedes Columbus's discovery of America in 1492 by seven decades.

6.4 **A landscape of Ming tombs, China.**
Standing among persimmon orchards at the foot of the Huangtu mountains, these Ming tombs were built mostly in the 15th, 16th and 17th centuries for 13 emperors. Set within a pleasing agricultural landscape, they represent a climax in Chinese mortuary architecture.

6.5 **The 1502 Cantino Planisphere.**
The Portuguese navigator Pedro Álvares Cabral explored the coast of Brazil in 1500. This portolan map also shows the entire African continent. Bartolomeu Dias was the first European to round the Cape of Good Hope in 1488, followed by Vasco da Gama in 1497. Progress in navigational triangulation led to improved precision in cartography.

6.6 *The Ideal City*, *c.*1485.
No one is certain who the artist of this painting was, but it may have been either Piero della Francesca or Leon Battista Alberti. The combination of a single-point perspective and the sublime light and illusion of space embody all the promise of Italian Renaissance humanism.

6.7 **Page from the treatise on perspective by Leon Battista Alberti.**
The approach to the design of constructed space seen here would have a tremendous impact on the way landscapes are perceived and shaped.

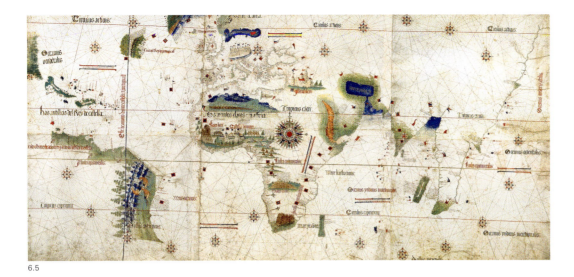

6.5

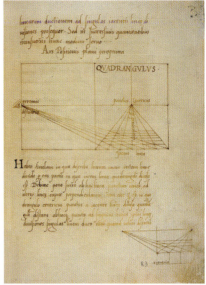

6.7

6.6

British Isles.[3] Landscape thus became the necessary expression of good governance, as illustrated in Lorenzetti's fresco, *Allegory of Good Government* [6.2]. As it progressively opened up, the Renaissance landscape organized itself around existing centres and new settlements occupying prominent sites with panoramic views of fields, roads and orchards.

Further afield, the old Silk Road of Central Asia and the spice routes that arrived in Venice via the Indian Ocean and the Red Sea were blockaded by the Ottomans in the 15th and 16th centuries, preventing the passage of European ships and trade through the eastern Mediterranean.[4] This encouraged alternative maritime ventures, including routes around Africa and new footholds in the Americas, and introduced an era of ocean mapping and navigation on an unprecedented scale. The portolan charts that first appeared in Genoa and Venice during the 13th and 14th centuries attest to a new accuracy in map-making. Using compass readings and the North Star to chart a ship's course in terms of time and distance, the charts, drawn on sheepskin, did not take the curvature of the Earth into account and were therefore most reliable when used for short distances in and around the Mediterranean basin. The one drawn up by Pietro Vesconte in Genoa in 1311 attempts to trace the entire Atlantic coast of Africa and Europe, and to note all ports of call at their correct geographical locations. Two centuries later, the Portuguese Cantino Planisphere of 1502 shows for the first time part of the coast

of Brazil and the Caribbean [6.5]. Such progress in mapping astronomically observed latitude would gradually be taken up on land, resulting in the first accurately triangulated maps of the world by the end of the 17th century.[5] Following the discoveries of Copernicus and Galileo, maps and globes of the Renaissance were drawn according to geodesic principles. The orthographic projection of cylindrical segments of the world was further perfected by cartographers and globe-makers such as Gerardus Mercator in the 16th century.[6]

In other areas, too, scientific advances were rapidly changing society. The mathematician Fibonacci, as we saw previously, introduced Arabic numerals, algebra and the 'golden spiral' to Western culture in his *Liber Abaci* (1202). This knowledge, acquired from trading partners in Algeria and Cairo, would prove invaluable for further developments in the arts and sciences. The celebrated Fibonacci sequence prepared the ground for the golden ratio, which would govern all the rules of proportion and perspective in the Renaissance. Artists took time to adopt the basics of perspective in their works. 'Primitive' painters such as Giotto tried to create an illusion of space using various methods, including differentiated degrees of shading and converging lines, while the system of linear perspective as we recognize it today was invented by Filippo Brunelleschi in the early 15th century and codified by Leon Battista Alberti in 1435–36 [6.6, 6.7].[7] It was further put to use by the painter Piero della Francesca and others. The use of the golden ratio and linear perspective became axiomatic in architecture, remaining relevant over the course of four centuries, from Bramante's Belvedere in the Vatican (1506) to the Ideal Villa Stein at Garches devised by Le Corbusier (1927). Perspective constituted a definite break from the centripetal order that had been established during the Middle Ages, instead describing a dynamic that expanded outwards towards the infinite horizon, as can be seen in Leonardo's landscape scenery of the Annunciation [6.8]. These advances in perspective transformed not only the painter's way of shaping the world: the combination of proportional and geometric structure led to one of humankind's greatest revolutions in conceptual thinking balancing both space and historical time, as can be seen in Botticelli's *Banquet in the Pine Forest* sequence [6.9]. Each 'project' could now map out its own position, purpose and direction and tell its own story.

Villas and gardens

Mercantile exchanges with Africa and the Middle East and, eventually, new trade routes to America brought considerable wealth to Italy in the 15th and 16th centuries, leading to the emergence of a rich aristocratic merchant caste in such city-states as Venice, Genoa, Siena and Florence.[8] It was through commerce that the Medici banking family accrued wealth and power, becoming leading patrons of art, architecture and science in Florence. Within this compelling cultural context,

the Renaissance garden became an expression of the highest artistic, scientific and philosophical meaning. Perspectival projection combined with mythological themes constituted the core theme of the landscape narrative, with results that were precise, directive and effective.

In the same way that artists readjusted their focus, so the treatment of gardens in the Renaissance triggered a change of attitude towards nature. Landscapes began to draw their narrative inspiration from Ovid's *Metamorphoses* and other seminal texts. Ancient stories involving satyrs and fauns, such as Silenus and Pan, muses and goddesses return, once more playing a central role in the meaning and atmosphere of a garden. The gardens of the Villa d'Este (1560–72), designed by Pirro Ligorio for Cardinal Ippolito II d'Este, are a prime example of the desire to integrate ancient mythology into the landscape narrative.[9] Located in Tivoli, the gardens feature mythical figures from antiquity such as the Fountain of Diana of Ephesus, designed by the Flemish sculptor Gillis van de Vliete and placed at the very bottom of the garden axis, which offers a chronological perspective reaching back to remote times [6.10].

The Renaissance garden reflects a conscious reawakening of our ancient understanding of nature that, in the West, had been silenced for over a millennium. In the famous romance known as the *Hypnerotomachia Poliphili* (1499) [6.11], attributed to Francesco Colonna and published

During the Renaissance, perspective was not only about drawing and architectural design. Exchanges between Egypt, Syria and the West in the late medieval period had opened up some of the most precious texts of the ancient world, most of which were unknown to European scholars: works of Classical philosophy, mathematics and literature that had been either lost or forgotten during a thousand years of Christianity. The recovery of Greek mathematics through Euclid, Aristotle and Plato opened up a treasury of knowledge. It is precisely this sense of perspective – or, rather, a retrospective interest in antiquity – that is such a hallmark of the period.

6.8

6.9

6.10

6.8 *Annunciation* by Leonardo da Vinci, with Andrea Verrocchio, *c.*1475.
Behind the angel Gabriel the landscape extends to infinity in a perspective of extraordinary depth and a wealth of fine detail that announces something beyond biblical significance. Verrocchio painted the Virgin, while the angel and background were left to Leonardo, his pupil.

6.9 *The Banquet in the Pine Forest* by Sandro Botticelli, 1483.
In this panel depicting a scene from Boccaccio's *Decameron*, Nastagio, who has been rejected by the woman he loves, has cut down trees to make space for a banquet. He knows the forest is haunted by an infernal hunt in which a rejected lover on horseback perpetually chases the naked object of his love and kills her. Having witnessed this, Nastagio's beloved changes her mind.

6.10 The Fountain of Diana of Ephesus, gardens of the Villa d'Este, Tivoli, by Pirro Ligorio, 1560–72.
The integration of ancient mythological references in this garden is unmistakable. Here, the multi-breasted Diana, goddess of the moon, can be seen as a Renaissance version of Ishtar. In Ephesus, a city founded by the Amazons, she took the form of a sculpted wooden figure.

6.11 Woodcut from the *Hypnerotomachia Poliphili* by Francesco Colonna, 1499.
The hero Poliphilo walks though a forest strewn with ruins and remains of the past. The book became an important document for landscape narratives in the Renaissance.

6.11

6.12

6.13

6.12 The Villa Medici at Fiesole, with views of the River Arno and Florence, Italy.
Built in the mid-15th century, this villa, later the seat of Lorenzo de' Medici, the Magnificent, was a place of prestige. Cut into a stony hillside, small gardens on terraces held exotic pomegranate, lemon and orange trees in the shade of cypress trees.

6.13 Lunette of the Villa Poggio a Caiano by Giusto Utens, 1599.
Commissioned by Lorenzo de' Medici and designed by Giuliano da Sangallo, work on the villa began in 1485. It is unusual in looking outwards, over a productive landscape of fields and orchards, and became a reference for other villas in the region.

in Venice, the hero, Poliphilo, tormented by his love for Polia, dreams he has arrived in a forest on his way to Cythera, the island of love. In this forest, strewn with ruins and mysterious remains from a long-forgotten past, Poliphilo encounters gods, goddesses, nymphs and fauns.[10] He then stumbles on the paradise garden belonging to a forgotten castle in the woods, where Venus and Cupid finally save his love. It is not so much the story, but rather the staging of historic myths, that really matters in this book. This marks the beginning of a long-standing tradition in landscape design of including mythological personifications and interpretations – an approach that lasted throughout the Italian Renaissance and well into the English Picturesque movement 400 years later.

Beyond the newly acquired stylistic elements to be found in their lavish gardens, the villas of the Italian Renaissance were also responsible for transformations in the surrounding landscape. The concept of the villa related not only to the house itself: rather, it embodied an entire country estate, with its composite parts held in balance by a common topology. The Villa Medici at Fiesole and its estate were bound together visually, rather as scenery unfolding before the house for the benefit of its owner [6.12]. The landscaping of an estate became a tool of pictorial experimentation: a device that opened up, and at the same time encompassed, a precise piece of territory with infinitesimal precision, extending all the way to the horizon. The geometry of the garden reaches

far beyond the terraces of the villa itself, incorporating a line of sight that projects and directs.[11] It is perspective – a device developed for the purposes of painting and architecture – that now becomes a powerful tool for ordering and dominating the landscape, an experience conveyed by the painting by Giusto Utens (1599) of the Villa Poggio (1485) [6.13]. The concept of the Renaissance *veduta*, set within the framework of an estate, has its roots in Petrarch's text of his ascent of Mont Ventoux in Provence, and the expansive prospect he enjoyed at its summit, but it took on a fuller significance when villas of powerful families were constructed with this strong sense of proprietary space and visual projection over their dominion, like the Villa Castello in Florence [6.15]. Here, as the viewer gazes out across the landscape, nothing is left to chance.

The earliest gardens of the Renaissance were full-scale testing grounds not only for the science of perspective, but also for the staging of human history and its stories. It is the period when, more than ever, the garden became a construct, requiring a high degree of technical skill and erudition, where precise modelling, triangulation and mapping of the terrain were married to the arts of proportional composition, illusionism and horticulture, as seen in the elaborate topiaries of the Villa La Petraia [6.14]. For the first time in history, a garden like that at the Villa Castello in Florence embodied a complete chronological narrative within its boundaries, moving from the allegoric realm of antediluvian mythology,

6.14 Gardens of the Medici Villa La Petraia, Florence.
The geometric, labyrinthine layout of the terraced garden design dates from 1588. Clipped box hedges and low-growing perennials preserve the open view out towards Florence.

6.15 The Medici Villa Castello, Florence.
Designed by Niccolò Tribolo in 1538, this is the first important Medici garden completed in Florence. The formal garden features clipped hedges in a labyrinth and fruit trees.

6.14

6.15

6.16 *Appennino* by Bartolomeo Ammannati, 1563.

The personification of the Apennines sits on a rock in the midst of a reservoir, hugging himself as if shivering from cold, with water trickling down over his head. Set against the backdrop of a rustic forest at the Villa Castello, it is to be understood as an allegory of man's place in the world. Nature is to be fought, wrought and tamed for the sake of our comfort.

6.17 Diagram from *De revolutionibus orbium coelestium* **by Nicolaus Copernicus, 1543.**

Copernicus's revolutionary theory of a heliocentric universe stated that the Earth revolved around the sun like the other planets, overturning ideas held since antiquity and questioning over a millennium of Christian dogma.

6.18 A terrestrial globe.

It is hard for us to imagine now that Galileo was put on trial by the Inquisition for claiming an obvious law of nature – that the Earth is round and spins on its axis, while tracing an annual orbit around the sun.

6.19 Anonymous painting of the Conquista of Brazil.

Trade with the Americas was a source of great wealth for Europe, but also a cause of great distress and destruction to the landscapes of the New World and its peoples. The way in which native peoples were depicted as man-eating savages left an indelible mark on our consciousness.

6.16

6.17

An important break from the medieval worldview occurred between the invention of linear perspective in the early 15th century and the appearance of Italian Renaissance gardens in the mid-16th century. Columbus's first contact with the Americas in 1492 [6.19], combined with Copernicus's demonstration of a heliocentric universe in 1543, turned established ideas about the world upside down [6.17].[12] At the beginning of the 17th century, Galileo's assertion that the Earth was round and turned on an axis challenged the geocentric dogma that had lain at the heart of medieval Christianity [6.18].[13] These discoveries had an impact on our understanding of the universe and proposed a new order of things in which the conquest of new landscapes would come to play an essential role.

6.18

6.19

By the mid-16th century, maps were being used for plotting maritime trade routes between Europe, Equatorial Africa and the West Indies. With the discovery of new territories came the beginnings of agricultural and industrial slavery; allied to these were the birth of modern financing, commerce, and the spice, sugar and textile trades. Most of the exquisite gardens produced in 16th-century Italy were the indirect result of profits from the so-called 'triangular trade' that grew up between Europe, Africa and America.[14] The first banks, created in Siena and Florence, became rich through such trading. America was in fact named after the Florentine explorer Amerigo Vespucci, who first worked for the Medici and then the king of Spain.[15] He wrote several influential accounts of his travels to the new continent, possibly without ever having set foot there.

through the tales of antiquity, towards humanism and the rational regularity of scientific enlightenment. This spatial and humanist progression through time was drawn from an established pictorial tradition: it was the work of architects and painters such as Leonardo and Michelangelo in the previous century that enabled the garden to incorporate this tremendous conceptual leap forward. One is also reminded of how Roman frescoes representing idealized idyllic scenes in their era influenced the later gardens of Pompeii.

The first true Renaissance gardens appeared more than a century after the studies of perspective by Leon Battista Alberti and Piero della Francesca. Following an apprenticeship and early career as a sculptor, Niccolò Tribolo returned to Florence in 1538 to build a garden for Cosimo I de' Medici's villa at Castello.[16] The garden took the form of a Classical *hortus conclusus* with golden-section proportions, backed by a wild wood or *macchia*, in which scenes from Ovid's *Metamorphoses* were staged. Thirty years later, the architect Jacopo Vignola arrived in Viterbo to build his famous perspective garden for the Villa Lante at Bagnaia. The rules of perspective that Vignola put into use at the Villa Lante had been tested out on paper and canvas long before they were translated onto the landscape. All of these gardens use the same narrative in slightly different ways. The grounds of Villa Castello, Villa Lante and Villa Aldobrandini in Frascati present a similar conceptual structure, in which

an archaic mythological wilderness is played against designs that symbolize the reason and destiny of humankind. The celebrated bronze fountain of *Appennino*, by Bartolomeo Ammannati (1563), also known as *Gennaio*, at Castello, seen crouching, seemingly frozen, on a pile of rocks in the middle of a primitive pool, is set against the backdrop of the Apennines in a dense oak woodland above the formal garden [6.16]. The uncomfortable naked figure takes on a particular untamed quality in which the 'wild', mythologically inspired form of rusticated nature epitomizes this quest for ancient origins and is typical of artists of the period.

Unlike examples in Roman times, the Renaissance garden was not primarily about lust, but rather about the juxtaposition of primeval chaos with orderly gardens shaped by reason. Villa Lante and Villa d'Este were commissioned at a time when the church had reached a peak in terms of power. But the willingness of cardinals to demonstrate an openness to advances in the art of landscape and memory did not extend to marked advances in science. When Copernicus, himself a monk, proposed his heliocentric model of the universe, or Galileo claimed that the Earth was a sphere turning on its own axis, the church was not so ready to listen and leap into the unknown [6.17, 6.18]. The discovery of the New World in 1492 marked also the beginning of the Spanish Inquisition which was to leave its indelible mark on the colonies [6.19].

Villa Lante, Italy

At the Villa Lante, Jacopo Vignola was able to translate perspectival effects from a two-dimensional plan directly into a three-dimensional landscape scheme thanks to the 'Lanci device', as it was called.[17] This mechanism combined the possibility of panoramic surveying with perspective drawing. It could trace a view on to a cylindrical surface, and project level sight lines upon a terrain like an advanced *groma*. These lines were then set to converge on the horizon, in a perspectival mode. Vignola used this instrument to construct the singular axial perspective of the garden and to control the views. Depending on whether the garden was viewed from above or below, the proportional effects of perspective became either compressed or extended as can be seen in plan [6.21].

The garden at the Villa Lante, designed for Cardinal Gambara from 1568, takes the form of a figurative landscape.[18] The visitor enters the garden from the main gate facing the town of Bagnaia, and stands before a cruciform basin and fountain at the centre of large open terrace named the 'Quadrato', with a central circular basin [6.33]. Although more regular and compact, it inspired the Isolotto of the Boboli Gardens in Florence, achieved in the early 17th century [6.20]. On the opposite side of the parterre at Lante stand two identical square villas or *casini*; as one looks between them a series of stacked terraces rises towards the wooded hill beyond [6.26]. The impression is of a garden steadily retreating in time to its primeval origins. This optical effect of chronological historical compression is reinforced by an ascending path, which becomes narrower and steeper in the upper reaches of the garden. There is a distinct sense of progressive enclosure as one steps up between the twin houses and passes the so-called 'Fountain of the Lanterns', with its jets sparkling in the sunlight [6.37].

On the next terrace, a long stone table filled with still water reflects a grotesque fountain flanked by two nonchalant river gods [6.0]. Then come the rushing rivulets of the 'water chain', leading to a small terrace at the top of the formal axis flanked by two *loggias* called the 'Houses of the Muses' [6.31, 6.42]. These frame the recessed Fountain of the Deluge, which surges from a rough but man-made grotto that echoes the surrounding hills [6.38]. Behind the grotto is an area of planted woodland, at the edge of which is a large tank that supplies the garden's water features. At its centre four bearded heads of gigantic proportions spout water [6.44]. This cistern and the garden's entire water system were designed by Tommaso Ghinucci, a hydraulic engineer from Siena.

6.20 The Boboli Gardens, Florence, Italy.
Initially designed by Niccolò Tribolo for Cosimo I de' Medici before 1550, the Boboli Gardens are typical of the formal Italian style that would influence projects across Europe. The Isolotto is a 17th-century creation by Alfonso Parigi, with a circular island garden reached by bridges replicating the microcosmic principles of the Maritime Theatre at Hadrian's Villa.

6.21 Reconstruction of the Villa Lante and its park, overlooking Bagnaia, Italy.
Designed by Jacopo Vignola in the second half of the 16th century, the Mannerist garden and forest park of the Villa Lante were constructed around an elaborate water scheme, developed by the engineer Tommaso Ghinucci.

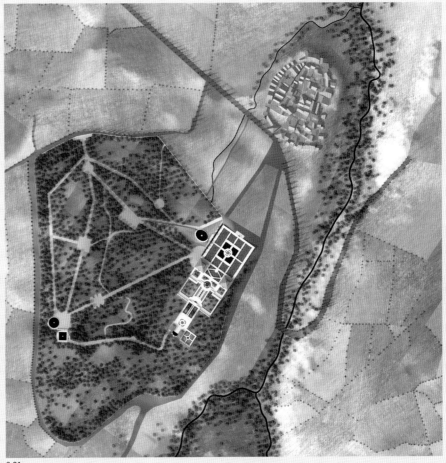

6.21

6.22a

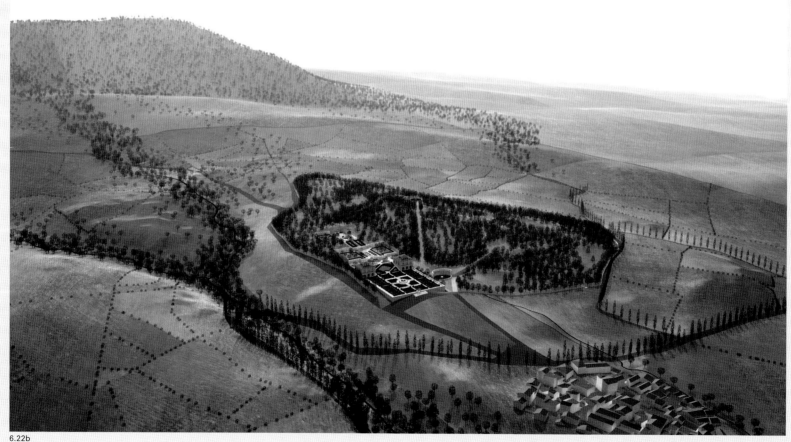

6.22b

6.22a, 6.22b Reconstructed before and after views of the site at Bagnaia, near Viterbo.
By the 16th century the entire landscape around Viterbo had been deforested and grazed. The project by Vignola inserts a piece of artificial forest alongside a formal Mannerist garden. For the Italian Renaissance the creation of a *bosco* or wood was just as significant as the garden.

6.23 Aerial view of the Villa Lante.
The square parterre of the Quadrato replicates the quadrant archetype of the walled garden. At the centre, water converges on the Fountain of the Moors, an obvious reference to the garden's Islamic influences. The artificial forest that works as a backdrop provides a 'natural' landscape setting that adds historical perspective to the narrative thread of the entire project.

6.23

The hilltop wood is reminiscent of the forest described in *Hypnerotomachia Poliphili*, the difference being that it was planted and staged entirely for the benefit of the garden [6.47]. This was probably the first time since the Hanging Gardens of Babylon that a newly planted forest formed an integral part of the scenography of a garden [6.22a, 6.22b]. Here, there is no expression of Eros of any sort, nor a lingering pastoral ideal, as would have been the case in Roman times. What we find instead is a contrast between rugged wilderness and a design representing human order and purpose [6.45]. The garden of the Villa Lante demonstrates a complete control over nature and time; it is a microcosm of precision meant to draw us away from bestiality and lust towards the path of structured reason [6.23]. The moral premise in which Christian good and pagan evil are juxtaposed here reappears; the Renaissance garden harnesses the thrust of time, history and perspective to further assert this Manichaean dogma within the dynamics of an entirely new moral and scientific order [6.41]. The artificial wood is an integral part of the garden design, forming a necessary rustic counterpoint to the refined clarity of the perfectly square Quadrato [6.25].[19] Here we see the two landscape archetypes – the forest and the walled garden – juxtaposed with one another but never quite mixing, in an arrangement that recalls the cultural clash between the barbarian and the Classical over a thousand years earlier [6.27].

The visitor reaches the top of the garden and turns around, and is presented with an extraordinary perspective, exquisitely proportioned through rectangular terraces and trimmed hedges. The all-encompassing view from the top of the garden is focused, orderly and symmetrical [6.29]. The main axis of the garden falls away within the natural terrain, which is carefully balanced on both sides for the sake of perspective. Flanking the water chain as it makes its way down the hill are terraces, some of which are carved out of bedrock [6.32]. Viewed from above, the rushing waters are framed and tamed into horizontal stillness; each step of the way, water is deviated and slowed down through an intricate arrangement of lateral fountains [6.30]. Their basins, which are placed on axis, gradually become more rational, geometric and abstract as the water moves down. When it reaches the long stone table on the penultimate terrace, the water is finally muted and transformed [6.28].

Water as an allegory of nature is a quintessential feature of this garden. The antiquarian Pirro Ligorio with the help of Tommaso Ghinucci worked on its aquatic scenography. The same can be said of the geometrically constructed garden, levelled to match the terraced pendants delineated by carefully constructed walls [6.39]. Together, these stepped terraces bring unity and symmetry to what would have been an overgrazed hillside with irregular outcrops of rock.

6.24

6.25

6.24 Diagonal side alleys of clipped boxwood leading up to the Quadrato casini (villas).
The break in both diagonals at the centre of the view corresponds to the passage of the central perspectival axis, left to right.

6.25 View from the second terrace looking north.
Looking back towards the Quadrato, the village of Bagnaia is today visible beyond the garden. Originally the village was further down the hill and did not interrupt the horizon in this way.

6.26

6.26 Diagonal view across the Quadrato towards the two *casini* with their roof lanterns.
An elaborate arabesque parterre of clipped box frames the Fountain of the Moors to the right. The fountain occupies the centre of the quadrant on the main perspectival axis due south.

6.27 Fresco of the Villa Lante by Raffaellino da Reggio, 1575.
The fresco in the Palazzina Gambara, one of the two *casini* situated on the Quadrato, gives a perspective view of the entire Mannerist garden and its newly planted wood. The Quadrato in the foreground reads literally as a walled *chahar bagh*, with the strong central axis moving uphill, southwards.

6.27

6.28

6.28 The water chain tumbling north and down the slope.
The gushing waters come to a halt in the tranquil water table below, just before reaching the Fountain of the Lights. In the distance, water spouts vertically in the Fountain of the Moors, in an allegory of wild water tamed in the name of reason, in parallel with the narrative of the rest of the garden.

6.29 Reconstructed view of the garden, seen from above.
The garden surrounded by the newly planted trees represents a clearing in the rustic forest. The linear perspective can also be understood as an axis in time, progressing from the ancient Deluge grotto set among wild trees and ruined colonnades to the south, with the garden descending in steps gradually to the Quadrato, a symbol of mathematical reason and control over nature.

6.29

6.30

6.31

6.32

6.30 Detail of a stairway balustrade at the Fountain of the Lights, on the second terrace. Water is orchestrated with such minute precision to delight the ears, and with such parsimony and craft with respect to the precious liquid, that the inspiration is undoubtedly Oriental.

6.31 View of the water chain looking south and upwards towards the Deluge grotto. The clipped box hedges create an architectural enclosure with narrow paths, enhancing the physical presence of water and its acoustic resonance.

6.32 View from the third terrace looking up. The wall of the fourth terrace on the eastern side is carved from bedrock. In the background the forest wraps around the stepped terraces that stand out as geometric clearings.

6.33

6.34

6.33 The Fountain of the Moors, on the main central axis.
The statues hold aloft the heraldic device of Cardinal Montalto in the shape of a star, set between the symmetrical twin *casini* behind.

6.34 Looking down from the third terrace balustrade over the grotto of Neptune.
The view encompasses the second terrace and the first terrace of the Quadrato. As the garden descends, the vegetation becomes more reduced and controlled, before finally reaching the parterre.

As the visitor descends again towards the wide, open parterre, the sense of geometric balance and centripetal order becomes predominant [6.34]. Here, nature is consciously pared back, taking the form of low, clipped box hedges and water mirrors [6.24]. The centre of the parterre contains a circular fountain with four Moorish figures, which was built later. The presence of this circular symbol at the centre of the Quadrato was perhaps designed to neutralize, albeit for an instant, the guiding thrust of perspective [6.35].

We are reminded of the Arabic heritage in this garden, and in particular the return of Euclidian geometry, without which perspective would never have occurred in Western culture. The Quadrato parterre is a perfect quadrilateral that derives from the earlier Persian tradition of the *chahar bagh*, although the four rivers of life converging at the centre are absent here. Instead we have an explicitly cruciform gravel path leading towards the main fountain, in a scheme inherited directly from medieval cloisters. This archetypal strength would serve many Baroque gardens to come.

The garden's axis, which runs from north to south – from the darkest recesses of woodland to the orderly clarity of a wide, open square – follows the rule of perspectival projection. The contrast between the geometric parterre, with its trimmed hedges and mirror-like basin, and the seemingly chaotic rock formation of the 'Deluge', with irregular stands of trees as backdrop, could not be more striking. Beyond

this point, the winding forest paths – strewn with fragments reminiscent of the past – reproduce a place where Poliphilo might have got lost [6.46]. The first visitors to the villa were drenched by a sudden release of water from the Deluge fountain, triggered as they approached the Houses of the Muses [6.40]: not a subtle joke, but one that carried a clear moral message. The way in which the garden design takes the raw force of nature and gradually harnesses it by the power of reason could be seen as the embodiment of a cultural war waged against this force.

In what appears to have been a conscious design, the 'evil' woodland is mostly to the left of the central axis as one looks down upon the cruciform garden [6.43]. As we know, the word 'left' translates as *sinistra* in Italian, reflecting old superstitions about the 'sinister' side of things. The Italian Renaissance garden thus represents an elaborate construct in which nature must be tamed for the purpose of humankind, paving the way for an attitude that would become a constant in Western culture [6.36].

6.35

6.36

6.35 Reconstruction of the Villa Lante garden looking south-east.
The entrance portico leads to the terrace of the Quadrato, framing the perspective axis on the central fountain. The Fountain of Pegasus to the right opens the way out to the forest.

6.36 The Fountain of Pegasus with the wall of muses.
The statue of Pegasus stands in the middle of an elliptical pool. Legend has it that when the flying horse struck the earth of Mount Helicon with its hoof, a spring burst forth.

6.37

6.38

6.37 The Fountain of the Lanterns.
Located on the second terrace between the twin *casini*, this fountain expresses enlightenment through the mastery of water.

6.38 The Foutain of the Deluge, with recessed nymphaeum.
The fountain and grotto are set in a narrow space between two rusticated loggias. The water can be understood as the origin of time, and is present throughout the garden. Early visitors here were drenched by trick water spouts, to the amusement of the host – hence the Deluge.

6.39 Section through the Villa Lante, on the south to north perspectival axis.
The terraces from the Quadrato upwards become proportionally smaller. The same is true of the paths, which become gradually narrower as one ascends, receding in time. The backdrop of the forest contributes to an overall feeling of primeval enclosure.

6.39

6.40

6.40 The twin loggias of the Deluge.
These loggias echo the two *casini*, but in a
diminutive way, as if their ghosts. Cardinal
Montalto would come here with guests to be
refreshed, converse and listen to the sound of
the muses.

**6.41 Detail of a balustrade between the forest
and the Deluge terrace.**
The subtle play between the organic and
inorganic, the dark and the light, the living and
the dead reaches its full expression here, as if
in Poliphilo's dream.

6.42 The Fountain of the Dolphins.
Located on the upper terrace of the garden
before the loggias of the Fountain of the Deluge,
this fountain comprises 16 dolphins paired
around an octagonal base. It is said that visitors
would get sprayed with water if they sat on the
benches. This is the fountain of life that feeds
the water chain just below. A ruined colonnade
stands in the background at the forest edge
as a reminder of time passing.

6.41

6.42

6.43

6.44 (label on lower left photo)

6.43 **The dark forest of the Villa Lante with the water cistern, *il conservone*, in the foreground.**
The cistern was fed by an aqueduct that was built some time prior to the garden. The terraced garden can be seen in the background.

6.44 ***Il conservone*, the main cistern at the Villa Lante.**
The primitive Titan heads emerging from the centre of the pool are reminiscent of *Appennino* at the Villa Castello. This 'capture' of water marks the first wilful act against nature in the garden.

6.45 **A fountain set in a lawn at the Villa Lante.**
The juxtaposition of a formal basin set in a verdant forest clearing is unique to this particular period, and would strongly influence both the Baroque and English landscape gardens.

6.46 **A ruined bench on a plinth in a clearing.**
As in the dream of Poliphilo, the visitor stumbles across inexplicable fragments from a long forgotten past. Landscape becomes the melancholic receptacle of unfathomable memories, real and fictitious, good and bad, all for the sake of love and humankind.

6.47 **A narrow path deep in the woods.**
The aesthetic of the hunting ground converted into a park becomes an important reference for subsequent landscapes.

6.45

6.46

6.47

The legacy of the Renaissance garden

As the Renaissance progressed, the attitude to nature changed. The landscape acquired a new sense of purpose through the use of perspective, while the garden defined itself as a human creation working 'against' nature. The Renaissance garden left a humanistic imprint on the world that remains a reference point to this day. The modern clipped-hedge gardens of Carl Theodor Sørensen in Denmark would not have happened without reference to the late Renaissance Rosenborg Gardens in Copenhagen (1624)[6.52]. The Renaissance introduced the idea of the terraced garden with all-encompassing views, distantly related to the ancient concept of the hanging gardens. The grounds of the Getty Center, Los Angeles (1977), suspended above the city skyline, show an almost literal interpretation of this archetype [6.58]. As a counterpoint, Muso Soseki gave birth to a new kind of forest garden at the Saiho-ji moss garden in Kyoto (1339) that was to become the polar opposite of Renaissance gardens in style [6.57].

The estate of the *Sacro Bosco*, 'sacred wood', designed by Pier Franceso Orsini with Pirro Ligorio in a late Mannerist style in Bomarzo (1552–64), used diminutive buildings and oversized monster sculptures as part of its woodland scenery [6.53, 6.54, 6.55].[20] Both Lante and Bomarzo featured artificially planted woodland that would inspire the creators of the first English Picturesque gardens two centuries later. Unlikely as it might appear, the English garden owes its origins to Italian Mannerism, but in the meantime attitudes towards nature underwent a complete reversal. There is an uncanny likeness in plan between the wood and garden axis of the Villa Lante and Ray Wood at Castle Howard, Venus's Vale at Rousham, and the Temple of British Worthies at Stowe. The artificial forests in each case stand out like intriguing patches of darkness to the left of the main garden axis.

Renaissance style spread through Europe in the 16th century, influencing Loire châteaux like Villandry [6.51] and Fontainebleau, and the Jacobean box knots and labyrinths at Hampton Court and Chatsworth [6.48, 6.49].[21] But in this period of conflict between Protestants and Catholics, the garden became an emblem of religious and ideological allegiance. The Hortus Palatinus in Heidelberg was never completed, but was intended to represent a repository of scientific knowledge under Catholicism.[22] The same applies to the Tuileries gardens in Paris, which became a form of scientific laboratory under Bernard Palissy.[23] The riches of new colonies encouraged powerful families like the Medicis to project their might across the surrounding landscape. Europe was not yet at the point when nations would claim entire continents, as France, Spain, Portugal and England would do in the Baroque period. During the late Renaissance, following villas in Rome, Fiesole and Castello, the next Medici project would be in Paris, where the Jardin du Luxembourg – first created for Marie de' Medici in 1612 – still stands today [6.56].

6.48 Circular pool and Irish yews with clipped hornbeam hedge, Chatsworth, England.
A more abstract manifestation of clipped topiary and a play of the informal and the formal add a note of humour to the incipient Baroque style.

6.49 Herm statue of a devil in a recess of clipped hornbeam, Chatsworth.
This statue welcomes guests on their way to the labyrinth. The transfer of a Renaissance narrative from Italy into the English landscape is very clear here.

6.48

6.49

6.50

The Renaissance coincided with the great Ming period in China, where the art of the garden reached its peak in Suzhou [6.50].[24] Few exchanges relating to garden design took place between Italy and China, and it is interesting to note how their landscape cultures developed in different directions. In Suzhou, for instance, the location of a garden's paths would have been dictated by the forces of geomancy and not geometry. The traditional Chinese garden was understood as an allegory of nature, replete with strongly coded symbolism, rather than of man's dominion over it, and its principal archetypes were the twin notions of 'mountain' and 'water'. Despite this difference, China would come to exert an influence on European gardens through the 'Anglo-Chinese' style that flourished in Europe during the 18th century.

6.50 Entrance to the Yi Pu garden, Suzhou, China.
This Ming dynasty garden was first established in the second half of the 16th century by Yuan Zugeng, and was called the Zui Ying Tang, 'Garden of Inebriated Talent'. It was then named Yi Pu, 'Angelica Garden' by a subsequent owner. The garden features elaborate rockwork and tall walls amid a labyrinth of pools, plantations and small stone bridges.

6.51 The Renaissance garden at Villandry in the Loire Valley, France, designed 1540.
The quadratic parterres and broad terraces are reminiscent of early Italian gardens of the same period. The château's owner, Jean Le Breton, was ambassador to France in Rome and certainly visited Bramante's Belvedere at the Vatican.

6.52 The King's Garden, Rosenborg, Copenhagen, Denmark.
Dating from the early 17th century, this Renaissance rose garden influenced countless landscape designers, including the 20th century's Carl Theodor Sørensen, known for his clipped elliptical hedges. Today the garden is still used by sun seekers, who shelter within geometrical hornbeam recesses.

6.51

6.52

6.53

6.53, 6.54, 6.55 Three views of the *Sacro Bosco*, Bomarzo, Italy, 1552–64.
Phantasmagorical sculptures of monsters and mythical creatures stage a complex and sometimes irreverent narrative against a backdrop of seemingly wild and untouched nature. The design of the garden in late Mannerist style is attributed to Pirro Ligorio, with sculptures by Simone Moschino, at the request of Pier Francesco Orsini in memory of his deceased wife.

6.56 The Medici Fountain in the Jardin du Luxembourg, Paris, France.
The Palais des Medicis and gardens built by Marie de' Medici in 1630 were modelled on the Palazzo Pitti and Boboli Gardens in Florence. The fountain has been moved and modified since then.

6.57 The mid-14th-century garden of the Saiho-ji temple in Kyoto, Japan.
Designed by the Buddhist monk Muso Soseki, the garden provides an interesting counterpoint to the European Renaissance. Its Golden Pond, with three islands originally carpeted with white sand, evolved naturally into a moss garden over time. The timeless, undisturbed contemplation of nature as opposed to a struggle against it is of the essence here.

6.58 The Central Garden, Getty Center, Los Angeles, USA, 1977.
This formal garden comprising mixed borders, clipped hedges and lawn was designed by the California artist Robert Irwin. A sublime expression of power, the sheer scale of this elaborate updated parterre reminds us of precedents including Hadrian's Villa, the Villa Lante and Vaux-le-Vicomte.

6.54

6.55

6.56

6.57

6.58

7. The Measure of Reason

'For, after all, what is man in nature? He is nothing in comparison with the infinite, and everything in comparison with nothingness, a central point between all and nothing.'
Blaise Pascal, *Pensées*[1]

To speak of the European Age of Reason without considering the vast landscapes at Vaux-le-Vicomte [7.0] or the allegorical paintings of Nicolas Poussin would seem an oversight [7.1], but not to mention the Dutch Golden Age as an important precedent in designed landscape geometry would be to ignore a revolution in mathematics, philosophy and technology that brought about considerable advances in modes of production and commerce to Europe.[2] The origins of the Dutch Golden Age lie in part in 15th-century political upheaval. In Spain, Ferdinand and Isabella imposed unity through religious conformity, establishing the Inquisition and forcing the conversion of non-Catholic communities. The immediate result was a massive exodus from Spain, Portugal and Flanders to Holland. Fleeing populations brought centuries of accumulated technical, philosophical and mathematical knowledge, inherited from the Arabs of al-Andalus, Egypt and the Middle East, to these inhospitable, marshy reaches of north-western Europe. The Dutch had popularized such technologies as the windmill, the river levee and the water pump, inherited from canal-builders of 8th-century Baghdad and themselves the result of earlier Persian inventions.[3] These three technologies were considerably improved, and together with the new migrants, aided land reclamation, allowing agricultural and urban development that would ultimately set the scene for the Dutch Golden Age. In addition, the arrival of advanced banking practices from northern Italy helped the Dutch East India Company to become the unchallenged leader in world commerce during the 17th century.[4]

The Dutch Republic of the early 17th century could be likened to a contemporary think tank. It boasted a concentration of wealth, knowledge and technical know-how,

7.0 (opposite) Looking south across the third terrace at Vaux-le-Vicomte, France.
The tall vertical edge of a trimmed wood at right angles to a reflective pool directs the view to the horizon. Just beyond, another pool seems unbalanced as it points to a distant clearing. Baroque gardens constantly play with the dichotomy between apparent intention and physical reality.

7.1 *Hymenaios Disguised as a Woman During an Offering to Priapus* (detail) by Nicolas Poussin.
The scene painted in 1638 evokes an ancient male fertility rite that can be traced back through Greek and Roman cultures to the Egyptian myth of Osiris and the Nile. Both Nicolas Poussin and Claude Lorrain worked in Rome and had a great influence on the Baroque and the Picturesque.

7.1

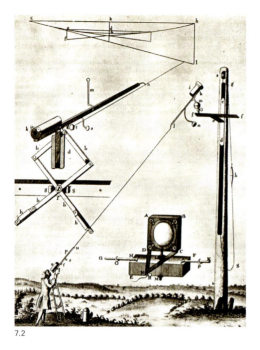

7.2

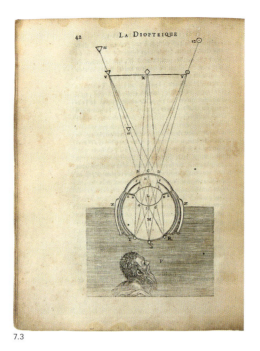

7.3

7.2 Illustration of the telescope without a tube.
Devised by the Dutchman Christiaan Huygens with his brother Constantijn in 1683, the tubeless or aerial telescope had an eyepiece for the observer on the ground and a focal objective on top of a pole aligned by a taut silk thread.

7.3 Diagram from *La Dioptrique*, René Descartes.
Descartes' diagram explains the phenomenon of image inversion on the retina of the eye. A preoccupation with measuring and optics was at the heart of scientific concerns at this time.

7.4 A diagonal view at the Beemster Polder.
When looking diagonally across two squares of the Beemster polder towards the village of Middenbeemster, our gaze becomes distorted: although the roads leading to the church steeple are at a right angle to each other, they appear to form a single flat horizon line in the distance.

7.5 Plan of the Beemster Polder, North Holland.
Overseen by the architect Jan Leeghwater, a former inland lake 3 metres (10 feet) below sea level was drained and the 7,000-ha (17,300-acre) polder laid out with a regular grid of squares measuring 900 metres (3,000 feet) each side. Each was then subdivided into five lots, following patterns of access and drainage.

and a thriving university at Leiden that attracted people such as the French Philosopher René Descartes [7.3] – an atmosphere that facilitated a liberal exchange of ideas between intellectuals, engineers and traders.[5] Without this rich discourse, involving Sephardic Jews, Italian heretics (Galileo's *Discourse* was smuggled to Leiden and published there), French Huguenots and Calvinist Dutchmen, the Dutch Republic would probably never have produced such remarkable scientific figures as the astronomer, timekeeper and mathematician Christiaan Huygens [7.2].[6]

A question of topography

Although, at first sight, there is no stylistic link between Baroque gardens and the vast, windswept polders of Holland, both in fact require great topographic precision, geometric rigour and superlative organization and discipline to maintain. The Dutch accumulated considerable wealth from what had been seen as the region's two major drawbacks: unusable marshland and too much wind. Through large-scale earthworks and water-management systems, they would finally gain control over the natural floodlands of North Holland and Zeeland. The paintings of the Dutch artist Jacob van Ruisdael show this new industrious spirit at work in the landscape [7.7]. The most emblematic project of this period is perhaps the Beemster Polder, located near Haarlem [7.4]. Created by the engineer Jan Leeghwater between 1609

and 1612, this was the first windmill-drained polder. Once it was dry, this large area of reclaimed land was divided up geometrically into squares, following a regular grid of drainage canals. This grid is of particular interest for the period, for it shows an unprecedented degree of control as well as visual and cartographic abstraction [7.5].[7] Baroque landscapes were not, therefore, only an invention of the French, and their triangulated cartography of a hundred years later could not have developed without this vital precedent [7.11]. Ironically, although most Baroque landscapes were born out of absolute monarchies in France and Austria, a significant portion of the applied surveying knowledge derived from the liberal culture of the Dutch Republic.

The Dutch landscape was sustained by an ingenious engineering system: dykes were protected by wind-powered water pumps drawing excess water from the soil and releasing it into the sea via canals. Wind-powered sawmills produced by the mid-17th century enough timber for the 15,000 vessels of the Dutch East India Company.[8] Huygens's invention of a reliable pendulum clock made possible the timekeeping for the collective management of polder lands, keeping track of tidal intervals and plotting maritime navigation. The painting *The Ambassadors* by Hans Holbein (1533) encapsulates well the beginning of this period of great technical and commercial expansion [7.6].[9] By the end of the 16th century Amsterdam had grown into a model of technical urbanity.

The French philosopher René Descartes, who is sometimes known as the 'father of modern philosophy', spent over twenty years of his adult life in the Dutch Republic, refining his reflections on reason, proportional mathematics and dualistic metaphysics. Between 1628 and 1649, Descartes profited from the country's extraordinary climate of intellectual questioning that flourished during that time. One is tempted to draw a parallel between the geometric shape of the early Dutch polders and Cartesian diagrams devised to express algebraic equations in a two-dimensional coordinate system.[10] The influx of intellectuals transformed the Republic and, more particularly, the new town of Amsterdam into one of the most lively intellectual environments in Europe.

7.4

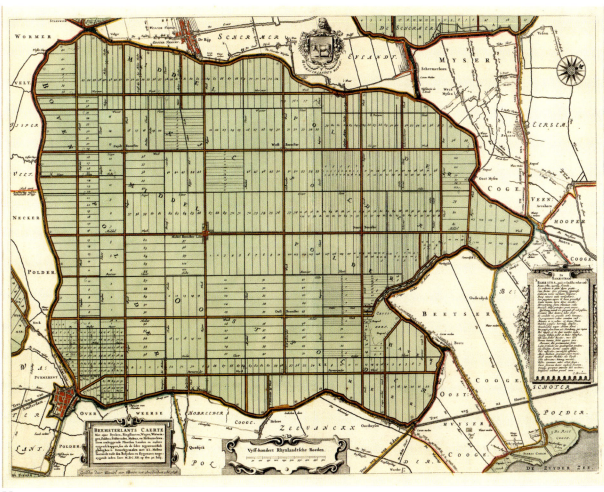

7.5

7.6

Perspective came to play a significant role in Baroque gardens. In artworks anamorphic compositions were conceived in such a way that they would be revealed only as the viewer found the correct vantage point. *The Ambassadors* (1533) by Hans Holbein has an anamorphic skull at the bottom of the composition [7.6]; and its terrestrial globe pre-dates Gerhardus Mercator's invention of orthographic projection allowing for a spherical map to be flattened into a two-dimensional chart.[11] These experiments with geometry seen as examples of 'Baroque play' or the mastery of changing form created a new type of manipulated space and perception, and thus new works of the imagination.

7.7

7.8

7.6 *The Ambassadors* **by Hans Holbein, 1533.**
Two powerful men pose before a collection of mathematical instruments used to measure both space and time. But it is the anamorphic skull that can only be viewed from the bottom left that makes this painting famous.

7.7 *The Windmill at Wijk bij Duurstede* **by Jacob van Ruisdael, 1670.**
The painting encapsulates the Dutch constructed landscape and its relationship to water: the banks of the dyke are held in place by bundles of brushwood, and the windmill towers over the village under menacing skies.

7.8 Map of Amsterdam by Joan Blaeu, 1649.
The city is shown at the peak of the Golden Age when it was still expanding within its concentric ring of semicircular canals. The new Baroque defence line is being traced on adjacent polders.

7.9 The *graphometre*.
First devised at the end of the 16th century, the *graphometre* was used to create precise terrestrial cartography. Surveyors would triangulate between church steeples and other prominent features in the landscape and could then draw accurate maps.

7.10 Design for a *parterre de broderie* **by Dezallier d'Argenville.**
D'Argenville's 1709 book on French garden aesthetics, entitled *La théorie et la pratique du jardinage*, went through thirteen editions before the French Revolution.

7.11 The *Cartes des Chasses* **drawn by Jean-Baptiste Berthier from 1764.**
The map of the royal hunting grounds in the greater Versailles region reveals how the process of triangulation developed by French land surveyors over the preceding century strongly influenced the shaping of territory.

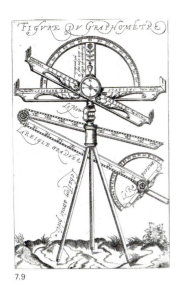

7.9

7.10

The Netherlands and France developed a set of precise surveying tools during the 16th century. The *graphometre* had two parts: a graduated semicircle with a compass at its centre, and a 180° recording instrument resting on paper for transcribing information [7.9]. Invented for mapping purposes, the *graphometre* came to be used extensively with a range-finder in 17th- and 18th-century parks and gardens, like the 1764 *Carte des Chasses*, where the tasks of plotting extended well beyond the boundaries of the garden [7.11]. It left an imprint on triangulated *patte d'oie* landscapes – a pattern typical of formal gardens of the 17th century in which straight paths branch off from a single point. The tool also allowed great precision in the definition of planar surfaces for ornamental gardens [7.10].[12]

7.11

Amsterdam became a 'Venice of the North', boasting concentric rings of canals flanked by the townhouses of wealthy merchants [7.8]. Politically, it became the symbol of a new liberal, democratic prosperity, embodied in the paintings of Rembrandt and Vermeer, that was in striking contrast to the despotic palatial monarchies of neighbouring countries. The city attracted wealthy Jewish families from Antwerp, Toledo, Lisbon and elsewhere, who contributed not only to its uncontested position as a mercantile and agricultural leader during the 17th century, but also to its intellectual development, with polemic philosophers such as Spinoza.[13]

Isfahan and Europe

As trade among seafaring nations expanded, so the world provided additional sources of inspiration that would influence the development of the formal garden. Historically, Persia was a point of exchange between East and West, lying between Venice and China on the Silk Road. But the geopolitics of Central Asia changed at the end of the 16th century with the Safavid rule of Shah Abbas in Persia [7.12].[14] Shah Abbas maintained diplomatic ties with Mughal India, with the Maidan in Isfahan serving in part as model for projects like the Taj Mahal laid out in 1632 under the Mughal emperor Shah Jahan [7.18].[15] But Abbas also established links with Europe at the turn of the 17th century in order to combat the Ottoman Empire.[16] He asked the architect and mathematician

Shaykh Baha' al-Din – also a great master of topography – to help him conceive a new capital on the Iranian High Plateau, where it was crossed by the Zaindeh River at the southern edge of the Great Salt Desert. In their scale and refinement, the gardens and palaces at Isfahan represented an impressive example of urban planning and landscape design fifty years before anything comparable was built in Europe [7.16].

Isfahan boasted the Royal Maidan, perhaps the biggest urban square in the world at that time, which was inspired by the typology of the caravanserai in its vast courtyard surrounded by shops and monuments [7.14]. Shah Abbas received ambassadors from India, China and Europe in the Music Room of the Ali Qapu royal palace, which overlooks the Maidan and its mosques [7.17]. Isfahan's main avenue, the Chahar Bagh, is planted with trees and slopes gently down to the Zaindeh River; on either side it was flanked by four square gardens, including the Chehel Sotun and the Hasht Bihisht [7.13].[17] The Chahar Bagh meets the river at the Si-o-seh Pol, or 'Bridge of 33 Arches', and the Khajou Bridge, which both feature a series of alcoves above the water [7.15]. The scale of the urban project at Isfahan was well known in European circles at the turn of the 17th century, as was the absolutist rule of Shah Abbas. Exchanges that took place between early Safavid Persia and Baroque Europe are well documented. Shakespeare's *Twelfth Night* (1601–2) already contains a reference to the Shah, or 'the Sophy', as he is called.

7.12

7.13

7.12 Isfahan, the new Safavid capital of Persia.
Designed for Shah Abbas by the architect Shaykh Baha' al-Din in 1598 and completed in 1630, the plan for the capital boasted splendid avenues, gardens, palaces, mosques and bridges set around a vast Maidan square. At that time Isfahan had no rival, and attracted countless visitors from Europe and China.

7.13 Mid-17th-century Safavid palace, Isfahan, Iran.
The sumptuous loggia with its twenty slender columns merges with the garden. A long cooling pool before the main entrance reflects the refined structure, hence its name: Chehel Sotun (Palace of Forty Columns).

7.14

7.15

7.16

7.17

7.18

7.14 Aerial view of the Maidan, Isfahan.
The Maidan was completed in 1629 and
measures 560 metres (1,840 feet) long.
The rooftops of the Bazaar are visible in the
foreground; the Shah Mosque is at the end of
the square, with its axis turned towards Mecca.

7.15 The Khajou bridge, Isfahan.
Built in the mid-17th century over the Zaindeh
River, this bridge rivals in beauty the Si-o-seh
Pol upstream. People sit here to meet and listen
to the rushing sound of the river.

7.16 The Maidan with the Shah Mosque, Isfahan.
Once a vast caravanserai courtyard open to
travellers and merchants from distant lands, this
has been transformed into a tourist destination,
with fountains and clipped trees.

7.17 Music Room of the Ali Qapu palace, Isfahan.
Shah Abbas entertained foreign guests here
with music, dancers and food. The extravagant
papier-mâché decoration has survived well for
400 years.

7.18 The Taj Mahal garden, Agra, India.
Designed by Ali Mardan Khan in 1632, the garden
is subdivided into sixteen sunken parterres. Its
scale was unrivalled at the time; Versailles was
begun four decades later. Accounts tell of a
paradise with countless fruit trees and flowers;
the British Empire changed all that to lawn.

7.19

Vaux-le-Vicomte, France

The garden at Vaux-le-Vicomte, begun in 1653, is a unique achievement, crafted out of the desire to transform a banal stretch of rural countryside into a complex arrangement of exquisite geometric illusions [7.20]. The manipulation of this rolling terrain (*vaux* means 'vales' in French) into a series of extensive terraces flanking a central axis divided by a low-lying canal recalls the Grand Canal (1609) developed nearby at Fontainebleau during the reign of Henri IV [7.19], but also the Mughal gardens of India and the Chahar Bagh of Isfahan completed half a century before.[18] But it is the impression of a wide, almost metaphysical openness at Vaux-le-Vicomte that makes the garden strikingly different from any other previously invented. This masterwork of landscape scenography designed by André Le Nôtre unfolds to the horizon and was made for Nicolas Fouquet, a rich French nobleman.[19] We are no longer experiencing a constrained, tunnel-like perspective, as at the Villa Lante, but a more open and elemental space that explores the physical limits of Euclidian geometry and human perception [7.22].[20]

Standing outside the house, one has a sense of ordered immensity facing south towards the horizon. The Cartesian balance and impeccable symmetry across the expanse of the grand clearing delivers a powerful message of enlightened reason.[21] Flat gravel terraces retained by stone walls are framed by straight lines of clipped hornbeam punctuated by topiary – conical yews and spherical box – mingling with elaborately embroidered parterres that recede regularly into the distance. Everything appears very orderly and controlled: a triumphant display of regular geometry and reason against the rougher backdrop of newly planted woodlands [7.21a, 7.21b]. The garden is conceived as an intellectual playground, a vast conceptual plane framed on all sides by tall hedges and woods, hence the clearing. Vaux-le-Vicomte creates the illusion of a broad paradise garden framed by a tall hedge set within a forest. Only a narrow, open slit on the forested hill, on axis with the house, enables the viewer to catch a glimpse in the far distance of the place where earth meets sky. Marrying the ancient archetypes of the forest clearing and the (hedged) walled garden, Vaux-le-Vicomte is made for metaphysical demonstration and earthly distraction.

The great achievement of Vaux-le-Vicomte is the way it creates an illusion of distance and warped proportion from the very beginning. Three identical, circular basins, seemingly equidistant from each other, as seen from the ballroom steps, reflect the sky at the centre of the garden terraces [7.23]. The first basin seen from the château is indeed large, round

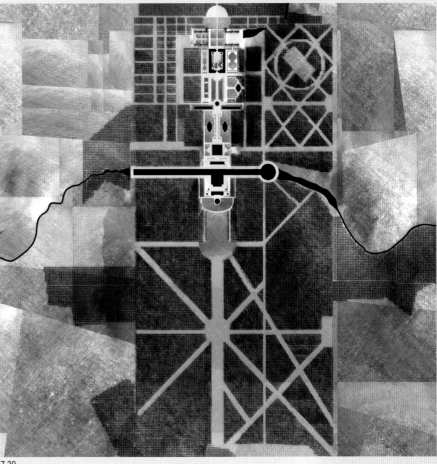

7.19 The Grand Canal, Fontainebleau, France.
Completed in 1609 in the reign of King Henri IV, the canal, almost 1,200 metres (4,000 feet) long and 50 metres (165 ft) wide, heralds a series of monumental reservoirs and canals that became the trademark of French Baroque gardens.

7.20 Plan of Vaux-le-Vicomte, France.
The château was commissioned by Nicolas Fouquet in 1653. The architect Louis Le Vau, landscape architect André Le Nôtre and artist Charles Le Brun were asked to reconceive the estate entirely.

7.20

7.21a

7.21b

7.21a, 7.21b Reconstructed before and after views of Vaux-le-Vicomte.
The original house and its terrain were much smaller and set in open farmland. A wood 3 km (1¾ miles) long and 1 km (⅔ mile) wide was then planted and the terrain carefully levelled to meet the strict optical requirements of perspective.

7.22 Aerial view of Vaux-le-Vicomte.
The château is the centrepiece of the project, where all optical illusions in relation to the park are focused. It is therefore set back proportionally in the garden, in order to enhance the effects of perspectival illusion.

7.22

and positioned on the central axis, but the two more distant basins flanking the axis are in fact oblong and several times longer than they are wide. They result from the precise anamorphic study of the garden, as seen from the house and are, therefore, quite deliberate and reasoned in their form.[22] This creates an illusion of consistency between the three separate bodies of water when viewed in this direction, compensating for the perspectival compression that naturally occurs in a vista of this depth. The visitor believes that the three circular basins are identical but, walking towards them across the first two main terraces, the reality of the illusion becomes apparent [7.25]. This play between physical response and intellectual perception and deception is a recurrent theme in Baroque gardens. It relates to the notion of Cartesian dualism, where the garden becomes a life-size laboratory in the service of enlightenment, demonstrating the inherent difference between body and mind as they relate to space. In other words, the body's failings are patent, needing constant correction and reinstatement on the path of reason (*raison*).

The garden has a moral element, where the place of man is measured against the greater forces of the universe – or of 'nature', if you will. The clipped vegetation reduced to minutiae at the foot of the house and on the central terrace is subjected to the will of man in the search of a higher truth [7.26]. What seems so clear and obvious at first sight becomes more complex as one moves towards the perspectival

goal on the horizon. It is only when the visitor completes the promenade at the end of the garden axis that a perfect reflection of the château appears in the large Square Basin. Beyond the canal, looking back north above the cascade, a complete view of the grounds is revealed. From this position, the house towers over a compressed one-point perspective, dominating the garden and sealing the entire horizon to the north [7.34].

Vaux-le-Vicomte plays with our blind faith in perspective, encouraging us to see what we think rather than to think what we see. Another splendid illusion staged at Vaux-le-Vicomte involves the first two terraces. Once again, as seen from the ballroom steps, the terraces appear to be square and equally proportioned, but in actual fact the second terrace, which is just a few steps lower than the first, is twice as wide and as deep as the first in order to compensate for perspectival compression [7.28]. The garden's metamorphosis and its distorted proportions become apparent only when the visitor is attentive to the illusory tricks at play. On an unconscious level, however, this might be one reason why visitors unfailingly find the walk along the garden axis far longer than expected, as if infinity were unrolling at their feet. The garden's illusory game becomes obvious once the visitor moves away from the house into the depths of the garden, which reveals itself as a highly abstract construct, a reflection of geometric rules in all their power and precision [7.35].

7.23

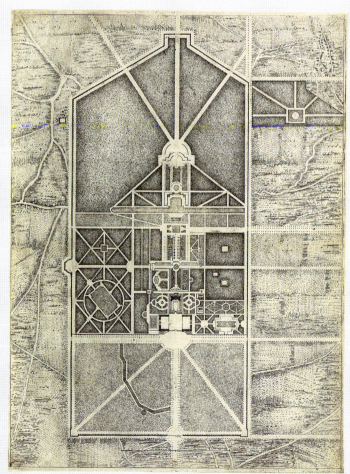

7.24

7.23 View from the ballroom steps.
It is from this viewpoint that the effects of compressed perspective and anamorphic distortion occur. The grotto at the end of the main alley appears to be at the same height as the viewer when in fact it is much lower. Likewise, three circular basins centred on the main axis seem to be similar in size and shape, but this illusion is shattered as one moves towards them.

7.24 Plan of Vaux-le-Vicomte by Israel Sylvestre, 1660.
The plan, drawn after the garden was laid-out, shows a strong geometric composition spiralling out of the château into the gardens and out towards the artificially planted forest. The perspective is not centred on the grounds, conferring a much stronger dynamic thrust to the project. The idea of landscape as a learned display of science and reason reaches a pinnacle here.

7.25 View from the third terrace towards the grotto.
The sequence here seems to repeat itself from that on the second terrace, but the intervals between objects become more expansive as the basin to the right unrolls its oblong form, and conical yews replace boxwood spheres leading the way towards a seemingly unattainable horizon.

7.26 Arabesque and spherical topiary on the second terrace, looking towards the woodland.
The clipped arabesque and neat lawn with a platonic boxwood sphere obey the language of reason, which requires that nature be thoroughly tamed. Vaux-le-Vicomte can be understood as a metaphysical forest clearing of sorts, where disordered and unkempt nature gets pushed out to the edges.

7.25

7.26

7.27 Sunken area left of the second terrace.
An elaborate construction of clipped yew, boxwood and hornbeam hedges is designed to compensate for the difference in height in this sunken area, where a river once ran, when viewed from the château and main alley. This maintains the optical balance across the broad expanse of the garden.

7.28 View of the first three terraces.
Seen in this direction, the differences in size and width of the terraces, the two oblong basins and the circular basin are quite noticeable. The sunken area is to the far right.

7.29 Main perspective at Vaux le Vicomte by Israel Sylvestre, 1660.
The engraving is an early perspective of the garden with visitors. The following year on 17 August 1661 Nicolas Fouquet threw his first and last grand party, with 6,000 guests in the presence of King Louis XIV. The sheer scale of the event became a founding reference for Versailles.

7.30 Engraving by Israel Sylvestre of a party at the Grotto on the south bank of the canal, 1660.
This is where mythology begins, distant from Reason left behind on the opposite shore. There are no terraces, just underworld recesses and a slope up to the statue of Hercules. It is difficult to appreciate how it must have felt, since most of the fountains, sculptures and trees were confiscated and taken to Versailles.

7.27

7.28

The appropriation of space through illusion

Ultimately, the illusionistic devices at play at Vaux-le-Vicomte had a concrete purpose, which was the demonstration of human power through the manipulation of 'natural' space. In the middle of the 17th century an aristocratic rebellion in France, known as 'la Fronde', had actively sought to weaken the power of the French monarchy. It was during this unstable period in French history, when monarchic rule was openly challenged, that Vaux-le-Vicomte came into being.

Nicolas Fouquet, the figure who commissioned Vaux-le-Vicomte, was a powerful aristocrat, financier and amateur of the arts and science. He was also rich, since his forefathers had made a fortune in the highly lucrative triangular slave trade between Africa, America and Europe. A very educated man, he selected the team for his project at Vaux-le-Vicomte with great care, choosing André Le Nôtre as landscape architect, Louis Le Vau as architect, Charles Le Brun as painter of interior decorations, and many other talents capable of bringing his vision into being, including the writers Jean de la Fontaine and Molière [7.29, 7.30].[23]

It would be mistaken to confuse the refinement invested in this first masterpiece of French Baroque garden design with the advent of the absolute monarchy of Louis XIV thereafter. Vaux-le-Vicomte is the product of sublime, liberal landscape invention at a specific moment in French history, when established rules of government and authority were questioned and conventions overturned. In his manners and taste, Fouquet was inspired more by his mentor, Cardinal Mazarin, and Catherine de' Medici than by the premise of absolute monarchy, of which he became one of the first victims.[24] To say, therefore, that the first French Baroque garden was the product of an enlightened despot is quite correct; but to say that it is the bare expression of French absolutism is to miss the essential point of its creation.[25] This garden is not only a manifestation of financial power, but an elaborate intellectual construct of great force and refinement, inscribed in a very long tradition of geometric garden design [7.27].

Vaux-le-Vicomte represents a showcase of state-of-the-art 17th-century landscape techniques. It was measured, terraced, drained and planted according to the finest technical precepts of the times. Few original plans of Vaux-le-Vicomte and subsequent gardens by Le Nôtre are known, probably because lines were traced, surveyed and triangulated directly on the terrain using ropes and chains, and with the help of precision surveying instruments [7.24]. The most important thing for the quality of Le Nôtre's design was the depth and refinement of the illusion at hand, based on the proportional precision of the first axial projection that was measured, traced and topographically adjusted upon the land.

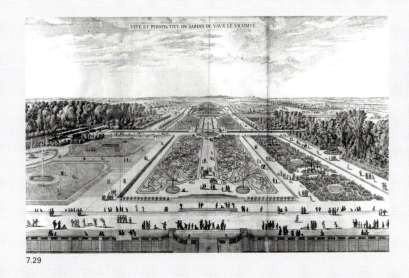

7.29

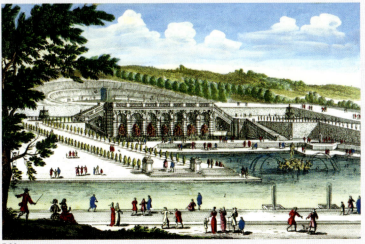

7.30

7.31

The garden sits in a gently rolling landscape amid open agricultural fields and scattered hedgerows. It is located 50 km (30 miles) to the south-east of Paris, on the road between Vincennes and Fontainebleau, two strongholds of French royalty. Over the course of eight years from 1653 to 1661, first with the architect Daniel Gittard, who laid out the terraces, and then with André Le Nôtre (1656), who completed the garden, three rivers were diverted and channelled underground and the small village of Vaux (1659) including the church and cemetery were demolished.[26] Using up to 1,800 labourers, the work was done 'secretively' to avoid any suspicion from the king. The terrain was significantly modified into a set of stepped terraces, geometric reflecting ponds and canals [7.32]. A natural, pre-existing declivity to the south-east of the house, due to a stream, was formally squared out and incorporated into the Baroque framework of the garden [7.27, 7.45].[27]

The extraordinary water features throughout the garden – its canal, cascade, basins and grotto – were designed for the dual purpose of illusion and perspectival delight, with countless allegorical statues and herms providing a strong mythological timeline [7.37]. Water was used in the creation of illusionistic effects as a reflective device [7.31]. The celebrated reflection of the house in the square basin at the end of the third terrace conveys a sense of mastery and extraordinary precision; that in the round basin across the

canal creates an almost cosmic impression, as if the facade were suspended above all worldly concerns [7.33]. At Vaux-le-Vicomte, water becomes as elemental as air, earth and light in its degree of abstraction; repeatedly obstructing our path, forcing us to depart or at least deflect from the intended trajectory.

The deceptively open perspective of the central terrace contrasts strongly with the complexity of the maze of hedges set towards the sides [7.44]. The dichotomy between vision and physical progress is all the more obvious as one approaches the perpendicular canal. Here, the difference between what is seen on axis and what is physically possible becomes evident; the visitor can either make a detour to the head of the canal on the left-hand side, where an idyllic pastoral scene awaits, before returning after a long walk to the central axis on the other side, or can take an even longer route to the right [7.43]. This delay in space and time before one reaches the other shore, with its grotto and statue of the *Farnese Hercules* beyond [7.39, 7.40, 7.41], is in fact a temporal device quite similar to the chronological compression expressed at the Villa Lante, reaching back to mythological times.[28]

Vaux-le-Vicomte and its moral dimension
For a very short moment in time, the gardens at Vaux-le-Vicomte became a prominent Baroque landmark.

7.31 The moat separating the château from the grounds.
Designed not as a defensive line but rather as a calm surface to reflect the sky, this moat is the ultimate metaphysical device, creating the illusion that the garden is suspended in mid-air.

7.32 Section across the first, second and part of the third terraces.
The terrain steps down in level terraces as it approaches the canal towards the right, and the forest in the background mirrors this scaled progression. The château stands at the highest point to view the perspective, at the heart of a rational space and in the midst of a geometric clearing as distant from the trees and nature as possible.

7.33 The château above a pool.
A small circular pool placed at the end of the garden axis seems to encompass the entire garden as the visitor glances back to view the house. The illusion that the entire garden and house are suspended above this elliptical form is short lived. At Vaux, man stands at the centre of all things, and it is human reason and not spiritual mystique that is here to guide us.

7.34 Perspective of the garden facade of the château at Vaux-le-Vicomte by Israel Sylvestre, 1660.
The engraving frames a broad optical 'pyramid' that shortens the perspective of the garden significantly. In this compressed view the house itself, which appears elevated and prominent, seems to hover over the world.

7.32

7.33

7.34

7.35

7.36

7.37

7.38

7.35, 7.36 Two side views of Vaux-le-Vicomte.
The garden is framed by a tall hornbeam hedge which appears to be part of the château's architecture, holding back the forest. In another view the lateral pool articulates the transition from the first to second terraces and creates a strong barrier, forcing movement perpendicular to the main axis.

7.37 A herm at the east entrance to the garden.
This archaic herm figure is positioned off to one side away from the main axis at the very edge of the forest clearing. Unlike Villa Lante, where mythology was aligned chronologically on the perspectival axis, here myth is found on all sides and has to be held on the periphery.

7.38 Reconstructed aerial perspective.
The edge of the forest on the right gradually encroaches towards the central axis as it progresses through the garden. This increases the illusion of depth through a forced perspective, making the garden seem deeper than it actually is, adding to the optical effects.

7.39

7.40

7.39, 7.40 The _Farnese Hercules_.
The statue was part of the original scheme, but Fouquet's arrest prevented its placement and it was only added in the late 19th century. Hercules plays a vital role in this garden of illusions. Seen from the château, the gigantic figure seems much like the people walking along the terraces, and it also punctuates the finale of the story with a parabolic return to humanism.

7.41 View looking north.
The entire perspective is so compressed in reverse that the narrow gap in the woods from this viewpoint seems to be as wide as the three terraces beyond the canal leading back towards the house.

7.41

7.42

7.43

It should be understood as an open labyrinth, a divine, geometric fingerprint comprising infinite folds that would please both Pascal and Leibnitz in their factorial complexity [7.38]. The garden could appear to unfold and multiply, depending on the visitor's propensity to stray away from the axis of reason.

The Baroque axis running through the garden's centre thus becomes a line of pure intention, gliding over all physical obstacles, detaching itself completely from the intricate paths that trap the body. Vaux-le-Vicomte becomes an abstract theatre of spatial manipulations utterly detached from nature. The surface of the garden can be likened to the weave of a fabric, operating according to a given set of folds, pleats and patterns that play with the very fibre of the landscape in multiple directions [7.36]. Time becomes elastic and full of surprises, despite the garden's apparent formal structure. The idea of the early Baroque landscape is that a higher level of meaning can be attained at each step, where each inflection and fold ultimately reveals the greater design of nature.

There is a constant interaction between matter and form at Vaux-le-Vicomte, expressed in the intrinsic difference between the garden's structure and its ornament. This could be interpreted as a proto-modernist separation of form and function. The reconciliation of these two elements at Vaux-le-Vicomte is not as literal as in previous Renaissance

gardens such as Villandry: the embroidered parterre in front of the ballroom vanishes into the distance, becoming an almost immaterial expression of structure, texture and light [7.46]. Vaux-le-Vicomte provides a strong physical counterpoint to its own framework, creating a sense of indefinable spatial displacement within an apparently placid setting. In its intent, it is a divine embodiment of Blaise Pascal's notion of the void, and the complex moral play that stands between human rectitude and our inclinations [7.42].[29]

The gardens of Vaux-le-Vicomte went on to inspire those designed by André le Nôtre at Chantilly, Sceaux, St-Germain and Versailles, with their axes and countless bosquets. All became places of learned explication and narration, where higher reason would be revealed. This eventually led to the idea of landscape narrative in the Picturesque, and the avoidance of complete geometric abstraction. In the French Baroque tradition, nature must be seen as an abstract moral and physical dimension that can in no way be understood as 'naturalistic'. According to Descartes, man continually strives against nature; unfortunately, our recent evolution fails to contradict this statement in any way.

7.44

7.45

7.46

7.42 The château at Vaux reflected in the moat.
As if floating in space and in time, the château advances on the path of reason. All the elements in nature are controlled with the utmost precision and refinement, and it is only the path taken by man that is liable to stray, with fatal uncertainty.

7.43 The grand canal at Vaux.
Roughly the same size as that at Fontainebleau, built 50 years earlier, the canal at Vaux runs perpendicular to the central axis and creates a fundamental break between the realm of reason on the château side and that of mythology, which stretches towards the *Farnese Hercules*. Getting around it on foot requires time, patience and faith in some distant history.

7.44, 7.45 Exterior and interior views of the edge of the second terrace.
A curving hedge encloses the pool at the edge of the second terrace. Both images show how differently the same space unfolds relative to the point of view, and invites us to take a second look from the small balustrade at the forest edge. This is the essence of Baroque duplicity and counterpoint in design.

7.46 The vista of illusion.
Behind the apparently simple formal structure of the garden lie many surprises, folds and forced detours interwoven with visions and illusions that contribute to a challenging experience. It offers for an instant the illusion of gliding metaphysically over all obstacles to escape our corporeal trappings, but we are soon brought back to reason and to try to find our way on earth.

Versailles: absolutism by design

Although the park at Versailles appears to be designed in the same formal manner as that at Vaux-le-Vicomte, the difference is that it was meant solely as a piece of royal scenography and propaganda as can be seen in the plan made by the Abbé Delagrive in 1746 [7.47]. Versailles is interesting because what it lacks in terms of proportional refinement and exquisite balance, it compensates for in sheer scale and extravagance. Vaux-le-Vicomte was certainly the inspiration for this grandiose project of Louis XIV, which marked an important turning point in the politics and scale of landscape thinking in Europe. But Versailles became the instrumental emblem of French absolutism and possessed neither the finesse nor the pristine intimacy of Vaux-le-Vicomte; those were not the king's objectives. The dominant spatial idea at Versailles was centrality, since paths leading from the town and the gardens were designed to converge on the Sun King's apartment [7.51].

Projection and control on an intercontinental scale

Because of its magnitude, Versailles became a prime testing ground for everything from topography to hydrology, with the Latona Fountain on axis with the Fountain of Apollo and infinity, and the Parterre du Midi [7.52, 7.53] sheltering the Orangerie [7.49, 7.50] with its microclimate and horticulture.

Triangulated paths laid out in *patte d'oie* pattern optimized visibility for hunts, military exercises and surveying. In the period of Louis XV the wider environment was surveyed for the king's needs and those of his armies. The notion of territorial management developed by Louis XIV's minister of finance, Jean-Baptiste Colbert, was not limited to Versailles: it became a template for the whole territory, as exemplified in his 'humble' domain at Sceaux [7.54, 7.55, 7.56]. New towns, new roads, new forests, new fields and canals were needed to improve the plight of Europe's most populated country. Using the *graphometre* and level range-finder in the early 18th century, cartography brought the science of surveying to a new degree of precision [7.48]. Such instruments allowed the Cassini family, beginning in 1744, to triangulate the French territory for the purposes of cartography.[30] These advances helped in the creation of new waterways, such as the Canal du Midi (1667) by Pierre Paul Riquet and the Canal de Bourgogne (1775), by Antoine de Chézy. Closer to the centre of government, the construction of the elaborate water-collecting system of the Plateau de Saclay (1679) by Thomas Gobert, and the pumping station on the Seine known as the 'Machine de Marly' (1684) by Rennequin Sualem [7.58], provided water for Versailles and were made possible by these instruments.

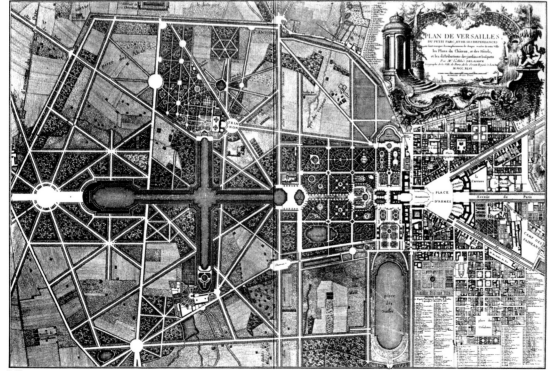

7.47

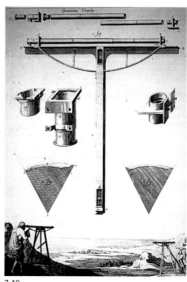

7.48

7.47 Plan of the Château of Versailles, France.
Here André Le Nôtre was answerable to
Louis XIV, and the main structure of the park
and town was radial and convergent on the
seat of absolute power. Versailles, with its
vast geometric park of bosquets, alleys and
cruciform canal, must be understood as a grand
experiment in landscape propaganda and design.

7.48 A surveying device with a level range-finder.
This instrument was developed by l'Abbé Picard
in France in the mid-17th century. By the middle
of the 18th century, 1744 to be exact, the accurate
mapping and triangulation of the entire country
of France was begun.

7.49, 7.50 The Orangerie.
The Orangerie at Versailles by Jules Hardouin-
Mansart (1686) could produce ripe citrus and
figs – remarkable at the time. Together with
the Potager du Roy, designed by Jean Baptiste
La Quintinie in 1683, the Orangerie excelled in
advanced horticulture. To conform with royal
'etiquette', straight trunks were considered the
rule, though whether they produced better fruit
is not known.

7.51 Late 17th-century painting of Versailles.
The Fountain of Apollo is in the foreground, on
axis with the canal and king's quarters, behind
which the planned town radiates out. The first
bosquet to the right shows the circular peristyle
built in 1685 by Jules Hardouin-Mansart,
replacing Le Nôtre's Bosquet des Sources. By the
end of Louis XIV's reign Versailles was a bustling
place, and the garden, bosquets and château
were the location for intrigue and entertainment.

**7.52 View of the park at Versailles and the
Latona Fountain.**
The unprecedented size of the park at
Versailles dwarfs mere humans and remains
overwhelmingly impressive to this day, when
landscapes and gardens have become much
simpler and less ornate.

**7.53 Versailles: Parterre du Midi above the
Orangerie, facing south towards the Pièce d'Eau
des Suisses.**
Compositionally speaking, this is probably one
of the most successful areas of the park by Le
Nôtre. The large pond was dug out of a swamp
and completed by the Swiss Guard in 1678. An
equestrian statue of the king by Bernini stands
at the far end of the perspective.

7.49

7.50

7.51

7.52

7.53

7.54 A cascade in the park at Sceaux, France.
At Sceaux, the scale and topography is quite different from other projects by Le Nôtre. He achieves a degree of subdued elegance and modesty, in keeping with his client, Jean-Baptiste Colbert, minister of finance under Louis XIV and rival of Nicolas Fouquet.

7.55 Canal at Sceaux.
The simple arabesque motif used by Le Nôtre on the canal's edge at Sceaux expresses both strength and minimal simplicity, as do the Lombardy poplars reflected in the water. The landscape contributes to the place's deep sense of serenity.

7.56 Perspective view of Sceaux.
Le Nôtre handles the topography of the great green carpet at Sceaux with the simplest of means: the slight hollow in the middle allows an underground spring feeding the canal to pass through. The single yew is a gentle reminder of the avowed modesty of Colbert in relation to his monarch. It is a design beyond suspicion, as much elegant as banal.

7.57 The Great Map of La Nouvelle France and Louisiana by J.B. Franquelin, 1684.
The East Coast of the USA was initially plotted by the French emissary Giovanni de Verrazzano in the early 16th century. Louis XIV of France claimed a vast territory stretching from the Gulf of Mexico to the Great Lakes; Franquelin's map used advanced surveying techniques to chart this territory.

7.58 'Machine de Marly'.
Because of insufficient water at Versailles, Louis XIV commissioned a monumental pump to lift the waters of the Seine at Bougival up to Marly and Versailles. Rennequin Sualem, a master carpenter, built the extraordinary contraption in 1684 and it operated for well over 100 years, providing abundant water to the fountains of Versailles.

7.54

7.55

7.56

The pressure on natural resources was such in 17th-century France that nothing was left of its original forest. Other factors exacerbated the problem; the 'Maunder Minimum', a period of extremely cold weather, affected all of Europe in the late 17th century, leading to a vast consumption of wood. Colonial expansion, wars and the slave trade meant that the shipbuilding industry also required massive amounts of timber. The result was a pressure on food supply and land resources. These factors explain the purpose underlying the French landscape garden, not only as a token of absolutist exuberance, but also as a symbol of territorial determination and organization that could be exported, as seen in this late 17th-century colonial map of La Nouvelle France [7.57].

Le Nôtre provided advice on a few plans for parks in England, such as Hampton Court and Greenwich [7.60]. Another example of a 'French' landscape plan on foreign soil is the National Mall in Washington, D.C., designed by Pierre Charles L'Enfant (1791) [7.63].[31] By this time the English landscape movement was thriving, but L'Enfant deliberately chose to import the triangulated motifs of the *patte d'oie* to demonstrate his allegiance to General Lafayette and to mark out the American capital as free from English influence [7.64]. Could it be that the French garden style was also capable of expressing liberty, humanism and democracy? The idea would certainly appeal to Fouquet, Descartes, Le Nôtre and others who contributed to its early development. The surveying tools

and methods that were tested in 17th-century France formed the basis of modern cartography. The Jeffersonian grid, which was applied to the entire territory of the USA, through the Land Ordinance of 1785, was a direct descendant of French land surveying. What has pertained to this day is not the geometric style of gardens, but rather the entire engineering system that underlined their purpose. This form of geometric thinking applied to the wider landscape evolved into the geodesic triangulated mesh that today serves as the universal basis for the geographic information system (GIS).

Despite attempts to export the Baroque garden to China, in the 'Western Mansions' at the Old Summer Palace, Beijing as late as 1747, most geometric landscape designs had peaked by the middle of the 18th century [7.62].[32] Germany developed impressive Baroque gardens in Karlsruhe (1715), Kassel (1689) and Herrenhausen (1676) [7.59]. In St Petersburg, the formal gardens of the Peterhof Palace (1714) opened onto the boreal forest and the Baltic Sea [7.61]. It seems that what started at Vaux and continued at Versailles has prevailed to this day, supplying the tools to civil engineers, geographers and developers the world over. Brasília, designed by Lucio Costa and Oscar Niemeyer, and Chandigarh, laid out by Le Corbusier, are two 20th-century cities whose plans tap directly into the rationality of Descartes and the Dutch Golden Age. Whether we realize it or not, we all ultimately owe our tacit acceptance of modernity to the Beemster Polder.

7.57

7.58

7.59

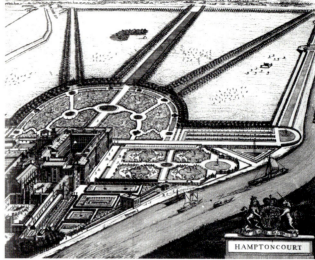

7.60

7.61

7.62

7.59 View of the Baroque city of Karlsruhe, Germany.
The circular radial plan designed in 1709 by the Margrave Karl Wilhelm von Baden-Durlach differs from other Baroque cities. The absolutist castle stands at the hub of 32 avenues radiating out. The built triangular segment represents a third of the ideal city, with the remaining two-thirds dedicated to parks and agriculture.

7.60 Late 17th-century Baroque plan of Hampton Court, England, under William and Mary, by Christopher Wren and George London and Henry Wise.
The absolutist landscape style was in vogue in England at this time, as at other places such as Stowe and Blenheim. It is said that Le Nôtre had a hand in drawing up this scheme.

7.61 Monplaisir Palace, Peterhof, Russia.
The summer palace at Peterhof was designed by Peter the Great and begun in 1714. The Grand Cascade and canal lead directly to the Baltic Sea and it was possible for visitors to reach the Baroque gardens by boat from St Petersburg.

7.62 Remains of the Western Mansions (Xiyang Lou) in the Old Summer Palace (Yuan Ming Yuan), Beijing, China.
The structures were designed by two Jesuits, Giuseppe Castiglione and Michel Benoist, for the Qianlong emperor in 1747; the elaborate fountains took ten years to build. The Old Summer Palace was looted and burned to the ground a hundred years later by Franco-British troops in 1860, during the Second Opium War.

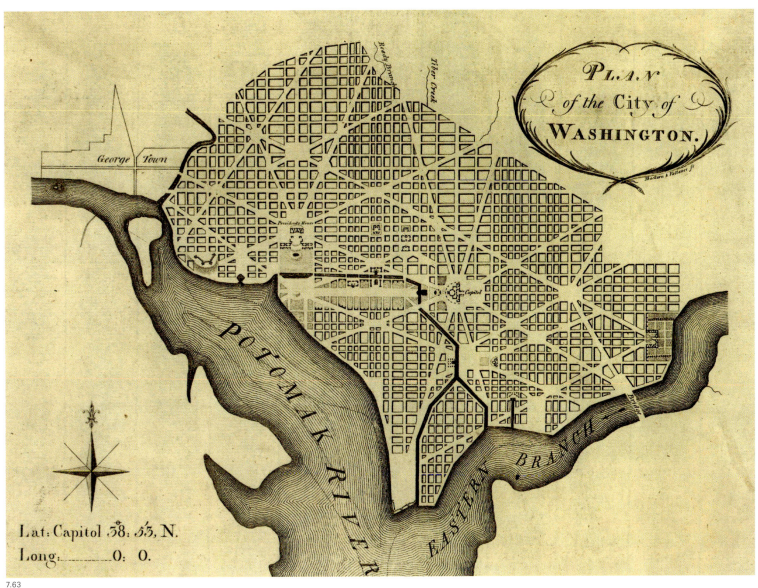

7.63

7.63 Plan of Washington, D.C., USA, by Pierre Charles l'Enfant, dated 1791.
This can be seen as a hybrid of two systems, where Le Nôtre meets Hippodamus, and a *patte d'oie* triangulation so typical of French absolutism meets the grid of Miletus, Piraeus and the birth of Greek democracy. The only question in Washington, D.C. is whether the grid runs parallel to the Mall or vice versa.

7.64 Aerial view of the Capitol and Mall in Washington, D.C.
The spirit of Le Nôtre and Versailles is evident in the central axis and *patte d'oie* avenues shooting out to the horizon. The main difference here is not so much the scale, but the political and symbolic significance. Instead of converging on an absolutist palace, the city and parks converge on the House of Representatives.

7.64

8. Gravity
The Constant of Nature

'Nature and Nature's laws lay hid in night; God said,
Let Newton be! and all was light.'
Isaac Newton's epitaph by Alexander Pope[1]

We have come to a moment in the evolution of landscape architecture when nature is entirely rethought and redefined in terms of perception and style. Conceptual breakthroughs redefining man's place in the world are triggered by a new philosophy of science arising from Isaac Newton's discovery of the gravitational constant. William Blake's opposition to enlightenment, epitomized by his monotype of Newton (1795), was a plea against a rising scientific materialism [8.1].[2] More than at any other moment in history, landscape becomes the ideological receptacle of a new concept in physics, which opens up fresh scientific horizons and an entirely new aesthetic. One witnesses a shift from the specific patterns of the Baroque garden to the more general appearance of a seemingly informal landscape, from the exclusive domain of a hedged paradise to an all-inclusive, common territorial dominion as with the great slope in Rousham, overlooking the River Cherwell, designed by William Kent [8.0]. This dominion also harkens back to the early model of the forest clearing, which – ironically – came to symbolize a return to nature in its original form.

This opening up of the landscape was very much linked to the philosophical discourse and political climate of late 17th-century England. The Glorious Revolution of 1688 set England on the path of modern parliamentary democracy, spelling the end of absolute monarchy.[3] Philosophers and learned gentlemen actively sought to mark this schism with texts on individual freedom, redesigning their gardens to distinguish them from those of kings and those built in the French tradition. A great number of landscape experiments were staged on landed estates throughout Britain during the following century, contributing to the development of what we now know as the English landscape style. The English

8.0 (opposite) The garden at Rousham, England.
Designed by William Kent, the understated simplicity of the green clearing on a slope, the low-lying grazing meadow and some freestanding clumps of trees expresses the quintessence of the English landscape tradition.

8.1 *Newton* by William Blake, 1795.
One hundred years after the publication of *Principia*, Blake depicted Isaac Newton as a creature fallen in the dark abyss of gravity – he is shown naked, head down over a scroll tracing lifeless geometry. Blake's reticence about scientific materialism expressed in Newton's Law of Universal Gravitation was founded in his view of science as barren. He was opposed to the Enlightenment and its effects on artistry and the human soul.

8.1

8.2

'natural' style did not, therefore, develop spontaneously following Newton's scientific revolution: several generations of inventive architects, gardeners, politicians and poets were needed to process the conceptual consequences of his discoveries. Within a century, the formal expression of the English Picturesque garden changed radically in favour of an archetypal and more banal expression of nature, devoid of mythological artefacts or ornament. This shift from the specific to the general spelled the end of Baroque humanist exclusiveness and paved the way for an entirely new, more reduced and scientific interpretation of landscape and nature, exemplified by the early transformation by John Vanbrugh and Nicholas Hawksmoor of the Ray Wood (1710) and gardens at Castle Howard into an English-style park (1715) [8.2, 8.3].[4]

The Newtonian revolution

Throughout the Baroque period, the expression of nature in landscape architecture was extremely controlled and Cartesian in essence. Clipped plant materials displayed on planar terraces were an almost perfect metaphysical expression of Leon Battista Alberti's perspectival space. The Baroque landscape itself was defined by a set of structured, self-determined, symmetrical parameters, in which geometry was crystallized into intricate microenvironments. These were architectural folds created according to reason, a measured architecture governed by the higher expression of humanist

ideals and bound by the static, hierarchical order of things. But the publication of Isaac Newton's *Philosophiae Naturalis Principia Mathematica* ('Mathematical Principles of Natural Philosophy') in 1687 revealed an entirely new order, greater than that established by man, which would change our perception of universal space, refute the earlier humanist construct of nature and render it obsolete almost overnight [8.5].[5] This is exemplified by the transformation of the front lawn at Chatsworth, reduced to a simple bowling green played out against the backdrop of a 'natural' landscape park designed by Lancelot 'Capability' Brown (1759) [8.4].[6]

Scientific enlightenment marked a conceptual watershed with regard to our understanding of invisible forces like gravity that ruled the universe. A starry night was described as the limitless play of celestial spheres, left to unwind in infinite space in myriad parabolic ellipses and tangents guided by some almighty hidden natural centripetal order, as depicted in Thomas Wright's concentric drawing of cosmic universes (1750) [8.6].[7] This notion ran completely counter to the perception of infinity still visible in the metaphysical thrust of the Baroque axis – one that was essentially based on the perspectival and optical canvas of man. This breakthrough in knowledge helped us to harness nature in a manner that was quite unprecedented in both scale and scope. It was now possible to calculate the effect of natural laws precisely and express their constant at all possible scales. The impact

8.2 Ray Wood and the great lawn at Castle Howard, England.
Begun in 1699, this is considered to be the oldest English garden. The woodland arranged with serpentine paths, allegorical statues, pavilions and water features contrasts with the simple open lawn. Designed by John Vanbrugh and Nicholas Hawksmoor it reaffirms the archetype of the forest clearing.

8.3 The water reservoir at Castle Howard.
Built at the heart of Ray Wood, the reservoir reproduces an archetypal circular clearing. Its setting is strongly reminiscent of the forest cistern at Villa Lante, 200 years earlier, although *il conservone* is square.

8.4 The South Lawn at Chatsworth, England.
Originally designed in the late 17th century by Henry Wise and George London as a formal parterre, this is now simply framed by a double row of clipped lime trees framing a circular Sea Horse Fountain. The hillside backdrop with groups of trees was entirely modelled and landscaped in a natural English style by Capability Brown in the late 18th century.

8.5 Newton's manuscript describing his Law of Universal Gravitation.
Later to become the cornerstone of a scientific and industrial revolution, Newton's *Principia Mathematica* proposed a model for the measurement of forces in the physical universe that completely transformed the mechanical world in which we now live.

8.6 A plethora of cosmic universes by Thomas Wright, 1750.
Wright's vision of the newly found complexity of the world was inspired by the questions raised by Newton's discovery. It was a new era in which Newtonian physics would indelibly change our relationship to the natural world. This went hand in hand with industrial progress, which saw our natural innocence gradually being lost to scientific materialism.

8.4

8.5

8.6

8.3

of the Newtonian equation was dumbfounding in both its instrumental power and simplicity, changing the course of our world irreversibly. Although Newton had discovered only a general law that was inherently natural, its application to society meant that our attitude towards nature, inherited from the Greeks and held right up to the Baroque period, had to be completely reassessed.

Landscape architecture was better suited to expressing a fundamental shift in the conceptual embodiment of nature than architecture, as seen in the fantastic naturalistic thrust of the new park at Castle Howard (1710) [8.7]. Newton's revelations gradually came to inform a new form of landscape, one that was essentially opposed to the geometrically confining rules of symmetry embraced by the Baroque. The apparent disorder in the natural landscape was understood as guided by some hidden natural forces, far superior to those imposed by man. The Newtonian revolution ushered in a new worldview and aesthetic, but also introduced a double-sided interpretation of nature. On the one hand, landscape could be made to appear as 'natural' and untouched, while on the other it could be harnessed as an instrumental force for improved productivity. In fact, early 18th-century England was far from natural: the land known as 'countryside' was already depleted, severely overgrazed and deforested, and marked by settlement clusters, with their hedgerows, woods, fields and meadows [8.11]. As the

scientific revolution sparked industrial progress, the art of landscape gardening in England evolved from a structured, narrative, Picturesque style that related to Classical painterly aesthetics into a more typical landscape style that represented a 'remake' of what one could understand as nature.[8]

The garden was thought of as an ideological laboratory, designed to elucidate man's evolving sense of the world and mirror his transient relationship with the universe. Whereas the Baroque gardens of Vaux-le-Vicomte sought to demonstrate humankind's unquestioned mastery over nature, the intention of the English garden can be understood as quite the opposite. It tells a story about the hidden truths of nature, and alludes to man's diminutive place within the new cosmic order. The history of the English garden style most likely begins in the private garden of the poet Alexander Pope, which he and William Kent designed in 1719 in Twickenham, on the banks of the River Thames [8.8]. This first 'dissident' garden was inventive, although quite eccentric and clumsy in its eclectic design. It displayed a variety of esoteric motifs inspired by elements of the Grotesque and Rococo, but the jumbled mix of plantings around a dislocated axis within vaguely labyrinthine borders represented a bold and irreverent departure from established perspectival tradition [8.9]. Pope's repute as a celebrated man of letters meant that the published plan of his garden and sketches had a significant influence on a broad public of readers.[9]

8.7

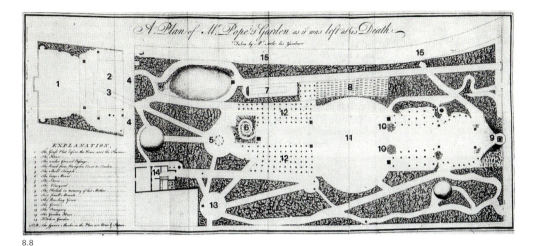

8.8

8.9

8.10

8.11

8.7 The South Lake, with the great lawn and Ray Wood, Castle Howard, England.
The forest became a place of myth and isolated retreat, whereas the lawn was the extension of the castle for large gatherings and celebrations. This early project begun in 1710 and completed by John Vanbrugh and Nicholas Hawksmoor in the 1720s combines the three essential ingredients of the English garden: lawn, wood and water.

8.8, 8.9 Alexander Pope's garden, Twickenham, England, by William Kent.
The garden was begun in 1719 and the crooked altar in the foreground of the drawing hides a grotto built in 1725. The plan, with its oblong shapes and winding paths, is a precursor to many urban parks to come.

8.10 *Pastoral Landscape* by Claude Lorrain, 1645.
The French School in Rome in the 17th century became a source of inspiration for the English Picturesque style in the following century. Here landscape realism recalled the idyllic landscapes of antiquity and their mythology.

8.11 A typical view of English countryside, with hedgerows, agricultural fields and pasture.
The 18th-century English countryside we have come to accept as natural was in fact a seriously altered environment essentially designed for productive purposes. The great strength of the English garden movement is to have incorporated this natural reduction in its style.

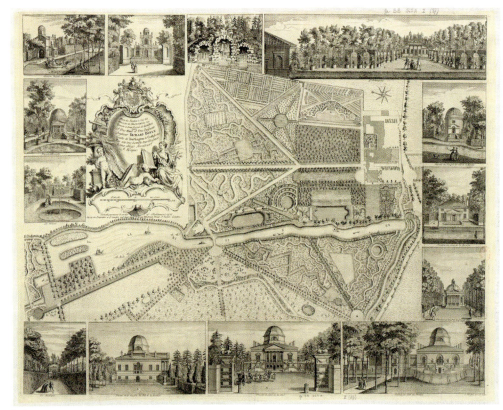

8.12

8.12 Plan of Chiswick House, London, England, by Lord Burlington and William Kent, 1729.
The experimental nature of the plan plays irreverently with Baroque absolutist garden syntax in a humorous way. For instance, the main axis with a rather flimsy *patte d'oie* completely misses the Palladian house and heads instead straight for a cul-de-sac of convoluted hedges in the other direction.

8.13 The Chiswick House *exedra* by William Kent.
Statues and herms instead of being aligned obediently in a row start to play with one another, allowing dogs to chase around them in defiance of proper etiquette. The liberty with which Kent and Burlington experiment with established taboos finds its roots in the Glorious Revolution of 1688 that challenged despotic order.

8.14 Herms and statues in the *exedra* of clipped hedges, Chiswick House.
The playfulness with which statues and herms are interspersed in the *exedra* is in fact a hidden statement about the greater order of things, disrupting established rules of garden geometry and opening on to the unknown.

8.15 Statue of a sphinx at Chiswick House, 1729.
Mythology played quite a different role in the English Picturesque than in Renaissance and Baroque times. Myth became a dynamic part of everyday life and was not solely confined to some historic narrative or perspective. It is the rather overt playfulness of such references that became the seal of this nascent style.

8.16 The great lawn at Chiswick House.
Children play on the grass and a majestic cedar of Lebanon rises above. In the foreground the stylistic cards have been reshuffled, with urns on pedestals interspersed with a diminutive cypress tree.

8.13

8.14

8.15

8.16

The garden at Chiswick House, in west London, is an example of early experimentation in the English garden.[10] Begun by Richard Boyle, 3rd Earl of Burlington, and the architect William Kent upon their return from Italy and completed in 1729 [8.12], it was created on the flat site of a dried-up meander of the Thames with no horizon or vista and has an atmosphere that is strongly introspective, epitomizing an intentional break from the formal garden tradition handed down since the Renaissance. The entrance axis was shifted to the side of the main Palladian villa, where it culminated, without the use of any kind of perspective, in a small temple with *trompe-l'oeil* decoration placed within a cul-de-sac of clipped hedges [8.19]. The alignment of statues on the great lawn defied the established rules of symmetry in a free arrangement that was quite whimsical [8.13, 8.14]. One gets the strong sense that the narrative structure of this early Picturesque garden, with its collage of diminutive temples, statues and sphinxes, is more concerned with dreamlike memories of Roman landscapes and ruins, recently visited by both designers, than with the accurate transliteration of Palladian elegance and proportion [8.15]. Whether Lord Burlington and William Kent took this course on purpose or were simply inept stylists is quite irrelevant. The fact remains that the new landscape style at Chiswick House shattered the rule of good manners in English garden art and thus opened the way for a more emancipated approach to landscape design.

The lawn as living carpet

The lawn at Chiswick House plays a new and interesting role in this early example of the English landscape garden. It springs from the Renaissance tradition of box motifs and parterres, and becomes a living carpet displaying an eclectic assemblage of artefacts. This lawn can be understood as a natural universe of sorts, without any designated paths on which visitors can move freely, instead immersing themselves in the immediate environment [8.16]. Overall the garden's paths are of secondary importance and serve only to link different sections in a very low-key manner. The rolling topography of the lawn leading down to the artificial lake on the west side of the estate creates an interesting asymmetrical counterpoint to the entrance axis and the ha-ha (sunken ditch) set on the other side of the lawn – a motif that Kent, together with Charles Bridgeman, later developed as a territorial system at Stowe in Buckinghamshire. Both the flat and the undulating surfaces at Chiswick are in fact quite artificial, and increased the garden's sense of heterogeneity and imbalance. An extraordinary maze of small paths set among tall clipped hedges functions as a backdrop for the larger areas of lawn, recalling the evergreen woodland often found in the surroundings of Italian Renaissance gardens [8.18].

Chiswick House constituted a truly fresh direction in landscape architecture, amplifying nature's irregularities,

8.17

8.18

8.17 The Ionic Temple in the Orange Tree Garden, Chiswick House.
The diminutive edifice based on the Pantheon in Rome was designed for two gentlemen to meet and philosophize. Orange trees in boxes were brought out in spring and set in rings around the obelisk pond, set in a concentric circular slope of lawn.

8.18 Detail of a convoluted hedge at the end of the *patte d'oie*, Chiswick House.
This arrangement introduces a labyrinthine world behind the scenes, in what was once a garden of geometric conformism, in defiance of predictable order and reason.

8.19 View of the main axis at Chiswick House.
The path completely misses the Palladian villa designed by Lord Burlington and William Kent, with the green carpet of lawn replacing it in front of the house. Note the random interplay between urns and cypresses on either side of the redundant axis.

undermining the powers of symmetry and proportion, and playing with statuary as if to jumble up historical references. The new laws of nature discovered by Newton and celebrated by Alexander Pope epitomized a return to an essential truth, one that had been masked and distorted by decades of Classical thinking and geometrically rigid falsehoods. William Kent's architectural experiments, with their characteristically awkward and diminutive proportions, like the playful Ionic Temple and obelisk in the Orange Tree Garden, represent a parallel search for 'new' laws in architecture [8.17]. Chiswick House may even be regarded as a first attempt to establish a vocabulary in landscape architecture that reinstated the magnitude of nature and diminished the significance of man and his architectural creations.

The collective rebellion of the English aesthetic

At the turn of the 19th century, as the Industrial Revolution was picking up speed, the transformation of landscape through infrastructure and industry was a far cry from the utopian ideal gardens designed 100 years earlier. The English garden had been developed by a handful of learned gentlemen reacting to the spirit of intellectual liberalism that prevailed in England at the time and best exemplified by projects like Stowe House [8.20, 8.21. 8.22].[11] Men like Charles Bridgeman and William Kent who promoted this new conception of landscape had little respect for the ideological precepts

of papal symbolism inherent in Renaissance and Baroque gardens. Their revolt condemned absolutism in favour of Newton's higher laws of nature. Humanity could no longer keep nature at bay, but instead become part of its universal forces, as embodied in the Temple of the Four Winds by John Vanbrugh at Castle Howard [8.23].[12] With the rise of the landed gentry and the decline of royal power, members of the English nobility were eager to rework their estates in a manner that broke with established tradition, memorably illustrated in the film *The Draughtsman's Contract* (1982) by Peter Greenaway [8.24].

Inspired by travels to Italy and by the 17th-century landscape paintings of Nicolas Poussin and Claude Lorrain these early advocates turned to the romantic leanings of the Picturesque, in which nature was seen as taking over the ruins of civilization [8.10].[13] It is the invention of a nature without apparent artifice that forms the subject of this particular aesthetic revolution, combined with an outright refutation of all previous styles of landscape art. It is precisely this getting rid of superstition and ancient culture in favour of scientific pragmatism that released the potential for the style's global development and territorial expansion. In the face of rapid industrialization, the cultural challenge for landscape architecture was to make the environment look more 'natural' at the same time as allowing industrial development to take place.

8.19

8.20

8.20 A ha-ha at Stowe House, England.
Designed in the 1730s to protect William Kent's 'Elysian Fields' from unwanted intrusion, the sunken ditch keeps out sheep and cattle. The stone wall with its raised plinth articulates a sort of *temenos* between the sacred and the profane. The ha-ha is a key feature of the English garden, permitting a visual continuity between distinct entities.

8.21 View over the great lawn at Stowe House.
Capability Brown partly erased earlier versions of the park to produce his English style around 1750. What was once an intricate garden became a vast swathe of axial lawn, effacing decades of fine work by designers such as Lord Cobham, Charles Bridgeman and William Kent.

8.22 The Palladian Bridge at Stowe House.
Designed by James Gibbs in 1744 under the supervision of William Kent, the bridge is an Arcadian reference set within a vast wet meadow against a wooded backdrop. It represents the icon of the English Picturesque at Stowe.

8.23 The Temple of the Four Winds, 1730, Castle Howard, England.
Originally known as the Temple of Diana, designed by John Vanbrugh, it stands at the end of a green esplanade on the edge of Ray Wood. It commands a dominant view towards Hawksmoor's Mausoleum (1740). The narrative of this early Picturesque garden is a mix of esoteric nostalgia and languor.

8.24 A scene from *The Draughtsman's Contract* by Peter Greenaway, 1982.
Here the landscape architect fixes the vistas at his easel in the garden. This interplay between pictorial representation, design and innovation is a fundamental trait of the Picturesque and its dedication to landscape narratives.

8.21

8.22

8.23

8.24

Rousham, England

The garden at Rousham in Oxfordshire shows William Kent's approach to garden design, first mapped out at Chiswick, reaching full maturity.[14] The project was begun in 1738 and centred on a series of small clearings staged in a rolling, wooded topography. Together with the park at Castle Howard by Nicholas Hawksmoor and John Vanbrugh, it is one of the most interesting examples of early English landscape design [8.25]. Rousham demonstrates a rejection of previously established geometric landscape traditions, and shows instead a tactful handling of the peculiarities of the existing site. This small property overlooking the River Cherwell, with its north-eastern exposure, is far from hospitable, but its unique challenges have been skilfully negotiated, giving it a strong sense of belonging and orientation [8.26, 8.28]. The great bend in the river is not only integrated into the project, but made the pivotal feature of the entire garden [8.27a, 8.27b].

Rousham avoids the overt eccentricity and diminutive scale of Pope's garden at Twickenham. It is more concise and intent on its message, confirming Kent's emancipated role as father of an entirely new style. The eccentric frills of Chiswick House, with its labyrinthine hedges, clumsily scattered statues and frustrated axes, are absent here. Rousham is instead a masterpiece of staged microenvironments, in which zones of brilliant light contrast with zones of intense darkness, and where areas of absolute flatness, like the bevelled Bowling Green designed earlier by Charles Bridgeman, are juxtaposed with significant declivities like the great slope remodelled by Kent [8.31, 8.32]. The garden adapts itself exquisitely to the theatrical potential of the terrain, dissolving gently into the surrounding farmed countryside and sometimes allowing a glimpse of a Gothic Seat *trompe l'oeil* or the Eyecatcher [8.30, 8.35]. Despite the tight planting of trees to add definition to the clearings, the design intentions remain understated, through a masterfully handled narrative introducing landscape alterations that allow the garden to look as 'natural' as possible. The entire staging appears both purposeful and discreet, as if Kent had wanted to deliver a hidden message of nature yet to be decrypted. Kent's design follows a winding path through a succession of small clearings replete with suspense and a surprise scenography, in which small temples alternate with clusters of sculpted animals, Classical nudes and wild fauns [8.34]. The diminutive size of the picturesque temples and pyramids strewn around the garden was intended to heighten the sense of power of their natural surroundings, playing on the nostalgia for a lost past that was very much of its time [8.36, 8.37].

8.25 The Mausoleum at Castle Howard, England, designed by Nicholas Hawksmoor, 1740.
The view is from the New River and New River Bridge, also designed by Hawksmoor around the same time, demonstrating how the Picturesque approached landscape design as a totality. The sheer scale of the setting is not only impressive, it is also daunting and characterizes a complete Picturesque experience.

8.26 Plan of Rousham.
The plan reveals a modest estate, with a few patches of trees framing small clearings along a bend in the River Cherwell. The power of Rousham lies in its subtlety, not its size, and in its topography and small recesses, not its expanse. It was designed by William Kent in 1738 following Charles Bridgeman's 1720 project. Rousham is the quintessence of the early English Picturesque garden.

8.26

8.27a

8.27b

8.27a, 8.27b Reconstructed before and after views of Rousham.
The original Baroque terraces of Charles Bridgeman designed in 1720 step down to the river. Kent's scheme retained Bridgeman's Bowling Green and enlarged the house, converting the terraces into a single concave slope. Kent added clearings – or rather he planted dense woods to create Venus's Vale, the Pyramid Meadow and Apollo's Glade.

8.28 Aerial photograph of Rousham.
The diminutive scale of the garden is quite striking, and one would not expect at first sight that the history of English gardens would unfold in this small piece of designed nature.

8.29 The Bowling Green with an old ha-ha to the left.
The view is looking towards the great slope, with the grazing meadow and Eyecatcher in the far distance. The framing of this levelled lawn by tall trees creates a striking contrast between the natural, with a pronounced vertical orientation, and the cultural, which is flat.

8.30 The Gothic Seat and Palladian Doorway designed by Kent.
Situated in the distance beyond the Bowling Green, the ha-ha and grazing field, these were fabricated as *trompe l'oeil* theatrical props.

8.28

8.29

8.30

8.31

8.32

8.33

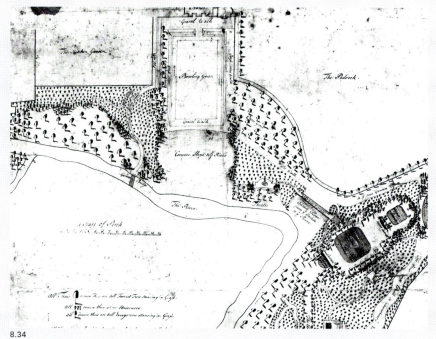

8.34

8.31 Bowling Green and statue.
Standing further back from the statue, the bevelled edge of the Bowling Green is revealed as a jewelled plinth in the landscape. Beyond the slope, the grazing field and the old Heyford Bridge open out to the countryside beyond.

8.32 The great slope.
Next to the garden seat in the background, a tall oak guards the dark entrance to the forest. To the right, a trimmed hedge of yew frames the neat Bowling Green, while to the left along the slope nothing appears trimmed. This progression can be understood as an allegory of gravitational pull and the freeing of geometric form.

8.33 Statue of a lion attacking a horse.
The dramaturgy with which this piece designed by Peter Scheemakers (1740) is set at the cusp of the great slope evokes all the force and brutality of nature embodied in gravity. It also demonstrates that Kent studied scenography with Niccolò Tribolo during his stay in Italy.

8.34 Original plan of Rousham, by William White.
Drawn in minute detail, each tree positioned and accounted for with the greatest attention, the plan shows a mature handling of the landscape spaces, circuits and proportions. The most prominent aspect is the 'Concave Slope to the River', replicating a ballistic curve in a complete break with established landscape tradition.

8.35 The Eyecatcher.
William Kent built this device in a distant field across the valley, roughly on axis with the Bowling Green. He probably saw a similar portico on his tour of Italy at Bomarzo. Its purpose is to tie the surrounding borrowed landscape back into his designed project.

8.36 The Pyramid Meadow.
The pyramid, also designed by William Kent, fits closely in the hillside, framed by woods that lead to the Bowling Green and house. It adds a surreal, esoteric atmosphere to the whole garden.

8.37 Reconstructed view of the Pyramid Meadow and the concave slope.
The woods define the edge of the slope in a strong chiaroscuro and set the stage for the pyramid designed by Kent in the adjacent meadow. Placed in a relatively isolated location, the building was used probably as a place of seduction and initiation.

8.35

8.36

8.37

8.38

8.38 The concave slope.
The slope leading down to the river has something irreversible about its pull, like entropy – once you reach the river it feels almost impossible to climb back up again. Compared with the time-framed narratives at Villa Lante and Vaux-le-Vicomte, here the visitor is propelled down through history and beyond by the force of gravity.

8.39 The Praeneste terrace.
Perched mid-slope on a narrow ledge offering an open view of the countryside, the Praeneste with its seven alcoves, is intended to provide an 'Augustan' tone to the garden. An urn stands at either end as symbols of antiquity.

8.40 *The Dying Gladiator*, or *The Dying Gaul*.
The statue is positioned on top of the Praeneste terrace, overlooking the river bend. An atmosphere of deep melancholy pervades the scene – a presentiment of death just before heading down towards Venus's Vale.

8.41 View from the Praeneste terrace looking down to the river.
The slope is much steeper here and forces the visitor to move sideways in the opposite direction, towards Venus's Vale and the Octagon Pond.

8.42 Section through Rousham House, the Bowling Green, the concave slope and the river.
The parabolic curve of the concave slope is reminiscent of one of Newton's early ballistics diagrams in reverse. Across the grazing field is the Gothic Seat, with a countryside of open fields and hedgerows beyond.

8.39

8.40

8.41

8.42

The sculptures at Rousham are not only fewer and farther between than at Chiswick, they are free of any axis whatsoever, and are positioned 'naturally' throughout the park, as visitors in their own right. This naturalism is underscored by the fact that human figures, mostly male, are naked and life-size; they were apparently painted pink when the garden was first completed.[15] Take the statue of Apollo in the glade beneath the Temple of Echo, with its melancholic demeanour reminiscent of Antinous, the Bythnian youth so cherished by the emperor Hadrian [8.50]. It could be that such references to Antique Rome provided Kent with a pretext for showing the human body in an ideal state, foreshadowing Rousseau's theory of the 'natural human'.

What works at Rousham is the garden's dramatic scenography and the carefully managed transition operated by Kent between flat and sloped areas [8.38, 8.42]. The breaking point is located at a cusp in the terrain, where the flat Bowling Green reaches towards a natural drop marked by the sculpture of a lion violently attacking a horse [8.33]. Two benches stand on either side by thresholds planted with yews that act as gateways [8.29, 8.46]. That to the left invites us to Venus's Vale, while the one to the right leads us to the Pyramid Meadow just below. Passing the Praeneste from the sunlit green into darkness, the visitor is suddenly blinded and lost, and feels a strong attraction exerted by the sloping terrain as gravity begins to take effect [8.39]. The pull becomes even

stronger as we reach the edge of Venus's Vale and are greeted by full-sized fauns [8.44, 8.47]. It is this abstract sensation of falling, staged in darkness, down a winding path that connects us with all the hidden mysteries of the Newtonian universe.

Rousham evokes a strong sense of modesty and innocence. Even the Praeneste arcade overlooked by the statue of *The Dying Gaul* appears diminutive [8.40, 8.41]. But the most sublime moment in the garden occurs as one encounters Venus standing awkwardly naked over a fountain in the midst of a vale [8.45]. A powerful atmosphere of trees, fauns, water and natural topography recalls the enchanted primeval realm of an archaic forest clearing [8.43]. All paths dissolve into the lawn, which becomes a natural carpet blending seamlessly all things. Venus's Vale plays on the notion of a 'disorderly' nature becoming the garden's principal feature. The vale itself is sloped, and could express the 'bedevilled' fall of man. A rill, which spills out in a rather disorderly manner over the edge of a hexagonal basin invaded by lilies and weeds, leads one back via the Cold Bath into the woods to its source, at the foot of the Temple of Echo [8.49, 8.51]. The gently winding rill traces a 'line of beauty' later codified by Hogarth [8.52, 8.53]. The Platonic form of the hexagon pool in Venus's Vale is blurred by nature, its perfect geometry transfigured by natural growth and the surrounding topography, creating a timeless illusion [8.48]. At Rousham Cartesian rules have been left to moulder under the sediments of a new natural order.

8.43

8.44

8.43 Reconstructed aerial view of Rousham.
In the centre is Venus's Vale with the upper and lower cascades, the Octagon Pond and upper ponds; the Praeneste stands to the left. The simplicity of the setting with its contained clearing framed by tall trees is compelling, re-enacting as it does a primeval archetype and staging a story of Venus, Bacchus and Pan.

8.44 Statue of Pan.
A devilish, hoofed creature, Pan stands at the entrance of Venus's Vale as one descends from the Praeneste and Bowling Green. His rough, dark and inhospitable figure embodies a universal force of nature with which we have to contend, and need to tame.

8.45 Statue of Venus overlooking the Octagon Pond.
The goddess stands awkwardly in her nudity in the midst of the vale where Pan and Bacchus tease her. Her discomfort reminds us of *Appennino* (p.152), shivering in the cold in his nakedness.

8.46 View from the forest edge looking west over the Bowling Green.
Next to the garden seat a secret passage opens to the Praeneste and Venus's Vale. The uneven, natural ground in the sequoia tree's dense shade contrasts with the pristine surface of the Bowling Green in the light.

8.47 The dancing figure of Bacchus.
As if springing out of a hedge, Bacchus catches the visitor by surprise. William Kent was inspired by picturesque descriptions in Edmund Spenser's 'The Faerie Queen'.

8.48 Venus's Vale seen from the lower cascade.
The magic at Rousham lies in the staging of elemental characters at play; it is a place where life, death and the ultimate transience of things are made apparent. Kent takes the dark forces of nature and puts them on a stage.

8.45

8.46

8.47

8.48

8.49

8.49 The Temple of Echo and the forest seat.
Rousham was conceived first and foremost
as a place of tranquil meditation and Augustan
delight.

**8.50 The statue of Apollo, with a verdant
tunnel leading back to the Praeneste.**
The nonchalant, almost effeminate figure of
Apollo was formerly painted pink. Some think
in fact that it was probably intended as a statue
of Antinous, Emperor Hadrian's lost lover.

8.51 Reconstructed view of Rousham.
The glade watched over by the statue of
Apollo leads down to the first bend of the
River Cherwell. A forest path leads back to the
Praeneste arcade, with the Cold Bath and Rill
situated just above, and the Temple of Echo
stands on the right. In the distance are the
concave slope and Bowling Green leading
back to the house.

8.52 The Cold Bath and serpentine Rill.
These intriguing features have something
of a rite of initiation about them. Just as one
leaves Venus's Vale and heads upstream towards
the Temple of Echo, this octagonal pool stands
in the way. It can be understood as a place for
ablution and lustral purification on one's way
to the origins of time.

8.53 The Rill end.
The story of Rousham ends enigmatically
with the Rill at the foot of the Temple of Echo.
It is as though the entire story of our humanity
is tied to this endless slender loop of matter
and memory.

8.50

8.51

8.52

8.53

Stourhead and the English landscape style

Rousham served as reference and model for many other prestigious gardens, such as those at Stowe in Buckinghamshire (from 1741), Stourhead in Wiltshire (1741–72) and Woodstock Park at Blenheim Palace in Oxfordshire (1764–74). However, these later projects were notably less concise in their expression of nature. The garden at Stowe almost appears like a vastly enlarged version of Rousham, repeating Kent's motif by laying out the woodland to the left of the central axis in order that the Elysian Fields stand in strong contrast to a forested backdrop.

The garden at Stourhead achieves an exquisite scenography, blending with the surrounding wooded hills and meadows. It employs for that purpose picturesque vistas of the Pantheon set against an artificial lake, reminiscent of the painting *Landscape with Aeneas at Delos* (1672) by Claude Lorrain [8.55].[16] But what Stourhead gains intellectually, in terms of artistic references and picturesque effect, it loses in freedom of movement and physical sensation. The visitor follows a path in closed circuit around a lake that is determined by a Picturesque trail which constitutes the garden's main narrative thread [8.59]. It reminds one strongly of the Japanese *shakkei* principle expressed in the Shugaku-in in Kyoto (1659), where this hermitage garden borrows its views from the surrounding rural landscape to enable serenity to set in. In this Japanese garden achieved roughly a hundred years before Stourhead, the path is also set in a closed circuit around the artificial Yokuryuchi pond, with its islands and two tea pavilions, that plays against the dramatic topographic backdrop of the Higashiyama mountains [8.57]. Similarly, the emphasis at Stourhead is placed on the timeless picturesque views of a series of small Classical buildings like the Temple of Apollo positioned carefully against a 'natural' backdrop producing a highly theatrical effect [8.56]. Here, the lawn is not treated as a 'liberated' carpet as at Chiswick House, nor is it motivated by the downward pull of gravity, as at Rousham; at Stourhead the visitor must follow an established circuit as beautiful as it is contrived.

Despite the fact that Stourhead has come to epitomize the English Picturesque style, the garden, designed by the banker Henry Hoare, appears quite artificial and calculated. This did not, however, prevent its landscape forms, including its control of space and circulation, from becoming a reference for many later parks in Europe and North America [8.58]. The approach to site topography at Stourhead, and to the garden's immediate environment, is far less sensitive and respectful than that at Rousham. The dam built across the valley of the River Stour in order to create the lake feels quite cumbersome today; and the exquisite views of the various temples do not compensate for the overly engineered aspect of this massive earth structure, which rises some 20 metres (66 feet) above the valley floor [8.54]. Ironically, the dam

8.54

8.55

8.56

8.57

8.58

8.54 View of the Pantheon, bridge and lake, Stourhead, England.
Everything in this idyllic setting is artifice and illusion. The small scale of the Pantheon makes it seem further away than it really is, and the lake, too, is illusory, held in place by a dyke across the entire vale. But Stourhead remains the most emblematic Picturesque project of its time.

8.55 *Landscape with Aeneas at Delos* by Claude Lorrain, 1672.
This painting was clearly a source of inspiration for the Picturesque garden at Stourhead. Painted one hundred years earlier, it is ironic that it was influential in the demise of the French Baroque garden style.

8.56 View towards the Temple of Apollo, Stourhead.
The perfect layering of the garden scenery together with the careful orchestration of planting yields a sense of depth and perspective. The scenes are almost all inspired by the paintings of Claude Lorrain and Nicolas Poussin.

8.57 Shugaku-in, Yokuryuchi pond, Kyoto, Japan, 1659.
Set against the backdrop of the Higashiyama mountains, the Shugaku-in adopts the principles of *shakkei*, incorporating views from the surrounding rice fields and setting a promenade with vistas of pavilions around an artificial lake one hundred years before Stourhead.

8.58 Path to the Temple of Apollo, Stourhead.
The rusticated stone arch is held together without cement in perfect stereotomy. The visitor is invited to ascend and travel back to the roots of mythology.

8.59 Plan of Rousham by Frederik Magnus Piper, 1779, showing sight lines.
The path makes a circuit around the entire lake, with scenic spots and narratives like a Japanese water garden. The visitor must follow this circuit, and unlike the unbridled freedom found at Rousham, it confines one to the path, as in some contemporary theme parks.

8.59

8.60

8.60 The Pagoda, Kew Gardens, London, England, designed by William Chambers, 1757.
Chambers's design for the Oriental Garden brings the role of the exotic in the landscape into full focus. After mythology in the Picturesque, it is now the turn of pragmatism to take over. Plant curiosities and collectibles became an attraction for a much broader public, and the Pagoda worked as exotic branding for Kew from the beginning.

8.61 Plate from *Methodus plantarum sexualis in sistemate naturae descripta*, Leiden, 1736.
The plate by George Dionysus Ehret follows Linnaeus's taxonomy divided into 24 classes. Taxonomy completely changed our perception and understanding of the plant world, and botany became a science.

8.62 The Palm House, Kew Gardens, designed by Decimus Burton, 1848.
Built to house a collection of rare palms and tropical plants brought back from the colonies, the greenhouse of glass and wrought iron needed to be heated artificially in winter to keep both temperature and humidity constant.

8.63 The great lawn at Badminton, England, by Canaletto, 1748.
The Baroque radial structure of the garden by William Kent was replaced by a single, vast lawn designed by Capability Brown. The original radial slits can still be seen between the trees on the horizon. Unfortunately almost nothing remains from Kent's designs, subsequently erased by Brown.

8.64 A view of the great lawn and Badminton House.
Little has changed since Capability Brown's time and the tree clumps (mostly oaks) laid out on a grid recede towards the house that sits on the distant horizon. It is the impressive scale of this open green vacuum that confers all the power to this archetypal landscape.

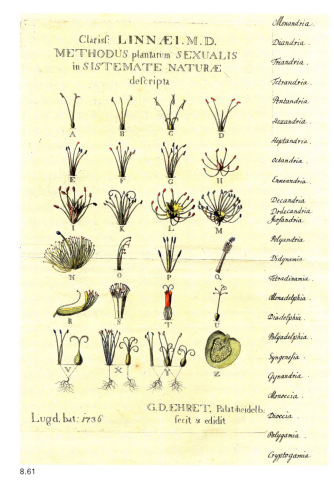

8.61

8.62

8.63

8.64

is adjacent to the miniature Pantheon, which has become the iconic image of Stourhead. Even if its aesthetic expression takes on a more romantic form, the artificiality needed to create this wide lake in a steep vale is most apparent. In this sense, the instrumentalization of nature at Stourhead is not so different from that at Vaux-le-Vicomte, and far less integrated than the dam holding up the Yokuryuchi pond on the hills of the Shugaku-in in Kyoto.

With the establishment of the Royal Botanic Gardens at Kew (1757), in south-west London, the conservation of species became a central preoccupation in British scientific circles.[17] The guiding idea behind Kew Gardens was to collect plants from all over the world and arrange them in a park-like setting according to Linnaeus's taxonomic classification developed in the *Species Plantarum*, 'The Species of Plants', (1753) [8.61].[18] The 'natural' style at Kew was for the most part devoid of any Picturesque references and was essentially based on the aesthetic qualities suggested by the plants themselves. There is no specific narrative to this garden, simply that of taxonomic classification. One moves through a sequence of outdoor plantings and greenhouses such as the huge Palm House, added a century later (1848), to admire the acclimatization of, and experimenting with, exotic plants [8.62]. The experience brings together elements from all parts of the globe, glorifying the position of Britain as a world power by assembling a palette of collectable curiosities in a manner similar to

Hadrian's Villa. The difference here is that the plant world of colonies takes centre stage in the landscape collage. A tall, red Chinese pagoda (1757), completely removed from its cultural context, was installed by William Chambers at the heart of an 'Oriental Garden', where it functioned as a combined symbol of adventure and exoticism [8.60].[19]

Industrialized landscapes

The revolution that Newton unleashed in science, offering the possibility of extraordinary precision, opened the door to mechanization in the landscape. On a wider scale, his laws of motion became the backbone of classical mechanics and accelerated technical progress in the Industrial Revolution. Probably the most remarkable landscape design of that period, reflecting on the law of motion, is the great lawn at Badminton designed first by Henry Wise and Charles Bridgeman followed by William Kent, with his initial tree clumps sheltering small huts and hermitages (1746) and depicted by Canaletto (1748)[8.63]. The sheer scale of the vacuum produced by this vast semicircular expanse of lawn set upon 'invisible' perspective rays in front of the house is simply breathtaking. Looking back at the countless clumps of oaks added later by Lancelot 'Capability' Brown to create a reverse, receding perspective that dwarfed Badminton House in the distance, one imagines the countless human and animal events that were staged here [8.64].[20]

Abstraction and reduction

The speed with which the garden revolution took hold of England also affected the development of the style, resulting in further simplification and reduction in a move towards a more pragmatic abstraction of nature. The large estates became laboratories for such landscape abstraction by the most fashionable landscape architect of the era, Lancelot 'Capability' Brown.

During the latter part of his career, Brown, who succeeded Kent on most notable projects, more or less obliterated all geometric references from the landscape, partly destroying the creations of his predecessors and replacing them with vast expanses of lawn strewn with tree clumps, as at Blenheim and Badminton and to a lesser extent Stowe and Chatsworth. His most exemplary project is the thorough transformation of the Woodstock Gardens at Blenheim (1764–74), where he overturned the work of predecessors such as John Vanbrugh in favour of a more open landscape style.[21] The sheer scale of the park is just stupendous, and its central Baroque axis, which is now pastoral in feel, still leaves an impression of empty monumentality [8.65]. The Great Lake was modified and considerably enlarged by Brown, submerging a significant part of the massive Baroque bridge designed by Vanbrugh over the tiny River Glyme (1710) [8.67], but it is Brown's systematic use of stands of trees to break down the landscape along the edges of the axial perspective

framing the Marlborough column that really characterizes the unique 'English' style of the place [8.66]. Instead of creating a clearing surrounded by trees, Brown created an archetypal inversion of sorts by planting huge clumps of copper beech trees surrounded by even vaster productive meadows [8.68].

The art of landscape Capability Brown employed to re-create an image of nature took place in an already distorted world. By the end of the 18th century, the poetry of William Wordsworth and Samuel Taylor Coleridge, from the Lake District in northern England, marked the arrival of English Romanticism.[22] Their lyrical poems express an unequivocal love of idyllic nature, but one that is also tinged with melancholy and a hope that our world can be changed for the better. The 'Lakists', as they were called, coincided precisely with the birth of the Industrial Revolution, as a result of which the world became circumscribed – a finite entity in which progress could compete. This is the period when Adam Smith wrote about the international division of labour and the origins of wealth.[23] By the end of the 18th century England had overtaken the Dutch Republic to become a world power, burgeoned by the Royal African Company's lucrative slave commerce and the exploitation of new colonies, including India [8.69].

Humphry Repton began his career in 1788 and formed a new dedicated profession, that of the landscape gardener and surveyor. The discourse was no longer painterly

8.65

8.65 The Column of Victory, Blenheim, England.
The impressive column commemorating the 1st Duke of Marlborough and his victories in battle stands on axis with the house and sets the monumental tone of the entire estate.

8.66 A ring of lime trees, Blenheim.
Based on Vanbrugh's original plan, this feature recreates a semblance of an archetypal clearing but without a proper sense of scale and proportion – it simply befits the expression of immense power.

8.66

8.67 The Grand Bridge, Blenheim.
Originally designed by Vanbrugh, with work
beginning in 1708, it spanned two hillocks and
contained numerous rooms on the ground floor.
When Capability Brown converted the park
and gardens at Blenheim in 1764, destroying
most of its Baroque features, he considerably
enlarged the artificial lake on the River Glyme,
partially flooding the extravagant bridge.

**8.68 A monumental group of copper beeches
on a hillside at Blenheim.**
The tree clump is Capability Brown's landscape
signature, reviving an archetypal quality,
although inverted: now the tree clumps are
themselves surrounded by an even vaster
open clearing.

8.67

8.68

8.69

8.70a

8.70b

8.71

8.69 *The Town of Lanark*, by John Clark, 1824–25.

With the transformations of the Industrial Revolution it became harder to find suitable places for idealized landscapes. The contradiction between mechanization and nature inherent in the Newtonian Revolution became all the more apparent.

8.70a, 8.70b *The Fort near Bristol*, by Humphry Repton, 1801.

The design for a project from one of Repton's 'Red Books' was published as part of his book *Observations on the Theory and Practice of Landscape Gardening* (1805). Landscape becomes a screen to disguise unwanted buildings and restore some semblance of an original pastoral splendour. It is ironic that few of Repton's proposed projects were ever built, and he is remembered more for his dioramas and visual simulations.

8.71 St James's Park, London, England.

Designed by John Nash in 1814, this old royal garden was remodelled into a public park. It displays a mature English pastoral style creating the complete illusion of a forest clearing just a stroll away from Piccadilly and Victoria. The art of masking surroundings would become the trademark of the English Garden Movement.

8.72 The English-style Muskauer Park, Germany–Poland.

The park, crossed by the River Neisse that defines the border between the two countries, was designed in 1815–44 by Prince Hermann von Pückler-Muskau, a close friend of Repton. The trees serve as markers indicating where paths meet on the vast expanse of the lawn.

8.72

but, rather, of an aesthetic that could accommodate the upheavals occurring in the British landscape at the time. Repton's 'Red Books' – bound volumes of manuscript text and accompanying watercolours – are full of suggestions that follow a formula: the unsightly must be hidden, and the beauty of what is left of nature must be heightened, with no effort spared [8.70a, 8.70b].[24]

A new world order came to fruition with the French Revolution (1789), the breaking down of absolute monarchy and democracy. Royal hunting grounds throughout Europe, such as Hyde Park and St James's Park in London, the Englischer Garten in Munich and the Bois de Boulogne in Paris, gradually became common spaces for the benefit of all [8.71]. By that time, the English landscape style had developed into a finely tuned instrument, capable of being employed on a scale previously unimaginable, which confirmed its extraordinary versatility. The fact that it essentially replaced a rich tapestry of indigenous landscapes with a single version of 'nature' itself can be seen as the ultimate stylistic victory.[25] The 'naturalistic' expression of the English landscape, in all its romantic humility, would henceforth be used to cover up the devastating effects of accelerating industrial progress. One could even say that this simulacrum of nature, the so-called English style, served industry more often than the general interest. It was so robust and simple that it could be applied to any given context, triggering a cultural revolution

of sorts that took less than a century to spread throughout the Western world. It inspired countless examples from René Louis de Girardin's humble garden in Ermenonville, France (1766–76), to Hermann von Pückler-Muskau's extensive 560-hectare (1,384-acre) Muskauer Park, in South Brandenburg (1815–44) [8.72].[26]

The fundamental contradiction between a philosophical understanding of the universal law of gravity, and its application in mechanical science would become more significant over time. The natural laws of motion were the pretext for all kinds of technical experimentation in the environment, including the gradual acceleration of human travel. This confirmed that scientific truths were part of the constant of nature that governed the universe, and did not fall within the 'arbitrariness' of the cultural sphere. This was taken as an excuse to treat nature as a mere commodity, devoid of cultural significance, to be shaped by the material necessities of humankind – triggering a fundamental change in spirit and attitude towards the world.

9. Combustion
Escape into the Exotic

'Nature never deceives us; it is always we who deceive ourselves.'

Jean-Jacques Rousseau, *Emile: Or, On Education*[1]

At the beginning of the 19th century, the effects of industrialization on the European environment started to become noticeable. The harnessing of steam power for transport, mining and industry had a direct effect on the atmosphere and a lasting impact on the infrastructure of landscapes on both rural and urban scales, as depicted by J. M. W. Turner in *Rain, Steam, and Speed* (1844) [9.1]. The burning of coal polluted the city air, and the quality of rivers deteriorated rapidly to the point that they became massive industrial and urban sewers. This period marks a significant turning point in the history of landscape architecture, as the reason and purpose of design lose their traditional, mythological and aristocratic roots to become essentially economical and societal. The park at Ermenonville (1770)

by René Louis de Girardin, where the 18th-century philosopher Jean-Jacques Rousseau looked to nature to mirror the just and rightful origins of man, became the model for an idealized form of nature suited to the city [9.2].[2] Concerned as he was with social justice, Rousseau entertained a certain idealized nostalgia for man's primitive state, seeing a just and equal return to nature, before the existence of proprietary rights, as the only possible salvation from the decadence of civilization. As he wrote in his *Discourse on Inequality* (1754): 'Nothing is so gentle as man in his primitive state, when placed by nature at an equal distance from the stupidity of brutes and the fatal enlightenment of civil man.'[3]

Many of the motifs used in 19th-century public parks like the Parc des Buttes-Chaumont in Paris (1867) by Adolphe Alphand were borrowed from the Picturesque tradition of the previous century and adapted to the constraints of congested urban contexts [9.0]. Some of the early public parks had been aristocratic hunting grounds, and whereas formerly they had

9.0 (opposite) The Temple of Sibyl, Parc des Buttes-Chaumont, Paris, France.
Rather than a temple, this is in fact a park belvedere designed by Gabriel Davioud in 1866. There are no prophecies and no Sibyl to be heard here; mythology is used only as a picturesque device, and if a voice of nature can be heard it is that of applied horticulture.

9.1 *Rain, Steam, and Speed* by J. M. W. Turner, 1844.
Turner painted this scene at Maidenhead Bridge over the Thames near London. The blurred, gaseous image addresses the radical shift in landscape perception that steam engines and speed locomotion brought about by the mid-19th century.

9.1

9.2

9.3

9.2 The park at Ermenonville, north-east of Paris.
Jean-Jacques Rousseau died and was originally
buried here, on the Île des Peupliers surrounded
by a ring of poplars. Designed by René Louis
de Girardin in the 1770s, the park's vistas were
strongly influenced by the writings of Rousseau.
Later parks like the Tiergarten in Berlin found
inspiration in the spirit of Ermenonville.

**9.3 *Wanderer Above the Sea of Fog* by Caspar
David Friedrich, 1818.**
The painting epitomizes German Romanticism:
a young man stands gazing out above the
fogs of the industrial world. In this improbable
terrain he perhaps comes close to an untainted,
Rousseau-like communion with nature. The
mountains depicted are in fact a collection
of peaks from various parts of Germany.

9.4 Regent's Park, London, England.
Designed by John Nash in 1810, it was partially
opened to the public in 1835. The original park
was part of an exclusive real estate scheme for
the wealthy, with 56 planned villas of which only
eight were ever built. The park worked as a vast
open space in a rapidly growing London, with
a primary purpose being benefits to health.

**9.5 Crystal Palace, Great Exhibition, 1851,
London, England.**
Designed by Joseph Paxton, head gardener at
Chatsworth, the glass and iron structure covered
10.5 hectares (26 acres) in Hyde Park. It housed
over 100,000 exhibits and specimens, including
some full-grown trees. Over 6 million visitors
came to see the exhibition in the space of the
six months for which it was open.

**9.6 *Over London – By Rail* by Gustave Doré,
1872.**
Doré's engraving shows the squalor of 19th-
century working-class housing in the British
capital, though conditions were comparable
in Berlin, Paris and New York. The misery of
such housing led the English social reformer
Edwin Chadwick to write a *Report on the
Sanitary Condition of the Labouring Population
of Great Britain*, which resulted in the Public
Health Act of 1848.

9.4

9.5

9.6

represented nature, they now performed the role of urban social lubricant. The Industrial Revolution was a great period for the creation of large parks, which in urban environments became highly artificial enterprises. It is striking to note that almost no cultural or stylistic boundaries hindered the spread of the romanticized image of nature inherited from the English style developed a century before. Its universal language had its roots in the scientific revolution that was under way, in which the Linnaean system of classification allowed nature to be itemized and classified methodically.[4] The great scientific inventory of the planet had begun.

Industrialization provoked the mass exodus of people from poorer rural areas towards cities and areas of high production served by railways, roads and waterways. Cities and industrial districts were not sufficiently planned and, more often than not, improvised settlements turned into squalid, overcrowded living quarters with tremendous problems of sanitation [9.6].[5] Both cities and factories grew tremendously fast without much concern for local workers or their living environment. By the mid-19th century, countless political upheavals and revolutions began to influence the actual shaping of cities. The changing status of the citizen, and more particularly of the growing urban middle class, increased concerns relating to health, hygiene and comfort. Landscape thus became a vital tool of urban planning and public works. Large parks, such as Regent's Park in London,

planned by John Nash in 1810, were designed privately and then handed over to the public [9.4].[6] All these parks had a strong moralistic purpose, and at the same time were thought to be beneficial to the health of the individual because they provided a symbolic connection with nature. The landscapes that appeared in the cities of Europe and the Americas during this difficult, crowded period of 19th-century urban history reflected a particular ideal of nature based on the exotic. Their invention was timely and quite a feat at a time when public space was more or less completely absent from the city.

Landscape and horticultural shows offered a type of escape from urban squalor, in which various forms of nature became symbols of a relentless and important mastery of the plant world, as exemplified in Joseph Paxton and Charles Fox's extraordinary Crystal Palace (1851) in London [9.5].[7] There had been a tradition of learned plant collection in botanical gardens since the early Renaissance, but 19th-century public parks displayed collections of imported plants not so much for scientific reasons as to present an exotic dream of nature that allowed for a temporary escape from the urban grind. This of course reminds one of the notion of a primal return to nature and humankind reverting to its 'original' state, as contained in the writings of William Wordsworth and Jean-Jacques Rousseau.[8] This romantic sentiment is also epitomized in the painting by the German artist Caspar David Friedrich, *Wanderer Above the Sea of Fog* (1818) [9.3]. This highly aesthetic approach towards nature, underpinned by a prominent moral aspect, became the dominant trend in landscape thinking of the period. Combined with a strong streak in 19th-century enterprise, it yielded some invaluable landscape projects that have remained extremely consistent up to the present today. Translated into the highly engineered urban public park, landscape became the 'natural' palliative of its time – a cure intimately linked to Enlightenment notions of progress, modernity and social justice.

Progress in the industrial age

During the 19th century science progressed in giant leaps, particularly following Nicolas Léonard Sadi Carnot's theory of thermodynamics in 1824.[9] In what would later form the basis of the second law of thermodynamics, Carnot defined the concept of entropy as the inevitable dissolution of energy towards a state of equilibrium. Entropy came to be understood as a constant in physics that could be applied universally. Its impact on our understanding of the environment would also have significant consequences for the development of art in that century as depicted in J. M. W. Turner's incredibly abstract vortex painting *Snow Storm – Steam-Boat off a Harbour's Mouth* (1842) [9.10].

In 1859, Charles Darwin published his revolutionary book *On the Origin of Species*, which described species as both reactive and adaptive to a variety of specific environmental conditions.[10] In some earlier notes dated 1837 Darwin sketches-out the idea of an evolutionary tree [9.8]. In its conclusion that man evolved ultimately from primates, this work overturned the belief in man's God-given supremacy. With its concept of causality, evolutionary theory would also have an impact on ecological thinking, especially the notion of cause and effect. Alexander von Humboldt similarly mapped entire natural systems, drawn through careful observation, such as his extraordinary phenotype section of Tenerife Island (1799) [9.7].[11] Such scientific advances tended to overlook human culture while concentrating distinctly on the much broader world of natural phenomena.

Science gradually liberated the relationship that had held between city and natural landscape for so long. Rapid urban expansion led to a broader definition of landscape architecture, in which it also came to denote a constructed natural environment cut off from its rural background and adapted to the functional and societal constraints of the city. This strong relationship between landscape architecture and urban design developed in countries including Germany, England, France, America and Argentina. Its success attests to the extraordinary coherence of the projects it inspired. There were, however, a few shameful shortcomings. The Jardin d'Acclimatation in the Bois de Boulogne, Paris [9.9] (to take one example of many such human zoos across Europe and America at the time), founded by Geoffroy Saint-Hilaire in

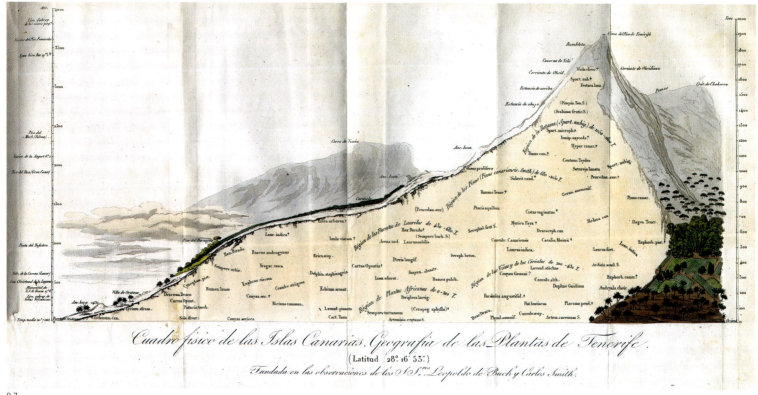

Cuadro fisico de las Islas Canarias. Geografia de las Plantas de Tenerife.
(Latitud 28° 16′ 55″.)
Fundada en las observaciones de los Sᵉˢ Leopoldo de Buch y Carlos Smith.

9.7

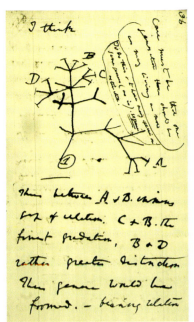

9.8

9.9

9.10

9.7 Profile section of Tenerife by Alexander von Humboldt, 1799.
The section labels the natural vegetation of the island, with lists of biomes and plant communities at varying altitudes. The natural sciences displaced the art of landscape representation away from the poetic and sacred and towards the scientific and analytical.

9.8 Charles Darwin's first sketch of the evolutionary tree, 1837.
The sketch represents Darwin's early theorizing that he developed in his revolutionary book *On the Origin of Species* (1859). In this he questioned creationist views of the world and replaced them with a systematic and scientific understanding of nature. The book provoked outrage, but has had a lasting effect on our appreciation of the natural world.

9.9 Kalina peoples of Guyana exhibited at the Jardin d'Acclimatation in Paris, 1892.
The theory of evolution could be applied in a negative way: in the later 19th century racial theories in physical anthropology claimed the natural superiority of the white man over 'primitive' peoples, and the practice of exhibiting them was widespread across Europe.

9.10 *Snow Storm – Steam Boat off a Harbour's Mouth* by J. M. W. Turner, 1842.
In this painting the forces of nature are pitted against a small ship dissolving in a tremendous vortex of wind, steam and water. Turner's intuition about man's relentless struggle with the elements in unmistakable.

Scientific discoveries of the 19th century had an impact on the world of art as well. Under the influence of J. M. W. Turner, for the first time painters showed the world dissolved into a whirlpool of light and motion [9.10]. Turner's works in particular would pave the way for the development of Impressionism and abstract Cubism. As Jonathan Crary states, it was in the early 19th century that vision was no longer defined merely in relation to an exterior image: the eye was no longer what defined the 'real world'.[12] The influence of modern science and industry on Turner's paintings is recognized, particularly in the way form is dispersed into speed, light and other atmospheric effects.

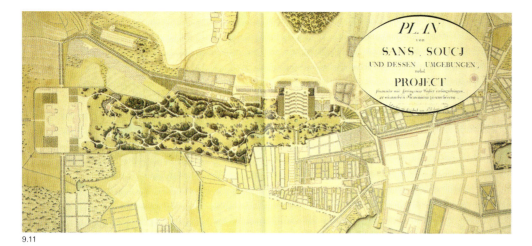

9.11

9.12

9.11 Plan of Sanssouci by Peter Joseph Lenné, 1816.
The plan shows a complete hybridization between French Baroque and English styles, blending a strong axis with gentle clearings. Moreover, the articulation of the numerous meandering lateral paths is a precursor of public park designs across Europe and America in the 19th century.

9.12 View of the Bornstedt church and Ruinenberg in Potsdam, 1850.
The painting by Julius Hennicke depicts the outskirts of Sanssouci in the fashionable Italianate style. The vegetation carefully recreates a sense of a Mediterranean Arcadia – the tall Lombardy poplars and oaks could be mistaken for cypress and olive trees.

1860, was designed to display exotic plant species, animals – and non-European ethnic groups.[13] Nubians, Eskimos and Pygmies, to name a few, were all displayed as if they were in a zoo, for the enjoyment and curiosity of the crowds. Tragically, some of the 'exhibits' did not survive the experience of a Parisian winter. Exoticism was analogous to an empirical science, in which progress resulted from a morally questionable process of trial and error. The scandalous nature of such an ethnographic venture shows how far removed European colonial thinking was from Rousseau's recognition of universal human rights.

It is during this period of rapid industrialization and unbridled urban and social growth that the first school of landscape architecture was born. The Gardener Academy in Potsdam, established by the landscape architect Peter Joseph Lenné in 1823,[14] became the crucible for an entire generation of Romantic landscape architects who worked hand in hand with Neoclassical architects and urban planners at developing the image of the modern Prussian capital – Berlin. Stylistically speaking, Lenné had trained as a Romantic. Though his projects did not invent a new style *per se*, he transferred elements of the Picturesque and the French Romantic into a 'hybridized' landscape vocabulary for the city park. He had trained at Ermenonville, north-east of Paris, in his youth under followers of René Louis de Girardin, and was deeply marked by the social theories of Rousseau and his notion of

a salutary return to nature. Lenné even went so far as to build a 'Rousseau island' in the Tiergarten in Berlin, in memory of the spot at Ermenonville where Rousseau had been buried [9.15].[15] Collaborating with the architect Karl Friedrich Schinkel, he altered the landscape in Potsdam and Berlin to fit a highly romanticized, Italianate ideal that had little to do with the natural ecology of Brandenburg, as can be seen in an idealized painting by Julius Hennicke [9.12]. His landscapes contributed to an exotic escape from the pressures of urban development epitomized by Berlin's sordid tenements.

Lenné drew up parks and gardens, developed new street typologies and, as early as 1840, proposed an urban green belt system around Berlin called the *Grünzug* [9.14]. The industrial city was an integral part of his ideal, as long as it allowed room for an integrated landscape network. Lenné's first major project was Sanssouci Park (1816) in Potsdam, which presented a rare blend of formal landscape with informal motifs [9.11].[16] The stylistic vocabulary that he developed here – clumps of trees in large clearings to signal forks in the footpaths, for example, or the way he combined the usual winding circulation system with a more axial approach – would be applied to most urban parks across Europe and America thereafter. This understanding of a need to diversify patterns of circulation marks an important initial step in the creation of the first public parks. Lenné went on to produce a remarkable plan for the Tiergarten (1818) [9.13], which linked

9.13

9.13 Plan of the Tiergarten by Peter Joseph Lenné, 1818.
This early plan shows clearly how access and circulation had become important features of the architecture of the park. No longer a closed private microcosm for the gentry, the park is opened on all sides to the city and its inhabitants. Alphand and Olmsted, who followed in Lenné's footsteps in Paris and New York, became masters of circulation.

9.14 Plan of the *Schmuck und Grünzug* around Berlin by Peter Joseph Lenné, 1848.
This is the first 'Jewel and Green Belt' plan ever designed for Berlin, and has remained incomplete to this day. It was a precursor by at least four decades of those that appeared in Paris and Boston.

9.15 The Rousseau Insel in the Tiergarten, Berlin, Germany, by Justus Ehrenreich Sello, 1797.
In the 1830s Lenné integrated the small island of the previous park in his Tiergarten plan, but modified the lake into a 'river'. It is still the most intimate and successful spot of the Tiergarten. A wooden urn stands in a ring of alders, in honour of the man who proclaimed a 'return to nature'.

9.14

9.15

9.16

9.17

9.18

9.19

9.16 Naturists in the Tiergarten, Berlin, Germany.
Some customs in the Tiergarten, Berlin, and the
Englischer Garten, Munich, have evolved since
they were first opened. So-called *Liegewiese*
(sunbathing lawns) invite people to commune
with nature on hot summer days.

**9.17 A typical star-shaped crossing in the
Tiergarten forest.**
Lenné employed asphalt paths here for the first
time. The radical use of materials contrasting
with the natural forest floor is the signature
of this urban park. Little has changed in terms
of approach over the past two centuries.

**9.18 A bucolic autumn walk in the Tiergarten,
painting by Johann Heinrich Stürmer, 1835.**
The early part of the 19th century saw the park
become a prominent public space in Berlin.
People would meet there for leisurely strolls
and conversation. Germany was one of the first
countries to experiment with this entirely new
type of public space.

**9.19 Ice skating around the Rousseau Island
in the Tiergarten, Berlin, 1902.**
This public park evolved and by the turn of the
20th century became a place where Berliners
could meet and parade around the 'river'
on their skates and on other occasions, thus
escaping for a while from the squalid conditions
of the *Mietskaserne* or workers' tenements.

**9.20 The long meadow clearing in the Englischer
Garten, Munich, Germany.**
From its opening in 1792, the oldest public park
in Europe was an outstanding amenity for the
city, with its Monopteros temple and Chinese
Tower. Without Friedrich Ludwig von Sckell's
perseverance over three decades, the park could
never have reached its present state and form.

the city centre of Berlin with the district of Charlottenburg to the west. The layout of paths – consisting of different-sized diagonal paths in *patte d'oie* formation, appearing at regular intervals and transecting the main axis, combined with a more informal curved path running the length of the park – gave the plan the appearance of a large urban loom, with countless threads connecting various parts of the city on both sides [9.17]. In this sense Lenné was certainly the first to invent such a landscape style based on functional pragmatism.

Early urban parks

The first recorded example of an urban park being handed over to the public in Europe was the Englischer Garten in Munich.[17] An existing aristocratic hunting ground, covering over 417 hectares (1,030 acres), was gradually transformed from 1789 in the English Picturesque style and opened to the general public in 1792. The park's designer, Friedrich Ludwig von Sckell, working under Charles Theodore, Elector of Bavaria, and supervised by Benjamin Thompson (Reichsgraf von Romford), a Massachusetts-born military man, shaped the vast garden according to the archetypal principles of the English landscape style with forested areas and picturesque vistas of monuments alternating within clearings. The grounds had previously been subject to frequent flooding by the Isar River, but were now protected by a levee. Without the talent, dedication and perseverance of von Sckell over

three decades, the park would never have been achieved in its present form. Today, after over two hundred years, the park, which is even larger than Central Park in New York or Hyde Park in London, still offers a tranquil view of the Munich skyline over vast expanses of woods and lawn where people flock year round [9.20].

The significance and impact of the Englischer Garten on other early examples of the genre in Germany and elsewhere is considerable. Without this precedent Lenné would have never been asked to work on the Tiergarten in Berlin, which became an important haven of new leisure activities in winter as in summer [9.18, 9.19]. On hot sunny days, the Tiergarten in Berlin and the Englischer Garten in Munich attract, among others, a public of dedicated naturists of all ages, who take the opportunity to commune with nature [9.16], entertaining thus a certain nostalgia for Rousseau's plea for a return to our primitive state.

Following the model of the Englischer Garten, public gardens sprang up in other parts of Europe and America, where the public was also given access to vast grounds. The scale and location of these projects was important: they would not have the force they do were they not located at the very heart of important cities. Examples include Regent's Park (1835) and Hyde Park (1850) in London, and the Bois de Boulogne (1854) and Bois de Vincennes (1863) in Paris, and Central Park (1858) in New York.[18]

9.20

9.21

Parc des Buttes-Chaumont, France

Most major industrial cities of the 19th century adopted similar designs for their early public parks. They were drawn up in the English Pastoral or Picturesque styles, with an open heart comprised of meadows framed by woods and a dense network of interweaving paths fringing the urban edge. Prospect Park (1867) designed by Frederick Law Olmsted and Calvert Vaux is a good example of such a blend of styles, with an artificially made cascade at Fallkill Falls reproducing a 'natural' mountain scene at the heart of Brooklyn [9.21]. The park (237 hectares, or 585 acres) set on an old glacial moraine with a ravine, works admirably with the natural topography. It is also the site of the Battle of Long Island (1776) in the American War of Independence.

It appears as though landscape architecture spoke a common 'language of nature' across nations and continents, a language that suited the hygienist theories of the period.[19] The design philosophy behind 19th-century parks, coincided with a rare moment in history when urban politics, design, techniques and the arts succeeded in working together hand in hand. The completely new parks – that is, those not occupying former hunting grounds or estates – were often sited on difficult terrains with slums, abandoned quarries and rubbish dumps. Considerable ingenuity and technical expertise were required to produce the desired results. One notable case in point is the Parc des Buttes-Chaumont in Paris (1867), which was not the most expansive of projects, but demonstrated the highly successful adaptation of an extremely challenging site [9.22].[20] Despite its relatively modest scale (25 hectares, or 62 acres), it is one of the most outstanding examples of adaptive reuse in 19th century landscape architecture, and the degree of technical control and topographic integration on display within the small site are impressive. The park is located in a working-class district of north-eastern Paris on the site of an old gypsum quarry, whose steep cliffs were surrounded by squalid proletarian housing and smoke-belching industry. When work began in 1863, the old quarry had been used as a rubbish dump since the Revolution and as a gallows hill before that. The park took three years to build and was inaugurated during the Paris Exposition Universelle of 1867.[21]

The extraordinary skill with which the raw, almost Cubistic topography of the old quarry at Buttes-Chaumont was transformed into an agreeable, picturesque garden, with a tightly knit network of winding paths, shows the level of accomplishment that the art of the landscape architect and civil engineer had achieved.[22] The project required steam

9.21 Fallkill Falls in Prospect Park, Brooklyn, New York, USA.
The park was designed by Frederick Law Olmsted and Calvert Vaux in 1867. This artificial piece of natural scenery works as a piece of the American 'wilderness', reproducing an idea of nature that is proper to this working-class district. The project was inspired by prevailing social concerns about health and hygiene at the time.

9.22 Plan of the Parc des Buttes-Chaumont, Paris, France.
Designed by Adolphe Alphand in 1867, the park is recognizable by its convoluted pathways resulting from circulation patterns imposed by the topography of the site. Straight lines through this extreme terrain were not possible.

9.22

9.23a

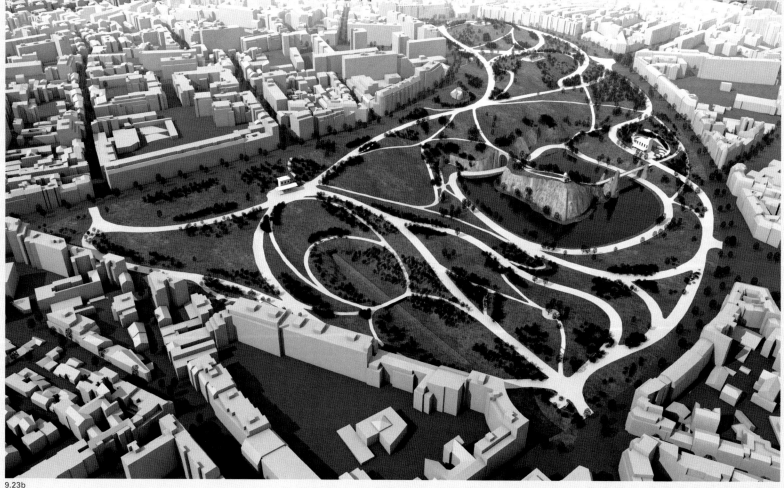

9.23b

9.23a, 9.23b Reconstructed before and after views of the Parc des Buttes-Chaumont. Originally an abandoned gypsum quarry with undefined terrain and scattered housing, it became an elaborate park, with winding roads and paths, and including an underground train line and a central water collector. Situated in a working-class district of Paris, the new park attracted better quality housing around its perimeter.

9.24 Aerial view of Buttes-Chaumont. The park is now set like a green island in the densely built urban fabric of Paris. Some shaded avenues radiate from it into neighbouring districts. The steep topography is visible at the far end of the park, where the street (rue de Crimée) reaches down the hill to the left.

9.24

engines, dynamite, horses and the manpower of over 1,000 labourers to be completed on schedule. Since the original gypsum quarry was covered in a layer of infertile clay hardpan, the drainage substrate, topsoil and vegetation all had to be brought in from elsewhere [9.23a, 9.23b]. In fact, the reason that this space was transformed into a park was that the quarry subsoil was too dangerous and almost impossible to develop for building. A public park, therefore, was one solution that would improve the standing and value of the neighbourhood. The landscape architect Adolphe Alphand, the engineer Eugène Belgrand, the architect Gabriel Davioud and the gardener Jean-Pierre Barillet-Deschamps worked as a team to bring this piece of idealized landscape into being, and went on to produce other projects as part of Baron Haussmann's transformation of Paris.[23]

The idea of placing a public park at the heart of a run-down district of Paris is of particular interest [9.25, 9.26]. Buttes-Chaumont is certainly not the first such landscape implantation: Berlin, London and New York all have good examples. But the Parc des Buttes-Chaumont was a somewhat experimental field, in which the finest techniques in contour-line surveying, terrain-modelling and road and rail tunnel construction were used [9.30]. Paths were made of asphalt, a revolutionary new impermeable elastic material. A system of drains and ponds at the park's lower levels collected rainwater [9.29]. In addition, everything down to the smallest piece of urban furniture was designed to work within an overall concept. The furniture developed by Alphand in Paris and by Olmsted in New York has to some extent come to symbolize the cities themselves [9.28].

The Parc des Buttes-Chaumont embodies an entirely new form of introverted landscape, in which the surrounding neighbourhoods face a single, elegant but much reduced icon of nature [9.24]. Entering the park via a series of shaded, winding paths that offer picturesque views of the Temple of Sibyl, built on a spur above both the lake and the Paris skyline, the visitor catches a glimpse of a towering cascade and a grotto [9.32]. But they offer no respite from the city: the grotto is no longer the timeless mythological refuge it would have been in the Renaissance, but rather an attraction. After passing the kiosk surrounded by a splendid assortment of exotic trees, one arrives at a single-arched span leaping a chasm over to the belvedere. Viewed from here, the Temple of Sibyl, rising above the city, has an almost intimate touch, but the rest of the park below our feet seems so small and frail against the immense, encroaching city [9.27]. The illusion that one experiences here is not a result of optics so much as an inversion of scale, in which an insular landscape is encapsulated in an idealized and nostalgic microcosm [9.38]. As one descends from the belvedere over Gustave Eiffel's suspended footbridge, a broader, more hostile city environment emerges from under the trees [9.35].

9.25

9.26

9.27

9.28

9.25 An early photograph of Buttes-Chaumont by Charles Marville, 1866.
The site of the park is being cleaned up, dynamited and given form. Note the complete absence of vegetation: huge quantities of soil had to be brought in and stabilized before any planting could take place.

9.26 Reconstruction view of Buttes-Chaumont from the same angle.
This shows how the park design was fitted into the context. We are far from an Elysian atmosphere of the early English garden and closer to a harsh urban reality of the 19th century.

9.27 The great lawn at Buttes-Chaumont.
The ground of the quarry had to be entirely reworked and stabilized with vegetation. The great lawn was given an incline in certain parts on a 2:3 ratio with artificial slopes, which have held without erosion for 150 years. For this purpose the paths help control runoff and erosion, with water channelled down to a central pool at the foot of the promontory.

9.28 Buttes-Chaumont 150 years later.
The park is now an extraordinary urban oasis, with the enigmatic miniature temple giving an illusion of distance and depth. The benches designed by Alphand line the asphalt road and have become a trademark of Paris. Good landscape requires time to grow.

9.29 Section across the cascade at Buttes-Chaumont.
The impressive change of level is mitigated by lateral paths and roads, parallel to the height lines. Water on the other hand runs perpendicularly to the slope and collects at the low point by the lake. The city has grown to its full extent in the background and wraps around the park.

9.29

Buttes-Chaumont can be viewed as the successful creation of a landscape that forms a congruous, albeit reduced, slice of nature within an industrialized city. It is nature far removed from the wild and the sacred, replete with attractions and distractions, but it is nature pragmatically conceived for the benefit of a great number of inhabitants [9.37]. It was made for the elegant Parisian *flâneur* as well as the immigrant worker, and provides a relaxed space where the chance of encountering others matters as much as the scenery at hand.

The landscape encapsulated at Buttes-Chaumont is of its time. It is not the expression of the French landscape tradition *per se*, but of a Romantic sentiment that prevailed in industrialized cities during that period [9.36]. The paths of Buttes-Chaumont are strikingly reminiscent of those drawn by Peter Joseph Lenné in Potsdam forty years before, but also of the much earlier Ming gardens at Souzhou, and the slopes of the Fragrant Hills in Beijing. The main achievement of Buttes-Chaumont, with its ornamented cement handrails, cascades and steps, is how it managed to transpose a prevalent style onto the extraordinarily difficult topography of this old quarry [9.31]. The park plan can be understood as an example of control and engineering for the purpose of landscape aesthetics, in which the surface-to-movement ratio is maximized and every square metre of space is profitably employed [9.39]. After all, Alphand was an engineer who trained at the prestigious École Polytechnique; it is only because he understood the site's topographical constraints that he was able to produce this feat of landscape engineering.

What lessons can be learned from the Parc des Buttes-Chaumont? The park incorporated a variety of circulation methods – vehicular, pedestrian and rail – without hindering general use in any way [9.33, 9.34]. Moreover, the site's extraordinary discrepancy in levels (the highest point is some 50 metres, or 164 feet, above the lowest) within a narrow band of terrain allowed the landscape architect to separate, and even superimpose, different uses that would otherwise have been in conflict. This understanding of how to incorporate complex circulation patterns within a park derived from observations Alphand shared with his colleague Frederick Law Olmsted, both in New York and in Paris.[24]

Olmsted himself had been inspired by the ingenious overlay of street and path he had seen in the English Picturesque gardens at Birkenhead [9.42],[25] designed by Joseph Paxton, or the earlier garden at Stourhead by Henry Hoare. The precision with which the path network was laid out at Buttes-Chaumont is a precursor of 20th-century theme parks such as Disneyland, which developed highly controlled landscape environments for the purpose of entertainment, augmenting the visitor's spatial experience within a strictly confined area.

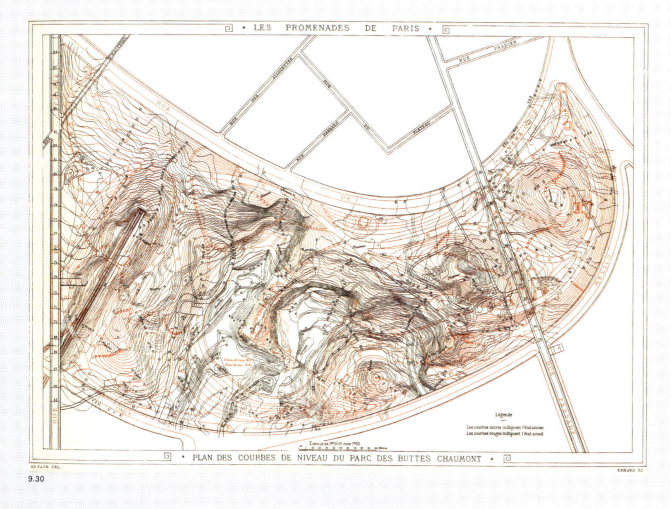

9.30

9.31

9.32

9.30 Topographic plan of the Parc des Buttes-Chaumont by Adolphe Alphand.
This engraved plan is exquisitely crafted, with each 1 metre (3 foot) height line inscribed. It is both a feat of engineering and a work of art.

9.31 Original ferro-cement handrail imitating rustic logs.
Alphand was radical both in his topographical plans and use of details. Just as Lenné introduced the asphalt path to his parks, Alphand introduced cement features that have lasted and branded the park.

9.32 The great cascade.
The immense grotto is a remnant of the quarry, with water fed from the Canal de l'Ourcq nearby. Though the cascade is artificial, the city noise is lost in its splashing sound, inviting us to return and imagine archaic times for an instant.

9.33 The tip of the park at its west end.
An artificial mound created from dynamited rubble produced during construction provides a viewing platform over the city. The absence of trees in the foreground is to maintain the view. The curving road operates a 180° turn back into the park, defining the foot of the mound.

9.34 The island in the Parc des Buttes-Chaumont.
The suspension bridge was designed by Gustave Eiffel, and this mix of archaic landscape design and high-tech engineering marks a shift in the approach to problem solving. The island could have remained unattainable and sacred, but by giving priority to circulation Alphand paved the way for other considerations and uses.

9.33

9.34

9.35

9.35 View from the pillar of Eiffel's suspension bridge towards the rock and the Temple of Sibyl.
Japan was in vogue in France at the time and the red bridge is reminiscent of a Japanese garden. But the spirit is different. The visitor is suspended too high above the water to find solace and must move on.

9.36 Flowering plum trees leaning into the slope over the railway tunnel.
Almost fifty species of trees were planted at the onset, ranging from cedars of Lebanon and ginkgos to humble fruit trees like these. It is fascinating to observe how each plant has adapted and survived in this park of extremes over time.

9.37 Users of the Parc des Buttes-Chaumont today.
The slope does not permit formal sports to take place, but allows for impromptu games and gatherings. The visual generosity of the great lawn was intended by Alphand as the centrepiece of his scheme, although in his day people were strictly confined to the paths.

9.38 The Buttes-Chaumont outcrop in spring.
The outcrop works as the centrepiece and natural jewel of the park, expressing seasonal change and displaying a reduced form of nature very much like an island in a Japanese garden. Its base is inaccessible to visitors and has become a sanctuary of sorts.

9.39 Plan of the Parc des Buttes-Chaumont by Adolphe Alphand, 1867.
The precision with which the park was drawn allows all forms of possible circulation – from train to meandering on foot and by carriage – to be represented. Alphand was an engineer, and as such his drawings of the park were not just elegant, they were also efficient, economical and robust.

9.36

9.37

9.38

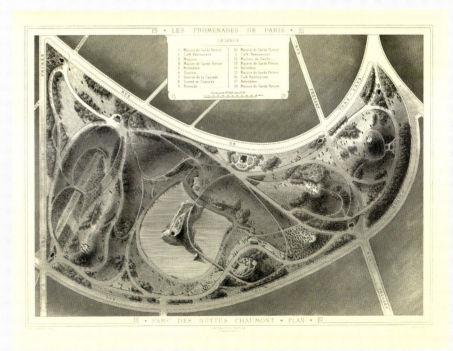

9.39

Parks and the wider urban framework

Today, the steeply sloping lawns of the Parc des Buttes-Chaumont are meant for casual relaxation and for viewing the skyline of north-eastern Paris under the shade of mature ginkgo trees. Most visitors are unaware of its complex history, and it is quite remarkable how this park, now almost 150 years old, has matured and come to fit the scale and character of the neighbourhood. Its collection of exotic plants (over fifty different species), planted at the onset, is now well established, and its canopy of trees – including cedars of Lebanon and oriental planes – interacts admirably with the natural declivity of the steep slopes, creating a pleasant alternating pattern of sunny clearings and shaded groves. The structure of the park reaches out beyond its gates to incorporate the surrounding streets that were planted according to Alphand's plans and sections of avenues and boulevards for the rest of the capital [9.40].[26]

Buttes-Chaumont was constructed as a distinct landscape component, but set within a larger urban framework of parks and promenades, similar in concept to Lenné's *Grünzug* around Berlin proposed forty years before. The Emerald Necklace in Boston (1878) by Olmsted appeared a decade later and was done in a more suburban style and on a different engineering scale altogether. It linked the Boston Common to Franklin Park via a necklace of parks and avenues including the Back Bay Fens draining back into the Charles River [9.43].[27] In many cases the landscape work that Olmsted performed was intended to drain land and allow for an integrated urban development and road work to take place. This type of landscape thinking on a wider scale should have informed urban developments of all cities into the next century: Buenos Aires is one city that continued with the park-and-boulevard tradition, through the works of Carlos Thays, the city's landscape director from 1892 to 1920, who shaped avenues and gardens around an immense (700-hectare, 1,730-acre) botanical garden (1898).[28] He experimented with unknown native plants including the jacaranda tree, which produced alignments of the most striking effect when the trees blossomed blue [9.41]. Although strongly inspired by the works of Alphand, with whom he had trained, Thays went on experimenting by plotting avenues on a different scale, with innovative plantations that conferred a particularly exotic touch to the city. But other places around the world were less fortunate and prevented from following a similar course by war or dramatic change in the economy that worked to the detriment of a continued landscape vision.

Most 19th-century parks now seem taken for granted, yet they resulted from a heated political debate about their merits at the time. Central Park in New York took almost 15 years from 1844 until 1857 before a competition was launched.[29] The 283 hectares (700 acres) of reclaimed land had been formerly settled by African-Americans and Irish

9.40 Plate from *Les Promenades de Paris* by Adolphe Alphand.
The section drawing shows the Boulevard Richard Lenoir as it passes over the Canal St Martin. The plate also includes an entire design palette of elements that branded Paris lastingly.

9.41 El Rosedal or Rose Garden by Carlos Thays, Buenos Aires, Argentina, 1898.
After working in Paris, Thays moved to Buenos Aires and sought to replicate what he had learned. Yet two fundamentals differed: the climate and the scale. This, combined with a local vegetation that has grown to unwieldy heights, confers a unique character and spirit to his projects.

9.42 Birkenhead Park by Joseph Paxton, 1847.
Birkenhead Park, on the the River Mersey in north-western England, is not comparable in scale to Central Park, but offers a detailed microcosm of circulation patterns that befits the style that Olmsted sought to promote.

9.43 Plan of the Emerald Necklace, Boston, USA, by Frederick Law Olmsted, 1878.
The Emerald Necklace project by Olmsted proposed to link Boston via the Charles River to the Back Bay Fens, the Arnold Arboretum and Franklin Park in the south-west. The ambitious scale of this landscape project was entirely new.

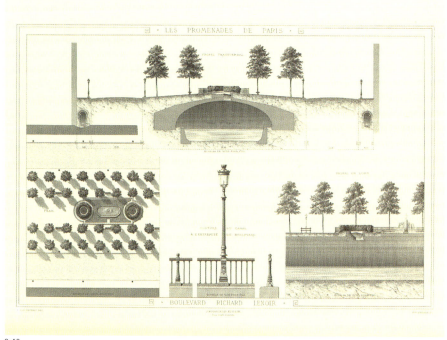

9.40

9.41

9.42

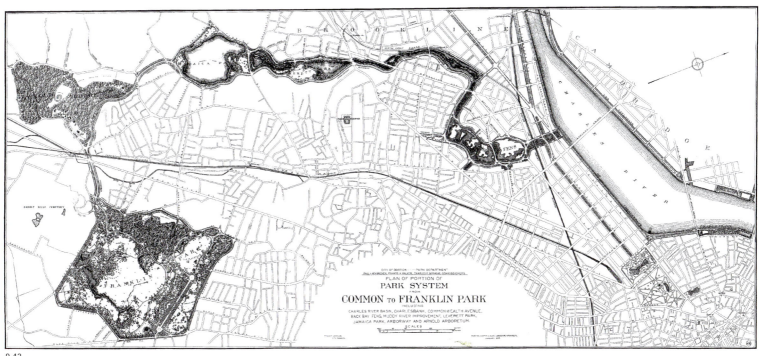

9.43

10. Acceleration
Landscapes of the 20th Century

'Perfection of means and confusion of goals seem – in my opinion – to characterize our age.'
Albert Einstein, London, 2 October 1941[1]

The last utopians

Where the 19th century delivered tangible landscapes for the city, the 20th century offered utopias and contrasting ideologies. Optimistic schemes, like the Parc de la Villette in Paris (1984) designed as a manifest Deconstructivist urban project served only to hasten a further detachment from nature, owing to the accelerated rhythm of material and societal change [10.0]. Similarly, Marcel Duchamp's *Nude Descending a Staircase (No. 2)* (1912) decomposed the accelerated movement of the human body abstractly [10.1]. It is difficult to tell whether a man or a woman is descending; the image has lost most character traits in favour of an embodiment of pure light and motion. Accelerated motion is probably the main reason why the urban park-and-promenade movement, begun a century earlier, was unable to integrate itself in the expanding suburban tissue. With the arrival of motorized mobility, the rules of urban development changed radically, as large reserves of land dwindled beneath suburbs, highways, airports and parking lots. This made replicating the 19th-century urban model almost impossible, particularly in extended peripheral areas. Landscape gradually transformed into the bare notion of 'green', with no particular historical or mythological references in mind. The green belt as protection against spreading urbanism became the creed of utopian thinkers such as Ebenezer Howard.[2]

Ebenezer Howard, father of the Garden City concept (1902), believed that it was possible to define universal rules for town planning that would support more balanced growth. Using a set of circular diagrams reminiscent of medieval *mappae mundi*, he illustrated the perfect ring-like structure of a utopian garden city, showing its living quarters, working quarters, productive agricultural land, schools, green belt

10.0 (opposite) Red folly at the Parc de la Villette, Paris, France, 1987.
This *folie* inspired by Russian Constructivist architecture is intended as a children's workshop. Set along the main north–south axis of the park, called Galerie de la Villette, it confers on the place a character more that of an elaborate public amusement park than a representation of nature.

10.1 *Nude Descending a Staircase (No. 2)* by Marcel Duchamp, 1912.
Human movement down a staircase is deconstructed using abstract elements. Inspired by the 'chronophotography' of Étienne-Jules Marey and Eadweard Muybridge of the late 19th century, it announces the cinematic 'dematerialization' of our vision and the body through motion.

10.1

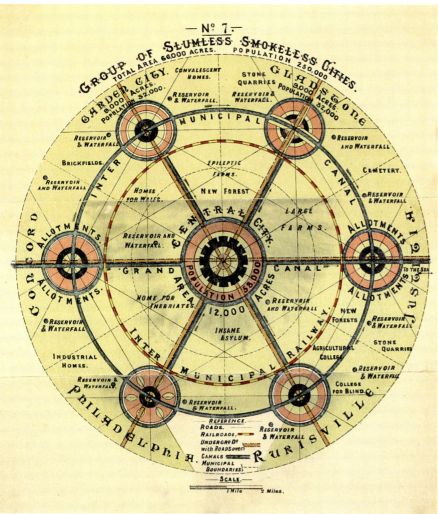

10.2

10.2 Diagram of the ideal garden city by Ebenezer Howard.
Small circular satellite towns are connected to each other by rings of railways and canals and to the central city by radial roads. Each person fits into the system, and landscape is repetitive and monotonous, with allotments, farmland, new forests and reservoirs. What remains at the centre is simply circulation.

10.3 Aerial view of Letchworth, England, laid out by Raymond Unwin in 1903.
Based on the principles of Ebenezer Howard, this is the world's first garden city. It could proudly boast the first roundabout in the UK, dated 1909, and banned pubs and alcohol in public premises until 1958. Its town centre was green but very quiet at night. Letchworth inspired countless other new towns around the world.

10.4 The Horseshoe Estate, *Hufeisensiedlung*, Berlin, Germany, by Bruno Taut, 1925–30.
Designed by Bruno Taut with landscape architect Leberecht Migge and architect Martin Wagner, the project is one of the most archetypal examples of post-war urban planning in Germany. The balance between green space, allotment gardens and urbanization distinguishes it from previous garden cities such as Letchworth, which were more suburban.

10.5 The trenches of the Somme, France, 1916.
The atrocities of World War I left an indelible mark on the landscape. Reaching the utter limits of annihilation, not only was Europe left with 16 million dead and 20 million wounded, but the wastelands of mud left behind would never recover their original spirit.

10.6 The Stadtpark Hamburg, Germany, completed by Fritz Schumacher in 1914.
One of the last great urban parks conceived in Europe, it covers 150 hectares (371 acres). The vast lawn fronting a lake surrounded by trees leads to a water tower by Otto Menzel (1915), later converted into a planetarium. It is strangely reminiscent of the Mausoleum at Castle Howard.

10.3

10.4

10.5

10.6

and so on [10.2].[3] The first new town to be born of these principles was Letchworth in Hertfordshire (1903), with the help of the architect Raymond Unwin [10.3].[4] Letchworth was actually quite different: it was rooted in a strong anti-urban sentiment and symbolized an approach in which 'green' land, detached from any obvious productive or cultural context, was meant to play a major role in town life. Early garden cities in Germany, inspired by the theories of Moritz Schreber, and later influenced by the architects Hermann Muthesius and Heinrich Tessenow, reflected some aspects of Howard's innovations.[5] It is to Howard that we owe the generic term 'green belt', which forms part of the planner's abstract vocabulary for defining suburban limits to this day. The garden city lacked clear references to established landscape archetypes and in this sense it was truly utopian. How such a universal form of greenery, removed from any cultural context and cleansed of its history, was adopted by the Modernists remains an enigma. The Garden City movement failed to deliver concrete solutions to problems of cities prone to increasing land value and sprawl. It coincides with a precise moment in history when landscape disengaged itself from the city core it had so painstakingly conquered a century before.[6]

World War I left in its wake countless human casualties, social and environmental upheaval and a landscape of rural wastelands [10.5]. The unprecedented level of human and environmental annihilation effected a deep change in attitude towards our world. Urban models, such as those developed by Ebenezer Howard in Letchworth and Hampstead before the war, offered small beacons of hope. Raymond Unwin's projects in Britain were praised by Hermann Muthesius, and inspired exchanges with German urban landscape avant-garde figures including Fritz Schumacher, Leberecht Migge and Bruno Taut.[7] In the Horseshoe Estate in Berlin (1925–30), Taut reinterpreted the concept of the radial garden city, but with a much higher density of housing [10.4]. The principles of the garden city were also adapted to developing areas of Hamburg and Berlin with housing projects that provided municipal gardens and new urban parks called Volksparks. The Volksparks were more pragmatic than their 19th-century forerunners, acting as a strong anchor for neighbourhoods and providing a public amenity in areas that had lacked any such benefit. Their design was functionalist, responding to society's need for sport, recreation and local identity. It allowed a geometric 'clearing' of sorts to materialize as gathering places within the growing urban fabric.[8] Their distinctive style was focused on a large, flat central lawn area for games, surrounded by groves of trees planted in regular patterns. The most notable example – which pre-dates the war – is the Stadtpark Hamburg (1914) by Fritz Schumacher [10.6]. It gave character to a new district of Hamburg, providing a large playing field, a lake and other opportunities for leisure.[9] This set a remarkable precedent for the rest of Germany.

10.7

10.8

Attempts to define a resolutely Modernist style of landscape, however, took time. Early Modern gardens were displayed at the Exposition des Arts Décoratifs in Paris (1925), with projects by the architects Gabriel Guevrekian and Paul Vera. A 'Cubist' garden at the Villa Noailles in Hyères (1927) followed, where Guevrekian set an abstract matrix of colourful plantings within a triangular walled promontory offering a splendid sea view [10.7].[10] Yet these isolated experiments had little effect on the general evolution of the Modernist movement that remained seemingly oblivious to questions of landscape. In terms of scale and impact, the Volkspark and garden city survive as the last generic forms of public landscape of the 20th-century city. The banal green of the Siemensstadt (1929–31), designed by Bauhaus architect Walter Gropius in Berlin, marks a break from any previous landscape forms [10.8].[11] The stretches of open and sparsely planted lawns designed by Leberecht Migge for 2,600 tenants retained little of a secular landscape tradition where notions of comfort, appropriation and belonging had prevailed.

The Modernists and CIAM

The ideological precepts of Modernism first established by Le Corbusier and his followers significantly reduced the prominence of landscape architecture and public space in 20th-century urban thinking.[12] Le Corbusier displayed an ambivalent understanding of nature, probably grounded in his childhood in the harsh environment of La Chaux-de-Fonds. The Plan Voisin for Paris (1925) is the illustration of his desire for radical modernity applied to a historic city [10.10]. The entire right bank of Paris would have been razed and replaced by tower blocks and stretches of 'green'.[13] Less brutal – but much more dogmatic – the Ville Radieuse (1933) was an elegant zoning plan for a vertical city laid on an orthogonal road system punctuated by tall housing, office and industry buildings set in green open spaces [10.9]. The project published in the Athens Charter aimed to promote an international style of architecture inspired by a socialist ideology detached from local culture and historical context as established by CIAM (Congrès Internationaux d'Architecture Moderne).[14]

The plan of the Ville Radieuse imitated Ebenezer Howard's ideal city diagram somewhat uncritically, vastly increasing its scale, thereby adding a particularly alienating dimension to the modern city. Le Corbusier first presented the Ville Radieuse at the 1930 third CIAM congress in Brussels on the topic of Rational Land Development as a grid of towering blocks, interspersed with industrial buildings, surrounded by rapid circulation systems set in 'green'. He had just returned from the USSR, where he had presented a similar plan to replace Moscow with an entirely new and unique Modern city.[15] His ink sketch of the Ville Radieuse reveals a rather fantastic scenery, with gigantic trees along broad paths linking distant building blocks with a disquieting loss of

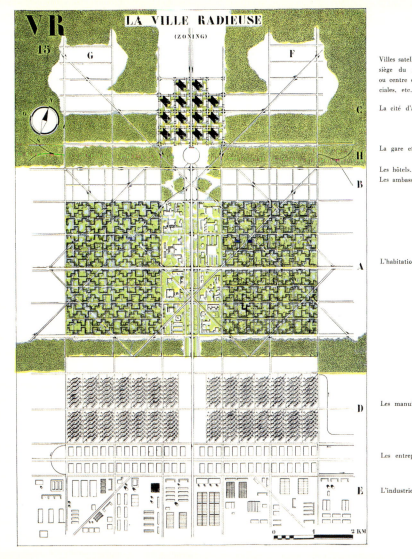

La Ville Radieuse (Zoning)

VR 15

Villes satellites, par ex.: siège du gouvernement ou centre des études sociales, etc.

La cité d'affaires:

La gare et l'aérogare.

Les hôtels.
Les ambassades.

L'habitation.

Les manufactures.

Les entrepôts généraux.

L'industrie lourde.

0   1   2 KM

10.9

10.7 Garden at the Villa Noailles, Hyères, France, by Gabriel Guevrekian, 1927.
This Cubist garden advances like the prow of a ship in the landscape of Provence. The composition plays out two geometries within a triangular garden wall: multiple facets along the walls are symmetrically juxtaposed with a parterre of square beds and pools set in coloured concrete.

10.8 Block of flats at the *Jungfernheideweg* by Walter Gropius, Siemensstadt, Berlin, Germany.
The district laid out following a master plan by Hans Scharoun, 1929, marks the shift from garden city to Modernist town, where landscape is reduced to a barren strip of lawn. Both the Bauhaus and CIAM neglected landscape in their schemes, confusing quantity with quality.

10.9 The Ville Radieuse zoning plan by Le Corbusier, 1933.
Drawn with clockwork mechanical precision, the plan imagines the city of the future as a vast circulation matrix interspersed with tall buildings and green spaces. There is nothing archetypal to be found here, and the project borrows uncritically from the zoning diagrams of Ebenezer Howard developed three decades earlier.

10.10 The Plan Voisin model by Le Corbusier, 1925.
In this model the centre of Paris has been flattened to make way for a high-density neighbourhood with green open space. This iconoclastic project itself became the icon of radical modernity promoted by CIAM.

10.11 Le Corbusier's sketch of the park at the Ville Radieuse.
The landscape no longer refers to any sort of archetype; it is green space without a scale. The discomfort is further enhanced by the diminutive size of people walking under giant trees trying to reach the next building on the horizon.

10.10

10.11

human scale [10.11].[16] Despite the claim that it would consist of 88 per cent parkland and 12 per cent construction, the Ville Radieuse plan shows scant landscape quality in a dense weave of overlapping motorways and streets punctuated by huge towers, each housing more than 1,000 inhabitants. The Modernist utopia professed a clear break from old bourgeois values with an interest in creating friendly and healthier environments, but more often than not produced quite the opposite – something akin to a pedestrian's windswept nightmare. An example is the mass-housing project in Marzahn (1977) in East Berlin, built on the site of an old Romani labour camp in communist DDR [10.12]. Landscapes in these Modernist peripheries were conveniently linked to the progressive social ideologies of authoritarian regimes, which could rid themselves of the burdensome cultural and ideological associations inherited from the previous century.

The frequently made criticism of Modernist utopian projects built after World War II, from Paris to Berlin and Chandigarh to Brasília, it is that they often lacked a sense of belonging and human scale. The pilot plan of Brasília by the architects Lucio Costa and Oscar Niemeyer (1957) was clearly inspired by CIAM principles.[17] The new city gives the impression of a powerful vacuum structured by the automobile, culminating with the Esplanade of Ministries representing the seat of Brazilian government symbolically removed from the city centre and outlying housing areas

[10.13]. It is the failed interaction between human being, building and landscape that remains the core problem of the Modernist utopia: these vast, open spaces, designed with the car in mind, were of course premonitory, yet went unappreciated because they remained approximate at the scale where a sense of memory and appropriation matter most. Because of its renunciation of the past, the International Style promoted by CIAM would have a big impact on architecture and urban development in Europe, the USA and Asia after World War II. This in part explains the continued denigration of landscape architecture as a valid tool of urban design, particularly in the immediate post-war period that was resolutely critical of the past and turned towards progress.

There were positive exceptions. For his utopian Broadacre City project (1932), Frank Lloyd Wright proposed a Midwestern model of suburban development that, in terms of context, remained closer to the original precepts of Ebenezer Howard, who himself had drawn inspiration from his time spent in Nebraska and Chicago [10.14]. But Wright's scheme, far from being universal, was clearly anchored in the specific cultural and territorial context of America and the Jeffersonian grid, and unlike CIAM his design principles were not transferable elsewhere in the world. This is what gave it all its appeal in terms of variegated landscape development.[18]

In Europe, some countries developed an attitude to modern town design that was different from CIAM, while

10.12

10.13

10.14

10.12 The Marzahn estate, Berlin, Germany, 1977.
The estate was built in the communist period of the DDR on the site of an old forced labour camp for Romani and followed CIAM principles closely. Here, as with other Modernist developments across the suburbs of the world, a sense of belonging is lacking, in spite of the availability and abundance of 'public space'.

10.13 Esplanada dos Ministérios, Brasília, Brazil, 1960.
The plan by Lucio Costa and Oscar Niemeyer also followed CIAM principles closely, but what works for fast-moving cars is less successful for pedestrians in the blazing heat of the Brazilian plateau. Viewed on axis from the Cultural Centre, the esplanade conveys a sense of immensity, vacuum and power.

10.14 The utopian city of Broadacre in the American Midwest, 1932.
A futuristic suburban development set within the Land Grant Grid designed by Frank Lloyd Wright, it balances radical innovation with a respect for existing landscape structures including roads, gardens, stadiums and fields. Broadacre offered each family an acre of land and people could move around by car, train or aerogyro.

remaining open to innovation. In Denmark, landscape had its traditional place and was considered unique in its peculiar scale, topography and locality. The campus at Aarhus University, Jutland (1931), designed by Carl Theodor Sørensen to complement the buildings of Kay Fisker, C. F. Møller and Povl Stegmann, is a prime example of this blend of tradition and modernity [10.16].[19] Sørensen carefully integrated the buildings into the rolling landscape of the campus. Oaks were planted as acorns in groves and left to grow. In microcosm, the campus re-created the spirit of a secular Danish oak landscape at the same time as adding modern functions such as rainwater rills and ponds, asphalt paths, parking areas and a green amphitheatre for ceremonies. The critical modernity expressed at Aarhus was in no way formulaic, nor was it universal in its style. Another remarkable modern landscape project is the Skogskyrkogården cemetery in Stockholm, Sweden (1920), designed by the architects Gunnar Asplund and Sigurd Lewerentz.[20] Here an archetypal working with the 'mythical' forest clearing is evident. A long formal alley through a vast open meadow leads up to the modern chapel and crematorium at the edge of the forest [10.15]. The project combines the weight of physical gravity with a sentiment of sorrow, and the tombs scattered through the woods unfold in a different order reminiscent of ancestral, animistic times. This form of culturally rooted landscape sensitivity is precisely what makes early Scandinavian modernity so unique and interesting.

The parkway

The surge in motorized transport called for new roads, which deeply affected our view of landscape. The parkway is an American invention of the late 19th century, and first appeared in its motorized high-speed form on the East Coast in 1906 with the Long Island Motor Parkway.[21] Robert Moses, Park Commissioner of New York in the 1920s, promoted it as a successful motif in landscape aesthetics.[22] The parkway sought to combine the experience of motoring while staging landscape scenery along the drive. The parkways were ground-breaking ways of connecting the suburbs to the city while experiencing the landscape [10.17]. Driving was the expression of radical modernity, since cars were faster than horses, and now able to speed uninterrupted along broad, open parkways connecting the city to natural scenery. The skilful handling of vegetation hid suburban settlements from the driver's view, enhancing the perceived 'naturalness' of the driving experience. This marriage of two opposites – the moving automobile and a 'natural' environment masking the city and lining the road – marked the beginning of an entirely different attitude towards landscape, here understood as a screen.[23]

Ironically, the only real challenge to CIAM's dogmatic position on the generic green spaces of the Ville Radieuse came from Nazi Germany and Hermann Göring, Minister of Forestry in 1933, where the idea of landscape tradition

10.15

10.16

10.17

10.15 The Skogskyrkogården cemetery, Stockholm, Sweden, by Gunnar Asplund and Sigurd Lewerentz, 1920.
Built on the site of old gravel quarries, this is probably one of the most remarkable examples of expressive sacred landscapes of the 20th century. Its subtly crafted contouring plays against a splendid pine forest backdrop. Lewerentz, who worked on the landscape, thought of it as a tranquil environment of pre-Christian beauty.

10.16 A peaceful meadow on the campus at Aarhus University, Denmark.
It is the timeless quality of this project designed by Carl Theodor Sørensen in 1931, at the onset of the modern age, that surprises and delights. Sørensen simply replicated the archetype of a clearing at the heart of the campus. Perhaps landscape architecture does not need to reinvent its motifs for the sake of modernity?

10.17 The Merritt Parkway from New York to New England, USA.
The road opened the hinterland to suburban development and completely changed our relationship to landscape as cars were pushed through suburbia in a tunnel of green.

10.18

10.19

10.18 Naturist women dance in a ring at the Wannsee near Berlin, Germany, 1926.
Gerhard Riebicke promoted *Nacktkultur* (nudism) through photography as early as the 1920s. Nakedness as a way to demonstrate a genuine closeness to nature later became an object of Nazi propaganda.

10.19 The Zeppelinfeld, Nuremberg, Germany, 1936.
This gigantic party rallying ground was one of Albert Speer's first projects for the Nazis. At almost 2 km (1¼ miles) across, the disproportionate scale of this overblown archetype is intended to impress a sense of dominance and power on people at the mass rallies. The bandstand at the centre, 380 metres (1,248 feet) wide, is modelled on the Pergamon Altar, but ten times the size.

10.20 The *Reichsautobahn* over the Bavarian Alps, Germany, designed by Alwin Seifert, 1930s.
Seifert drew influence from the American parkways, but the *Autobahn* became also a tool of racial propaganda, promoting the idea of rapid movement through a scientifically 'authentic' German landscape. Texts on 'German Nature' by Willy Lange promoted this view and served as an ideological basis.

10.21 Aftermath of the atomic bomb, Hiroshima, Japan.
The atomic bomb dropped on 6 August 1945 destroyed 12 sq. km (4.6 sq. miles) of the city in seconds, killing over 150,000 people. The photograph, taken shortly after the explosion, leaves an eerie impression of annihilation. Hiroshima, one of the oldest and most sacred cities of Japan, had just been wiped off the map. Humankind was now able to destroy the physical world as never before.

and natural authenticity was taken very seriously for its ideological and symbolic associations with 'blood and soil' ascendancy.[24] The naturist movement, which had sprung up in Germany and Scandinavia at the turn of the 20th century, showed a marked sympathy for the cult of the healthy naked body immersed in the natural environment [10.18]. This and other, similar movements flirted with notions of Aryan supremacy, as can be seen in the works of Hans Suren and Gerhard Riebicke.[25] Photographs by Riebicke of a ring of naked women dancing in a clearing at the Wannsee near Berlin are far from natural; they are contrived in that they aim to show racial superiority. Naturalist landscape theories were thus drawn into the nationalist cause of Nazi Germany and skilfully mixed with the traditionalist products of the Heimatstil – a style promoted by the architect Paul Schmitthenner and inspired by Heinrich Tessenow that privileged modest materials, pitched roofs and regional characteristics.[26]

Architects and landscape architects under Nazi rule worked assiduously on architectural and landscape styles that would symbolize Aryan ascendancy and the thousand-year Reich. Albert Speer, a student of Tessenow, was its most prominent figure: it was he who designed the Zeppelinfeld stadium in Nuremberg (1936), where massive populist rallies were held each year [10.19]. For the Nazi regime, nature was a highly ideological, symbolic subject, to be utilized at all possible levels of cultural and scientific propaganda. To give one example: in 1934, under Hermann Göring, the concepts of 'German nature' (*deutsche Natur*) and 'German forest' (*deutscher Wald*) became a canvas for nationalistic, anti-modern, racist and biological manipulations.[27]

The Third Reich's head landscape architect under Göring, Alwin Seifert, went as far as to apply notions of purity to plant species, distinguishing for the first time native plants from non-native plants that did not belong to German soil.[28] Despite its supposed scientific objectivity, the concept of separating plants in this arbitrary manner was very much in keeping with other separationist tendencies of the Nazi period. That notwithstanding, this new kind of natural ideology had a lasting effect, and became one of the guiding dogmas of environmental conservation after World War II.[29]

Alwin Seifert also had a hand in developing the first *Reichsautobahn* in Germany (1934–41), when 3,650 km (2,270 miles) of motorway were built. The planning of the motorway took ideological and aesthetic considerations into account, since it was designed to allow Germans to enjoy the country's different iconic landscapes [10.20]. The parkways of Robert Moses certainly inspired Seifert, but the aesthetic theory underpinning the *Reichsautobahn* was, to all intents and purposes, quite different. For instance, Seifert sought to line the motorways with native (*einheimischen*) plants in accordance with Nazi ideology, making this the first

10.20

10.21

known example of an 'ecologically' founded project.[30] In addition, even across the flattest plain of Lower Saxony, the *Reichsautobahn* curved and swayed as it made its way into Hanover. It seems probable that the purpose of these curves was to express the line of beauty so dear to William Hogarth and his followers – a line that could bring even the most boring stretch of scenery to life through the road's swerving course. According to this reading, Seifert indirectly promoted nationalistic propaganda by using the subliminal device of the 'S' curve, thought of as pre-eminently feminine, to bring appeal to even the dullest of German landscapes. More prosaically, it was said that the curves on the *Reichsautobahn* were designed to keep the driver alert.

It is sad to think that pre-war Modernists as a whole failed to grasp the importance of landscape symbolism and identity, or to define an aesthetic position of their own on this vital topic. Why did the Bauhaus and CIAM not challenge the racist theories of National Socialism on this ground and ignore the tremendous potential that a modern landscape movement could offer? Rejecting the secular language of nature entirely as something old fashioned and bourgeois was an obtuse absurdity. Doing otherwise would have certainly helped to counter the Nazis' nationalistic landscape approach, with its concern for the perennial virtues of a 'true' German nature. Because of this failed Modernist debate – and the fact that matters relating to nature conservation

in post-war Germany were overseen by ex-Nazi officials such as Seifert who was elected president of the Bavarian '*Heimatschutz*' (Nature Conservancy) in 1946 – landscape was deemed reactionary and resolutely suspect, losing even more credibility in the progressive eyes of CIAM.[31]

Science and industry reached a historic turning point on 6 August 1945 when the atom bomb, originally conceived to annihilate Nazi Germany, was dropped on Hiroshima instead, wiping it out completely in a matter of seconds [10.21]. This single act of violence was of overwhelming political and humanitarian significance, but also confirmed that a fundamental shift of power had occurred in humankind's overall relationship with nature. When Einstein published his general theory of relativity in 1916, he overturned the centuries-old theory of mechanics. Suddenly all motion became relative, and time and gravity were no longer absolutes.[32] Influential physicists such as Niels Bohr undertook ground-breaking work in quantum mechanics that allowed science to position itself as the principal interpreter of nature. With subsequent advances in a General Systems Theory, first published in 1950,[33] modern science became an all-encompassing field, capable of analysing and acting upon complex environmental situations irrespective of cultural context. This scientific advance significantly altered the perception of landscape and its purpose in relation to the wider natural environment. Science became a religion of sorts, capable not only of measuring natural factors, but also of influencing their course and thus affecting human destiny. Put prosaically, the impact of our faith in the scientific knowledge of nature left a deep and lasting mark. What symbolic role could landscape play in this modern scientific world order?

The masters of landscape

When Mies van der Rohe moved to America his first commission was to design the Resor House in Jackson Hole, Wyoming. There he discovered the overwhelming power of the Grand Teton mountains.[34] He produced a remarkable series of photomontage perspectives showing a minimal dematerialized interior comprised of a full floor-to-ceiling window with four slender cruciform columns. The power of the landscape, particularly the view towards the Grand Tetons, contrasts with the frail, diaphanous frame of the house [10.22]. Such a subdued architectural expression confronted by the American wilderness was in complete rupture with any European tradition. Conventional rules of perspective were inverted, with the highly contrasted view of the mountains substantiating the forefront and modern elegance of the building. It marks a significant shift in the architect's understanding of the bond between interior and exterior; its date of conception – 1939 – is not innocent and can be understood as a definite break from old world values.

The 20th century witnessed the rise of exceptional projects, essentially in the private sphere of garden design. Figures such as Pietro Porcinai in Italy, Thomas D. Church in America and Russell Page in England were able to encapsulate the spirit of Modernism. Their gardens became exquisite icons of the age, like Page's courtyard at the Frick Collection in New York (1977), realized in his later years, which replicated a walled courtyard garden archetype in a modern interpretation [10.23]. But earlier designs, such as Porcinai's garden for the Villa I Collazzi near Florence (1939), were a stark and powerful expression of Fascist ideals.[35] With its minimalist swimming pool lined with quartz, set at the centre of an expansive lawn framed by tall cypresses, it leaves a lasting impression of power [10.25]. This sober jewel embodies in its reductive essence the spirit of late 1930s rationalist design. But Porcinai was suspected of being a Fascist sympathizer, as was his Italian architect colleague Giuseppe Terragni.

The first American Modernist garden, untainted by the ideological struggles in Europe, was by Thomas D. Church in California.[36] In his distinguished work for private residences such the Donnell House in Sonoma, Napa Valley (1948), through his radically modern garden design, Church paid particular attention to the wider integration of the landscape, in this case some coast live oaks in an existing stand [10.24]. Rather than replicating an archetype, his garden forms were inspired by modern art, among others the work of Jean Arp.[37]

10.22

10.23

10.24

10.22 The Resor House, Wyoming, USA, by Ludwig Mies van der Rohe, 1939.
The discovery of the 'untainted' American wilderness of the Grand Tetons impressed Mies van der Rohe on his arrival at Jackson Hole, Wyoming. And the impact of the striking contrast between the frail minimalism of his house and the sheer magnitude and force of nature would never leave him. Centuries of codified cultural history from the old world vanished for him overnight.

10.23 Garden courtyard at the Frick Collection, New York, USA, by Russell Page, 1977.
The elegance of the garden walled on three sides taps into a familiar tradition and archetype. The rectangular pool at its centre and the delicate dappled shade of trees take us back to times immemorial and a paradise long lost.

10.24 The Donnell Garden, Napa Valley, California, USA, by Thomas D. Church, 1948.
The most famous icon of Modernist Californian landscape design, the pool's organic shape hewn into a hillside of coast live oaks overlooks the northern reaches of San Francisco Bay. The sculpture by Adaline Kent gives a sense of scale, and sets the tone for this pragmatic design meant for family life, relaxation and parties.

10.25 Garden at Villa I Collazi, Italy, by Pietro Porcinai, 1939.
Set in a historic garden framed by old cypresses and low trimmed boxwood hedges, the grey and white quartzite pool stands ominously at the centre of a vast green lawn like a rare gem. The stone trim recalls the austere Italian architectural style in vogue at that period; although minimal it is clearly an expression of absolute power.

10.25

10.26

10.27

10.26 The UNESCO Garden, Paris, France, by Isamu Noguchi, completed 1958.
Blending fragments of different landscape cultures into a common whole, elements of Japanese gardens are slotted into a larger walled frame, bound on one side by a cascade. The garden, built barely thirteen years after the bombing of Hiroshima, attempts to celebrate landscape as a form of universal culture.

10.27 The Parque del Este, Caracas, Venezuela, by Roberto Burle Marx, 1961.
The painterly plan reminiscent of the works of Joan Miró, Jean Arp and Henri Matisse, uses intertwined biomorphic shapes to define areas of activity and circulation. It is a project that breaks away from the weight of Latin American tradition by proposing a radically new form of space and vegetation. With its 82 hectares (200 acres) and diverse programme, it has become the most popular park in town.

10.28 Roberto Burle Marx's private hillside garden in Sitio near Rio de Janeiro, Brazil, 1950.
The garden was Burle Marx's laboratory for an extraordinary palette of Modernist compositions, which he then applied to a variety of projects. His work was particularly bold and refreshing, and since he was also a painter, his use of plants followed form, colour and texture.

10.29 *Double Negative*, Nevada, USA, by Michael Heizer, 1969–70.
Located in the high desert, *Double Negative* is a statement about the 'negative' effects of humans on their environment. Two huge trenches were excavated in a line, requiring the removal of 250,000 tons of rocks. The gap between the two trenches creates a void or absence – a negative.

10.30 *Tanner Fountain*, Harvard University, USA, by Peter Walker, 1984.
The fountain, with its 159 granite boulders set loosely in a ring, spreads over asphalt and lawn and under trees and uses mist sprinklers at its heart. It borrows from minimalist artist Carl Andre's work entitled *Stone Field Sculpture* from 1977.

10.28

10.29

10.30

In the post-war period Isamu Noguchi and Roberto Burle Marx created works of refreshing novelty. Noguchi's UNESCO Garden in Paris (1958) blended an understated Japanese garden aesthetic with a Western abstract approach to sculpted space [10.26]. It fused tradition and modernity together, affirming a new faith in humanity.[38] The artist botanist Burle Marx produced projects throughout Latin America in the 1950s and 1960s. His painterly manner revealed a love for nature in modern plant assemblages in a surprising reinterpretation of Brazilian culture. For Burle Marx, the post-war world had to be reinvented, and projects like the famous ocean front promenade at Copacabana were a leap into modernity. The Parque del Este in Caracas (1961) was a radical departure from conventional park stylistics, comprising three major areas of undulating grass fields with a lake, a forest with densely meandering paths and a Cubist garden [10.27].[39] His private studio in Sitio (1950), near Rio de Janeiro, is an exuberant botanical repertoire of 3,500 tropical plant species arranged in a luxuriant garden on the slopes of the estate [10.28].

The land art movement that appeared in the 1960s and 1970s, whose rugged style was markedly oblivious to nostalgic reinterpretations of nature, was initiated by emblematic figures such as Robert Smithson, Walter De Maria, James Turrell and Michael Heizer. The movement remained a predominantly American phenomenon, confined to barren stretches of the West, devoid of obvious cultural ties and offering a setting for conceptual experimentation with earthworks.[40] Double Negative (1969–70) by Michael Heizer, located in South Nevada, is emblematic of the period. A pair of mirrored trenches is carved directly into rhyolite cliffs overlooking the Virgin River Mesa. The abstract piece plays with the 'absence' set in between the positive and negative space of the two excavated trenches, which are beginning to erode [10.29].

One offshoot of the land art movement was a trend launched by the landscape architect Peter Walker in the early 1980s called 'landscape as art'. It drew inspiration directly from conceptual artists such as Carl Andre and Andy Goldsworthy, whose works were reinterpreted to fit common landscape projects including car parks, urban plazas and rooftops. The Tanner Fountain (1984) located on the Harvard campus is probably the most emblematic and successful 'minimalist' project of that movement [10.30].[41] Designed by Peter Walker in collaboration with the sculptor Joan Brigham as an art installation, it used boulders set in asphalt animated by lawn sprinklers. The fountain has become a casual place to meet for students. This trend later found resonance in Europe, particularly Germany, England and the Netherlands, and was seen as a reaction to the nascent environmentalist movement which condemned landscape aesthetics as something unnatural and formalistic.

10.31

10.32

Progress in the post-war period

The rise of mechanized modernity happened without much understanding for old world values epitomized by the Arcadian project of the artist Ian Hamilton Finlay and his wife Sue Finlay in Little Sparta near Dunsyre (1966) [10.35].[42] With its Classical citations carved in stone set in the landscape of the Pentland Hills of Scotland, the work was anachronistic, but it strongly influenced Postmodern landscape architecture in Europe, particularly the work of Dieter Kienast. Meanwhile countless suburban developments were created across Europe for logistical convenience, transport and economy rather than inherent landscape qualities. The iconoclastic film *Mon Oncle* (1958), by Jacques Tati, pinpoints with acerbic precision the absurdity of modern suburban living at the time [10.31]. Copenhagen, with its green 'finger plan' (begun in 1947), as well as Stockholm and Helsinki were the exceptions; their central park systems incorporated larger visionary landscape schemes for the periphery. This is when Sørensen's remarkable Cubist hedge garden in Herning, Jutland (1956), became an icon of Scandinavian modern landscapes [10.32].[43] The Hansaviertel in Berlin (1957–61), developed by the architect Hans Scharoun and landscape architect Hermann Mattern, demonstrated a mix of radical modernity in architecture and eclectic naturalism in landscape, serving as critical reference to Germany's past. In France, however, most architectural offices dogmatically followed the precepts of CIAM after

the war. According to Michel Corajoud, who worked at the Atelier d'Urbanisme et d'Architecture (AUA), green spaces were directly drawn on to a plan without any prior site visit. This absence of site reconnaissance led to projects of inherently poor quality.[44] The Parc du Sausset (1980–2000) on the northern outskirts of Paris was an attempt to compensate for CIAM planning in the area through a more traditional form of landscape. Claire Corajoud, Michel Corajoud and their team developed the 160-hectare (395-acre) park into four parts, planting a forest of 100,000 trees interspersed with large archetypal clearings [10.36].[45]

In America, these were times of unbounded social optimism. Garrett Eckbo and Dan Kiley, who were trained as Modernist landscape architects by Walter Gropius at Harvard, responded to the demands of corporate design and private housing.[46] Eckbo produced no fewer than 300 private residential gardens in Los Angeles, mixing modern materials like concrete, wood and steel in resolutely modern designs. The East Farm project (1951) in Vermont by Kiley is probably his most understated yet iconic example of the modern rustic garden that became his brand [10.33]. One rare example of successful Modernist public housing space is Lafayette Park in Detroit (1956–63) by Alfred Caldwell with the architects Mies van der Rohe and Ludwig Hilberseimer. It blends the scale of tall buildings with an open archetypal space comprised of woodlands interspersed by clearings [10.34].[47]

10.31 Scene from the film *Mon Oncle* by Jacques Tati, 1958.
Tati's film anatomizes the day-to-day drawbacks of French consumerist modernity. Set In a suburban house and garden full of dysfunctional contraptions, it turns every detail of daily life into humour.

10.32 Geometrical Gardens, Herning, Denmark, by Carl Theodor Sørensen, 1956.
Sørensen's project is part of a larger sculpture garden, where the play with scale and interior and exterior has a striking archetypal force. The interlocked patterns of hedges are both traditional and radical in their overt playfulness.

10.33 East Farm, Green Mountains, Charlotte, Vermont, USA, by Dan Kiley, 1951.
The regular structure of the terraces is both archetypal and modern. Together with Richard Rose and Garrett Eckbo, Dan Kiley, is one of the founding fathers of Modernist landscape architecture in America.

10.34 Lafayette Park, Detroit, USA, 1963.
Designed by Alfred Caldwell, with Mies van der Rohe and Ludwig Hilberseimer as architects, the 30-hectare (74-acre) project with its 7-hectare (17-acre) park embodied the hopes and spirit of Urban Renewal, with particular attention given to public and semi-private spaces.

10.35 Little Sparta, Dunsyre, Scotland, by Ian Hamilton Finlay and Sue Finlay, 1966.
The garden assembles 270 works that reflect Finlay's moral and philosophical intentions, and openly question contemporary political values. The 2-hectare (5-acre) setting allows for the artist's garden poems carved in stone to be displayed against the Scottish Arcadian hillside.

10.36 Parc du Sausset, Villepinte, France, by Claire Corajoud and Michel Corajoud, 1980–2000.
The 'clearing in the clearing' is the most intimate and secret part of this park of 160 hectares (395 acres) in the *banlieue* north-east of Paris. The archetype of the clearing returns in full force in this piece of French Postmodernist landscape.

10.33

10.34

10.35

10.36

10.37

Parc de la Villette, France

Together with the Schouwburgplein in Rotterdam by the office of West 8 [10.37], one remarkable project of late 20th-century Deconstructivist landscape architecture stands out. The Parc de la Villette (1984), in north-east Paris, epitomizes an ambitious conceptual approach to design through the concentrated overlay of functions and site programme upon a single plan [10.38]. Constructed on the site of a disused slaughterhouse and cattle market, the project transformed this industrial relic alongside the Boulevard Périphérique into a new kind of public experience. The park, designed by the architect Bernard Tschumi, remained true to many Modernist principles by seeking to detach itself from the weight of history, context and traditional landscaping. With the support of philosophers such as Jacques Derrida, Tschumi promoted the application of a radical style that would erase any reference to archetypal forms of nature; the park wilfully disregarded any romantic appendages [10.39a, 10.39b].[48]

The purpose of the Parc de la Villette is hard to grasp at first sight – it tries to create a place with no historical precedent, deliberately breaking away from habitual references to landscape architecture and shattering established spatial conventions through a 'cinematic' apprehension of space [10.41]. Tschumi's quest for a completely new identity was in line with the multi-layered and fragmented urban reality of the site. The spatial quality of the park is based essentially on human experience and shifts in scale. Although strongly axial and geometric in feel, the layout of the park remains disconcerting for the first visitor because the intertwined paths and bitty spaces create a kaleidoscopic effect that seldom matches the clarity of the plan [10.40].

The systematic overlay of a regular grid of red 'follies' on the 55-hectare (136-acre) park, combined with convoluted paths and fragmented surfaces, lends a deconstructed, serial character to the project that is in keeping with the dominant trends in art and philosophy of the time [10.45].[49] The grid of follies has a huge effect on the visitor's sense of scale and orientation. For instance, the scenic promise offered by the 'cinematic' path turns out to be diminutive in scale. The moments of surprise one would expect to find strewn along the way don't always match the narrative thread of the place [10.44]. This betrays an inherent flaw in the park's management of the project's initial programmatic ambition, where the serial complexity promised by all the follies looked good. Tschumi's idea of combining function and purpose through a complex web of points, lines and planes was inspired by Bauhaus artist Wassily Kandinsky [10.48, 10.49].

10.37 The Schouwburgplein, Rotterdam, The Netherlands, at night.
Designed in 1996 by Adriaan Geuze and his office, West 8, the Schouwburgplein quickly became an icon of late Deconstructivist landscape architecture. Made essentially of metal, rubber and wood, the roof garden of 1.2 hectares (3 acres) boasts a complete absence of vegetation and trees; instead, three giant red swivelling and bending lights animate the square.

10.38 Plan of the Parc de la Villette, Paris.
Built along a canal on the site of an old cattle market and slaughterhouse, the park comprises a grid of red follies interwoven by 'cinematic' paths following a logic of points, lines and planes. It offers various attractions and events in what appear to be archetypal fragments of clearings and squares.

10.38

10.39a

10.39b

10.40

10.39a, 10.39b Reconstructed before and after views of the Parc de la Villette.
Initially, the cattle market and slaughterhouse stood on an open industrial site; the park, designed by Bernard Tschumi, with its 35 red follies, then appears. A considerable number of new buildings are added along the Périphérique ring road, so that first impressions are more of a new town than a park.

10.40 Aerial view of the Parc de la Villette.
Set against the backdrop of the Boulevard Périphérique and the *banlieue* districts of Aubervilliers and Bobigny, the park is a manifest statement of Deconstructivist design, with a grid of red follies confirming the overwhelming urban character of the area. The green spaces appear just as fragmented as the rest of the area crossed by roads, railways and canals.

10.41 The main north–south axis, or Galerie de la Villette.
A conventional planting of tree alignments has been replaced by a continuous undulating tensile structure. Open day and night, it provides shelter, light and shade to those visiting the Grande Halle across the way. Planting is kept to a strict minimum.

10.42 The Folie du Canal, Parc de la Villette.
This emblematic *folie* is reflected in the Canal de l'Ourcq and is bisected by a raised pathway that symbolically links Paris to the *banlieue*. The trees planted in the Prairie du Cercle have grown since this photograph was taken two decades ago; the site has also become more urban in character, with a massive new Philharmonic built.

10.41

10.42

10.43

The most obvious aspect of the project is its grid of bright-red follies placed at regular intervals across the park, which are meant to 'activate' each location as a substitute for more traditional vistas [10.42].

The overall impression left by the Parc de la Villette is of a place held together by a dense landscape structure of follies, organized in a combination of circulation routes and functions that reveal the spirit of the times. The open green surfaces that hem the multiple pathways feel like broken remnants of a forgotten whole [10.50]. The great circular lawn, visible at the centre of the section, is cut in half by an existing canal; the elements are clearly defined, but don't always connect [10.52]. The triangular lawn to the east of the Great Market Hall is the most successful area in the park, suitable for games, gatherings and multiple events. The park provides an oasis for the urban dweller, and favours human experience and interaction over contact with nature. The Parc de la Villette thus refuses romantic idealization and chooses instead to heighten an already existing urban disruption of place [10.43]. All things considered, setting a park in this difficult post-industrial context was no easy task, but applying the 'point, line and plane' overlay method – normally used by engineers in descriptive geometry – to the scale of an entire site overcomplicated matters tremendously [10.49].[50] The park is rapidly urbanizing on the fringes and has fallen victim to its own programmatic and conceptual ambitions. It is interesting to note that this programmatic overlay method invented by Bernard Tschumi became the trademark of an entire genre of landscape mapping in the decades that followed.

The Parc de la Villette represents a moment of strong stylistic affirmation rather than 'natural' expression, but it leaves the essential question of a possible role for nature in the city unanswered [10.48]. In summer, the park is animated day and night, hosting an abundance of concerts, outdoor cinema and cultural events that make it popular with young visitors. In this respect, the Parc de la Villette fulfils its cultural ambition entirely and can be understood as the last in a long lineage of 'pre-ecological' parks focused essentially on Parisian lifestyle. Although announced by its designer as a revolutionary park for the 21st century, it has remained an exception rather than a model for subsequent projects [10.51]. There must be a reason for this; and criticisms of the park's poor public image and security and maintenance issues cannot be solely blamed on the design itself, but rather on the proximity of the *banlieue* ghettos. At best, the Parc de la Villette is an interesting relic of an expensive 20th-century architectural utopia, out of touch with current ecological needs and the simple expectations of a populous neighbourhood. The Cité de la Musique, with its new philharmonic designed by Jean Nouvel, is expanding along the Boulevard Périphérique, confirming what Tschumi said all along: the park will deconstruct, becoming an entirely new piece of city.

10.43 The Fontaine des Brouillards designed by Alain Pellissier, 1987.
At the heart of the park, the fountain offered a wild and unique experience for the visitor. The fog generated was at times so thick that people strolling by would occasionally be robbed, making the situation too difficult to control in a public open space and the fountain was subsequently closed down.

10.44, 10.45 Two views along the 'cinematic' path.
A triplet of stainless steel rubbish bins are wedged into a solid granite bench, and the Garden of Mirrors creates the impression of a forest from a few reflected trees. The diminutive scale of the path, understood as the thematic backbone of the park, produces a feeling of awkwardness and questions the Deconstructivist spirit of the place.

10.46, 10.47 Two reconstructed views of the park.
The first view looks over the Alley of the Belvedere, and some of the follies, with the Prairie du Triangle in the middle ground, where numerous events are staged. The other shows the point where the Canal de l'Ourcq intersects with the Prairie du Cercle.

10.44

10.45

10.46

10.47

11. Terrain Vague

'The task of perception involves pulverizing the world, but also spiritualizing its dust.'
Gilles Deleuze, *The Fold: Leibnitz and the Baroque*[1]

The fragmentation of 20th-century territory created a phenomenon that prevails in almost all cultural and geographical contexts: the *terrain vague*. The *terrain vague* is the by-product of our age, in which outrageous violence done to a particular strip of ground results in the obliteration and amalgamation of traces. The term, adopted by Ignasi de Solà-Morales, designates a ground condition that has been subject to uncontrolled aggression and subsequent dilapidation.[2] As such, it is the complete antithesis of conscious landscape design, though clearly the work of humans. It is not a picturesque terrain with romantic ruins evoking the beauty of ancient glories, but, rather, a ground zero of complete cultural and environmental annihilation in the age of the 'Anthropocene', characterized by severely eroded and often contaminated land.[3] The site of Dungeness on the coast of Kent in England, near Derek Jarman's cottage, where a general sentiment of natural and human desolation prevails, comes to mind [11.0]. *Terrain vague* is about failing care and disrepair, about land that expresses no particular quality *per se*. It forms the most abstract and unnatural kinds of landscape: a piece of ground straddling the aftermath of successive depredations in the unlikelihood of future promise.

The term *terrain vague* is itself oxymoronic: *terrain*, meaning 'ground' in French, expresses the impact of successive human and mechanical acts. This might be visible in a layer of detritus covering the ground, comprising pieces of plastic, shards of glass, rusted metal, bone and so on. The work *Untilled* (2012) by the artist Pierre Huyghe at Documenta 13 in Kassel shows a reclining figure with a beehive set on the uncultivated ground of a refuse site [11.1].[4] The amorphous topography feels suspect, it betrays a history of upheavals that undermine its stability. The

11.0 (opposite) A column made from a piece of driftwood, Prospect Cottage, Dungeness, England.
The meaning of a landscape depends not only on its perception, but also on how it is acted upon and transformed through the unlikely poetics of place, as in the case of Derek Jarman who chose to make this his last garden.

11.1 Concrete figure of a reclining woman with a live beehive on her head, *Untilled*, by Pierre Huyghe, 2012.
Created for Documenta 13 in Kassel, this work, set in a *terrain vague* of sorts, makes a strong statement about our relationship with simple natural phenomena such as bees, from which we have become completely estranged.

11.1

11.2

11.3

11.4

11.5

11.2 A landscaped rubbish dump in the Netherlands, photographed by Bas Princen.
The lunar quality of the artificial mound attracts bikers who see in the slope a great opportunity to train. The people appear tall next to dwarfed trees on a severely eroded terrain, contributing to the awkward aesthetic of this *terrain vague*.

11.3 A slum of 'zoniers' near the Porte d'Italie, Paris, France, by Eugène Atget, 1913.
The poorest people lived here amidst detritus and dereliction. The *terrain vague* is always the mirror of an indigent human condition; it is where landscape and misery meet, producing this culture of poverty captured so well in Atget's photographic aesthetic.

11.4 Yosemite National Park, USA, by Ansel Adams, 1935.
It is through highly technical black-and-white photography rather than painting that the American wilderness aesthetic, with its roots in Greek philosophy, took hold in the public mind in the 20th century. Adams's images were widely published in the American press to promote National Parks.

11.5 The post-war suburbs of Rome, Italy, by Henri Cartier-Bresson.
A *terrain vague* is not only the human by-product of difficult social conditions, it also results from the upheavals of a highly technical society in which the powers of architecture and engineering stop short of making landscape. The complete absence of concern for soil and vegetation contributes to a general sense of abandonment.

11.6 *The Fountain Monument – Side View* from Robert Smithson's *A Tour of the Monuments of Passaic, New Jersey*, 1967
A row of pipes draining water into the Passaic River: Smithson's written observations describe nearby bulldozers as 'prehistoric creatures trapped in the mud' or 'extinct machines'.

11.7 A *terrain vague* in Catalonia by Jean-Marc Bustamante, mid-1980s.
The irony of this scene is that everything in the foreground is either man-made or man-induced unwittingly. The *terrain vague* has a destructive logic and power of its own that makes it look alike anywhere in the world.

11.6

11.7

term *vague*, 'elusive' in French, means that the piece of land is both anonymous and collective, as well as defiant and circumstantial. It reminds one of the view of a Dutch rehabilitated rubbish dump (2005) taken by Bas Princen representing landscape in a perpetual state of abstraction that encourages experimentation and creativity [11.2]. The 'vague' quality of a landscape resides in the fact that it cannot be attributed to a single hand or creator, but is an accidental product of surrounding human forces. The ambiguity of these sites is as pervasive as their ubiquity: cultureless and placeless, the *terrain vague* looks identical no matter where it is found.

Terrain vague is a universal artefact, yet always signifies a specific epoch, as in the depiction by the French artist Jean-Marc Bustamante of *Tableau 55A* (1982) showing a site under transformation in Catalonia [11.7]. *Terrain vague* combines two words that hint at an uncomfortable wave of uncertainty on what ought to be *terra firma*. The two terms put together express both an end and a turning point: an end because one instinctively seeks to limit the annihilation of a landscape; and a turning point because of the paradigm shift in aesthetic appreciation that such a place endorses, pushing the potential to act further. *Terrain vague* marks a finality: the 'mud bottom' of civilization. There is no easy return to nature from the Gomorrah of a *terrain vague*, even though we are repeatedly asked to create landscapes that somehow reinstate a pristine form of nature, or a semblance thereof.

Terrain vague has not only caused a shift, but also effected a profound, and very critical, transformation of our appreciation of landscape aesthetics.[5] It has crippled our ability to design conventionally and relegated our two original archetypes to the distant past. However, it is by no means a new phenomenon. We find artistic eulogies of desolation in the photography of Charles Marville and Eugène Atget, who elevated proletarian squalor to the highest level of poetic representation [11.3]. Atget depicted a slum of Paris (1913) with as much vigour and artistic persuasion as Ansel Adams when he photographed the American wilderness for the establishment of protected National Parks (1935) [11.4].[6] Through literature, photography, film and art, the *terrain vague* went on to acquire an extraordinary poetic presence in the latter part of the 20th century. The photographs of the land artist Robert Smithson, taken along the Passaic River in New Jersey (1967) a century after Marville's records of Paris, elevated the most wretched signs of industrial decrepitude and environmental dejection to the level of picturesque rusticity and elegance [11.6].[7] Bolstered by photography and film, particularly the wave of Neo-realism of the 1950s and 1960s, the *terrain vague* aesthetic, epitomized in Henri Cartier-Bresson's depictions of the periphery of Rome, transgressed all national boundaries and, with its potent nihilistic vision, came to symbolize the aftermath of modernity [11.5].

Ecological upheaval

The destructive forces exemplified in the *terrain vague* caused observers to question the roots and purpose of the prevailing canons of landscape architecture. As an indirect result, a plethora of artistic and philosophical interpretations – combined with new ecological and environmental pressures – provoked a schism in landscape architecture at the beginning of the 1970s. The artist Joseph Beuys, for instance, promoted ecological consciousness through a polemic project called *7000 Oaks* (1982) in which the very act of tree planting became the symbol of anti-establishment rebellion [11.9].[8] In the midst of such ideological upheavals, many landscape architects abandoned a secular artistic design tradition, and proclaimed themselves 'nature-makers' and environmental healers whose remit was endorsed by 'objective' scientific evidence.

The remarkable efforts of the environmental movement promoting nature conservation were taken as a starting point in computer science for those seeking to develop 'design methods'. The Delmarva project (1967), using the SYMAP system developed by Professor Carl Steinitz at Harvard, produced the first computerized series of analytical landscape maps inspired by the methods of Ian McHarg [11.8].[9] This marriage of extremes between ecological convictions and positive faith in computer science gave birth to modern-day GIS technology.[10] The promise of a return to nature, combined with a concern for desolate wastelands, gave birth through the action of the Dutchman Louis Le Roy to the ruderal movement in Europe.[11] The word 'ruderal' comes from the Latin *rudus*, meaning 'rubbish', and in this sense refers to rubble. The new ideology advocated complete design abstinence, whereby aesthetic issues were considered irrelevant. In fact, any form of human intervention in ruderal environments was considered with suspicion. The Schöneberger Südgelände (1945–99) experiment that took place in a bombed-out rail yard in Berlin is probably the most emblematic project of this peculiar kind of early 'landscape ecology', where the prohibition of any human presence over decades allowed for the unbridled, spontaneous growth of vegetation to occur undisturbed, creating a parallel world completely detached from the common urban reality of Berlin [11.10].[12]

Leftover landscapes

Extraordinary ruderal experiments took place in Germany during the 1970s, in places like Berlin, Duisburg and Essen, where abandoned industrial sites were left to grow into urban jungles from another age. They posed a serious challenge to the history of gardens, maintaining that landscape archetypes were obsolete, formal and non-ecological. Under the pretext of a return to an 'original' nature – which was in fact unattainable – designers began to speculate awkwardly about the rightful place of native versus non-native species within their schemes. They could justify this discriminatory attitude

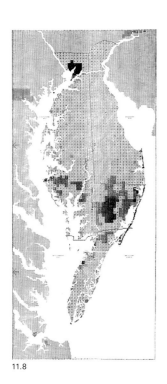

11.8

11.9

11.10

11.8 Delmarva Peninsula Project maps, 1967.
This is the first map using SYMAP (Synographic Mapping System) produced by Carl Steinitz at the Laboratory for Computer Graphics and Spatial Analysis founded by Howard Fischer at Harvard. The landscape analysis was grid based and influenced nascent geographic information system (GIS) technology.

11.9 Joseph Beuys with volunteers tree planting, 1982.
The project for Documenta 7 in Kassel entitled *7000 Oaks* (*7000 Eichen – Stadtverwaldung statt Stadtverwaltung*) played with words, confounding 'city forestation' with 'city administration'. Seven thousand oaks were planted, each with an upright basalt stone next to it. The oaks live on and contributed to growing ecological consciousness.

11.10 The Schöneberger Südgelände rail yard, Berlin, Germany, transformed into a 'nature park', 1945–99.
After this 18-hectare (45-acre) site was bombed in World War II, decades of uncontrolled natural growth were encouraged by forbidding all human access. Nature gradually reclaimed the site as a so-called '*Urwald*' ('forest of the origins'). By the mid-1980s, in theory, an original Brandenburg biome would have grown there, but ecologists did not take into account the seeds carried in over time by countless trains. The result was a stunning and unexpected mix of vegetation, both foreign and native. Urban ecology had to be rewritten. This peculiar blend of 'ruderal' rail yard aesthetics and spontaneous vegetation would influence a range of landscape projects, including the High Line in New York.

11.11

towards a longstanding horticultural tradition since they now embraced the higher truth of a science of 'designed nature'.

Landscape architects started experimenting with various forms of nature relating to ecology. One of the more remarkable and courageous examples is the General Mills Entry Landscape in Minneapolis (1991) by the office of Michael Van Valkenburgh [11.11]. In this project located at the General Mills corporate headquarters, seasonal burning became part of the annual maintenance to encourage the growth of rare native prairie grasses and flowers. The native grassland planted with Heritage River birch trees was meant as a proactive statement about the vanishing original prairie; it was demolished by the client after only a decade. Cultural distinctions in matters of landscape symbolism have been inherited from the remote past, but whether prairie burning befits a corporate image in an age of climate change remains debatable. Beyond the discussion surrounding this new faith in ecology, *terrain vague* must be thought of positively as an opportunity rather than an end – a starting point for a landscape of another kind. The Lüneberg Heath in northern Germany is an interesting case in point. It is probably one of the oldest *terrains vagues* of sorts in Europe [11.12].[13] Systematically deforested and overgrazed since Neolithic times, and after thousands of years of environmental abuse, its eroded heath strewn with beautiful patches of heather now stands as one of the most celebrated 'natural' treasures of

Germany. Understanding the *terrain vague* as a potential tool for transforming our approach to nature will challenge many of our preconceptions of ecology and design. The task that lies ahead has less to do with historical references or plant 'nativeness' than with invention through a form of creative destruction, tapping future landscape potential in unexpected combinations and situations.[14]

New hope
Tommy Thompson Park (2005) in Toronto is an example of the regeneration of a derelict site – in this case a dredge heap – through biodiversity of a new order. The 'Urban Wilderness Park', occupying a long spit of contaminated dredge material on the shore of Lake Ontario, has become one of the most valuable wildlife habitats in the region [11.13].[15] But beyond its ecological merits, it has also attained an almost mythological status among city dwellers by transcending persistent, habitual tales of environmental degradation and dismay as portrayed in Rachel Carson's book *Silent Spring*.[16] It is as though the wildlife that returned to the site washed away some of the city's past sins. Thanks to the work of landscape architect James Corner and his office, Field Operations, Tommy Thompson Park has now been incorporated into the larger Lake Ontario Park project, and public access will be monitored in order to preserve wildlife diversity. The scheme provides a good example of

11.11 General Mills Entry Landscape, Minneapolis, USA, by Michael Van Valkenburgh, 1991.
The seasonal burning of a reconstituted native grassland area took place annually in front of the General Mills corporate headquarters. This radical project, alluding to the loss of native grassland to cereal production, applied a strong ecological principle directly on site. Although it was relatively short-lived, it demonstrated the power of applied ecology in landscape design.

11.12 A hillside of purple heather at the Lüneburg Heath, Lower Saxony, Germany.
The heath results from environmental abuse from logging, clearing and overgrazing since Neolithic times. Despite its tragic history and the complete disappearance of original forest, it is one of the best-known symbols of natural beauty in Germany. Could it be that ecology, nature and beauty are all just constructs in the making?

11.13 Tommy Thompson Park, Toronto, Canada, 2005.
Originally the site of a 5-km (3-mile) long spit retaining dredged waste composed of contaminated sand and silt from the inner harbour, this is a story of *terrain vague* turning into an 'accidental wilderness'. Designed by Field Operations as a public park, it now forms the largest bird sanctuary of Lake Ontario.

11.12

11.13

11.14

11.14 The Reserva Ecológica Costanera Sur, Buenos Aires, Argentina, 1982.
The reserve was planned originally as the locus of government buildings under the military junta in the 1970s, but history has had it otherwise.

11.15 *Arches* by Andy Goldsworthy at Gibbs Farm, New Zealand, 2005.
The appearance of archaic dislocated ruins from a lost civilization, set against an entirely natural coastal backdrop, plays with a strongly picturesque idea of landscape and culture.

11.16 Gilles Clément, Creuse, France.
Clément's concept of 'The Garden in Movement' promotes a vision of nature without 'racial' connotations. To him plants are dynamic natural forces competing with each other, rather than belonging to a scientific classified native identity.

11.17 Temporary community gardens, Hardturm stadium, Zurich, Switzerland.
Abandoned and subject to ill-fated urban developments, the site has become a place for community interaction. Flowers and vegetables are grown in carefully tended containers.

11.15

11.16

11.17

environmental redemption, whereby a new form of nature has returned to a formerly impoverished site of dejection.

Another extraordinary example of natural regeneration is the Costanera Sur Ecological Reserve (1982) in Buenos Aires, Argentina [11.14]. Huge amounts of rubble from buildings demolished for new motorways were used as landfill on a site offshore. The military junta had planned that this area would become the new seat of government but it was left unfinished after the Falklands War. This piece of landfill gradually became a mute symbol of all the oppression and destruction that Buenos Aires had suffered during the years of terror. The area, covering 400 hectares (990 acres), was spontaneously colonized by wind-blown flora from the Pampas and water-borne flora from the Parana River. Today it has become an 'untouched' urban jungle and a vital symbol of redemption in the city's history. The fact that this improbable refuge was never a product of human design, but rather the result of negligence, is a moral lesson: it reminds us that nature can recover from political tyranny to embody social justice. Both the Toronto and Buenos Aires examples point to a complete absence of design, as if conscious aesthetic choices no longer mattered in appropriate landscape design.

Following the premonitory warnings of *The Limits to Growth* (1972), climate change was acknowledged in the first IPCC report (1990), and has led to an unstable situation in which the founding myth of a nurturing 'mother' nature has run aground with the prospect of much more threatening and destructive natural forces.[17] Two attitudes towards nature now prevail: one of melancholy and abandonment; the other of engagement and active adaptation. These attitudes are inherently contradictory. The first sees the inevitability of natural ruin as an aesthetic goal in its own right. It is epitomized by the artistic arrangements of Andy Goldsworthy such as his stone arcade at Gibbs Farm in New Zealand (2005) [11.15]. This project is both easy to understand and very picturesque, but it offers few solutions for future challenges. The second attitude strives for active adaptation and is harder to grasp: it calls for a new mode of landscape intervention. Certain protagonists like Gilles Clément claim that this change of attitude must be more local and active [11.16].[18] Through 'The Garden in Movement' he promotes a transformed relationship to nature in which human interaction plays an essential role. We may thus uncover a new language of nature by anticipating problems with humility in preparation for changes to come. When confronted with desolation, there is always a chance to cultivate a new garden. This is the case of the temporary gardens on the *terrain vague* of the abandoned Hardturm stadium in Zurich (2014). The small-scale family garden is, after all, a familiar cultural trope, a handiwork that represents perhaps humankind's most ancient productive and immediate relationship with a form of humanized nature in the making [11.17].

11.18

Prospect Cottage, England

When the artist-filmmaker Derek Jarman began his makeshift garden at Prospect Cottage in Dungeness, he knew little about gardening. With determination, however, he began to gather fragments of flotsam found on the shore to create a refreshing aesthetic that intuitively reinterpreted the art of topiary.[19] What drove Jarman towards this venture was a personal quest for meaning amid a sense of finality – the result of a terminal diagnosis. Unlike the artificial Dutch *terrain vague* photographed by Bas Princen in the Netherlands [11.18], Dungeness is a barren yet natural, wind-swept stretch of fat pebbles strewn with flotsam and clumps of yellow gorse on the Kent coast [11.19]. The key to the poetry of this garden was not its rugged, almost primitive craftsmanship, but the extraordinary assemblage that Jarman forged between fragments that would otherwise have remained stranded. What Jarman achieved at Prospect Cottage was conceptual integrity, creating meaning out of nothingness by arranging weathered wood, rusted steel and succulent plants against an expanse of beach and a stark industrial backdrop, achieving in the process strong cultural symbiosis. His 'naive' planting beds take on the form of clumps and archetypal circles [11.20, 11.22]; and his unusual, priapic assemblages of *objets trouvés* standing upright in the pebbles give visitors their bearings and reflect something of Jarman's relentless, if not obsessive, search for pattern and human meaning in a place of desolation [11.23]. In the shadow of Dungeness nuclear power station, which looms on the horizon, he was able to create a place of irreverent beauty, where life was allowed to slow down [11.24].

The extraordinary artistic freedom exhibited at Prospect Cottage was partly the result of necessity, but also reflected its author's need for creative self-expression [11.21]. Nonetheless, the reason Jarman's garden remains important and meaningful to us is that it expresses the fragile miracle of human life [11.25]. Its design is far from conformist and remains embryonic in this *terrain vague* of sorts, yet it constitutes an artistic statement about the power to create, reinvent and destroy that we all carry within ourselves [11.26]. Jarman the filmmaker turned the raw material he found in his everyday life into scenery and exquisite poetry. He embraced the environment of Dungeness – with its marooned skiffs and stranded wooden huts and nuclear reactor – in all its derelict splendour, turning it into a place that fully embraces the moment as a gift of unconditional beauty. Jarman was not trying to make a dogmatic, self-righteous statement regarding his environment, but rather show his deep admiration for, and acceptance of, the wonder of it all.

11.18 Artificial Arcadia in the Netherlands, by Bas Princen, 2004.
This *terrain vague* of sorts is the active result of countless human interventions, with tyre marks in the foreground and heaps of soil of uncertain origin in front of a camping site where Dutch people come to enjoy a holiday. The image is a mirror of a strong daily reality, where landscape projection and reception meet and blend, outside any kind of archetypal prefiguration.

11.19 Aerial view of Dungeness, England, with the nuclear power plant.
Dungeness is considered to be the only true 'desert' in England, and in that sense it can also be seen as a *terrain vague*. In his garden at Prospect Cottage on the shingle shore, Derek Jarman gathered plants and pieces of flotsam and debris, crafting them into a distinctive new creation.

11.19

11.20 View from Prospect Cottage looking over the front garden.
A crown of bright yellow gorse, endemic to the area, forms a rough circle around a small totemic piece of driftwood. Derek Jarman reached back instinctively to archaic figures in the landscape, reinventing this language of nature.

11.21 The entrance leading to Prospect Cottage.
The path to the old fisherman's hut is not clearly defined; the approach is simply through loose arrangements of plants and material salvaged from the beach. It is as though the rules of composition were still in the making and not yet fixed.

11.22 Miniature stone circles.
Rings of stones are arranged as if to recreate a sacred Neolithic microcosm of sorts. It is the hand of Derek Jarman the artist at work, expressing his own physical suffering and existential questioning.

11.20

11.21

11.22

11.23

11.24

11.23 A field of wooden posts set upright in totemic fashion.
The complete absence of any planting around these posts evokes the barren lifeless landscape of this *terrain vague*. It has an ontological and almost painful feeling, invoking the injustice of Jarman's terminal illness and death.

11.24 View towards the Dungeness nuclear power plant from Prospect Cottage.
Here the garden ends and nature takes over, with its random patches of sea kale and debris stretching out to the horizon. This shift from careful archaic symbolic design to utter randomness makes this project very compelling.

11.25

11.26

**11.25 The south wall of Prospect Cottage
with John Donne's poem 'The Sun Rising'.**
Donne's poem is an ode to the sun and the
mysteries of our own terrestrial existence.
The expanse of shingle, with no plants, in front
of the wall is reminiscent of the gravel garden
of a Japanese shrine, though here unkempt.

**11.26 Back garden at Prospect Cottage, with a
collection of sculptural *objets trouvés*.**
This Postmodern garden plays with its context
in a sublime way: everything negative is turned
into positive symbols. Jarman said of his own
creation: 'Paradise haunts gardens, and some
gardens are paradises. Mine is one of them.'

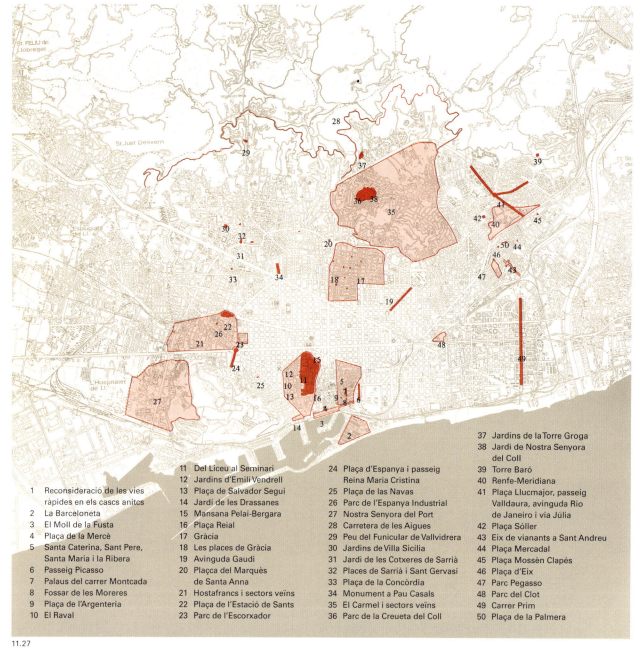

11.27

1	Reconsideració de les vies ràpides en els cascs anitcs	11	Del Liceu al Seminari
2	La Barceloneta	12	Jardins d'Emili Vendrell
3	El Moll de la Fusta	13	Plaça de Salvador Segui
4	Plaça de la Mercè	14	Jardí de les Drassanes
5	Santa Caterina, Sant Pere, Santa Maria i la Ribera	15	Mansana Pelai-Bergara
6	Passeig Picasso	16	Plaça Reial
7	Palaus del carrer Montcada	17	Gràcia
8	Fossar de les Moreres	18	Les places de Gràcia
9	Plaça de l'Argenteria	19	Avinguda Gaudi
10	El Raval	20	Plaça del Marquès de Santa Anna
		21	Hostafrancs i sectors veïns
		22	Plaça de l'Estació de Sants
		23	Parc de l'Escorxador

24	Plaça d'Espanya i passeig Reina Maria Cristina	37	Jardins de la Torre Groga
25	Plaça de las Navas	38	Jardi de Nostra Senyora del Coll
26	Parc de l'Espanya Industrial	39	Torre Baró
27	Nostra Senyora del Port	40	Renfe-Meridiana
28	Carretera de les Aigues	41	Plaça Llucmajor, passeig Valldaura, avinguda Rio de Janeiro i via Júlia
29	Peu del Funicular de Vallvidrera	42	Plaça Sóller
30	Jardins de Villa Sicília	43	Eix de vianants a Sant Andreu
31	Jardi de les Cotxeres de Sarrià	44	Plaça Mercadal
32	Places de Sarrià i Sant Gervasi	45	Plaça Mossèn Clapés
33	Plaça de la Concòrdia	46	Plaça d'Eix
34	Monument a Pau Casals	47	Parc Pegasso
35	El Carmel i sectors veïns	48	Parc del Clot
36	Parc de la Creueta del Coll	49	Carrer Prim
		50	Plaça de la Palmera

11.28

11.29

Even in the most destitute of places, a clear landscape vision has the power of a dream that reaches far beyond the physical bounds of a location. The transformation of the entire Mediterranean city of Barcelona into an ambitious cultural mosaic would have seemed impossible during the time of General Franco's rule in Spain. The scheme comprising fifty landscape projects, launched as a single plan by the architect Oriol Bohigas (1980), is still of great cultural and political importance today [11.27]. Marking Catalonia's refusal to defer to the rest of Spain after forty years of humiliation, it incorporated the whole of the city in a composite vision of public spaces, parks and promenades, forging a new identity for Barcelona.[20]

Bohigas's scheme restored some original names of places that had been banned. In other areas, particularly the dense populous districts of the Barrio Gotico, by demolishing building blocks he created a series of small public spaces. A large stretch of the old industrial seafront, extending from the old port as far north as the mouth of the River Besòs, became a laboratory of innovative experiments. The harbour-front promenade of the Barceloneta (1994) by Olga Tarrasó and Jaume Artigues opened the way towards the seafront which had been blocked for so long with a subtle play in surface topography [11.28]. The new Plaça del Mar (1996), located at the southern tip of the Barceloneta, also by the same team, opened to the broad blue horizon of the Mediterranean

Sea by articulating a subtle transition between the hard paved surfaces of the city and the newly restored beach [11.29]. People who stroll along the shoreline today, with its modern art exhibits, cannot remember, or even imagine, how destitute the entire waterfront of Barceloneta had been – an area of *terrains vagues*, slums and abandoned factories [11.30]. Bohigas's interventions worked like local landscape acupuncture, activating neighbourhoods that had been moribund. The effort was minimal, yet the entire feeling of Barcelona was transformed in a short space of time and had a resounding impact abroad.

The IBA Emscher Park project in the Ruhr (1989–99) re-branded an entire industrial valley, placing an emphasis on the ecological and cultural recovery of abandoned steel mills and slag heaps. After a hundred years of intensive coal mining, the entire floor of the Emscher Valley had slowly collapsed, sinking more than 30 metres (98 feet) and causing enormous problems in an area inhabited by millions of people. Faced with such a serious situation, the federal German government unanimously voted funding to help solve the Ruhr's acute environmental problems.[21] The IBA Emscher Park developed over the course of ten years, and produced some landscape icons. Richard Serra's art piece *Slab for the Ruhr* (1998), consisting of a great steel fin planted on top of the Schurenbach slag heap, became a strong identifier for the region [11.31].

11.30

11.27 Plan of Barcelona, Catalonia.
When Catalonia regained some autonomy after the death of General Franco, the city of Barcelona organized a series of urban landscape projects visible on this plan. These projects transformed often derelict *terrains vagues* that were scattered along the coastline and inner city into proud new symbols of a reborn civil society.

11.28 The harbour esplanade at the Barceloneta, by Olga Tarrasó and Jaume Artigues, 1994.
This is probably one of the most successful urban spaces designed in Barcelona during its revival. The generous dimensions, the simplicity of materials and open planting of Parkinsonia trees are an invitation for a leisurely stroll on what used to be a restricted industrial dock.

11.29 View of the Plaça del Mar, Barcelona.
Beneath the trees is a work by Juan Muñoz entitled *Una habitació on sempre plou* ('A room where it always rains'). The space, created on *terrains vagues* of abandoned industries, symbolizes a figurative and literal liberation from oppression. The caged-in figures are a lasting reminder of the past, at the same time as a new landscape opens to the horizon.

11.30 *Homenatge a la Barceloneta* ('Homage to the Barceloneta'), by Rebecca Horn, 1992.
A rusty leaning tower with industrial windows creates a play with the crisp horizon of the sea. It evokes the toil that went on here in recent times, with smoke-belching industry and a beach that consisted of noxious waste.

11.31

11.31 The *Schurenbachhalde*, Essen, in the Ruhr region of Germany.

This *terrain vague* of industrial waste is capped with asphalt and crowned by a sculpture entitled *Slab for the Ruhr* by Richard Serra. Created in 1998, this 15-metre (46-feet) high sail of rusted Cor-ten steel acknowledges the region's heavy industries of coal and metal smelting, somehow justifying the heap on which it stands.

11.32 Duisburg Nord landscape park, Germany, by the office of Peter Latz.

The landscape rehabilitation of the site of an old steel-mill, this was constructed in the 1990s during the 'exhibition' IBA Emscher Park. Simple natural elements like flowering cherry are interspersed with industrial ruins creating a very particular aesthetic reminiscent of the Gas Works Park by Richard Haag in Seattle of the early 1970s.

11.33 One of the highly contaminated decantation pits at the Duisburg Nord project.

The archetype of the walled paradise garden is obvious, but it is a garden to be looked at and not walked in, with 'mutant flora' growing tightly packed in serial rows.

11.34 Gas Works Park, Seattle, USA, by Richard Haag, 1975.

Once seen as a place of dejection, the island, with its industrial ruin set in a generous new lawn, became a symbol of community gathering and play. The aesthetic inversion here led to the acceptance of post-industrial landscapes as an aesthetic category in their own right. This pioneer project became the emblem of environmental redemption, not so much in ecological but more in social terms, and influenced many later projects, including the IBA Emscher experiment of the 1990s.

11.35 Still from *Pina*, by Wim Wenders, 2011.

The film honours the late German choreographer Pina Bausch and her Tanztheater Wuppertal. We see two dancers move and strive expressionistically in the dust of a no-man's-land in the Ruhr, while another carries a lone tree in a rare ode to hope in the *terrain vague*, hinting at the sublime.

11.32

11.33

11.34

11.35

11.36

11.37

11.36 Novartis Campus, Basel, Switzerland, by Vogt Landscape Architects, 2006.
Set on top of an underground car park, these carefully constructed strata of soil work like a rudimentary section through geological time, reverting back to a form of landscape narrative invented during the Renaissance.

11.37 Botanical Garden, Bordeaux, France, by Catherine Mosbach, 2001.
In the Galerie des Milieux a series of huge soil transplants set on top of concrete slabs represent different plant communities of the region, ranging from sand dunes to oak forests. These samples are exhibited like so many ecological curiosities.

11.38 Extension of the Parc Paul Mistral, Grenoble, France, by Alexandre Chemetoff, 2008.
A former roadway is definitively closed down and changed into a promenade. Such shifts in usage are becoming increasingly common as more ecologically conscious designers set their sights on parts of the established urban territory.

11.39 The Vache Noire roof park, Arcueil, France, by Agence TER, 2007.
Built on the rooftop of a large shopping centre, this park does not seek to mask reality behind some form of ecological pretext or narrative – instead it works playfully to show precisely the artificiality of the whole concept.

This theme reappears in Wim Wenders's film *Pina* (2011), which showcased ritual dances staged by the late choreographer Pina Bausch in desolate terrain settings of the Emscher Park [11.35].[22] This play on lost identity was further reinforced in the Duisburg Nord Park project (1994) by the office of Peter Latz, where a heavily contaminated site was patiently recovered by vegetation, producing an ecological aesthetic in its own right [11.32, 11.33].[23] The irony of this contaminated industrial site turned into a landscape park is reminiscent of the Gas Works Park project (1975) in Seattle, USA, by Richard Haag a decade before, where a disused industrial ruin stood as the centrepiece of the park [11.34].[24] The suggestive ecological power of all these projects does not, however, negate a strong sense of belonging. The Ruhr region was designated as the European Capital of Culture in 2010 and millions of visitors flocked to acknowledge that a terrible form of beauty was born: name it urban ecology, if you will.

Terrain vague is the ground zero of an evolution towards absolute landscape reduction. The development of successive periods of landscape remains an indelible part of our imagination, impacting on the way we perceive and shape our environment.[25] The new Botanical Garden in Bordeaux (2001), designed by the French landscape architect Catherine Mosbach on top of a protective slab covering an old oil refinery site, proposes a 'Gallery of Milieux', where large ground samples representing biomes specific to

Aquitaine are exposed as botanical 'transplants' [11.37].[26] In a similar way the Novartis Campus Park in Basel (2006), by the office of Vogt Landscape Architects experiments with an ecological narrative on top of subterranean parking. Geomorphic islands reconstituted with sedimentary layers covered with appropriate vegetation represent a cross-section of the Rhine Valley at that location [11.36].[27] Can we create a desire for original landscapes as strong as the disgust that modern construction practices provoke? The question is of fundamental importance. Using a topological approach designers tools should have tools that enable them to work knowingly in complex situations. The Vache Noire roof park in Arcueil (2007) by Agence TER expresses such a difficult urban condition [11.39].[28] It covers the roof of a shopping centre with artificial planting, while acting as a public open space replete with a water feature. It chooses not to play the ecological register, in order to accentuate artificiality.

What we are missing today is an aesthetic language capable of bridging the banal and reinventing ecological myths that recover what is there.[29] The extension of the Parc Paul Mistral (2008) in Grenoble by Alexandre Chemetoff and the Bureau des Paysages works precisely on the question of reappropriation of existing roads into a park [11.38]. As we have seen, whether on a local scale or that of the city, the range of possible transformations for *terrains vagues* remains tremendous.

11.38

11.39

12. Topology
Rediscovering Meaning in the Landscape

'Topology is precisely the mathematical discipline that allows the passage from local to global…'

René Thom, *Topologie et Signification*[1]

Throughout history, places have achieved meaning through rules and structures at various scales that give shape to landscapes. From old archetypes to modern, fragmented cityscapes and artificial topologies like the Sigirino Mound (2014) in Ticino, landscapes have changed and are now nothing more than a metaphor of nature to be reconciled with our industrial dwelling habits [12.0]. The examples we have seen throughout this book express a particular 'intelligence' of nature, one that is immediately graspable as a specific reaction to, and modification of, the environment within a specific period. Between ubiquity and uniqueness, the meaning of a landscape remains consistent and unequivocal, linked as it is to the prevailing physical, spatial and cultural constructs. Whether a landscape bears significance depends on what is ingrained in the terrain as much as in the minds of the living.

Landscape is allegorical and reflects a true story – that of our journey through life. *Wave Field* (1995) created by the artist Maya Lin in memory of a young student is an example of ground work acting as a topological catalyst on our sentiments and memories [12.1].[2] The power of a landscape has always relied on the duality of inclusion and exclusion, good and evil, natural and unnatural (consider paradise). Landscapes, through centuries and across different cultures, have proven capable of bestowing meaning through the reinterpretation of archetypes. A strong landscape topology can be food for both the body and the soul, but at present it seems to want to escape the old archetypal rules.[3] How can topology develop into a new language of landscape? Our faith in ecology has attempted to itemize natural biotic features on the surface of the earth, but all too often it appears to miss the sublime aesthetic of human experience and spiritual potential.

12.0 (opposite) AlpTransit Sigirino Mound, Ticino, Switzerland, 2014.
The Sigirino Mound represents a volume of 3.5 million cubic metres (124 million cubic feet) of excavated material from the Sotto Cenere tunnel. An old terrace wall stands in front of the artificial topography at the foot of Monte Ferrino, where abandoned vineyards give way to chestnut woods. The 'skin' of the mound is enriched with humus to encourage vegetation and promote slope stabilization.

12.1 *Wave Field* by Maya Lin, 1995.
A natural wave pattern is transformed into an earthwork in memory of the late François-Xavier Bagnoud at the University of Michigan in Ann Arbor. The artist sees it as: 'pure poetry. It is a very gentle space that exists on a very human scale. It is a sanctuary, yet it's playful … with the changing shadows of the sun …'

12.1

The poetics of the garden are indeed ambiguous for they contain mixed notions of growth and decay, of the abject and the divine, which in turn affect human fate. The walled Persian garden is an archetypal figure that one finds in the most remote references of Buddhist Japan and all the way back to Renaissance Italy. Hafez, the poet of Shiraz quoted at the beginning of this book, lived 700 years ago in a city of gardens at the edge of the harshest desert in the world: the Dasht-e Lut. He wrote verses that celebrated landscape as an act of wonder, reclaiming a sense of the sublime infused with the symbolic power of a nature made by man. He often spoke as an oracle to immediate human sentiments such as love and hate. His tomb, erected within the walled Musalla Gardens of Shiraz (1390), is a place where young people still come to meet, converse and embrace life's coincidences and mysteries [12.2].[4] It is this avatar of a paradise garden that speaks to them, and confers deep trust, comfort and wholeness to the place, through the recognizable topology of a central void around this tomb paved in marble, surrounded by fragrant orange groves and roses framed by alcoves and cypress trees.

Are we able to reinvent anew places in our ecological age that are capable of such timeless resonance? A garden always remains bound to sentiments as it interacts with a nature that is cared for; it is the opposite of a *terrain vague*, which promotes a feeling of abandonment. Think of the reaction of Derek Jarman to the 'desert' of Dungeness:

to what end did he seek to transform the immediate surroundings of his cottage into an archetypal garden of sorts? A successful landscape is one that speaks to the heart through a play of opposites, one where decrepit flotsam and rusted steel scraps combine poetically. Over the course of centuries landscapes sought to connect mutually opposed facets of nature into a meaningful whole. In the flattened clearing of Avebury there always was a deep pit; and beside the sacred *temenos* of the Apollo sanctuary at Delphi lay the profane wastelands of the Phaedriades ravines.[5]

We all share common memories of ubiquitous landscapes through established topologies that form an indelible part of our collective understanding of place. These memories continue to affect the way we think about, value and act upon our world. The Diana, Princess of Wales Memorial Fountain in Hyde Park in London (2004) is undoubtedly the most striking example of such a project to have been produced in recent times as an avatar of the forest circle. The project's success is due to Kathryn Gustafson's artistic sensibility and keen sense of topology. The granite fountain carved in the shape of a 'perpetual' ring of water is carefully crafted and embedded in a small meadow clearing beside the Serpentine [12.3]. This astonishing piece of rushing water has become a vivid place of remembrance, layering a powerful statement about the loss of the princess and her vitality on top of the most ancient landscape archetype of the ring [12.4, 12.5].[6]

12.2

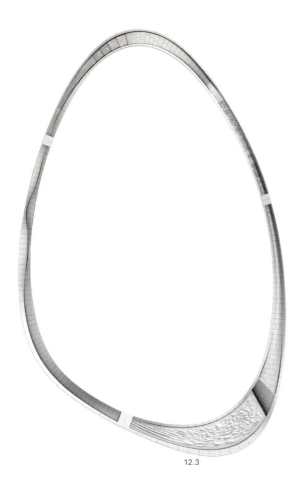

12.3

12.4

12.2 Orange grove at the Tomb of Hafez in the Musalla Gardens, Shiraz, Iran.
The tomb was first built shortly after the poet's death in 1390 by Babur, then redesigned by Shah Abbas and again by André Godard in 1935. The original topological essence of the *Hafezieh* remains, as the youth of Shiraz meet at dusk amid the heady scent of orange blossom.

12.3 Plan of the Diana, Princess of Wales Memorial Fountain, Hyde Park, London, England, 2004.
Designed by Kathryn Gustafson and the office of Gustafson Porter Landscape Architects, the fountain takes the form of an unusual and expressive ovoid sculptural shape, with water running in both directions.

12.4 Aerial view of the Diana, Princess of Wales Memorial Fountain.
The ring of flowing water is set within a planted meadow dotted with trees near the Serpentine lake. The oval plays with aspects of the park's gently rolling terrain, inviting people to meet and celebrate and remember.

12.5 Detail of the Diana, Princess of Wales Memorial Fountain.
Made from machine-milled Cornish granite, the exact shape of the fountain was carefully studied through precise models. The speed of water varies according to texture and topology of the ring, intended to express different phases in the life of the princess.

12.5

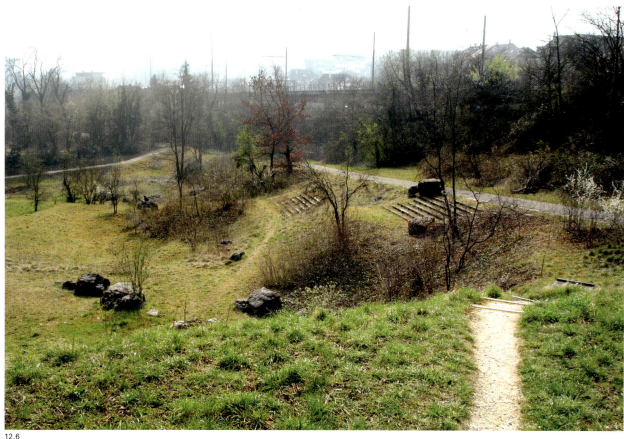

12.6

Nature fabricated

With the rise of ecology in an age of climate change, we have tended to lose sight of landscape archetypes and their significance, and concentrated our thoughts on the survival of our small planet instead. How should we actually set about making landscapes in this new era, and according to which criteria should they be produced? Landscapes reflect a world of striking extremes, in which science and poetry at present seldom reconcile. Landscape architecture has shifted roles and adopted a more global position, becoming both custodian and provider of 'real' nature, rather than producer of a symbolic nature as before. The dry grassland Jura meadow project by Dieter Kienast at the Brüglingen park in Basel (1980) sets an important precedent in the context of archetypal change [12.6]. An artificial meadow on limestone substrate was created on a railway embankment for the 'Grün 80' garden show in Basel.[7] Wild seeds were sown and a 'true' Jura grassland biotope emerged in this most unlikely suburban context. Years have passed, and the dry meadow has now become a major icon in Swiss nature conservancy. Kienast achieved a form of designed ecology that was no longer bound to any sort of cultural referent. His ecological approach set a precedent that had far-reaching effects on the status of the landscape profession in Switzerland and elsewhere. It effected a significant withdrawal from the realm of garden aesthetics and proposed a roster of natural species on an artificial topography instead. One could question whether a piece of fabricated Jura dry meadow really belongs to a banal railway embankment in Brüglingen. But beyond its recognition as something authentic and natural, it is the avowed separation between people and nature here that remains problematic. The topology of this exemplary meadow is not intended for people to gather comfortably, but rather to show us a piece of rugged, unkempt nature.

The Fürstenwald cemetery in Chur (1997), designed a decade later by Dieter Kienast, was animated by a different ecological spirit; it was conceived as an archaic place where native clipped hedges and a linden grove integrated a part of Alpine folklore [12.7].[8] In this sense it is a piece of deep cultural ecology, reinstating a sense of natural rootedness within a strong symbolic whole. Kienast treated the cemetery as an archetypal plinth on a slope at the edge of a forest clearing. The cemetery is neither forest nor meadow, but a topology for the dead in which a humanized nature expresses deep secular meaning. In a comparable way, the Invalidenpark in Berlin designed by Atelier Phusis (1997) plays on the spirit of an old Prussian memorial grove of oaks against a sunken wall and basin set on a raised plinth of granite [12.8].[9] The remaining stand of 'native' oaks was preserved, in marked contrast to the forecourt entirely stripped of its historical substance and planted with clumps of 'non-native' ginkgo trees. The project juxtaposes the highly symbolic topography

12.7

12.8

12.6 Dry grassland biotope by Dieter Kienast, Brüglingen, Basel, Switzerland, 1980.
The landscape was designed by Kienast as an artificial piece of 'natural' topology for the 'Grün 80' exhibition and is now under strict environmental protection by law. It is ironic that this project by Kienast, who obtained a doctorate in the study of resilient urban weeds, is protected in this way.

12.7 The Fürstenwald Cemetery, Chur, Switzerland, by Dieter Kienast, 1997.
A wall leaves the forest edge, then swings back following the terrain from the belvedere to a funerary chapel set against the distant Alps. The horizontal axis underlines the topography and expresses a strong mortuary *temenos* that clearly separates the profane meadow from the sacred burial ground.

12.8 Invalidenpark, Berlin, Germany, by Christophe Girot and Atelier Phusis, 1997.
In a subtle modelling of terrain on this old military ceremonial ground in Berlin, a new plinth was raised above the existing ground level. People walking along the edge of the basin of water are elevated, like Giacometti sculptures, formulating a 'metaphysical' space of memory, emotions and history.

12.9

12.9 Lilacs in the sacred grounds of the 1,000-year-old Kiev Pechrsk Lavra Monastery, Ukraine.
It is the link between a sacred ground, a fundamental love of nature and ourselves that is at the heart of things. We need to respond to the fullest spectrum of the human senses in both spirit and mind – only then will a renewed faith in nature be born and science kept in balance.

12.10 A ginkgo on the central lawn of the Beijing University campus, China.
A marble crown of lotus buds set around the trunk is a symbol of prostration in Buddhism; it confers a sacred aura to the tree and its precinct. The ginkgo no longer exists in nature and has survived to this day only through the attentive care of humans.

12.11 An ancient hinoki cypress tree at the Ise Naiku shrine, Japan.
The Ise Naiku or Inner Shrine is the most sacred Shinto sanctuary, dedicated to the goddess Amaterasu-omikami. For over two millennia, people have come to venerate both the shrine and its spectacular trees. The bark of this tree has been polished by the hands of millions of devotees praying here since time immemorial.

12.12 The Berkshire Boardwalk, Massachusetts, USA, by the office of Reed Hilderbrand, 2011.
This elevated wooden path winds its way through natural wetlands for over 800 metres (half a mile). The topology of a path depends to a great extent on the sensitivity of its designer to draw out elements of discovery, surprise and mystique from the landscape. Ecology matters less at this point than the actual narrative and the thoughts that we accumulate along the way.

12.10

12.11

12.12

of a 'universal' layer of ginkgos in the front, with an ecological layer of more 'traditional' German oak forest at the back.

We all need to feel connected to something greater than ourselves. In many cultures, landscape represents a form of fabricated nature in which spiritual affinity can be found. Take the hillside gardens of the Pechrsk Lavra Monastery in Kiev (1051), filled with magnificent lilac groves. When spring comes, the lilacs delight the senses with vivid colours and heady scents. They embody a moment of sacredness and communion, when holding the flowers becomes a symbolic act of prayer [12.9]. Imported to Ukraine from Asia Minor and the Balkans, lilac is considered ecologically as an 'ergasiophyte', meaning that it can only survive there in cultivated form. Nonetheless, it remains highly emblematic of deep religious ties with the Byzantine Orthodox tradition. In another register, an old ginkgo tree on the campus at Beijing University embodies secular cultural values [12.10]. The ginkgo can no longer be found in nature – in theory it is a fossil plant that is ecologically extinct – but thanks to monks it has been carried into the present.[10] The tree stands in a quiet corner of the main lawn, and its foot is circled by a ring of marble lotus flowers, a symbol of prostration in the Buddhist faith. It is a resplendent symbol of ancestry, outliving those that tread in its dappled shade each day.

Tree veneration is cross-cultural and archaic. At the Ise Naiku shrine in Japan, a stand of hinoki cypress trees is subject to intense animistic worship. The Shinto cult has its origins here, where the floor of an ecologically 'native' forest has been used for rituals from times immemorial. Trees in the immediate vicinity of the sanctuary dedicated to the goddess Amaterasu-omikami are themselves subject to prostration and prayer [12.11]. The shrine, set in a rectangular clearing covered in a patch of white pebbles, is made of the same wood. Every twenty years, hinoki trees are sacrificed and felled to rebuild the shrine anew.[11] The Ise Naiku sanctuary has seemingly retained its ecological balance to this day through a deep commitment to nature and an even deeper cult of ancestry.

In contrast, our connection to more profane landscapes can be understood as individual layers of meaning inscribed over the course of time. The Berkshire Boardwalk project, designed by the office of Reed Hilderbrand in Massachusetts (2011), offers a new reading of a common New England marshland area through a path for ecological contemplation [12.12]. The frail-looking meandering boardwalk made of locally grown hemlock (tsuga) evokes the spirit of Walden Pond. It addresses an ecology rooted in 150 years of local 'transcendentalist' culture. There are no guardrails on the walk through this wooded marsh and so the wanderer is left exposed to the 'wild' elements in the self-reliant way of Henry David Thoreau.[12] In this instance, ecology signifies not so much the art of scientific safeguarding, but rather the potential for meditation on a return to nature.

12.13

12.13 Crissy Field, San Francisco, USA, by Hargreaves Associates, 1998.
The great success of this landmark is due not only to its exceptional location on San Francisco Bay, near the Golden Gate, but also to the intelligence with which subtle topological design blends with both ecological and anthropological concerns.

12.14 Model of a proposed park on the Ciliwung River, Jakarta, Indonesia.
The project, designed by ETH Masters students Shoshiro Hashimoto and Benedikt Kowalewski, clears riverside slums to make way for new low-rise housing and a river park that works as a promenade with gardens that help regulate some of the floods that occur in the neighbourhood year round.

12.15 The Letten area, Zurich, Switzerland.
Formerly a wasteland alongside derelict train tracks, this area was notorious as a place where crowds of drug users once gathered. It is without doubt the most vibrant and youthful waterfront in Zurich today. It is hard to believe that this bathing paradise on the Limmat River recovered its healthy status by simply providing cleaner water.

12.14

The search for a new language

In past decades remarkable examples, dense with relationships bridging ecology and design, have been established. The Crissy Field project (1998) by the office of Hargreaves Associates addresses ecological concerns while also pioneering innovative landscape design [12.13].[13] The conversion of this relentlessly flat military airfield at the Presidio on San Francisco Bay into a national park, including a recreation space as well as wetland and dune restoration areas, required a strong dose of topological invention. The project re-enacted several layers of recent geological history through the careful modelling of a series of stylized landforms ranging from artificial dunes to intertidal wetlands. As a result, Crissy Field offers a new form of remedial ecology bound together in an expressive topographic choreography that was truly ahead of its time. Ecological considerations were just one of many aspects taken into account to reveal the site's full potential. The project's ultimate success revolves around the expression of a trusted relationship with the forces of nature acting on the site in the interest of biodiversity. Cultural issues were also given a place – fostering, comfort, beauty and leisure – while acknowledging the forces of natural disruption that regularly act on the site.

On another register, the Ciliwung River project in Jakarta, Indonesia (2012), is an example where the fight against poverty and environmental degradation go hand in hand [12.14].[14] A research team at the ETH Future Cities Laboratory in Singapore worked for five years to develop restorative landscape ecology and appropriate housing to establish a stronger balance with nature in areas where the relationship to the river had been completely obliterated. The ambitious project proposes a radical topological change to the entire river profile, transforming it into a new urban park, and recovering environmental balance for the Indonesian megacity.

A shift in focus towards water quality in cities has been of fundamental importance in more recent projects. One of the best examples of river transformations occurred on the Limmat River in the Letten area of Zurich (2005), thanks to Rotzler Krebs Partner [12.15].[15] What was formerly a derelict railway track next to the infamous 'needle park' notorious for drug abuse in the 1970s became an extraordinary place for leisure two decades later. Physical changes in the project remain understated, but the water quality and ecology of the Limmat have improved fundamentally through considerable environmental efforts by the authorities. When the water temperature reaches 20°C (68°F) in summer, the Letten area fills with crowds of people eating, drinking and watching swimmers exercise in the swift flow. The change in topology here – accessing the water – is purely qualitative, and this makes a world of difference.

The Ribeira das Naus waterfront in Lisbon by the offices of PROAP and Global landscape architects (2013)

12.15

12.16

plays instead on the topology of local maritime history by reinstating a long forgotten shipyard at the heart of the city's civic space [12.16]. The project retains the strong geometric lines of the wharfs which produced the ships of the Great Age of Discovery. For centuries the wharfs were closed to the public, but they have now turned green, with a sloped lawn and trees, and are alive with people strolling on the subtle topography that edges and rolls down gently to the banks of the River Tagus (Tejo). The search for meaning in larger-scale riverine landscapes requires a strong political vision to make the consolidation of discontinuous spaces possible.

One of the most remarkable examples of such a determined landscape consolidation is the Cheonggyecheon River project begun in 2003 in Seoul, and completed during the following decade [12.17]. Although of a completely different order of magnitude, the story of this small stream is typical of countless other urban waterways: over the previous century it was packed with slums, then encased in concrete slabs and covered by an 8-km (5-mile) long elevated motorway. Nothing indicated that it would ever see the light of day again. With great courage the then mayor of Seoul, Lee Myung-bak, decided to demolish the motorway and restore the stream, albeit artificially with water pumped up from the Han River. Some 'deep ecology' militants complained that the Cheonggyecheon River was not restored to its 'natural' condition.[16] But the change in atmosphere has been so positive

that people flock to the river in their thousands each day, to stroll along its banks, listen to the water and hear birds sing.

The Cheonggyecheon River is a clear lesson against environmental fatalism, showing how a river landscape can become the centrepiece of civic life again. As with the example of the Letten in Zurich and the Ribeira das Naus in Lisbon, it shows how a riverfront can become a place to celebrate nature's emblematic return to the city. Although the political processes that gave birth to each project differ tremendously – some local and democratic, and others more autocratic – improved landscape value was achieved in all cases. The challenge at present is how to develop better and ecologically more relevant forms of engineered nature that could enhance social cohesion while establishing a stronger bond between society and nature, encouraging good governance, environmental stewardship and respect.

The channelized Kamo River in Kyoto, Japan, is a good example of a cultivated urban ecology that has lasted over a thousand years, maintaining an environment of relative harmony and diversity while preventing floods. Schoolchildren jump across the river's stepping stones in the precinct of the Shimogamo Shrine, embracing the river scenery with its clear water and ducks [12.18]. In spring, the banks of the river are entirely transformed by clouds of cherry blossoms under which crowds gather to rekindle their connection with nature. The good relationship between the inhabitants of

12.17

12.16 **The Ribeira das Naus, Lisbon, Portugal, by PROAP and Global, 2013.**
What was once an enclosed precinct along the Tagus River in the city centre became one of Lisbon's major public open spaces overnight. The careful attention with which the topology of the promenade is crafted, merging into the water step by step, feels as if it has always belonged here.

12.17 **The Cheonggyecheon River project, Seoul, South Korea, 2005.**
The Cheonggyecheon River project is a remarkable case of recovery, where once a concrete flyover used to cut the city in half for a distance of over 8 km (5 miles). The restoration of the buried river was criticized as being too artificial, but its popular success is incontrovertible.

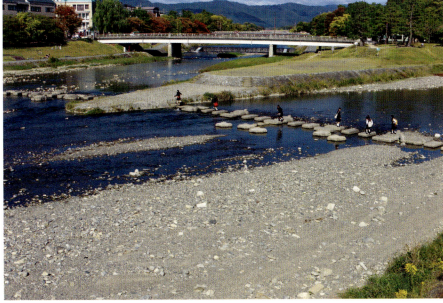

12.18

12.18 **The Kamogawa, Kyoto, Japan.**
The river's previously concrete banks have recently been naturalized and provide a beautiful link in the north of the city. Through such understated interventions, the ancient Japanese capital has successfully managed to maintain a natural link between its many treasured parks and gardens.

12.19

12.19 Houtan Park, Shanghai, China, by Turenscape, 2010.

This linear park shows how effective water decontamination can be achieved through the use of plants. Located on an environmentally degraded industrial site along the Huangpu River, it employs a rural aesthetic that is not in keeping with Chinese garden traditions, but borrows rather more from the English Picturesque.

12.20 The Tianjin Qiaoyuan Wetland Park, China, designed by Turenscape, 2008.

Couples meet in the semi-private shade of trees to commune with nature on a 'mountain' occupying an old contaminated industrial site. The project demonstrates a desire to reinterpret traditional Chinese garden themes within the new topology of the site.

12.21 One of the purification ponds in the Qiaoyuan Wetland Park.

The use of natural reeds to treat the highly contaminated water becomes a spectacle in itself. Although there is no traditional rock garden to be seen, the overall topology of the park juxtaposing 'mountain' and 'water' remains true to a particular Chinese landscape tradition.

12.22 Bishan-Ang Mo Kio Park, Singapore, designed by Atelier Dreiseitl, 2012.

A positive example of a rehabilitated storm-water system, the project manages the variation in runoff through a system of swales, pools and a meandering stream. The English park topology, with vast swathes of open green slopes, may be questionable in such a hot tropical climate calling for shade, but compared to the concrete culvert that it once was it is a resounding success, not to say a miracle.

12.20

12.21

12.22

Kyoto and their river is based on a subtle topological balance in the river's engineered design, which ensures environmental control while also allowing nature to prevail.

Ecological restoration is part of an ongoing environmental revolution in China that is transforming an ancient garden tradition into a discipline operating at a completely different scale. The Shanghai Houtan Park (2010) – by the office of Turenscape – has reshaped a ruined industrial site along the Huangpu River into an exemplary landscape project that treats water pollution through an elaborate succession of stepped gardens and seepage ponds [12.19].[17] It features an unexpected sequence of plantings that create a new kind of scenery that is so far unheard of in Chinese landscape culture. The park, which opened for the Shanghai Expo 2010, leads the way for a sensitive change in the symbolic treatment of nature within Chinese culture. Ecology in this case no longer responds to the canons of secular garden design, but it has helped to create a new landscape typology: one of reconciliation with troubled waters in Chinese cities.

Another project by the same office is the Qiaoyuan Wetland Park in Tianjin (2008), a good example of how ecological considerations can successfully be incorporated into large-scale civic transformations. Designed by the landscape architect Kongjian Yu, the project skilfully establishes a public park consisting of a series of

phytoremediating wetland ponds, on what used to be a heavily polluted industrial site [12.21]. It is the combination of active remedial ecology, in a broader framework of identifiable historical landscape signifiers like a 'mountain', a 'lake' and pavilions that makes the topology of this project truly innovative and remarkable [12.20].

Other places in Southeast Asia tackle urgent questions of storm-water management due to climate change in a different ecological way altogether. The Bishan-Ang Mo Kio Park in Singapore designed by Atelier Dreiseitl (2012) has created a complete 3-km (2-mile) long 'riverine' environment in replacement of an obsolete water culvert [12.22].[18] It has become a regional reference in matters of ecological storm-water restoration. The engineered concrete ditch was transformed into a generously open grass swale strewn with trees and small permanent water features. When a tropical storm strikes, park visitors are called back by the wardens and the landscape rapidly fills up with water that is either temporarily stored and percolated or conveyed away in case of over capacity. On dry days the park, located in a populous district of town, is filled with people and children playing in the water. The only irony about this form of 'renaturalization' is that there was never a river here in the first place. But this is not the point, the project clearly shows that we have entered an age of natural invention, where designed ecologies and topological experimentation will have a major role to play.

12.23

Sigirino Mound, Ticino, Switzerland

The shaping of future landscapes will be influenced by ecology and the tools and topological methods at our disposal. The digital revolution has helped produce three-dimensional models of complex environments with unprecedented precision. Advanced surveying technologies involving laser-scanning have revolutionized our ability to quantify and analyse terrain, changing the way we see, record and interact with the physical environment. This has been useful in the management of large-scale ecological projects, where modelling and simulation with a high degree of altimetric and planimetric precision is required [12.24].

The artificial mound at Sigirino in Ticino, undertaken by AlpTransit Gotthard AG, constructor of the new Gotthard and Ceneri Base Tunnels, was a highly challenging project that pushed the technical limits of environmental design. Examples of similar landfill projects such as the Garraf Waste project in Catalonia by the office of Batlle i Roig have remained creative while using more conventional surveying methods [12.23], but the Sigirino Mound used pioneering techniques in topology and morphing to allow precise topographic modelling and advanced visualizing to occur [12.25a, 12.25b]. The mound forms part of NEAT, an infrastructure project designed to connect Switzerland to Italy through a series of high-velocity rail tunnels under the Alps.[19] Huge quantities of material produced during tunnel excavation had to be disposed of, and artificial mounds were created. The Sigirino Mound represents 3.5 million cubic metres (124 million cubic feet) of gneiss rubble removed from the Ceneri Base Tunnel, reaching a height of 150 metres (492 feet) [12.26]. On completion, it will be visible from the San Gottardo motorway and local railway lines, as well as Monte Tamaro and the city airport of Lugano. Because of its location it will become a symbol of the high-velocity era. Great care was thus taken to integrate it ecologically into the landscape of Monte Ferrino.

Studies with engineers and environmental agencies took ten years to complete; the main challenges lay in the shape of the mound itself as it comes into contact with the original topography, combined with the difficulty of growing anything 'natural' on the bare slopes of the compacted excavation material. The goal was to make a landscape that could fit within a highly sensitive cultural setting and a vulnerable ecological environment. To this end, test strips of the outer surface of the mound, composed of raw excavation material mixed with compost, were sown with local wild seeds and native trees, and vegetation growth was monitored

12.23 The Garraf Waste Landfill project, Catalonia, by Batlle i Roig.
The project began in 2003 and will eventually become a major gateway to the new Garraf Natural Park. Transforming this contaminated site, once a waste dump, into a new topology and providing access to nature epitomizes the landscape irony of our times.

12.24 Plan of the Sigirino Mound, Ticino, Switzerland, designed by Atelier Girot.
The 3.5 million cubic metres (124 million cubic feet) of rubble produced during tunnelling were made to curve and become 'naturalized', at the request of environmental groups. The stepped slopes will alternate between forested areas and open meadows.

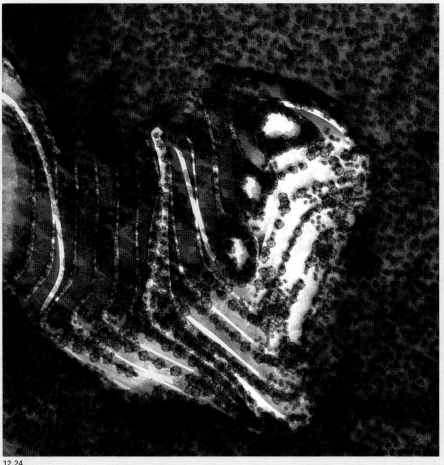

12.24

12.25a

12.25b

12.26

12.27

12.25a, 12.25b Before and after views.
What was once a small chestnut grove was cleared to receive the spoil from the AlpTransit Ceneri Base Tunnel. It took years of study, testing and deliberation to determine the definitive topology of this artificially forested hillside.

12.26 The Sigirino Mound under construction.
On the left is a recently cleared area, while on the right the first definitive green slopes emerge. The mound will be managed as an 'ecological' reserve with limited human access.

12.27 Point cloud scan of the Divan vale in Sigirino in the early stages of forest clearance.
Each pixel in such a scan is geo-referenced and triangulates precisely with satellites and terrestrial stations. When merged, several such scans can become a 3D geo-referenced model.

over the course of seven years [12.34]. To help in the shaping of an optimal form, the project team applied advanced modelling and visualizing techniques based on point clouds. This enabled the designers to test and present a variety of ecological options during the approval process.[20]

Point clouds: a tool for the future

Laser scanners used for advanced surveying and modelling produce images that are valued by engineers for their great precision in three-dimensions high resolution. But for the landscape architect, because of the way they reveal the terrain, they have an inherent aesthetic appeal [12.27, 12.28]. In the case of the Sigirino Mound, the site model itself became a piece of workable terrain that could be tested according to local constraints. The data sets enable for instance the landscape architect to determine precisely the point of contact between the artificially engineered topography of the mound and the steep, rocky slopes of Monte Ferrino [12.29, 12.33]. This level of engagement with the physical reality of a terrain is unprecedented and allows the team to grasp the situation at a glance and act upon it, saving considerable time. Ecologically speaking, every plant, every path and every slope in the surrounding valley can be precisely located, modelled and visualized; the virtual visitor can stand under each tree and look out in any direction from the inside out [12.32]. Inversely, the project can be viewed

and assessed from any location outside, thus introducing principles of spatial relativity in design. The landscape designer can model trends in the growth of vegetation over time, using a type of virtual reality that is not only aesthetically striking, but also more accurate with regards to terrain. Topology will spark off a significant conceptual revolution in landscape architecture, allowing the designer to question a virtual site model from all sides [12.30].

To appreciate fully how this approach affects work flow and design, we need to recognize the importance of physical reality through the aesthetic of the beauty and drama it creates [12.31]. Comparing the mound at Sigirino with Silbury Hill near Avebury, built some 5,000 years ago, may seem a little odd, since their methods of construction and their aims are obviously quite different [12.35, 12.36]. Yet both are artificial earthworks that express strongly the beliefs of their times: in the case of Silbury Hill, its purpose was religious and ritual, whereas for the Sigirino Mound it is cultural and ecological. What the comparison reveals is a leap of faith: Silbury was built at the dawn of civilization to form a clear contrast with its natural surroundings, whereas the mound at Sigirino, built at the tail end of the industrial era, is an artificial behemoth that tries to blend in ecologically with the surroundings. Topology is, therefore, about reinventing a language of nature in tune with its times.

12.28

12.28 Long-range Terrestrial Laser Scanner of the LVML in operation, 2012.
The extreme precision of this instrument enables the accurate mapping of difficult terrain in all three coordinates of the geographic information system. It enables landscape architects to work topologically with much higher precision in data-poor environments.

12.29 Point cloud model of the Sigirino Mound, 2009, inserted into the Swisstopo GIS mesh.
Working with such a precise topological tool has facilitated much simpler design solutions for the perimeter of the mound where it comes into contact with the natural terrain. Not one retention wall was required to hold the mound within its legal bounds.

12.30 Section through the valley bottom and Sigirino Mound.
This landscape project required a thorough understanding of the ambient topology where a steep artificial topography meets a natural one.

12.31, 12.32 The west face of the Sigirino Mound under construction.
Above is a photograph and below the same view modelled in a 3D geo-referenced image. Ironically, without the help of precision topological tools it would have been almost impossible to generate the 'organic' form requested by environmentalists. Here the aesthetics of ecology call for highly technical support.

12.29

12.30

12.31

12.32

12.33

12.33 **The first point cloud model of the Sigirino Mound generated in 2009.**
At the beginning of construction, the contrast between the stark geometric core and its natural background has been considerably attenuated by the 'renaturalization' process, despite the fact that the topology still reads as an entirely man-made object in the landscape.

12.34 **A meadow landscape on an artificial slope at the Sigirino Mound, Ticino, 2014.**
The result of careful studies of topology and substrates, and experimentation by landscape architects and engineers, what could have remained just another slag heap is a prime example of resilience and natural beauty.

12.35 **Silbury Hill, Avebury, England.**
No one is certain what it was that motivated people to build such a phenomenally massive structure made of chalk scraped from the surroundings 5,000 years ago. It is clearly the product of a highly organized society translating its beliefs into a constructed landscape.

12.36 **Profile of the slope of the Sigirino Mound.**
Although it resembles Silbury Hill, what differs is not so much the form as the belief behind the making of the object. Can this mound become the place of a new cult of nature? Or is it simply intended to remain a scientifically renaturalized green area, with no further meaning added beyond the mere ecological amenity it provides?

12.31

12.32

12.33

12.33 The first point cloud model of the Sigirino Mound generated in 2009.
At the beginning of construction, the contrast between the stark geometric core and its natural background has been considerably attenuated by the 'renaturalization' process, despite the fact that the topology still reads as an entirely man-made object in the landscape.

12.34 A meadow landscape on an artificial slope at the Sigirino Mound, Ticino, 2014.
The result of careful studies of topology and substrates, and experimentation by landscape architects and engineers, what could have remained just another slag heap is a prime example of resilience and natural beauty.

12.35 Silbury Hill, Avebury, England.
No one is certain what it was that motivated people to build such a phenomenally massive structure made of chalk scraped from the surroundings 5,000 years ago. It is clearly the product of a highly organized society translating its beliefs into a constructed landscape.

12.36 Profile of the slope of the Sigirino Mound.
Although it resembles Silbury Hill, what differs is not so much the form as the belief behind the making of the object. Can this mound become the place of a new cult of nature? Or is it simply intended to remain a scientifically renaturalized green area, with no further meaning added beyond the mere ecological amenity it provides?

12.34

12.35

12.36

Landscape vision

People should recognize landscape as a symbolic part of their social environment. Thoughtful designs can encourage respect and a better appreciation of the cultivated territory we inhabit. Such is the case with the rehabilitation of the Aire River near Geneva (2014) designed by Georges Descombes and the office ADR in Switzerland [12.37].[21] The flood bed of the river, which was channelled before, has been broadened considerably through precise topological work and a natural promenade created along its grassy banks. The landscape of the Aire was subtly carved out of the floodplain, and the landscape atmosphere crafted through the exquisite sketches of Descombes. The creative efforts concentrated on this small suburban stretch of river over the past ten years have paid off. The project has now reinvented the Aire River with a more naturalistic appeal in the true spirit of Rousseau.

Climate change is a challenge to the established position and values of landscape architecture every day. Nothing is more unnatural than a seafront made of protective barriers, levees and polders. Although there is a long tradition of such landscapes around the world, the extent and pace of present 'remedial' operations is astounding. Entire coastlines and valleys – New Jersey, New Orleans, Jakarta and Melbourne to name but a few – are being re-engineered to protect them from floods, changing landscapes that are centuries old. In the Netherlands, where effects of climate change are most obvious, engineers are studying radical new flood-management measures with the Room for the River project.[22] One solution developed by students of the ETH around the city of Dordrecht (2011) would turn part of it back into an island; much of the hinterland would be left unprotected and subject to unpredictable tidal fluctuations [12.38]. It has not been easy for low-lying farmers to accept the necessity of flooded agricultural land, but such measures now being promoted by the office HNS show how acute the issue has become. The role of the landscape architect alongside the hydraulic and the civil engineer is now to oversee topological change and to develop new types of ecologies that have no precedent in history.

New York has also had its share of natural disasters and the new Ocean Flood Barrier project off Staten Island by Kate Orff and Scapestudio (2014) points towards a radically new way of conceiving large-scale subaquatic landscape 'reaches' along ocean coastlines [12.39].[23] Instead of raising a continuous protective barrier along the shore, the team proposes a series of 'reaches': underwater breakwaters functioning as reefs that mitigate wave action while providing vital habitat for ocean flora and fauna. It is the radical simplicity of the solution that won this project its success against more powerful engineering conglomerates promoting much heavier and costlier solutions. And it is the visionary scale at which an entire coastal topology will be changed to

12.37

12.37 Aire River project by the ADR, Geneva, Switzerland, 2014.
Precise topological considerations make this project one of the best natural river designs in Switzerland today. By extending the flood plain over what was formerly farmland, the Aire has been given back its liberty to expand freely, while also creating a new kind of promenade.

12.38 The Dordrecht flood control project designed and modelled by ETH students, 2011.
In this project, Archipelago, by Kristina Eickmeier and Annina Peterer, important tracts of agricultural land were conceded to the intertidal zone of the river in what is some of the oldest farmland in South Holland. The difficult decision to flood ancestral land has not been without problems in relation to local farmers.

12.39 The new Ocean Flood Barrier project, Staten Island, designed by Kate Orff and Scapestudio, New York, USA, 2014.
It is the shift in the kind of nature that landscape architects are being asked to design that calls for a new understanding of topology. In order to engage in such large-scale territorial projects they will need to work with engineers to recreate a culture of place.

12.38

Topological techniques have helped map important topographical qualities of the Dutch landscape. In Dordrecht, elements synonymous with historical notions of collective effort and trust have become the cornerstones of a strong landscape identity. Scenarios of flooding were developed by ETH students to help safeguard agriculture and preserve woods wherever they emerged from the waterline.[24] The extraordinary mosaic of possibilities, none of which were more than a few metres above the waterline, informed exactly where topography would yield to the natural forces of flooding, and where it could protect. Precise work in topology has become of vital importance in our age, and can help redefine the boundaries of established landscape settlements, by better understanding the interaction of river and tidal flows over time [12.38].

GREAT KILLS HARBOR

Annadale & Crescent Beach Reach

Lemon Creek & Wolfe's Pond Reach

RARITAN BAY

Tottenville Reach

PHASE 1: PILOT

⊚ Water hubs
🏠 Schools
🦪 Breakwaters

12.39

12.40

12.40 Madrid Rio project, Spain, by West 8 and MRIO arquitectos, 2011.
A remarkable series of landscape themes along the Manzanares River brings new shaded promenades to urban areas that previously lacked them and has reintroduced the river as a positive space in the city. The project's success is a result of the care with which it has created new links and a continual topology in this area of the city.

12.41 The High Line, New York, USA, 2011.
In a prime example of adaptive conversion, an old railway bridge has become a highly symbolic landscape crossing over the Meatpacking District of Manhattan. Designed by James Corner of the office Field Operations it has been a resounding success and has set a trend, although its purported ecological impact is far less notable than its remedial impact.

12.42 The Park Spoor Noord, Antwerp, Belgium, designed by Studio Associato Secchi-Viganò.
Since its opening in 2009 this park, built on 24 hectares (60 acres) of old rail yard, has been an unmitigated success for the neighbourhoods it links together by new circulation routes. Everything is just made for people to flow, gather and play.

12.43 The BeltLine project around inner Atlanta.
The project results entirely from the idea of Ryan Gravel, who first developed it during his Master's thesis at Georgia Tech in 1999. Now the ring of abandoned rail lines, 35 km (22 miles) long, is becoming a landscape reality, supported by grassroots associations, community groups, public transport authorities and private investors.

12.41

12.42

12.43

become an agent of environmental resilience that marks a real paradigm shift in landscape practice.

Topology can translate into an act of public interest, belief and perseverance to create a better urban ecology in difficult contexts. The Madrid Rio project on the Manzanares River by the office of West 8 and MRIO arquitectos (2011) shows how careful topological work on the urban floor can give coherence and repair environments that have been severely dismembered by heavy infrastructural engineering [12.40]. Here 6 km (3 ¾ miles) of riverbank were freed of road infrastructure and transformed into a series of resplendent gardens. The Salon de los Pinòs, with its 8,000 pines planted on top of an underground motorway, has become a vital park and link between neighbourhoods, and the blossoming cherry trees of the Avenida de Portugal have become a popular emblem.

Landscape can actually change the value and image of an entire area, as in the case of the Meatpacking District of Lower Manhattan that has been transformed by the resounding success of the High Line project (2011) by James Corner and Field Operations [12.41].[25] An old derelict suspended rail line was transformed into a prestigious hanging ecological promenade, with a remarkable plant selection by Piet Oudolf that attracts countless nature-loving urbanites and tourists year round. The appeal of this landscape promenade has been so phenomenal that land

value has increased in the immediate vicinity of the project. Other cities in America have followed and embarked on more complex and ambitious visions. The BeltLine project in Atlanta (2015) started as an idea fifteen years before when Ryan Gravel proposed a radical idea for a green circuit around central Atlanta bringing together four disused rail belts into a single ring of public amenities, parks and transport [12.43]. Today, after over a decade of intensive community involvement as well as public and private lobbying, the BeltLine has become a tangible physical and political reality for the city and is now growing further. Projects are developing along it, and a pedestrian promenade and nascent tramline contribute to an entirely new kind of 'sustainable' lifestyle for this automotive city. The topology of the BeltLine works like a common thread along a 35-km (22-mile) circuit of footpaths, bike lanes and tramlines linking previously disconnected neighbourhoods together and opening up a vast array of community activities and possibilities.

In a similar way, but on another continent, the city of Antwerp decided to convert the disused rail yard of the Antwerpen Dam into a park. The Spoor Nord Park, covering 24 hectares (55 acres), designed by Studio Associato Secchi-Viganò (2009), brings together neighbourhoods that had been kept apart for over a century [12.42].[26] The subtle topological play connecting the west side to the east side turns the park into a natural place of convergence for sport, events and

12.44

leisure activities. A central water feature located by the Cargo Hall marks the cultural focus of the park, where people meet for concerts, games and food.

To transform large-scale environments through appropriate landscape methods requires an act of faith and strong political will. Without long-term support, it is not possible to sustain the scale of such an approach. In this instance, emphasis must be placed on landscapes that can function and be maintained as living frameworks. The case of the Parc aux Angéliques (2015) on the right bank of the Garonne River in Bordeaux is a good example of topological transformation [12.44].[27] By planting a broad selection of native trees in a series of lines perpendicular to the river on some disused industrial sites, the landscape architect Michel Desvigne has organized the entire waterfront as a potential 'natural' park that will eventually cover over 40 hectares (almost 100 acres). The landscape serves also as a prefiguration of the urban programme to come, with ecological zones, an urban farm, sport fields and bicycle trails framing three new neighbourhoods. The Plateau de Saclay Campus project (2014), also under the leadership of Michel Desvigne, shows another facet of large-scale landscape planning [12.45]. The site of Saclay, south-west of Paris, was structured and drained originally in Baroque times to provide water for the park at Versailles. The precision with which this piece of territory was engineered and maintained over four centuries is consciously inscribed in the topological approach of the project. The campus, which covers 7,000 hectares (17,300 acres), is intended to become the new 'silicon valley' of France, welcoming prestigious engineering and science schools as well as enterprises on a sustainable site with public landscape amenities and a mass-transit system. Desvigne has taken great care to integrate the long-standing drainage grid of the territory in his scheme. This is a top-down project in the best of French centralized tradition and it will be interesting to see how this mix of landscape tradition and ecological innovation will unfold. These two powerful examples clearly illustrate how designed landscapes on a territorial scale can be developed to such a degree that their topology becomes part of a new natural and ecological reality.

In the contemporary urban context, landscapes are often more fragmented, but are intended to reflect the values of human respect and ecological hope that make up the spirit of a place. The Parc Blandan project (2013) produced by the office Base on the 17-hectare (42-acre) site of an old military fort adjoins some of the most populous districts of Lyon [12.46]. The park is organized into three major zones that play skilfully with the topography, providing amenities for relaxation and play while maintaining distinct ecological zones for the local flora and fauna. Such a pragmatic approach to given site conditions and topology raises hopes of a new dawn in French landscape architecture.

12.44 The Parc aux Angéliques, Bordeaux, France, 2015.
Michel Desvigne's concept of prefigurative landscape reinforces the idea that landscape architecture can become the structural substrate of the contemporary city. By imprinting a landscape in Bordeaux with over 4,500 trees he has prefigured the framework of a city to come, while providing a strong public amenity for today.

12.45 The new campus plan for the Plateau de Saclay, France, by Michel Desvigne.
Here Desvigne prefigures the structure of a new university town. Careful attention to historic traces that have shaped this plateau since the times of Louis XIV brings a sense of balance and belonging and gives topological coherence to the entire project.

12.46 The Parc Blandan, Lyon, France, by BASE, 2013.
Created on the site of an old military camp, this has become the second-most used park in the city. A minimal approach to design combined with good programmatic planning means that most elements of the park including topography and vegetation already existed.

12.45

12.46

12.47 Pleated earth ridges at Schiphol airport, Amsterdam, The Netherlands, by HNS, 2014.
Through the combined work of an artist and a landscape office, a new typology has been invented that can considerably reduce ground noise around airports. Pleated earth ridges, 3 metres (10 feet) high, work playfully together to define a field that deflects sound and makes a strong topological statement at the same time.

12.48 The National 9 / 11 Memorial, New York, USA, by Peter Walker Partners, 2011.
The project draws on the very substance of the void left by the two fallen towers of the World Trade Center to recall a very strong topological experience. Like two vast square clearings in a forest of oaks, the memorial brings us back through this archetype to the very roots of our landscape culture.

12.49 The Central Garden, the Getty Center, Los Angeles, USA, designed by Robert Irwin, 1997.
Bright pink bougainvillea clambers over a cluster of artificial Cor-ten trees to provide a place to sit in the shade. The artificiality of these 'trees' does not contradict either their sense or their purpose; it is the notion of comfort and belonging that matters. Most landscape topologies that we will witness in our age will be, and will remain, artificial.

12.47

12.48

12.49

Shaping terrain

The cultural questions thrown up by new topological methods are truly fundamental. Since they pertain to landscape, they relate to the ground itself, in all its specificity. When it comes to reading and modifying the ground conditions of a site, topology draws a clear distinction between design on a physical model and the dream of an idealized plan. It marks a return to basic archetypal traditions where new forms of terrain can emerge, alongside an awareness of the pre-eminence of site. The Dutch land artist Paul de Kort working with the office of HNS (2014) created an extraordinary field of pleated earth ridges of 36 hectares (75 acres) that effectively reduce by half the low-frequency sound of planes coming from Schiphol airport before they reach adjacent neighbourhoods [12.47].[28] The ridges arranged in playful rhythmic patterns disperse the noise as it travels on the ground. The field is also an artistic invitation to wander, picnic and play.

Through a stronger awareness and sensitivity to topology, landscape architecture can also enhance expressions that place human concerns and emotions at their heart. The National 9/11 Memorial by Peter Walker Partners in New York (2011) is an archetypal project that symbolically reinstates the memory of the twin towers in a clearing in a highly emblematic forest of oaks [12.48]. The water falling down the two deep voids left by the footprints of the towers conveys a sense of vertigo to the visitor. The project fulfils the basic human need to create beauty out of what is odious, and to install meaningful forms of hope, rather than abandonment and oblivion, in the landscapes where we belong.

The hand of the artist often makes a difference to our appreciation of landscapes. The Central Garden at the Getty Center in Los Angeles designed by the American artist Robert Irwin (1997) marks a precise topological distinction by inventing a new realm of poetry, craft and sensitivity in the present language of landscapes [12.49].[29] The freedom with which the garden plays with up to 500 species of plants offers a colourful contrast to the visitor. Cor-ten baskets filled with bright red bougainvillea act like trees on the artificial ground.

A landscape only gains sense when it is fully recognized and accepted by people. Technological and scientific advances may help when it comes to issues of topology and ecology, but these notions often remain distant from more immediate human concerns. The possible meaning attached to parks and gardens may have changed at present, but not their ultimate destination. Imagine a city that could offer the luxury of peaceful gardens and ecology instead of stretches of wasteland – a place of human comfort and exchange instead of desolation and disgust. Notions of grounding and rootedness can be reaffirmed with topology to encourage a feeling that our world is permanently in the making. It is this faith in a design with nature on a human scale, in all its complexity and promise, that will deliver the landscapes of the future.

Afterword
Towards a Cultural Revolution in Nature

'*I am aiming at blurring the distinction between nature and society durably, so that we shall never have to go back to two distinct sets, with nature on one side and the representations that humans make of it on the other.*'

Bruno Latour, *The Politics of Nature*[1]

Early sedentary settlements marked the land with a distinct separation between societal space and the natural environment. Archetypes such as the forest clearing and walled garden embodied the mysteries of space, time and creation through thresholds where the rituals of nature and fertility were staged. The distinction between a place where nature was cared for and the surrounding untended wilderness came to be called landscape: a formal artefact of nature crafted for both utilitarian and symbolic purposes. The faith that once animated these archaic sites has gone, but looking at an old sanctuary in Kyoto, where fallen leaves are carefully skimmed from the surface of a pond to avoid

eutrophic conditions, one feels a strong aesthetic bond with nature [13.0]. Is the skimming of the leaves purely an aesthetic gesture or is it also non-ecological? With the recent rise of ecological concerns, the very purpose of landscape has changed drastically; notions of abandonment became part of a new ethical consideration, making things confused. For it is this lack of immanence, the manner in which a landscape remains uncared for, that introduces an element of doubt: although our natural world has become humanized to a large extent, has our reverence for nature become misconstrued?

A renewed willingness to conceive landscape as infused with symbolism, tapping into the signifiers of a culture, would help to recover sensitivity and meaning. Looking at the painterly power and beauty of Yves Brunier's Museum Park in Rotterdam (1993), we feel a bond towards nature [13.1].[2] Must we strive to unravel myths again, albeit ecological ones? Only then will we achieve a more respectful relationship towards our world, by giving a greater place to nature in society.[3]

13.0 (opposite) A gardener gathers fallen leaves from a pond in Kyoto, Japan.
This subtle gesture, full of sensitivity and care, is repeated each year and controls nature in a ritual that holds things in balance. Shaping landscape in this manner is an investment that should be at the heart of our concerns, for only through an active contact with the landscape can we reinstate a sense of respect for our world.

13.1 Museum Park, Rotterdam, The Netherlands, by Yves Brunier and Petra Blaisse of OMA, begun in 1989.
The park connects the city with the River Meuse through a series of highly evocative landscapes that play with moods in a juxtaposition of colours, textures and light. Brunier reintroduced a painterly manner in his practice through expressive artworks and collages; he died before seeing the extraordinary park he created.

13.1

13.2

Rapid urban growth has pushed landscape towards the fringes of society. There is an absence of purpose between a town and its immediate surroundings. A more meaningful interaction between dwelling and landscape requires a symbolic act – one which, unfortunately, seldom occurs. The scientific word 'biotope', borrowed from ecology, designates a biotic equilibrium inherent to 'un-manned' patches of nature that are residual. Yet what a biotope achieves ecologically, it often fails to deliver on a societal level.[4] Our task is to reconcile society with ecology, because the history of 'undesigned' ecologies is recent, and their adoption remains speculative, not to say unwieldy, as if we no longer can recall landscape aesthetics as the long-standing expression of our symbolic bond to nature.

Take the Seonyudo Island Park in Seoul (2003), which transformed an old sewage-treatment plant into an 'ecological' showcase [13.2].[5] Schoolchildren visit the park each day to learn about the virtues of ecology and admire a nature displayed within the disused cesspools. The project replicates stylistically the post-industrial IBA landscapes of the Ruhr, but misses an essential historical point, one deeply rooted in Korean culture, which inspired the Confucian poets and painters of the Joseon kingdom in the 16th century to revere this sacred island on the Han River. What matters are the signs of a greater devotion to nature; nothing can replace these profound moments that

are in resonance with the deeper beliefs of a people. Despite good intentions, showing a cesspool filled with water lilies to children falls somewhat short of the respect for nature one would expect here.

What we lack is a strong sense of poetics that would give voice to a new form of naturalism. Each culture has wrought symbolism from a cultivation of nature that is proper to its language and customs. Perhaps we should follow Alessandra Ponte's precepts, and allow notions of the Beautiful, the Picturesque and the Sublime to be resurgent and become more local and specific.[6] Only then can a shared understanding of nature return. The Barcelona Botanical Garden (1999) designed by the landscape architect Beth Figueras with the architects Carlos Ferrater and Josep Lluís Canosa embraces these notions, incorporating Mediterranean taxonomy with a zest of radical topology inspired by Catalan Cubism [13.3]. The angular Cor-ten steel walls set against exotic and endemic plant collections on the arid slopes of Montjuïc demonstrate how a serious interpretation of nature can remain culturally strong and creative. Contemporary systems thinking increasingly focuses on complex ecological networks, but misses an essential point: the possibility of a reconciliation between society and the cultural potential of nature.

We now live under a scientific conception of the world driven by a moral imperative that has reduced the range of

13.2 Seonyudo Island Park, Seoul, South Korea, 2003.
The island that once inspired Confucian poets and painters of the Joseon kingdom became a sewage-treatment plant in the 1970s, but was then transformed again into a park by the Ctopos office in 2003. Children are taught to observe 'ecology' in old settling tanks. This celebration of ruins is a Western concept that excludes Korean landscape aesthetics and the spirit of belonging.

13.3 The new Barcelona Botanical Garden, Montjuïc, 1997.
The project was designed by Beth Figueras together with the architects Carlos Ferrater and Josep Lluís Canosa. A completely modern landscape, the strong topographic design builds on a scenography of nature, with plants placed according to ecological affinity, but also in great swathes of colour and textures held in terraces by triangular Cor-ten steel panels. The poetic voice of the late designer can still be felt.

13.3

landscape design to a form of 'biomimicry'. Our new maxim is equity and biodiversity under the threat of global warming, and the new oracle is sustainable development. Preston Scott Cohen and Erika Naginski discuss an apocalyptic drama where the finiteness of resources is played out against the 'dismal' cycle of human production and consumption.[7] To what degree does this 'ontological primacy of bio-environment' and its inexorable constraints negate working with earlier landscape archetypes?[8] The empirical trend to 'naturalize' landscape has made it difficult to reaffirm a belief in a cultural continuum. The new trend in 'biomimicry' is uncritical of itself and profoundly ahistorical because it is a rejection of the social, 'symbolic life of forms' be they social, cultural or political.[9] But there are exceptions to this rule: the Nørrebro Park (2007) in Copenhagen, designed by Steen Høyer uses an archetypal form to enhance a stretch of urban park [13.4].[10] The gentle topography of the urban clearing invites people to relax year round. Human rituals have changed, but the specific topology of a place has not. The culture of forming landscape transmitted from one generation to the next has been blocked, and there is an urgent need to 'demystify the ecological and the sustainable while acknowledging the reality of new necessities'.[11]

A cultural revolution of nature is now necessary: deep ecology – understood as the fabrication of 'real' nature at the polar opposite of 'real' civilization – could replace history at a stroke, fulfilling a redeeming role as an empirically driven biological 'restart' for the planet. Up to now landscape has never been considered a simple act of biology, but rather as a complex, deeply symbolic cultural artefact. Yet ecology has not only superseded the meaning of history, but has actually transcended all established transformative traditions. Proponents of deep ecology believe that the planet should be saved from humanity, dismissing any reference to history as unworthy. This new messianic faith in nature finds worldwide appeal precisely at a time when natural destruction has never been so great.

We are heading for a brave new world of ecology, supported by the great scientific predictions of cybernetics. Yet we are also in a form of historical denial that has damaged the transmission of landscape culture durably. The beauty of a landscape is first and foremost human and not natural. Many landscape forms have been forgotten, but the question of form in design remains essential, and ecology alone cannot be a substitute for the symbolic meaning of nature ingrained in our collective memory. We need to renew our relationship with nature creatively, but will never retrieve a sense of wholeness from this empirically dissected reality.

We should trust our need for a deeper sense of purpose and humanity in a landscape, and it is precisely the substitution of an immanent understanding of landscape for a more profane scientific explanation that has left us

13.4

stranded. The first sedentary landscapes marked a clear break from nature, with strong intent and cosmological purpose, but these places conceived *in situ* also embodied an inherent wonder towards the living world.[12] Such early animistic rituals can still be witnessed in places like the Ise Naiku shrine in Japan, where tall hinoki trees are ritually sacrificed every two decades to erect the temples anew [13.5]. This re-enactment of tree sacrifice reaches back to time immemorial, and to Japan's ancestral links to the animistic tribes of Siberia, such as the Buryats. The cult of the ancestors that is associated with Ise asserts a deep belief in the equilibrium of memory, place and nature. Ecology may certainly play an important role in society, but without reaching a balance and clear correspondence with each cultural trope, custom and spiritual sensibility, it will find neither a resonance nor direction of its own.

Landscape is the crucible of human actions and reactions towards nature, and landscapes are the product of a deep cultural revolution that occurred at the dawn of human settlement 9,000 years ago. But the myths that originated then need to be seriously reconsidered in light of our present condition that is significantly removed from the natural world. Can a sense of the sublime in nature still prevail within our very muddled 'technoid' culture, or is it just a naturalistic mirage? Our planet is weary, and despite it green ecological make-up we instinctively know that something

fundamental has changed. The landscape ruins of today are no longer the enigmatic fabrications of 18th-century Anglo-Chinese gardens, nor the exquisite imperfections embedded in early Zen gardens; they are actually widespread and very real.

The purpose of this book was to place the reader back under an old grove of trees, to show how our relationship to nature has drastically changed. In our current environmentally anxious age, projects no longer seem to carry much mystery about them. To detach ourselves from humankind's immediate necessities seems unthinkable; but a new form of transformative landscape architecture will help reset the cultural paradigm. It will infuse an entirely new sense of being in the world, one that can nurture hope and reconcile our spirit with a simpler kind of existence while planting a younger grove of trees anew.

13.4 Nørrebro Park, Copenhagen, Denmark, by GHB landscape architects and Steen Høyer, 2007.
The very simple, almost banal terrain modelling allows this linear park at the heart of the city to create comfort by crafting an 'inside' where people can enjoy themselves even in the middle of winter. This topological gesture is archetypal in that it encourages landscape habits that have been with us since time immemorial.

13.5 The House of Nature at the Ise Naiku Shrine, Japan.
Landscape mirrors how we inhabit nature and find a balance – call it ecology if you will. The word ecology derives from the Greek word *oikos*, meaning house. At the Ise Naiku Shrine in Japan a house dedicated to the goddess Amaterasu-omikami invites a praying mantis to commune with us. It serves as an inspiration, balancing nature's mysteries with humanity, seeking a poetic language common to all that is stronger than science or reason.

13.5

Notes

Foreword

1 Report of the United Nations Conference on Environment and Development, Rio de Janeiro, 3–14 June 1992, Annex III, 'Non-Legally Binding Authoritative Statement of Principles for a Global Consensus on the Management, Conservation and Sustainable Development of All Types of Forests', Preamble (e) and (g).

2 Kolbert, Elizabeth, 'Unsafe Climates', in *The New Yorker*, 7 December 2015.

3 The term was coined by, among others, the chemist Paul Crutzen, who proposed the definition of a geological age beginning in the late 18th century as the Anthropocene.

Introduction

1 'C'est là que nous agissons par l'imaginaire, non pas en modifiant le monde, mais en le préparant. La literature est un levier puissant et c'est pour cela qu'elle ne peut disparaître.' J. M. G Le Clézio, 'La littérature est un levier puissant', interview with Eric Fottorino, in *Le Monde*, 5 October 2009. Translation Christophe Girot, 2012. Clézio was awarded the Nobel Prize for Literature in 2008.

2 The garden was designed by Charles de Noailles in the 1950s with the help of English gardeners on a terraced site in Grasse, with old olive groves on restored 'restanque' (terraced) cisterns.

3 The Cedron (Kidron) Valley cuts a topographic rift between the Temple Mount and the Mount of Olives in Jerusalem; its rocky terraces were landscaped not for cultivation but for the burial of the dead, and the Cedron's scarce water was meant to purify the bodies, before flowing down east through Judaea to the Dead Sea. This is where Jews, Muslims and Christians lay at rest. The picture was taken in May 2012 by a young French photographer Simon David, who passed away tragically the year after.

4 Stronach, David, *Pasargadae: A Report on the Excavation Conducted by the British Institute of Persian Studies from 1961 to 1963* (Oxford: Clarendon Press, 1978).

5 Descola, Philippe, *Beyond Nature and Culture*, trans. Lloyd, J. (Chicago: University of Chicago Press, 2013).

6 The park, designed by the landscape office of Zulauf, Seippel, Schweingruber and Hubacher Haerle architects, was planted with birch, cherry and paulownia on a dense 4 × 4 metre grid. Over time these will be thinned out to a maximum of an 8 × 8 metre grid. Moll, Claudia, *Zürich, ein Begleiter zu neuer Landschaftsarchitektur* (Munich: Georg D. W. Callwey, 2006).

7 Fery, Thekla, *Von der Restfläche zur neuen Landschaft – Das Schöneberger Südgelände in Berlin* (Berlin: Univ.-Bibliothek TU Berlin, 2005).

8 Esposito, Robert, *Bios: Biopolitics and Philosophy*, trans. Campbell, T. (Minneapolis: University of Minnesota Press, 2008).

9 Designed by the landscape architect Gustav Lange, the Mauerpark occupies an area that belonged to the no-man's-land running along the Berlin Wall. The site was rapidly taken over in the 1990s and covered with graffiti. It has become the stage for spontaneous musical events, which run day and night through the summer months. The park seems to survive on almost zero maintenance, and nature here is reduced to the bare essentials of a heavily used but decrepit lawn.

1. Roots

1 *Poems from the Divan of Hafiz*, trans. Bell, Gertrude Lowthian (London: W. Heinemann, 1897), 68.

2 Nebamun was an ordinary scribe and grain counter in 18th Dynasty Thebes. The wall painting on plaster from his tomb now on display in the British Museum shows a garden in the afterlife that resembles the gardens of the wealthy class to which he did not belong. Parkinson, Richard, *The Painted Tomb-Chapel of Nebamun* (London: British Museum Press, 2008), 63ff.

3 William Ryan and Walter Pitman had postulated a date of *c.* 5600 BCE for the event; other studies, which have carbon-dated freshwater mollusc shells found at the bottom of the Black Sea, appear to suggest that massive volumes of salt water swept into the depression in *c.* 7400 BCE – the date I have accepted here. See Ryan, William, and Pitman, Walter, *Noah's Flood: The New Scientific Discoveries about the Event that Changed History* (New York: Simon & Schuster, 1998). For the more recent research, see Romanescu, Georghe, 'Geoarchaeology of the ancient and medieval Danube Delta: Modeling environmental and historical changes. A review', in *Advancing Pleistocene and Holocene Climate Change Research in the Carpathian-Balkan Region*, Quaternary International, vol. 293 (April 2013), and Giosan, L. et al., 'Young Danube Delta documents stable Black Sea level since the middle Holocene: morphodynamic, paleogeographic, and archaeological implications', *Geology*, 34, 9 (2006), 757–60.

4 Gupta, Sanjeev, et al., 'Catastrophic flooding origin of shelf valley systems in the English Channel', *Nature*, 448 (2007), 342–45.

5 Hambledon Hill was occupied around 3000 BCE, at a time when the Blackmore Vale in Dorset along the Stour valley was still a heavily forested area. Mercer, Roger, and Healey, Frances, *Hambledon Hill, Dorset, England. Excavation and Survey of a Neolithic Monument Complex and its Surrounding Landscape, Vol. 1* (London: English Heritage, 2008).

6 A study led by Paul Wozencroft and Paul Devereux from the Royal College of Art in London (2014) established that the famous blue stones brought from Mynydd Preseli, 322 km (200 miles) away in Pembrokshire, south Wales, were actually metallic sounding 'lithophones' or so-called ringing rocks.

7 MacKillop, James, *Dictionary of Celtic Mythology* (Oxford: Oxford University Press, 1998).

8 Field, David, et al., 'Introducing Stonehenge', *British Archaeology*, 111 (2010), 32–35.

9 Gupta, Sanjeev, et al., 'Catastrophic flooding origin of shelf valley systems in the English Channel', *Nature*, 448 (2007), 342–45.

10 Malone, Caroline, *The Prehistoric Monuments of Avebury, Wiltshire* (London: English Heritage guidebook, 1994). Burl, Aubrey, *Prehistoric Avebury* (New Haven and London: Yale University Press, 1979).

11 Pitts, M., and Whittle, A., 'The development and date of Avebury', *Proceedings of the Prehistoric Society*, 58 (1992), 203–12.

12 Cohen, Chaim, 'Eden', in Berlin, Adele, and Grossman, Maxine, *The Oxford Dictionary of the Jewish Religion* (Oxford: Oxford University Press, 2011).

13 Discovered in the tomb of Meketre in Thebes in the 1920s, this wooden model of a paradise garden in the afterlife, now in the Metropolitan Museum in New York, shows scale and remarkable detailing.

14 Ghirshman, Roman, *Fouilles de Sialk près de Kashan, 1933, 1934, 1937, vol. 1* (Paris: Geuthner, 1938).

15 The poetry of Hafez of Shiraz captures the atmosphere of these refined and sensuous gardens: 'Last night, when Irem's magic garden slept, / Stirring the hyacinth's purple tresses curled, / The wind of morning through the alleys stept' ('The Birds of the Garden Sang unto the Rose'), *Poems from the Divan of Hafiz*, trans. Bell, Gertrude Lowthian (London: W. Heinemann, 1897).

16 Research reveals up to 75 small water mills along the stretch between the Bagh-i Fin and the city of Kashan. Pourjafar, Mohammad Reza, Amirkhani, Aryan, and Leylian, Mohammad Reza, 'Traditional architecture of Iranian water mills in reference to historical documents and the case studies', *Asian Culture and History*, 2, 2 (2010) 234–51.

2. Hydraulic Civilizations

1 Ferry, David, *Gilgamesh. A New Rendering in English Verse (Tablet XI)* (New York: Farrar, Strauss and Giroux, 1992), 81–82.

2 Jericho is known to have existed in the form of a small village built around a spring in *c.* 9000 BCE, but it was not inhabited continuously until the early 7th millennium BCE. Mithen, Steven, *After the Ice: A Global Human History, 20,000–5000 BC* (London: Weidenfeld & Nicolson, 2003; Cambridge, Mass.: Harvard University Press 2006), 57.

3 Ibid.

4 Service, Elman, *Primitive Social Organization: An Evolutionary Perspective* (New York: Random House, 1962).

5 Jacques Cauvin describes the early Anatolian settlement of Çatalhöyük, which drew its irrigation water from deep wells and stored it in large reservoirs. Its society thrived on this system until it was gradually decimated by malaria. Cauvin, Jacques, *The Birth of the Gods and the Origins of Agriculture*, trans. Watkins, Trevor (Cambridge: Cambridge University Press, 2000).

6 Ryan and Pitman's theory would solve the long-standing enigma surrounding the spread of the proto-Indo-European language, making it a direct consequence of tribes living on the Black Sea shores fleeing the flood in various directions. See Ryan, William, and Pitman, Walter, *Noah's Flood: The New Scientific Discoveries about the Event that Changed History* (New York: Simon & Schuster, 1998).

7 Kramer, S. N., *The Sumerians: Their History, Culture, and Character* (Chicago: University of Chicago Press, 1963).

8 We have inherited the Sumerian calendar and part of its belief system from ancient Mesopotamia, although most people would probably not, for instance, associate the astrological sign of Virgo in late summer with the Roman goddess Ceres, the Greek goddess Demeter or the Mesopotamian fertility goddess Ishtar.

9 Leonard Woolley's discovery at Ur of sacrificial tombs, in which rulers were accompanied by their attendants, attests to the power of religion in later Sumerian cultures. Woolley, Leonard, *Excavations at Ur* (London: E. Benn; New York: Barnes and Noble, 1963).

10 Anthony, David, *The Horse, the Wheel, and Language: How Bronze-Age Riders from the Eurasian Steppes Shaped the Modern World* (Princeton: Princeton University Press, 2007).

11 Spar, Ira, 'The Origins of Writing', Heilbrunn Timeline of Art History, The Metropolitan Museum of Art, http://www.metmuseum.org/toah/.

12 Aaboe, A., 'Scientific Astronomy in Antiquity', in *Philosophical Transactions of the Royal Society of London*, 276, 1257 (1974), 21–42.

13 Legend has it that Nebuchadnezzar II built the gardens in the 6th century BCE for his wife, Amytis of Media, who was pining for the fragrant mountain gardens of her homeland in Persia. In this case, the model was perhaps the ancient Bagh-i Fin garden near Kashan.

14 Dalley, Stephanie, *The Mystery of the Hanging Garden of Babylon: An Elusive World Wonder Traced* (Oxford: Oxford University Press, 2013).

15 Altaweel, Mark, 'Simulating the effects of salinization on irrigation agriculture in southern Mesopotamia, in Wilkinson, T. J., Gibson, M., and Widell, M. (eds), *Models of Mesopotamian Landscapes: How Small-Scale Processes Contribute to the Growth of Early Civilizations* (Oxford: Archaeopress, 2014), 219–39.

16 Schama, Simon, *Landscape and Memory* (New York: A. A. Knopf, 1995).

17 Base 10 mathematics appeared in Egypt in Tomb Uj at Abydos around 3000 BCE. Burton, David, *The History of Mathematics: An Introduction* (New York: McGraw-Hill, 2005).

18 Verner, Miroslav, *The Pyramids: The Mystery, Culture, and Science of Egypt's Great Monuments* (New York: Grove Press 2002), 386.

19 Rackham, Oliver, 'Observations on the historical ecology of Boeotia', *The Annual of the British School at Athens*, 78 (1983), 291–351.

20 The exodus mentions the parting of a 'sea of reeds', which would conform well with the topography of Lake Moeris. The opening of dammed waters on to the pharaoh's troops as they rode through a dry Joseph Canal is further offered as a plausible explanation. Hebrew: *Kriat Yam Suph* (Crossing of the Sea of Reeds) is part of the escape of the Israelites, led by Moses, from the pursuing Egyptians in the Book of Exodus 13:17–14:29.

3. From Temenos to Physis

1 Nagy, Gregory, *Homeric Hymn to Demeter*, Cambridge, Department of the Classics Harvard University, 2000 (Stanzas 7–17 condensed).

2 Early Minoan snake goddesses were most probably the representation of an earth goddess. Bonney, Emily M., 'Disarming the Snake Goddess: a reconsideration of the faience figurines from the Temple Repositories at Knossos', *Journal of Mediterranean Archaeology*, 24, 2 (2011), 171–90.

3 The first oracles appeared on the island of Delos and at Delphi in the 8th century BCE. Bowden, Hugh, *Classical Athens and the Delphic Oracle: Divination*

and Democracy (Cambridge: Cambridge University Press, 2005).
4 The Greek myth of Europa is first related in Homer's *Odyssey* in the 8th century BCE, but it refers to ancient landscapes of the Mesara Plain in Crete. Vidal-Naquet, Pierre, *Le monde d'Homère* (Paris: Perrin, 2000), 19.
5 Rackham, Oliver, and Moody, Jennifer A., *The Making of the Cretan Landscape* (Manchester: Manchester University Press, 1996).
6 Robinson, Andrew, 'The Phaistos code: Write only', *Nature*, 453 (2008), 990–91.
7 Smith, William S., *Interconnections in the Ancient Near East: A Study of the Relationships Between the Arts of Egypt, the Aegean and Western Asia* (New Haven: Yale University Press, 1965).
8 Dickinson, Oliver, *The Aegean Bronze Age* (Cambridge: Cambridge University Press, 2005).
9 Bowden, Hugh, *Mystery Cults of the Ancient World* (London: Thames & Hudson; Princeton: Princeton University Press, 2010).
10 Page, D. L., *The Santorini Volcano and the Destruction of Minoan Crete* (London: The Society for the Promotion of Hellenic Studies, 1970). Also, Manning, S. W., *A Test of Time and A Test of Time Revisited: The Volcano of Thera and the Chronology and History of the Aegean and East Mediterranean in the Mid-Second Millennium BC* (Oxford and Philadelphia: Oxbow Books, 2014).
11 The Linear B writing system from the Late Minoan period is clearly identifiable as an early form of Greek. Ventris, Michael, *Work Notes on Minoan Language Research and Other Unedited Papers* (Rome: Edizioni dell'Ateneo, 1988).
12 Halstead, Paul & Frederick, Charles (eds), *Landscape and Land Use in Postglacial Greece* (Sheffield: Sheffield Academic Press, 2000).
13 This is highly probable, unless it was the Dorians, who stemmed from the northern reaches of Macedonia and the Danube, who first introduced agriculture to Greece. Isager, Signe, and Skydsgaard, Jens E., *Ancient Greek Agriculture: An Introduction* (London and New York: Routledge, 1995).
14 Mayor, Adrienne, *The Amazons: Lives and Legends of Warrior Women Across the Ancient World* (Princeton: Princeton University Press, 2014).
15 Broad, William J., *The Oracle: The Lost Secrets and Hidden Message of Ancient Delphi* (New York: Penguin, 2006).
16 Frazer, J. G. (trans.), *Pausanias's Description of Greece*, Vol. 5, 314–18 (New York: MacMillan, 1913).
17 Fontenrose, Joseph, *Python: A Study of Delphic Myth and Its Origins* (Berkeley: University of California Press, 1959).
18 Parke, H. W., *A History of the Delphic Oracle* (Oxford: Basil Blackwell, 1939).
19 Dinsmoor, William B., *The Architecture of Ancient Greece* (New York: Biblio and Tannen, 1973).
20 Barnes, Jonathan, *The Presocratic Philosophers* (London: Routledge, rev. ed., 1982).
21 Hodgkin, Luke, *A History of Mathematics: From Mesopotamia to Modernity* (Oxford: Oxford University Press, 2005), Chapter 2 'Greeks and "Origins"'.
22 Diels, H. (ed.), *Simplicii in Aristotelis Physicorum Libros Quattuor Priores Commentaria* (Berlin: G. Reimer, 1882), Book IV, 24, 13. Simplicius, *On Aristotle's Physics*, trans. Fleet, B. (Ithaca: Cornell University Press, 1997).
23 Virgil, *Eclogues, Georgics, Aeneid*, trans. Fairclough, H. R. (Loeb Classical Library, Cambridge, Mass.: Harvard University Press, 1916).

4. Of Villas and Woods

1 Virgil, *Eclogues, Georgics, Aeneid*, trans. Fairclough, H. R. (Loeb Classical Library, Cambridge, Mass.: Harvard University Press, 1916).
2 Achilli, A., et al., 'Mitochondrial DNA variation of modern Tuscans supports the Near Eastern origin of Etruscans', *American Journal of Human Genetics*, 80 (2007), 759–68.
3 Torelli, Mario, *The Etruscans* (London: Thames & Hudson, 2000).
4 Mackay, Christopher, *Ancient Rome: A Military and Political History* (Cambridge: Cambridge University Press, 2004).
5 Von Stackelberg, Katharina, *The Roman Garden: Space, Sense and Society* (London and New York: Routledge, 2009).
6 Wiseman, Timothy P., *Remus: A Roman Myth* (Cambridge: Cambridge University Press, 1995).
7 Mann, J. C., 'The Settlement of Veterans in the Roman Empire', Doctoral Thesis University College London, 1956.
8 Laurence, Ray, *The Roads of Roman Italy: Mobility and Cultural Change* (London and New York: Routledge, 1999).
9 Lucretius, *On the Nature of Things: De rerum natura*, trans. Esolen, Anthony M. (Baltimore: The Johns Hopkins University Press, 1995).
10 Hodge, A. Trevor, *Roman Aqueducts and Water Supply* (London: Bristol Classical Press, new ed., 2002).
11 Sewell, Jamie, *The Formation of Roman Urbanism, 338–200 B.C.: Between Contemporary Foreign Influence and Roman Tradition* (Portsmouth, RI: Journal of Roman Archaeology, 2010). Krautheimer, Richard, *Rome, Profile of a City, 312–1308* (Princeton: Princeton University Press, 1980).
12 Meyboom, Paul G. P., *The Nile Mosaic of Palestrina: Early Evidence of Egyptian Religion in Italy* (Leiden: Brill, 1995).
13 Virgil, *Eclogues, Georgics, Aeneid*, trans. Fairclough, H. R. (Loeb Classical Library, Cambridge, Mass.: Harvard University Press, 1916).
14 Grimal, Pierre, *Les jardins romains* (Paris: Fayard, 3rd ed., 1984).
15 Rüpke, Jörg (ed.), *A Companion to Roman Religion* (Oxford: Blackwell, 2007).
16 Platner, Samuel Ball, *A Topographical Dictionary of Ancient Rome*, rev. Thomas Ashby (Oxford: Oxbow, 2002).
17 Grimal, Pierre, *Les jardins romains* (Paris: Fayard, 3rd ed., 1984).
18 Morrison, Donald R., *The Cambridge Companion to Socrates* (Cambridge: Cambridge University Press, 2010).
19 Inspired by the Villa of the Papyri at Herculaneum it was designed by architects Robert E. Langdon, Jr and Ernest C. Wilson, Jr, and opened in Pacific Palisades in 1974.
20 Adembri, Benedetta, *Hadrian's Villa* (Milan: Electa, 2000).
21 Boatwright, Mary T., *Peoples of the Roman World* (Cambridge: Cambridge University Press, 2012), 100–23.
22 Barker, Edmund Henry, *The Germany ... and the Agricola ...* (London: Longman & Co., 1828).
23 Hingley, Richard, *Hadrian's Wall: A Life* (Oxford: Oxford University Press, 2012).
24 Waldron, Arthur, *The Great Wall of China: From History to Myth* (Cambridge: Cambridge University Press, 1990).

5. The Rule of Faith

1 Sorrell, Roger, *St. Francis of Assisi and Nature: Tradition and Innovation in Western Christian Attitudes Towards the Environment* (New York: Oxford University Press, 1988), 60.
2 St Augustine, born in North Africa of Phoenician and Semitic descent, was brought up in the Manichaean faith before converting to Christianity. He established Christian theology around Manichaean notions of Original Sin, and constructed a dogma around the divinity of a single almighty God expressed through the Holy Trinity. He also introduced the cult of the Virgin Mary as the 'mother of god'. St Augustine proclaimed celibacy and chastity as the guiding rules of Christian priesthood and monastic life. Although he died during the siege of Hippo by the Vandals in 430 CE, his doctrine was widely adopted. Brown, Peter, *Augustine of Hippo* (Berkeley: University of California Press, 1967).
3 Gothic and Turkic tribes repeatedly invaded Europe during the 4th and 5th centuries, followed by Arab, Mongolian and Norman invasions thereafter. The Arab incursion into Spain lasted over 900 years, but this did not hinder the growth of monastic Christianity, first through the Visigoths and then through the subsequent Benedictine, Cistercian and Carthusian orders. Braunfels, Wolfgang, *Monasteries of Western Europe: The Architecture of the Orders* (London: Thames & Hudson, 1972).
4 According to legend, St Francis said to the wolf: '... O brother wolf, if so be thou no more offend them, and they shall forgive thee all thy past offences, and neither men nor dogs shall pursue thee any more'. Hudleston, Roger, *The Little Flowers of Saint Francis of Assisi* (London: Burns Oats & Washbourne, 1926), Chapter 21.
5 *The Lady and the Unicorn* is a set of six tapestries, each representing the mythical animal, which can be seen at the Musée du Moyen Âge (Musée de Cluny) in Paris.
6 Richard Koebner offers a detailed account of this 'colonization'; see 'The Settlement and Colonization of Europe' in *The Cambridge Economic History of Europe from the Decline of the Roman Empire, vol. 1, Agrarian Life of the Middle Ages* (Cambridge: Cambridge University Press, 2nd ed., 1966), 1–91.
7 There is a beautiful fictional account of Cistercian monks siting the future Abbaye du Thoronet in Provence in Pouillon, Fernand, *Les Pierres sauvages* (Paris: Seuil, 1964).
8 'The ground that the lord holds on behalf of his king, from his overlord down to the tenant farmer, where peasants toil year round, supports them all. In addition, the word "ground" should also imply the concept of distance. But Old French does not possess such a meaning: it appears only in around 1510, and derives from learned Latin circles. Before then one would mention "earth" only to designate what one tills and where one falls, where one rests, where one situates houses and churches, and where one will end up lying, awaiting the Final Judgment.' Zumthor, Paul, *La Mesure du monde* (Paris: Seuil, 1993), 73; translation Christophe Girot.
9 Williams, A., and Martin, G. H., *Domesday Book: A Complete Translation* (London: Penguin, 2003).
10 Braudel, Fernand, *L'identité de la France* (Paris: Arthaud Flammarion, 1986–87).
11 In Roman times, the forest of the Carnutes around Chartres had caused endless problems for Roman legions, who were constantly harassed by the local Celtic tribes who lived in the woods. A cathedral was then built on the remains of a Celtic temple and well, and the subsequent campaign to clear the forest for agriculture came to symbolize a triumph of light over darkness, of virtuous fertility over paganism and of productivity over idleness. Delaporte, Yves, *Notre-Dame de Chartres: Introduction historique et archéologique* (Paris: Hachette, 1957).
12 Davidson, Hilda Ellis, *The Lost Beliefs of Northern Europe* (London: Routledge, 1993).
13 The sap of the ash tree is still drawn each year in remote parts of Castelbuono in Sicily, where it is called manna, as if it were still considered a gift from the gods.
14 The cult of the Virgin Mary at Chartres, with its black Madonna made of polished linden wood which is paraded around the city during the summer harvest, could easily be likened to archaic fertility cults, such as those of Ceres, Demeter or Ishtar. Sumpton, Jonathan, *Pilgrimage* (London: Faber & Faber, 1975), 401.
15 Corvol, Andrée, *L'Arbre en Occident* (Paris: Fayard, 2009), 196.
16 Davidson, Hilda Ellis, *Myths and Symbols in Pagan Europe: Early Scandinavian and Celtic Religions* (Manchester: Manchester University Press, 1988).
17 Fulcanelli, *Le Mystère des cathédrales* (Paris: Jean Schmitt, 1926).
18 The pagan god Woden is mentioned in an old Saxon baptismal vow preserved in Vatican Codex 577: 'I forsake all devil's work and words, Thunear [Thor], Woden and Saxnot and all the monsters that are their retainers.' This clearly shows that forest pagans were still being Christianized during the 8th and 9th centuries. See Thorpe, Benjamin, *Northern Mythology: Comprising the Principal Popular Traditions and Superstitions of Scandinavia, North Germany, and the Netherlands* (London: Edward Lumley, 1851).
19 The 'Migration Period', also known as the 'Barbarian Invasions', was a time of human migration roughly between 300 and 700 CE. It is understood as marking the transition from Late Antiquity to the early Middle Ages. Geary, Patrick, *Myth of Nations. The Medieval Origins of Europe* (Princeton: Princeton Paperbacks, 2003).
20 The ransacking of Bath shortly after the fall of Rome in the 6th century is a good example of the outright rejection of this kind of refinement by subsequent tribes. Gerrard, James, 'The End of Roman Bath', *Current Archaeology*, 217 (2008), 24–31.
21 The garden of the Middle Ages was not only about divine contemplation and chastity, but was also the setting of a virtuous exchange between men and women, in which every single plant and detail was encoded with symbolic meaning. The tapestry series of the Lady and the Unicorn shows an extraordinary array of flowering plants within an enclosed space. Similar sets of tapestries are now in both the Musée du Moyen Âge, Paris, and the Metropolitan Museum

of Art, New York. Here, the columbine – to take one example – is a symbol of virtue and of the Virgin Mary. Freeman, Margaret B., *The Unicorn Tapestries* (New York: Metropolitan Museum of Art, 1956).
22 Bruun, Mette Birkedal, *The Cambridge Companion to the Cistercian Order* (Cambridge and New York: Cambridge University Press, 2013).
23 The name 'Poblet' stems from *populus*, the Latin name for the common poplar that grows naturally there on the banks of the Francolí River; the leafless tree blooms red each year around Easter time.
24 It is generally understood that the fall of Rome and the subsequent repulsion of Gothic and Vandal invaders by Mediterranean populations, particularly in North Africa and Spain, greatly facilitated the rapid penetration and establishment of Islam in Europe. Brunschvig, Robert, 'Ibn Abd al-Hakam et la conquête de l'Afrique du Nord par les arabes', *Al-Andalus*, 40 (1975), 129–79.
25 Watson, Andrew M., *Agricultural Innovation in the Early Islamic World: The Diffusion of Crops and Farming Techniques, 700–1100* (Cambridge: Cambridge University Press, 2008).
26 El-Bizri, Nader, 'A Philosophical Perspective on Alhazen's Optics', *Arabic Sciences and Philosophy*, 15 (2005), 189–218.
27 Øystein, Ore, *Number Theory and Its History* (New York: McGraw Hill, 1948).
28 Al-Khalili, Jim, *The House of Wisdom: How Arabic Science Saved Ancient Knowledge and Gave Us the Renaissance* (New York: Penguin, 2011).
29 Davidson, Herbert A., *Moses Maimonides: The Man and His Works* (Oxford: Oxford University Press, 2005).
30 Ettinghausen, Richard, and Grabar, Oleg, *The Art and Architecture of Islam, 650–1250* (New Haven: Yale University Press, 1987), 37–45.
31 Petrarca, Francesco [Petrarch], 'The Ascent of Mount Ventoux', in Cassirer, Ernst et al. (eds), *The Renaissance Philosophy of Man* (Chicago: University of Chicago Press, 1948).

6. Gardens of Perspective

1 Petrarca, Francesco [Petrarch], 'The Ascent of Mount Ventoux', in Cassirer, Ernst et al. (eds), *The Renaissance Philosophy of Man* (Chicago: University of Chicago Press, 1948).
2 It is said that Zhu Siben, born in 1273, designed the oldest bi-hemispherical world map. Although the example shown here is a 17th-century copy of the lost original, it appears that Chinese mastered this knowledge before the Europeans. Liu Gang, 'The Chinese Inventor of Bi-Hemispherical World Map', e-perimetron, 2, 3 (2007), 185–93.
3 LaFrenière, Gilbert, *The Decline of Nature: Environmental History and the Western Worldview* (Palo Alto: Academica Press, 2008).
4 Karpat, Kemal H., *The Ottoman State and Its Place in World History* (Leiden: Brill, 1974), 111.
5 Bagrow, Leo, *History of Cartography*, rev. ed. Skelton, R.A. (New Brunswick, NJ: Transaction Publishers, 2010).
6 Crane, Nicholas, *Mercator: The Man Who Mapped the Planet* (London: Phoenix, 2003).
7 Millon, Henry A., and Lampugnani, Vittorio Magnago (eds), *The Renaissance from Brunelleschi to Michelangelo: The Representation of Architecture* (London: Thames & Hudson, 1994).
8 Hibbert, Christopher, *The Rise and Fall of the House of Medici* (London: Penguin 1979).
9 Coffin, David, *The Villa d'Este at Tivoli* (Princeton: Princeton University Press, 1960).
10 Colonna, Francesco, trans. and intro. Godwin, Joscelyn, *Hypnerotomachia Poliphili: The Strife of Love in a Dream* (London: Thames & Hudson, 2005).
11 Ackerman, James, *The Villa: Form and Ideology of Country Houses* (Princeton: Princeton University Press, 1990).
12 Repcheck, Jack, *Copernicus' Secret: How the Scientific Revolution Began* (New York: Simon & Schuster, 2007).
13 Finocchiaro, Maurice, *Defending Copernicus and Galileo: Critical Reasoning in the Two Affairs* (New York: Springer, 2010).
14 Eltis, David, *The Rise of African Slavery in the Americas* (Cambridge and New York: Cambridge University Press, 2000).
15 Fernández-Armesto, F., *Amerigo: The Man Who Gave His Name to America* (New York: Random House, 2007).
16 Ballerini, Isabella, *The Medici Villas: Complete Guide* (Florence: Giunti, 2003).
17 Baldassare Lanci's perspectograph was used at Villa Lante. Jacomo Barozzi da Vignola talks about the surveying device in his book, *Le Due Regole della Prospettiva Pratica*, published in Rome in 1583.
18 Coffin, David, *The Villa in the Life of Renaissance Rome* (Princeton: Princeton University Press, 1979).
19 Battisti, Eugenio, 'Natura Artificioso to Natura Artificialis', in *The Italian Garden*, Dumbarton Oaks Colloquium on the History of Landscape Architecture, Coffin, David R. (ed.) (Washington, D.C.: Dumbarton Oaks, 1972).
20 Sheeler, Jessie, *The Garden at Bomarzo: A Renaissance Riddle* (London: Frances Lincoln, 2007).
21 Duchess of Devonshire, *The Garden at Chatsworth* (London: Frances Lincoln, 2001).
22 Salomon de Caus, *Le jardin palatin [Hortus Palatinus]* (Paris: Le Moniteur, 1981).
23 Palissy, Bernard, *Oeuvres Complètes* (Paris: Dubocher, 1844).
24 Dunzhen, Liu, *Chinese Classical Gardens of Suzhou* (New York: McGraw-Hill, 1993).

7. The Measure of Reason

1 Pascal, Blaise, *Thoughts*, trans. Trotter, W. F. (New York: Collier & Son, 1910).
2 Schama, Simon, *The Embarrassment of Riches: An Interpretation of Dutch Culture in the Golden Age* (New York: Knopf, 1987).
3 The city of Madinat as-Salam, founded by the Abbasid caliph al-Mansur in the 8th century and notable for its string of curvilinear canals, would later form the core of imperial Baghdad. Kennedy, Hugh, *When Baghdad Ruled the Muslim World* (Cambridge, Mass.: Da Capo Press, 2004).
4 Gelderblom, Oscar, and Jonker, Joost, 'Completing a financial revolution: The finance of the Dutch East India trade and the rise of the Amsterdam capital market, 1595–1612', *The Journal of Economic History*, 64, 3 (2004), 641–72.
5 Gaukroger, Stephen, *Descartes: An Intellectual Biography* (New York: Oxford University Press, 1995).
6 Andriesse, C. D., *Huygens: The Man Behind the Principle*, trans. Miedema, Sally (Cambridge: Cambridge University Press, 2005).
7 Sutton, Elizabeth A., *Capitalism and Cartography in the Dutch Golden Age* (Chicago: University of Chicago Press, 2015), 59–61.
8 Prak, Maarten, *The Dutch Republic in the Seventeenth Century: The Golden Age*, trans. Webb, Diane (Cambridge: Cambridge University Press, 2005).
9 North, John, *The Ambassadors' Secret: Holbein and the World of the Renaissance* (London: Phoenix, 2004).
10 Descartes, René, *Discourse on Method, Optics, Geometry, and Meteorology*, trans. Olscamp, Paul J. (Indianapolis: Hackett, 2001).
11 Crane, Nicholas, *Mercator: The Man Who Mapped the Planet* (London: Weidenfeld & Nicolson, 2002).
12 Dezallier d'Argenville, Antoine J., *La théorie et la pratique du jardinage* (Paris: Hachette, 2012 [1747]).
13 Schama, Simon, *The Embarrassment of Riches: An Interpretation of Dutch Culture in the Golden Age* (New York: Knopf, 1987).
14 Savory, Roger, *Iran under the Safavids* (Cambridge: Cambridge University Press, 2007).
15 The Chahar Bagh was built in 1603, while the Taj Mahal – a model of Mughal design – was begun in 1632 and completed in 1653. Koch, Ebba, *The Complete Taj Mahal, And the Riverfront Gardens of Agra* (London and New York: Thames & Hudson, 2006).
16 Intensive diplomatic exchanges through Armenian traders with Venice and Madrid, as well as with London and Moscow, as early as 1600 confirm the global ambition of the Safavids. The Safavid ambassador Husain Ali Beg travelled with the first Persian embassy to Europe between 1599 and 1602. There is a fresco in the Doge's Palace in Venice depicting the arrival of Persian ambassadors in 1599. Matthee, Rudolph P., *The Politics of Trade in Safavid Iran: Silk for Silver, 1600–1730* (Cambridge: Cambridge University Press, 1999).
17 Babaie, Sussan, *Isfahan and Its Palaces* (Edinburgh: Edinburgh University Press, 2008).
18 Hebert, Jean-François, and Sarmant, Thierry, *Fontainebleau: Mille ans d'histoire de France* (Paris: Éditions Tallandier, 2013).
19 Mariage, Thierry, *The World of André Le Nôtre*, trans. Larkin, Graham (Philadelphia: University of Pennsylvania Press, 1999).
20 Hazlehurst, F. Hamilton, *Gardens of Illusion: The Genius of André Le Nostre* (Nashville: Vanderbilt University Press, 1980).
21 Vaux-le-Vicomte can be seen as a manifestation of Cartesian dualism, in which the thinking mind is considered to be distinct from, and far subtler than, the body. Conan, Michel, 'New horizons of Baroque garden cultures', in *Baroque Garden Cultures: Emulation, Sublimation, Subversion*, Conan, Michel (ed.) (Washington, D.C.: Dumbarton Oaks, 2005), 1–37.
22 Farhat, Georges, 'L'anamorphose du territoire: les fonctions paysagères de la perspective topographique dans l'économie seigneuriale en France, autour de l'oeuvre d'André Le Nôtre (1613–1700)', Doctoral Thesis, Paris: Sorbonne, 2008.
23 Fumaroli, Marc, *Le Poète et le roi, Jean de La Fontaine et son siècle* (Paris: Éditions de Fallois, 1997).
24 Nicolas Fouquet was imprisoned for life shortly after his sumptuous inaugural party at Vaux-le-Vicomte in August 1661, arrested on the orders of a very young and suspicious Louis XIV. Nonethelesss, the gardens at Vaux served as inspiration for Versailles, and were subsequently depleted to provide material for the king's immense new garden.
25 The garden at Vaux-le-Vicomte, begun in 1653, was conceived by Le Nôtre at the request of Nicolas Fouquet during a period of regency when Louis XIV was only 15 years old, and had yet to seize fully the reins of power. It should, therefore, not be confused with the absolutist park at Versailles that ensued.
26 In the case of Vaux-le-Vicomte, Le Nôtre applied all the painterly knowledge he had acquired from his teacher, Simon Vouet, to the elaboration of the project. Bouchnot Déchin, Patricia, and Farhat, Georges, *André Le Nôtre en Perspectives* (Paris: Hazan, 2013).
27 For the plan of Vaux-le-Vicomte, Le Nôtre took as a starting point the Renaissance gardens of France and Italy, especially the Tuileries gardens in Paris, where he had been tutored by two generations of royal gardeners. When one compares the plan of the Tuileries with that of Vaux-le-Vicomte, one sees many formal and proportional similarities. The gardens are similar in width and length, and have the same features, in particular an elongated central axis extending towards the horizon. Both gardens are broad and rectangular in shape, balanced with parterres and woods on either side of the main axis. But the great difference at Vaux-le-Vicomte is the open perspective and the optical play with the concave topography of the terrain, which simply could not have happened in the same manner on the very flat terrain of the Tuileries gardens. What appears in plan to be the same is, in fact, significantly different on site.
28 According to Thierry Mariage the statue of Hercules was introduced only in 1895, almost 235 years after Fouquet's fateful party of August 1661, despite having been planned from the outset. Mariage, Thierry, *The World of André Le Nôtre*, trans. Larkin, Graham (Philadelphia: University of Pennsylvania Press, 1999).
29 'All our dignity resides in thought. By it we must elevate ourselves, and not by space and time, which we cannot fill. Let us endeavour, then, to think well; this is the principle of morality.' Pascal, Blaise *Pensées*, trans. Trotter, W. F. (New York: Random House, 1941), 347.
30 César-François and Jean-Dominique Cassini succeeded in mapping only parts of France in the mid-18th century, but, owing to the level range-finder and the *graphometre*, were able to do so with great precision. Pelletier, Monique, *Les cartes des Cassini, la science au service de l'état et des provinces* (Paris: CTHS, 2013).
31 Lafayette and French military engineers also trained the first US army engineering corps in the surveying techniques that had been developed in France. These would play a significant role in shaping the country – as a comparison between the southern states and those plotted according to the Jefferson grid reveals.
32 The so-called 'Western Mansions' were a series of European-style palaces and formal gardens designed by French Jesuit missionaries under the direction of Giuseppe Castiglione to satisfy the Qianlong emperor's taste for exotic buildings and objects. The same gardens were ransacked by French and British troops during the Second Opium War in the 19th century.

8. Gravity

1 Pope, Alexander, *The Poems of Alexander Pope*, Butt, John (ed.) (New Haven and London: Yale University Press, 1963), 808.

2 Ault, Donald, *Visionary Physics: Blake's Response to Newton* (Chicago: University of Chicago Press, 1974).

3 The Glorious Revolution of 1688 resulted in the deposition of James II and the accession of William of Orange (William III) and his wife, Mary, to the throne. During their coronation the concept of parliamentary supremacy over the king was formally established. Israel, Jonathan (ed.), *The Anglo-Dutch Moment: Essays on the Glorious Revolution and Its World Impact* (Cambridge: Cambridge University Press, 2003).

4 Ridgway, Christopher, 'Castle Howard', in *Chicago Botanic Garden Encyclopedia of Gardens*, Vol. 2, Shoemaker, Candice A. (ed.) (Chicago and London: Fitzroy Dearborn Publishers, 2001), 242–43.

5 Newton, Isaac, *The Principia, Mathematical Principles of Natural Philosophy*, trans. Cohen, Bernard, and Whitman, Ann (Oakland: University of California Press, 1999).

6 Brown, Jane, *The Omnipotent Magician: Lancelot 'Capability' Brown, 1716–1783* (London: Chatto & Windus, 2011), 124.

7 Wright, Thomas, *An Original Theory or New Hypothesis of the Universe* (London: H. Chapelle, 1750).

8 Lancelot Brown, generally known as 'Capability' Brown, and Humphry Repton are considered the fathers of the English Landscape style that superseded the Picturesque. Hunt, John Dixon, *The Genius of the Place. The English Landscape Garden 1620–1820* (London: Elek, 1975).

9 Alexander Pope had a number of followers – including Lord Burlington (who owned Chiswick House), Lord Carlisle (Castle Howard), Henry Hoare (Stourhead) and of course William Kent – who developed their gardens according to the precepts of the 'Augustan' style. This style aimed at reproducing the 'amiable simplicity of unadorned nature' and was meant to recall the 'golden age' heralded in by the Roman emperor Augustus after years of bitter civil war. The English style thus functioned as a metaphor in landscape for the peace brought about by the Glorious Revolution of 1688. Willson, Anthony Beckles, 'Alexander Pope's Grotto in Twickenham', *Garden History*, 26, 1 (1998), 31–59.

10 Harris, John, *The Palladian Revival: Lord Burlington, His Villa and Garden at Chiswick* (New Haven: Yale University Press, 1994).

11 Shurmer, James, *Stowe Landscape Gardens* (London: National Trust, 1997). Robinson, John Martin, *Temples of Delight: Stowe Landscape Gardens* (London: George Philip Publishers, 1999).

12 Ridgway, Christopher, 'Castle Howard', in *Chicago Botanic Garden Encyclopedia of Gardens*, Vol. 2, Shoemaker, Candice A. (ed.) (Chicago and London: Fitzroy Dearborn Publishers, 2001), 242–43.

13 Nicolas Poussin and Claude Lorrain were French painters of the 17th century who spent most of their working lives in Rome. Their works, showing mythological scenes within highly classicized depictions of nature and framed by elaborate perspectives, circulated throughout Europe and were much collected in England. Lagerlöf, Margaretha Rossholm, *Ideal Landscape: Annibale Carracci, Nicolas Poussin, and Claude Lorrain* (New Haven: Yale University Press, 1990).

14 Wilson, Michael, *William Kent, Architect, Designer, Painter, Gardener, 1685–1748* (London: Routledge & Kegan Paul, 1984). Weber, Susan (ed.), *William Kent. Designing Georgian Britain* (London and New Haven: Yale University Press, 2013).

15 In his scholarly study of Rousham and its scenography, Ulrich Müller asserts that most of the nude male statues were indeed pigmented in pink. Müller, Ulrich, *Klassischer Geschmack und Gotische Tugend, Der englische Landsitz Rousham* (Worms: Wernersche Verlagsanstalt, 1998).

16 At Stourhead, Henry Hoare expressed his Augustan convictions by creating an extraordinary oneiric (dream-like) space reminiscent of Claude Lorrain's painting *Landscape with Aeneas at Delos* (1672). The journey around the lake was in fact supposed to evoke Aeneas's descent into the underworld. Bergdoll, Barry, *European Architecture: 1750–1890* (Oxford: Oxford University Press 2000), 77.

17 Desmond, Ray, *The History of the Royal Botanic Gardens, Kew* (London: Royal Botanic Gardens, Kew, 2007). Parker, Lynn, and Ross-Jones, Kiri, *The Story of Kew Gardens* (London: Arcturus Publishing, 2013).

18 Linnaeus, Carl, *Species Plantarum* (Stockholm: Larentius Salvius Publisher, 1753).

19 Desmond, Ray, *The History of the Royal Botanic Gardens, Kew* (London: Royal Botanic Gardens, Kew, 2007). Parker, Lynn, and Ross-Jones, Kiri, *The Story of Kew Gardens* (London: Arcturus Publishing, 2013).

20 It is said that the Duke of Beaufort at Badminton first conceived of twenty radial avenues extending far into the country. Tuan, Yi-Fu, *Topophilia: A Study of Environmental Perceptions, Attitudes and Values* (New York: Columbia University Press, 1990), 140.

21 Turner, Roger, *Capability Brown and the Eighteenth-Century English Landscape* (Chichester: Phillimore, 1999).

22 Thompson, Ian, *The English Lakes: A History* (London: Bloomsbury Publishing, 2010).

23 Smith, Adam, *The Wealth of Nations* (New York: Bantam Classics, 2003 [1776]).

24 Repton's Red Books were the result of consultations with clients. Each book included before-and-after images of a project and was designed to show clients how landscape architecture could accompany the transformation of their estate. Many of these projects were in fact never executed. Daniels, Stephen, *Humphry Repton. Landscape Gardening and the Geography of Georgian England* (New Haven and London: Yale University Press, 1999).

25 Dixon Hunt, John, *Gardens and the Picturesque. Studies in the History of Landscape Architecture* (Cambridge, Mass.: MIT Press, 1997), 289.

23 Pückler-Muskau, Herman, *Hints on Landscape Gardening*, trans. Sickert, Bernhard (Boston: Houghton Mifflin, 1917).

9. Combustion

1 Rousseau, Jean-Jacques, *Emile, or On Education*, trans. Bloom, Alan (New York: Basic Books, 1979).

2 Jean-Jacques Rousseau died in July 1778 at Ermenonville while visiting his friend the Marquis de Girardin. He was buried on a small island in the middle of the park; his tomb became a place of pilgrimage after the Revolution, and it was only much later that his remains were transferred to the Panthéon in Paris.

3 Rousseau, Jean-Jacques, *Rousseau: The Basic Political Writings*, trans. and ed. Cress, Donald A. (Indianapolis: Hackett Publishing, 1987), 64.

4 Frängsmyr, Tore (ed.), *Linnaeus. The Man and His Work* (Berkeley: University of California Press, 1983).

5 Hamlin, Christopher, *Public Health and Social Justice in the Age of Chadwick: Britain, 1800–1854* (Cambridge and New York: Cambridge University Press, 1998).

6 Tyack, Geoffrey (ed.), *John Nash: Architect of the Picturesque* (Swindon: English Heritage, 2013). Summerson, John, *The Life and Work of John Nash Architect* (London: Allen & Unwin, 1980).

7 Designed for the 1851 World Exhibition in London by Joseph Paxton, with engineer Charles Fox, the Crystal Palace was made of cast iron and glass, its structure based on the leaf of the giant *Victoria amazonica* (*regia*) water-lily. McKean, John, *Crystal Palace: Joseph Paxton & Charles Fox* (London: Phaidon Press, 1994).

8 William Wordsworth epitomizes British 'Lakist' romanticism, through his writing entitled 'The Prelude', in which he sees man's salvation through a communion with nature. Wordsworth, William, *The Major Works* (Oxford: Oxford University Press, 2008).

9 Sadi Carnot, Léonard, *Réflexions sur la puissance motrice du feu et sur les machines propres à développer cette puissance* (Paris: Bachelier, 1824).

10 Darwin, Charles, *On the Origin of Species by means of Natural Selection* (London: John Murray, 1859).

11 Helferich, Gerard, *Humboldt's Cosmos: Alexander von Humboldt and the Latin American Journey that Changed the Way We See the World* (New York: Gotham Books, 2004).

12 Crary, Jonathan, *Techniques of the Observer: On Vision and Modernity in the Nineteenth Century* (Cambridge, Mass.: MIT Press, 1992).

13 Bergougniou, Jean-Michel, Clignet, Rémi, and David, Philippe, *Villages noirs et visiteurs africains et malgaches en France et en Europe: 1870–1940* (Paris: Karthala, 2001). Bancel, Nicolas, et al., *Zoos humains. De la Vénus hottentote aux reality shows* (Paris: La Découverte 2002).

14 Brüsch, Björn, 'Experimentalization of Gardening in Nineteenth Century Germany. Peter Joseph Lenné and the "Gärtner-Lehranstalt" at Wildpark/Potsdam'. Max Planck Institute for the History of Science, 2006.

15 Günther, Harri, *Peter Joseph Lenné: Gärten, Parke, Landschaften* (Stuttgart: DVA, 1985).

16 Hinz, Gerhard, P.J.L. *Das Gesamtwerk des Gartenarchitekten und Städteplaners*, 2 vols (Hildesheim, New York: G. Olms, 1989).

17 Dombart, Theodor, *Der Englische Garten zu München* (Munich: Hornung, 1972). Von Buttlar, Adrian, 'Der Englische Garten in München', in *Der Landschaftsgarten. Gartenkunst des Klassizismus und der Romantik* (Cologne: DuMont, 1989), 197–205.

18 Taylor, Hilary, 'Urban Public Parks, 1840–1900: Design and Meaning', *Garden History*, 23, 2 (1995), 200–21. Alphand, Charles-Adolphe, *Les Promenades de Paris* (New York: Princeton Architectural Press, 1984 [1867–73]).

19 Taylor, Dorceta E., *The Environment and the People in American Cities, 1600–1900s: Disorder, Inequality, and Social Change* (Durham: Duke University Press, 2009).

20 Strohmayer, Ulf, 'Urban design and civic spaces: nature at the Parc des Buttes-Chaumont in Paris', *Cultural Geographies*, 13, 4 (2006) 557–76.

21 Plazy, Gilles, and Legrain, Arnaud, *Le Parc des Buttes-Chaumont* (Paris: Flammarion, 2000).

22 Alphand, Charles-Adolphe, *Les Promenades de Paris* (New York: Princeton Architectural Press, 1984 [1867–73]).

23 Limido, Luisa, *L'Art des jardins sous le Second Empire: Jean-Pierre Barillet-Deschamps, 1824–1873* (Grenoble: Champ Vallon, 2002).

24 Waldheim, Charles, 'Landscape as Architecture', *Harvard Design Magazine*, 36 (2013), 19.

25 Olmsted, Frederick Law, *Walks and Talks of an American Farmer in England* (Ann Arbor: University of Michigan Press, 1967). Olmsted, Frederick Law, *Forty Years of Landscape Architecture: Central Park*, Olmsted Jr, Frederick Law, and Kimball, Theodora (eds) (Cambridge, Mass.: MIT Press, 1973).

26 Alphand, Charles-Adolphe, *Les Promenades de Paris* (New York: Princeton Architectural Press, 1984 [1867–73]).

27 Zaitzevsky, Cynthia, *Frederick Law Olmsted and the Boston Park System* (Cambridge, Mass.: Harvard University Press, 1982).

28 Berjman, Sonia, *Los Paseos Públicos de Buenos Aires y la labor de Carlos León Thays* (Buenos Aires: Librería Concentra, 2014).

29 Rosenzweig, Roy, and Blackmar, Elizabeth, *The Park and the People: A History of Central Park* (Ithaca, NY: Cornell University Press, 1992).

10. Acceleration

1 Einstein, Albert, 'The Common Language of Science', in *Ideas and Opinions* (New York: Crown Publishers, 1954), 335.

2 Howard, Ebenezer, *Garden Cities of To-Morrow* (London: Faber and Faber, repr., 1946), 50–57.

3 The book in which Howard's circular diagrams first appeared, *Garden Cities of To-morrow* (London: S. Sonnenschein & Co., 1902), is a landmark of utopian urban planning that influenced Modernism.

4 Unwin, Raymond, *Town Planning in Practice: An Introduction to the Art of Designing Cities and Suburbs* (Princeton: Princeton Architectural Press, repr., 1994).

5 Stalder, Laurent, *Hermann Muthesius 1861–1927* (Zurich: gta-Verlag, 2008).

6 Nonetheless, Howard's guidelines for polycentric garden cities – combined with the spatial theories of the German geographer Walter Christaller in the 1930s – would form the basis of many future Modernist developments. Christaller, Walter, *Die zentralen Orte in Süddeutschland* (Jena: Gustav Fischer, 1933).

7 Whyte, Ian Boyd, *Bruno Taut and the Architecture of Activism* (Cambridge: Cambridge University Press, 1983).

8 Haney, David, *When Modern was Green: Life and Work of Landscape Architect Leberecht Migge* (London and New York: Routledge, 2010). De Michelis, Marco, 'The Green Revolution: Leberecht Migge and the reform of the garden in Modernist Germany', in Teyssot, G. and Moser, M. (eds), *The Architecture of Western Gardens* (Cambridge, Mass.: MIT Press, 1991), 409–20. Galen Cranz, in *The Politics of Park Design* (Cambridge, Mass., MIT Press, 1982), identifies four distinct stages in the development of public parks in the US; one, which

she calls the 'Reform Park', corresponds closely to the concept of the German Volkspark.

9 Tate, Alan, *Great City Parks* (New York: Routledge, 2015), 185–95.

10 Imbert, Dorothée, *The Modernist Garden in France* (New Haven: Yale University Press, 1993).

11 Haspel, Jörg, and Jaeggi, Annemarie, *Housing Estates in the Berlin Modern Style* (Berlin: DKV-Edition, 2007).

12 Mumford, Eric, *The CIAM Discourse on Urbanism, 1928–1960* (Cambridge, Mass.: MIT Press, 2000).

13 Le Corbusier, *Urbanisme* (Paris: Grès et Cie, 1925).

14 The Athens Charter in which the Ville Radieuse project was published is a result of the 4th Congrès International d'Architecture Moderne (CIAM) held in 1933 under the direction of Le Corbusier. Curtis, William, *Le Corbusier – Ideas and Forms* (London: Phaidon, 2006).

15 Cohen, Jean-Louis, *Le Corbusier and the Mystique of the USSR, Theories and Projects for Moscow, 1928–1936* (Princeton: Princeton University Press, 1992).

16 In his essay on Le Corbusier, 'Nature as Inspiration', Tim Benton writes 'The idea that man should submit to the great system of forces – sun, water, fire – that governed the earth became a dogma in his book *La Ville Radieuse*.' In Cohen, Jean-Louis (ed.), *Le Corbusier: An Atlas of Modern Landscapes* (New York: Museum of Modern Art, 2013), 165.

17 Evenson, Norma, *Two Brazilian Capitals* (New Haven: Yale University Press, 1973).

18 Scully, Vincent, *Frank Lloyd Wright* (New York: George Braziller, 1996).

19 Andersson, Sven-Ingvar, Høyer, Steen, Whiston, Anne, and Avondoglio, Peter, *C. Th. Sørensen. Landscape Modernist* (Copenhagen: The Danish Architectural Press, 2001).

20 Treib, Marc, 'Woodland Cemetery: a dialogue of design and meaning', *Landscape Architecture*, 76, 2 (1986), 42–49. Constant, Caroline, *The Woodland Cemetery: Toward a Spiritual Landscape* (Stockholm: Byggförlaget 1994).

21 Kroplick, Howard, and Velocchi, Al, *The Long Island Motor Parkway* (Charleston, SC: Acadia Publishing, 2009).

22 Wallock, L., 'The Myth of the Master Builder, Robert Moses', *Journal of Urban History*, 17 (1991), 339–62.

23 The ultimate reference work on the landscape aesthetics of the American road is Appleyard, Donald, Lynch, Kevin, and Myers, John R., *The View from the Road* (Cambridge, Mass.: MIT Press, 1965).

24 Wolschke-Bulmahn, Joachim (ed.), *Nature and Ideology: Natural Garden Design in the Twentieth Century* (Washington, D.C.: Dumbarton Oaks, 1997).

25 Swedish naturalism, which reached its apogee in the 1920s, was a significant influence on the Nazis' theories of racial supremacy. See, among others, Sgard, Anne, 'Entre l'eau, l'arbre et le ciel', *Géographie et Cultures*, 66 (2008), 121–38.

26 Frampton, Kenneth, *Modern Architecture, A Critical History* (London: Thames & Hudson, 1985).

27 As part of this propaganda, the old German Volk from the forest was placed in irreconcilable opposition with the Jewish Volk who stemmed from the desert. In his research on 'Forest and Trees in the German Aryan Spirit and Cultural History', Heinrich Himmler clearly wanted to root Germany in a kind of original forest clearing. Zechner, Johannes, 'Politicized Timber: The German Forest and the Nature of Nations, 1800–1945', *The Brock Review*, 11, 2 (2011), 19–32.

28 Seifert worked with the botanist Reinhold Tüxen to contrive the scientific basis for such racial classifications. Rusinek, B.A., 'Wald und Baum in der arisch-germanischen Geistes- und Kulturgeschichte. Ein Forschungsprojekt des "Ahnerbe" der SS 1937–1945', in Lehman, A. & Schriewer, K. (eds), *Der Wald – Ein deutscher Mythos? Perspektiven eines Kulturthemas* (Berlin: Lebensformen, 2000), 267–363.

29 Radkau, J., and Uekötter, F., *Naturschutz und Nationalsozialismus* (Frankfurt: Campus Verlag, 2005).

30 Discherl, Stefan, *Tier und Naturschutz im Nationalsozialismus: Gesetzgebung, Ideologie und praxis* (Göttingen: V & R Unipress, 2012), 189–98. Zeller, Thomas, '"Ganz Deutschland sein Garten": Alwin Seifert und die Landschaft des Nationalsozialismus', in Radkau, J., and Uekötter, F. (eds), *Naturschutz und Nationalsozialismus* (Frankfurt: Campus Verlag, 2005), 277. Bramwell, Anna, *Blood and Soil: Walther Darré and Hitler's Green Party* (Abbotsbrook: The Kensal Press, 1985).

31 Seifert became the first chairman of the Bavarian Nature Conservancy and, together with other collaborators also in office, helped to push the dogma of 'nativeness', developed in the 1930s, into conservation legislation. In particular he was responsible for the law on Standortgerecht Bepflanzung ('place-specific planting') that predetermines the kind of 'native' plants that are appropriate to use in a given location. See: Radkau, J., and Uekötter, F. (eds), *Naturschutz und Nationalsozialismus* (Frankfurt: Campus Verlag, 2005).

32 Einstein, Albert, 'The Foundation of the General Theory of Relativity', in *The Collected Papers of Albert Einstein, vol. 6, The Berlin Years: Writings 1914–1917*, Klein, Martin J., Kox, A. J., and Schulman, R. (eds) (Princeton: Princeton University Press 1997), 146–200.

33 Von Bertalanffy, Ludwig, *General System Theory: Foundations, Development, Applications* (New York: George Braziller, 1968).

34 Schulze, Franz, and Windhorst, Edward, *Mies van der Rohe: A Critical Biography* (Chicago: University of Chicago Press, 2012), 184–86.

35 Matteini, Milena, *Pietro Porcinai, Architetto del Giardino e del Paesaggio* (Milan: Electa, 1991). Latini, Luigi, and Cunico, Mariapia, *Pietro Porcinai. Il progetto del paesaggio nel XX secolo* (Venice: Marsilio, 2012).

36 Church, Thomas, D., *Gardens Are for People* (San Francisco: McGraw-Hill, 1955).

37 Laurie, Michael, 'Thomas Church, California Gardens and Public Landscapes', in Treib, Marc (ed.), *Modern Landscape Architecture: A Critical Review* (Cambridge, Mass.: MIT Press 1992), 166–80. Treib, Marc, *The Donnell and Eckbo Gardens: Modern California Masterworks* (San Francisco: William Stout, 2005).

38 Noguchi, Isamu, *A Sculptor's World* (London: Thames & Hudson, 1967).

39 Berrizbeitia, Anita, *Roberto Burle Marx in Caracas* (Philadelphia: University of Pennsylvania Press, 2005).

40 Beardsley, John, *Earthworks and Beyond: Contemporary Art in the Landscape* (New York: Abbeville Press, 1984).

41 Walker, Peter, and Levy, Leah, *Peter Walker: Minimalist Gardens* (Washington, D.C.: Spacemaker Press, 1997).

42 Weilacher, Udo, 'Poetry in Nature Unredeemed – Ian Hamilton Finlay' (interview), in *Between Landscape Architecture and Land Art* (Basel: Birkhauser, 1999).

43 Treib, Marc, *The Architecture of Landscape* (Philadelphia: University of Pennsylvania Press, 2002), 44–45.

44 Blin, Pascale, *L'AUA, mythe et réalités: L'atelier d'urbanisme et d'architecture, 1960–1985* (Paris: Electa Moniteur, 1988).

45 Corajoud, Michel, and Prozynska, Vera, *Michel Corajoud Paysagiste* (Paris: Hartman Edition, 2000).

46 Treib, Marc, and Imbert, Dorothée, *Garrett Eckbo: Modern Landscapes for Living* (Berkeley: University of California Press, 1997). Treib, Marc, *Modern Landscape Architecture: A Critical Review* (Cambridge, Mass.: MIT Press, 1992).

47 Waldheim, Charles, *Case: Hilbersheimer/Mies van der Rohe, Lafayette Park Detroit* (New York: Prestel, 2004).

48 Tschumi, Bernard, *Cinégramme folie: le Parc de la Villette* (Princeton: Princeton Architectural Press, 1987), 32.

49 Derrida, Jacques, *Point de folie – Maintenant l'architecture*, in Tschumi, Bernard, *La case Vide: La Villette* 1985 (London: Architectural Association, 1986).

50 The original text written by Tschumi and his team for this project was handled like a manifesto for the park of the 21st century, in which the principle of overlay through points, lines and planes became the methodological credo. Girot, Christophe, Interview with Bernard Tschumi, *Documents 4*, 1994, 3–23. Girot, Christophe, 'Learning from La Villette', *Documents 4*, 1994, 26–44.

51 Reed, Peter, *Groundswell: Constructing the Contemporary Landscape* (New York: Museum of Modern Art, 2005).

52 Kurgan, Laura, *Close Up at a Distance – Mapping, Technology and Politics* (Cambridge, Mass.: MIT Press, 2013).

53 Scott, Emily, and Swenson, Kirsten, *Critical Landscapes* (Los Angeles: University of California Press, 2015).

11. Terrain Vague

1 Deleuze, Gilles, *The Fold, Leibniz and the Baroque* (London: Athlone Press, 1993).

2 Solà-Morales, Ignasi de, 'Terrain Vague', in Davidson, Cynthia C. (ed.), *Anyplace* (Cambridge, Mass.: MIT, 1995), 118–23.

3 Crutzen, P. J., and Stoermer, E. F., 'The "Anthropocene"', *IGBP Newsletter*, 41 (2000), 17–18.

4 Barikin, Amelia, *Parallel Presents: The Art of Pierre Huyghe* (Cambridge, Mass.: MIT Press, 2012).

5 Mariani, Manuala, and Barron, Patrick (eds), *Terrain Vague: Interstices at the Edge of the Pale* (New York: Routledge, 2014).

6 Alexander, J.A.P., *Perspectives on Place: Theory and Practice in Landscape Photography* (New York: Bloomsbury, 2015).

7 Smithson, Robert, 'A Tour of the Monuments of Passaic, New Jersey', New York, *Artforum*, 1967. Ursprung, Philip, trans. Elliott, Fiona, *Allan Kaprow, Robert Smithson, and the Limits to Art* (Berkeley: University of California Press, 2013).

8 Beuys, Joseph, *7000 Eichen (7000 Oaks)*, New York, Dia Art Foundation, 1995–2004.

9 McHarg, Ian, *Design with Nature* (New York: The Natural History Press, 1969).

10 Chrisman, Nick, *Charting the Unknown: How Computer Mapping at Harvard Became GIS* (Redlands: ESRI Press, 2004). Steinitz, Carl, *Computers and Regional Planning: The DELMARVA Study* (Cambridge: H.G.S.D., 1967).

11 The Dutch ecological pioneer Louis Le Roy, also called the 'wild garden man' of Herenveen in the Netherlands, claimed in his book *Natuur uitschakelen-natuur inschakelen* (Deventer: Ankh Hermes, 1973) that nature itself was a better designer anyway and would create an aesthetic quality in parks and gardens without the help of man.

12 Cobbers, Arnt, *Vor Einfahrt HALT – Ein neuer Park mit alten Geschichten. Der Natur-Park Schöneberger Südgelände in Berlin* (Berlin: Jaron Verlag, 2001).

13 Lüneburg Heath is the product of over 4,000 years of continuous overgrazing and deforestation, first by early Neolithic settlers, and then by medieval farmers and salt-packers. This activity led to a complete change of vegetation, from mixed oak forest to briar moorland, resulting in serious soil deterioration and acidification. The heath is now ironically considered one of Germany's major nature reserves, encompassing over 7,000 square km (2,700 square miles) of moorland. Ellenberg, Heinz, and Leuschner, Christoph, *Vegetation Mitteleuropas mit den Alpen in ökologischer, dynamischer und historischer Sicht* (Stuttgart: Ulmer Verlag, 1996).

14 Professor Ingo Kowarik at the Technische Universität Berlin founded an institute of urban ecology that accepts the notion of mixing native with non-native species; this has been measured in terms of real biodiversity and biomass. The findings are astonishing: cities such as Berlin were found to have much more biodiversity and to be more resilient than the surrounding Brandenburg countryside. See: Endlicher, Wilfred, et al. (eds), *Perspectives in Urban Ecology: Studies of Ecosystems and Interactions Between Humans and Nature in the Metropolis of Berlin* (Berlin: Springer, 2011). Kowarik, Ingo, *Biologische Invasionen: Neophyten und Neozonen in Mitteleuropa* (Stuttgart: Ulmer Verlag, 2010).

15 Tommy Thompson Park is part of a long lineage of such artificial 'natural' parks that perhaps started with Diaccia Botrona, created over 250 years ago near Grosseto in Tuscany. There, malaria-infested swamps were partly drained and transformed into what has become one of the most beautiful nature reserves in Italy.

16 Carson, Rachel, *Silent Spring* (Boston: Houghton Mifflin, 1962).

17 Two major reports, both based on systems theory and cybernetics, profoundly affected global attitudes towards the environment in recent decades. The first was a book entitled *The Limits to Growth* (New York: Universe Books, 1972), written by Donella Meadows, Dennis Meadows, Jørgen Randers and William Behrens for the Club of Rome, which predicted imminent global collapse due to the limited availability of resources for economic and demographic growth. The apocalyptic predictions of the book, developed through computer simulation, showed the consequences of unbridled human growth on the Earth's natural systems. There followed the first report on human-induced Climate Change by the IPCC that was published in 1990, which has become the major subject of concern in this century.

18 The French landscape ecologist Gilles Clément claimed that a new green revolution was coming in his book *Le Jardin en Mouvement* (Paris: Pandora, 1991). The field of ecology according to him would need to reinvent a language of its own in the coming years and generate entirely new combinations in this age of great climate change.

19 Jarman, Derek, *Derek Jarman's Garden* (London: Thames & Hudson, 1995).

20 The 50 new urban and landscape design projects launched across Barcelona during the 1980s completely changed the face of the city. See Bohigas, Oriol et al., *Plans i Projectes per a Barcelona 1981–1982* (Barcelona: Ajuntament, 1983).

21 The IBA Emscher Park, under the direction of Christoph Zöpel and Karl Ganzer, lasted from 1989 to 1999 and effected a lasting change on the entire Ruhr region. Over 120 projects were launched during that period, with a particular emphasis on water management, ecology, housing and the rehabilitation of industrial wastelands into parks. The equivalent of at least 2.5 billion Euros was invested in the project, two-thirds of which was public money. It set a European standard in terms of polluted water management and clean energy consumption, and became the largest landscape architectural project ever launched in Germany.

22 The Film *Pina*, produced in 3D by Wim Wenders and presented at the 2011 Berlinale, depicts dancers from Pina Bausch's Tanztheater Wuppertal lost in an eerie world of *terrains vagues* from the Ruhr stretching to the horizon.

23 Brae, Ellen, *Beauty Redeemed, Recycling Post-Industrial Landscapes* (Berlin: Birkhauser, 2015).

24 Saunders, William (ed.), *Richard Haag. Bloedel Reserve and Gas Works Park* (New York: Princeton Architectural Press, 1997).

25 In an essay first presented at the Landscape Architecture Positions and Oppositions Congress in Herrenhausen, June 2013, Vittoria di Palma set out an interesting thesis about the role of disgust and the ugly in landscape aesthetics. Di Palma, Vittoria, 'In the Mood for Landscape', in *Thinking the Contemporary Landscape*, Girot, Christophe, and Imhof, Dora (eds) (New York: Princeton Architectural Press, 2016).

26 Reed, Peter, *Groundswell: Constructing the Contemporary Landscape* (New York: Museum of Modern Art, 2005).

27 Vogt, Günther, *Miniature and Panorama. Vogt Landscape Architects, Projects 2000–06* (Zurich: Lars Müller Publishers, 2006).

28 Bava, Henri, Hoesler, Michel, and Philippe, Olivier, *Fragments de Paysage – Agence Ter* (Paris: ICI Interface, 2011).

29 Chemetoff, Alexandre, *Visits: Town and Territory, Architecture in Dialogue* (Basel and Boston: Birkhauser, 2009).

12. Topology

1 Topology is precisely what makes the distinction between a natural topography and a designed topography. It is about the form of intelligence applied to the shaping of a landscape, resulting in a modified topography, call it landscape design if you will. Thom, René, *Topologie et Signification, L'Âge de la Science 4* (Paris: Dunod, 1968), 219–42. Reprinted in Thom, René, *Mathematical Models of Morphogenesis*, trans. Brookes, W. M., and Rand, D. (Chichester: Ellis Horwood, 1983).

2 Wave Field, 33 × 33 metres (100 × 100 feet), created in 1995 by Maya Lin on the North Campus of the University of Michigan Ann Arbor was commissioned in memory of a fallen student named François Xavier Bertrand. Lin, Maya, *Topologies (Artist and the Community)* (Winston-Salem: Southeastern Center for Contemporary Art, 1998).

3 'Topology' is a term of landscape architecture that was recently coined to signify an all-encompassing design methodology: Girot, Christophe, Freytag, Anette, et al., *Landscript 3: Topology* (Berlin: Jovis Verlag, 2013), and Girot, Christophe, Freytag, Anette, et al., *Topology: Pamphlet 15* (Zurich: GTA Verlag, 2012).

4 Schimmel, Annemarie, 'Hafiz and His Contemporaries', in *The Cambridge History of Iran, Vol. 6, The Timurid and Safavid Periods*, Jackson, Peter, and Lockhart, Laurence (eds) (Cambridge: Cambridge University Press, 1986).

5 Burl, Aubrey, *Prehistoric Avebury* (New Haven: Yale University Press, 1979).

6 The Diana, Princess of Wales Memorial Fountain in Hyde Park was inaugurated in July 2004. It is made of 545 massive pieces of Cornish granite, which form a vast oval. The water, pumped up to the top of the oval, flows down on either side, framing a clearing. The two sides of the ring are treated quite differently – one is a smooth and gently rippled slope, while the other has marked steps and sharp curves – in a manner supposed to represent two aspects of Princess Diana's troubled life: happiness and turmoil. It was the work of the office of Gustafson Porter, London.

7 Freytag, Anette, Dieter Kienast, *Stadt und Landschaft lesbar machen* (Zurich: GTA Verlag, 2016).

8 Ibid.

9 Girot, Christophe (ed.), *Zeitgeist Berlin Invalidenpark* (Zurich: GTA Verlag, 2006).

10 Zhou Z, and Zheng, S., 'The missing link of Ginkgo evolution', *Nature*, 423 (2003), 821–22.

11 Hvass, Svend M., *ISE: Japan's Ise Shrines. Ancient Yet New* (Copenhagen: Aristo Publishing, 1998).

12 Thoreau, Henry David, *Walden, or Life in the Woods* (Tunbridge Wells: Solis Classics, 2013).

13 M'Closkey, Karen, *Unearthed: The Landscapes of Hargreaves Associates* (Philadelphia: University of Pennsylvania Press, 2013).

14 The Future Cities Laboratory in Singapore, with ETH students Shoichiro Hashimoto and Benedikt Kowalewski under the direction of Christophe Girot, developed a project to redesign the riverbed and the residential quarters in Kampung Melayu. The aim was to transform the Ciliwung River into a park in order to control the massive volumes of water flowing through the city during the monsoon season. The concept also focused on creating new public spaces such as squares and gardens of various sizes along the riverbanks. The project was shown at the Rotterdam Biennale for Architecture in 2014: 'Urban by Nature', catalogue (Rotterdam: IABR Publications, 2014).

15 The minimalist design of the Letten area was undertaken by the Swiss landscape office of Rotzler Krebs Partner of Winterthur in 2003–05.

16 Cho, Myung-Rae, 'The politics of urban nature restoration: The case of Cheonggyecheon restoration in Seoul, Korea', *International Development Planning Review*, 132, 2 (2010), 145–65.

17 Saunders, William S. (ed.), *Designed Ecologies: The Landscape Architecture of Kongjian Yu* (Basel: Birkhauser, 2012).

18 Dreiseitl, Herbert, and Grau, Dieter, *Waterscapes Innovation* (Hong Kong: Design Media Publishing, 2015).

19 Girot, Christophe, 'Landscape in Motion, From Tunnel Movie to Alp Transit', in *The Swiss Touch in Landscape Architecture*, Jacob, Michael (ed.) (Verbania: Tarara Edizioni, 2013).

20 The design of the Sigirino Mound was a collaborative effort between engineers of AlpTransit Gotthard, ITC & IFEC, and the Atelier Girot in Zurich. Its main morphological changes were managed by Christophe Girot and Ilmar Hurkxkens between 2008 and 2012.

21 The Aire River revitalization project by Georges Descombes and the ARD office received the Swiss 2012 Schulthess Prize for environmentally responsible landscape architecture.

22 The Room for the River is undoubtedly the most important Dutch flood control project of the last decade in the Netherlands. It implies the transformation of considerable stretches of river landscapes in South Holland. The Office of HNS was involved in this project from the outset and contributed significantly to the ongoing transformation of the landscape. Van Dooren, Noël, *'Gardening the Delta'. A Dutch Approach to Landscape Architecture*, HNS Landscape Architects, Jubilee Publication (2015).

23 Orff, Kate, *Toward an Urban Ecology, SCAPE Landscape Architecture* (New York: The Monacelli Press, 2016).

24 Several Dutch agencies, including the landscape office HNS under the direction of Dirk Sijmons, have tackled the issue of landscape transformation in the Rhine Delta, and schools including the Harvard Graduate School of Design and the ETH in Zurich have held studios on the topic. See Girot, Christophe, and Rossano, Frédéric, *Rising Waters, Shifting Lands*, Pamphlet 16 (Zurich: GTA Verlag 2012).

25 Corner, James, and Hirsch, Alison (eds), *The Landscape Imagination: Collected Essays of James Corner 1990–2010* (New York: Princeton Architectural Press, 2014).

26 The Studio Associato Bernardo Secchi Paola Viogano received the 2015 Belgian Building Award for the Spoor Nord Park.

27 Brae, Ellen, *Beauty Redeemed, Recycling Post-Industrial Landscapes* (Berlin: Birkhauser, 2015).

28 Bull, George, 'Ridge and Furrow', *Landscape*, Spring 2014, The Journal of the Landscape Institute, London.

29 Weschler, Lawrence, *Robert Irwin Getty Garden* (Los Angeles: Getty Trust Publications, 2002).

Afterword

1 Latour, Bruno, *Politics of Nature. How to Bring the Sciences into Democracy*, trans. Porter, Catherine (Cambridge, Mass.: Harvard University Press, 2004).

2 Koolhaas, Rem, and Auricoste, Isabelle, *Yves Brunier: Landscape Architect Paysagiste* (Berlin: Birkhauser, 1996).

3 Roland Barthes would argue that each and every generation reinvents its myths of life, death and nature. Could it be that ecology will bring forth entirely new ways of living the myth of an eternal return to nature? Barthes, Roland, *Mythologies*, trans. Lavers, Annette (London: Vintage Classics, 1993).

4 Latour, Bruno, *Politics of Nature. How to Bring the Sciences into Democracy*, trans. Porter, Catherine (Cambridge, Mass.: Harvard University Press, 2004).

5 The Seonyudo Park was completed in 2002 by the Seoahn Total Landscape office in Seoul. It was awarded the 2004 ASLA Award of Merit.

6 Ponte, Alessandra, 'Desert Testing', in *Architecture and the Sciences. Exchanging Metaphors*, Picon, Antoine, and Ponte, Alessandra (eds) (New York: Princeton Architectural Press, 2003), 80–117.

7 Scott Cohen, Preston, and Naginski, Erika (eds), 'The Return of Nature', in *The Return of Nature: Sustaining Architecture in the Face of Sustainability* (New York: Routledge, 2014), 1–8.

8 Ibid.

9 Ibid.

10 Nørrebro Park in South Central Copenhagen was designed in 2007 by Steen Høyer and GHB landscape architects.

11 Scott Cohen, Preston, and Naginski, Erika (eds), 'The Return of Nature', in *The Return of Nature: Sustaining Architecture in the Face of Sustainability* (New York: Routledge, 2014), 1–8.

12 The French thinkers Augustin Berque and Philippe Descola argue that for landscape to exist within a culture, a set of cultural preconditions needs to be fulfilled. Berque draws a clear distinction between the actor in the physical landscape and the thinker that conceptualizes it, and Descola in a similar way distinguishes landscapes made 'in situ' and landscapes made 'de visu'. Berque, Augustin, *Thinking Through Landscape* (London: Routledge, 2013).

Bibliography

1. Roots

Briard, Jacques, *Les Cercles de pierres préhistoriques en Europe* (Paris: Errance, 2000).

Caroll, Maureen, *Earthly Paradises. Ancient Gardens in History and Archaeology* (London: The British Museum Press; Los Angeles: J. Paul Getty Museum, 2003).

Cohen, C., *La femme des origines. Images de la femme dans la préhistoire occidentale* (Paris: Belin-Herscher, 2003).

Conan, Michel (ed.), *Perspectives on Garden Histories*, Dumbarton Oaks Colloquium on the History of Landscape Architecture vol. 21 (Washington D.C.: Dumbarton Oaks, 1999).

Gothein, Marie Luise, *A History of Garden Art, From the Earliest Times to the Present Day, Vol. 1 (Ancient Egypt to Renaissance)*, Wright, Walter P. (ed.), trans. Archer-Hind, Laura (New York: Cambridge University Press, 2014).

Hobhouse, Penelope, *The Story of Gardening* (London and New York: Dorling Kindersley, 2004).

Hunt, John Dixon, *Greater Perfections: The Practice of Garden Theory* (Philadelphia: University of Pennsylvania Press, 1999).

Kostof, Spiro, *The City Assembled. Elements of Urban Form through History* (London: Thames & Hudson, 1992).

Mosser, Monique and Teyssot, Georges (eds), *The History of Garden Design. The Western Tradition from the Renaissance to the Present Day* (London: Thames & Hudson, 2000).

Norberg-Schulz, Christian, *Architecture: Presence, Language, Place* (Milan: Skira, 2000).

2. Hydraulic Civilizations

Anthony, David, *The Horse, the Wheel, and Language: How Bronze-Age Riders from the Eurasian Steppes Shaped the Modern World* (Princeton, N.J.: Princeton University Press 2007).

Bonnechere, Pierre, and de Bruyn, Odile, *L'art et l'âme des jardins* (Antwerp: Fonds Mercator, 1998).

Calvet, Yves, and Geyer, Bernard, *Barrages antiques de Syrie* (Lyon: La Maison de L'Orient, 1992).

Cauvin, Jacques, *The Birth of the Gods and the Origins of Agriculture*, trans. Watkins, Trevor (Cambridge: Cambridge University Press, 2000).

Kramer, S. N., *The Sumerians: Their History, Culture, and Character* (Chicago: University of Chicago Press, 1963).

Mithen, Steven, *After the Ice: A Global Human History, 20,000–5000 BC* (London: Weidenfeld & Nicolson, 2003; Cambridge, Mass.: Harvard University Press 2006).

Petruccioli, Attilio, and Pirani, Khalil K. (eds) *Understanding Islamic Architecture* (London: Routledge, 2002).

Pregill, Philip, and Volkman, Nancy, *Landscapes in History. Design and Planning in the Eastern and Western Traditions* (New York: John Wiley, 1999).

Schama, Simon, *Landscape and Memory* (New York: A.A. Knopf, 1995).

Spar, Ira, 'The Origins of Writing', Heilbrunn Timeline of Art History, The Metropolitan Museum of Art, http://www.metmuseum.org/toah/

3. From Temenos to Physis

Barnes, Jonathan, *The Presocratic Philosophers* (London: Routledge, rev. ed., 1982).

Bowden, Hugh, *Classical Athens and the Delphic Oracle: Divination and Democracy* (Cambridge: Cambridge University Press, 2005).

Bowden, Hugh, *Mystery Cults of the Ancient World* (London: Thames & Hudson; Princeton: Princeton University Press, 2010).

Carratelli, Giovanni (ed.), *The Greek World. Art and Civilization in Magna Graecia and Sicily* (New York: Rizzoli, 1996).

Dickinson, Oliver, *The Aegean Bronze Age* (Cambridge: Cambridge University Press, 2005).

Fontenrose, Joseph, *Python: A Study of Delphic Myth and its Origins* (Berkeley: University of California Press, 1959).

Isager, Signe, and Skydsgaard, Jens E., *Ancient Greek Agriculture: An Introduction* (London and New York: Routledge, 1995).

Mayor, Adrienne, *The Amazons: Lives and Legends of Warrior Women Across the Ancient World* (Princeton: Princeton University Press, 2014).

Mylonas, George E., *Eleusis and the Eleusinian Mysteries* (Princeton: Princeton University Press, 1962).

Rackham, Oliver, and Moody, Jennifer A., *The Making of the Cretan Landscape* (Manchester: Manchester University Press, 1996).

4. Of Villas and Woods

Adembri, Benedetta, *Hadrian's Villa* (Milan: Electa, 2000).

Boatwright, Mary T., *Peoples of the Roman World* (Cambridge: Cambridge University Press, 2012).

Grimal, Pierre, *Les jardins romains* (Paris: Fayard, 3rd ed., 1984).

Jashemski, Wilhelmina F., *The Gardens of Pompeii* (New Rochelle: Caratzas Bros., 2nd ed., 1979).

Laurence, Ray, *The Roads of Roman Italy: Mobility and Cultural Change* (London and New York: Routledge, 1999).

MacDougall, E. B., and Jashemski, W. F., *Ancient Roman Gardens* (Washington, D.C.: Dumbarton Oaks, 1981).

Purcell, Nicholas, 'Town in Country and Country in Town', in *Ancient Roman Villa Gardens*, MacDougall, E. B. (ed.) (Washington, D.C.: Dumbarton Oaks, 1987), 187–203.

Torelli, Mario, *The Etruscans* (London: Thames & Hudson, 2001).

Virgil. *Eclogues, Georgics, Aeneid*, trans. Fairclough, H.R., Loeb Classical Library Volumes 63 & 64 (Cambridge, M.A.: Harvard University Press, 1916).

Von Stackelberg, Katharina, *The Roman Garden: Space, Sense and Society* (London and New York: Routledge, 2009).

5. The Rule of Faith

Braunfels, Wolfgang, *Monasteries of Western Europe: The Architecture of the Orders* (London: Thames & Hudson, 1972).

Brown, Peter, *Augustine of Hippo* (Berkeley: University of California Press, 1967).

Davidson, Hilda Ellis, *The Lost Beliefs of Northern Europe* (London: Routledge, 1993).

Ettinghausen, Richard, and Grabar, Oleg, *The Art and Architecture of Islam, 650–1250* (New Haven: Yale University Press, 1987).

Geary, Patrick, *Myth of Nations. The Medieval Origins of Europe* (Princeton: Princeton University Press, 2003).

Hennebo, Dieter, *Geschichte der deutschen Gartenkunst, vol. 1, Gärten des Mittelalters* (Hamburg: Broschek, 1962).

Irwin, Robert, *The Alhambra* (London: Profile Books; Cambridge, Mass.: Harvard University Press, 2004).

Johns, Jeremy, *Arabic Administration in Norman Sicily: The Royal Diwan* (Cambridge: Cambridge University Press, 2002).

Moynihan, Elizabeth, *Paradise as a Garden: In Persia and Mughal India* (London: Scolar Press, 1980).

Petrarca, Francesco [Petrarch], 'The Ascent of Mount Ventoux', in Cassirer, Ernst et al. (eds), *The Renaissance Philosophy of Man* (Chicago: University of Chicago Press, 1948).

Ruggles, D. Fairchild, *Gardens, Landscape and Vision in the Palaces of Islamic Spain* (University Park: Pennsylvania State University Press, 2000).

Watson, Andrew M., *Agricultural Innovation in the Early Islamic World: The Diffusion of Crops and Farming Techniques, 700–1100* (Cambridge: Cambridge University Press, 2008).

6. Gardens of Perspective

Bagrow, Leo, *History of Cartography*, rev. ed. Skelton, R. A. (New Brunswick, N.J.: Transaction Publishers, 2010).

Battisti, Eugenio, 'Natura Artificioso a Natura Artificialis', in *The Italian Garden*, Dumbarton Oaks Colloquium on the History of Landscape Architecture, Coffin, David R. (ed.) (Washington, D.C.: Dumbarton Oaks, 1972).

Coffin, David, *The Villa d'Este at Tivoli* (Princeton: Princeton University Press, 1960).

Coffin, David, *The Villa in the Life of Renaissance Rome* (Princeton: Princeton University Press, 1979).

Colonna, Francesco, trans. and intro. Godwin, Joscelyn, *Hypnerotomachia Poliphili: The Strife of Love in a Dream* (London: Thames & Hudson, 2005).

Dunzhen, Liu, *Chinese Classical Gardens of Suzhou* (New York: McGraw-Hill, 1993).

Levenson, Jay A. (ed.), *Circa 1492. Art in the Age of Exploration* (New Haven: Yale University Press, 1991).

Prest, John, *The Garden of Eden. The Botanic Garden and the Re-Creation of Paradise* (New Haven: Yale University Press, 1981).

Van der Ree, Paul, Smienk, Gerrit, and Steenbergen, Clemens, *Italian Villas and Gardens* (Munich: Prestel, 1992).

7. The Measure of Reason

Babaie, Sussan, *Isfahan and Its Palaces* (Edinburgh: Edinburgh University Press, 2008).

Conan, Michel (ed.), *Baroque Garden Cultures: Emulation, Sublimation, Subversion* (Washington, D.C.: Dumbarton Oaks, 2005).

Crane, Nicholas, *Mercator: The Man Who Mapped the Planet* (London: Weidenfeld & Nicolson, 2002).

Descartes, René, *Discourse on Method, Optics, Geometry, and Meteorology*, trans. Olscamp, Paul J. (Indianapolis: Hackett, 2001).

Dezallier d'Argenville, Antoine J., *La Théorie et la pratique du jardinage* (Paris: Hachette, 2012 [1747]).

Gothein, Marie Luise, *A History of Garden Art, From the Earliest Times to the Present Day, Vol. 2 (French Renaissance to 1914)*, Wright, Walter P. (ed.), trans. Archer-Hind, Laura (New York: Cambridge University Press, 2014).

Hazlehurst, F. Hamilton, *Gardens of Illusion: The Genius of André Le Nostre* (Nashville: Vanderbilt University Press, 1980).

Koch, Ebba, *The Complete Taj Mahal, And the Riverfront Gardens of Agra* (London and New York: Thames & Hudson, 2006).

Lablaude, Pierre-André, *The Gardens of Versailles*, trans. Biddulph, Fiona (London: Zwemmer, 1995).

Mariage, Thierry, *The World of André Le Nôtre*, trans. Larkin, Graham (Philadelphia: University of Pennsylvania Press, 1999).

Schama, Simon, *The Embarrassment of Riches: An Interpretation of Dutch Culture in the Golden Age* (New York: Knopf, 1987).

Sutton, Elizabeth A., *Capitalism and Cartography in the Dutch Golden Age* (Chicago: University of Chicago Press, 2015).

Steenbergen, Clemens, and Reh, Wouter, *Architecture and Landscape: The Design Experiment of the Great European Gardens and Landscapes* (New York: Birkhauser, 2003).

8. Gravity

Bergdoll, Barry, *European Architecture: 1750–1890* (Oxford: Oxford University Press 2000).

Brown, Jane, *The Omnipotent Magician: Lancelot 'Capability' Brown, 1716–1783* (London: Chatto & Windus, 2011).

Daniels, Stephen, *Humphry Repton. Landscape Gardening and the Geography of Georgian England* (New Haven and London: Yale University Press, 1999).

Harris, John, *The Palladian Revival: Lord Burlington, His Villa and Garden at Chiswick* (New Haven: Yale University Press, 1994).

Hill, Jonathan, *Weather Architecture* (Abingdon and New York: Routledge, 2012).

Hill, Jonathan, *A Landscape of Architecture, History and Fiction* (Abingdon and New York: Routledge, 2015).

Hunt, John Dixon, *The Genius of the Place. The English Landscape Garden 1620–1820* (London: Elek, 1975).

Hunt, John Dixon, *The Picturesque Garden in Europe* (London: Thames & Hudson, 2002).

Lagerlöf, Margaretha Rossholm, *Ideal Landscape: Annibale Carracci, Nicolas Poussin, and Claude Lorrain* (New Haven: Yale University Press, 1990).

Müller, Ulrich, *Klassischer Geschmack und Gotische Tugend, Der englische Landsitz Rousham* (Worms: Wernersche Verlagsanstalt, 1998).

Newton, Isaac, *The Principia, Mathematical Principles of Natural Philosophy*, trans. Cohen, Bernard, and Whitman, Ann (Oakland: University of California Press, 1999).

Robinson, John Martin, *Temples of Delight: Stowe Landscape Gardens* (London: George Philip Publishers, 1999).

Thompson, Ian, *The English Lakes: A History* (London, Bloomsbury Publishing, 2010).

Wilson, Michael, *William Kent, Architect, Designer, Painter, Gardener, 1685–1748* (London: Routledge & Kegan Paul, 1984).

9. Combustion

Alphand, Charles-Adolphe, *Les Promenades de Paris* (New York: Princeton Architectural Press, 1984 [1867–73]).

Berjman, Sonia, *Los Paseos Públicos de Buenos Aires y la labor de Carlos León Thays* (Buenos Aires: Libreria Concentra, 2014).

Crary, Jonathan, *Techniques of the Observer: On Vision and Modernity in the Nineteenth Century* (Cambridge, Mass.: MIT Press, 1992).

Darwin, Charles, *On the Origin of Species by Means of Natural Selection* (London: John Murray, 1859).

Dixon Hunt, John, *Gardens and the Picturesque. Studies in the History of Landscape Architecture* (Cambridge, Mass.: MIT Press, 1997).

Günther, Harri, *Peter Joseph Lenné: Gärten, Parke, Landschaften* (Stuttgart: DVA, 1985).

Helferich, Gerard, *Humboldt's Cosmos: Alexander von Humboldt and the Latin American Journey that Changed the Way We See the World* (New York: Gotham Books, 2004).

McKean, John, *Crystal Palace: Joseph Paxton & Charles Fox* (London: Phaidon Press, 1994).

Olmsted, Frederick Law, *Forty Years of Landscape Architecture: Central Park*, Olmsted Jr, Frederick Law, and Kimball, Theodora (eds) (Cambridge, Mass.: MIT Press, 1973).

Rosenzweig, Roy, and Blackmar, Elizabeth, *The Park and the People: A History of Central Park* (Ithaca, NY: Cornell University Press, 1992).

Strohmayer, Ulf, 'Urban design and civic spaces: nature at the Parc des Buttes-Chaumont in Paris', *Cultural Geographies*, 13, 4 (2006) 557–76.

Tyack, Geoffrey (ed.), *John Nash: Architect of the Picturesque* (Swindon: English Heritage, 2013).

Von Buttlar, Adrian, 'Der Englische Garten in München', in *Der Landschaftsgarten. Gartenkunst des Klassizismus und der Romantik* (Cologne: DuMont, 1989)

Zaitzevsky, Cynthia, *Frederick Law Olmsted and the Boston Park System* (Cambridge, Mass.: Harvard University Press, 1982).

10. Acceleration

Andersson, Sven-Ingvar, Høyer, Steen, Whiston, Anne, and Avondoglio, Peter, *C. Th. Sørensen. Landscape Modernist* (Copenhagen: The Danish Architectural Press, 2001).

Beardsley, John, *Earthworks and Beyond: Contemporary Art in the Landscape* (New York: Abbeville Press, 1984).

Berrizbeitia, Anita, *Roberto Burle Marx in Caracas* (Philadelphia: University of Pennsylvania Press, 2005).

Cohen, Jean-Louis (ed.), *Le Corbusier: An Atlas of Modern Landscapes* (New York: Museum of Modern Art, 2013).

Constant, Caroline, *The Woodland Cemetery: Toward a Spiritual Landscape* (Stockholm: Byggförlaget 1994).

Francis, Mark, Hester Jr, Randolph, *The Meaning of Gardens* (Cambridge, Mass.: MIT Press, 1990).

Haney, David, *When Modern was Green: Life and Work of Landscape Architect Leberecht Migge* (London and New York: Routledge, 2010).

Howard, Ebenezer, *Garden Cities of To-Morrow* (London: Faber and Faber, repr., 1946).

Imbert, Dorothée, *The Modernist Garden in France* (New Haven: Yale University Press, 1993).

Ingersoll, Richard, and Kostof, Spiro, *World Architecture: A Cross Cultural History* (New York: Oxford University Press, 2013).

Reed, Peter, *Groundswell: Constructing the Contemporary Landscape* (New York: Museum of Modern Art, 2005).

Treib, Marc, *Modern Landscape Architecture: A Critical Review* (Cambridge, Mass.: MIT Press, 1992).

Treib, Marc, and Imbert, Dorothée, *Garrett Eckbo: Modern Landscapes for Living* (Berkeley: University of California Press, 1997).

Tschumi, Bernard, *Cinégramme folie: le Parc de la Villette* (Princeton Architectural Press, 1987).

Waldheim, Charles, *Case: Hilbersheimer / Mies van der Rohe, Lafayette Park Detroit* (New York: Prestel, 2004).

11. Terrain Vague

Brae, Ellen, *Beauty Redeemed, Recycling Post-Industrial Landscapes* (Berlin: Birkhauser, 2015).

Chemetoff, Alexandre, *Visits: Town and Territory, Architecture in Dialogue* (Basel and Boston: Birkhauser, 2009).

Clément, Gilles, *Le jardin en movement. De la Vallée au jardin planetaire* (Paris: Sens & Tonka, 5th ed., 2007).

Corner, James (ed.), *Recovering Landscape: Essays in Contemporary Landscape Architecture* (New York: Princeton Architectural Press, 1999).

Girot, Christophe, and Imhof, Dora (eds), *Thinking the Contemporary Landscape* (New York: Princeton Architectural Press, 2016).

Le Roy, Louis, *Natuur uitschakelen-natuur inschakelen* (Deventer: Ankh Hermes, 1973).

McHarg, Ian, *Design with Nature* (New York: The Natural History Press, 1969).

Meadows, Donella, Meadows, Dennis, and Randers, Jørgen, *The Limits to Growth: The 30-Year Update* (White River Junction: Chelsea Green, 2004).

Scott, Emily, and Swenson, Kirsten, *Critical Landscapes* (Los Angeles: University of California Press, 2015).

Smithson, Robert, *The Collected Writings*, Flam, Jack (ed.) (Berkeley: University of California Press, 1996).

Solà-Morales, Ignasi de, 'Terrain Vague', in Davidson, Cynthia C. (ed.), *Anyplace* (Cambridge, Mass.: MIT, 1995), 118–23.

Waldheim, Charles (ed.), *The Landscape Urbanism Reader* (New York: Princeton Architectural Press, 2006).

12. Topology

Cache, Bernard, *Earth Moves. The Furnishing of Territories*, trans. Boyman, Ann (Cambridge, Mass.: MIT Press, 1995).

Corner, James, and Hirsch, Alison (eds), *The Landscape Imagination: Collected Essays of James Corner 1990–2010* (New York: Princeton Architectural Press, 2014).

Cosgrove, Denis, *Mappings* (London: Reaktion, 2002).

Freytag, Anette, *Dieter Kienast, Stadt und Landschaft lesbar machen* (Zurich: GTA Verlag, 2016).

Girot, Christophe, Freytag, Anette, et al., *Landscript 3: Topology* (Berlin: Jovis Verlag, 2013).

Leatherbarrow, David, *Uncommon Ground. Architecture, Technology, and Topography* (Cambridge, Mass.: MIT Press, 2000).

Leatherbarrow, David, *Topographical Stories. Studies in Landscape and Architecture* (Philadelphia: University of Pennsylvania Press, 2004).

Lin, Maya, *Topologies* (Artist and the Community) (Winston-Salem: Southeastern Center for Contemporary Art, 1998).

M'Closkey, Karen, *Unearthed: The Landscapes of Hargreaves Associates* (Philadelphia: University of Pennsylvania Press, 2013).

Orff, Kate, *Toward an Urban Ecology, SCAPE Landscape Architecture* (New York: The Monacelli Press, 2016).

Radkau, Joachim, *Nature and Power: A Global History of the Environment*, trans. Dunlap, Thomas (Cambridge and New York: Cambridge University Press, 2008).

Saunders, William S. (ed.), *Designed Ecologies: The Landscape Architecture of Kongjian Yu* (Basel: Birkhauser, 2012).

Acknowledgments

I would like first to thank my parents, Antoine and Annie, who raised me in England and then in France, close to 'Capability' Brown's Richmond Park and Le Nôtre's park at Versailles; without such memories, and the many travels thereafter, the founding thread of this book could not have been twined. My gratitude extends also to my school colleagues, students and teachers across continents – without them I would not have reached this point of maturity and reflection on the subject of landscape architecture. I would also like to thank my clients, as well as the collaborators and partners who have worked with me throughout my variegated professional practice, contributing invaluable experience to my knowledge of the design field.

Without generous support from the ETH in Zurich, this book would not have seen the light of day. My thanks extend particularly to President Ralf Eichler, the ETH School Board and Brigitte Schiesser of the Legal Department for their unflinching support in difficult times, when my previous publisher went bankrupt.

I am very grateful for the support received from the entire team at the Chair of Landscape Architecture of the ETH from the outset of this project. I would like to thank first and foremost Arley Kim for her engagement, dialogue and care in the early stages of the book. Her help in the conceptual phase with the choice of case studies, through to the first draft manuscript with its wonderful 'pinwheels' was invaluable. The project initially began when Martina Voser scouted up the Sacred Way at Delphi attesting to the sublime power of this Pythian site; she was followed by Anne Devaux, who searched relentlessly through ancient Sumerian and Greek literature, revealing the symbolic meaning of ploughing in all its depth. The Theory Lab then followed, with Anette Freytag, Albert Kirchengast and Dunja Richter engaging actively in the nascent debate on the subject of landscape topology. My thanks extend more particularly to the talent and contributions of Ilmar Hurkxkens, Magda Kaufmann, James Melsom and Elsa Tamvakera, of the LVML and Design Lab, who produced elaborate 3D models for each case study with beautiful renders and animations. Without repeated testing, cross-exchanges and long critical discussions, this book could never have reached this milestone of depth, quality and precision in illustration. In the closing stages, my thank goes to Marco Cascianneli for his perseverance at unravelling the best possible image sources under strenuous circumstances.

Without Georg Gerster's invaluable collection of key landscape sites taken from the air, this book could not have achieved the proper conceptual resonance it now has. I would like to thank him particularly for all the time spent selecting his precious slides and making them digitally available for this book. The case study of the Faiyum could never have been illustrated without the photographic mission led by Ben Gitai, who managed to follow the Bahr Yusuf from El Lahun in the Nile Valley all the way to Lake Moeris. I would like to thank him for the outstanding quality of his pictures that capture so well the mood of this extraordinary landscape artefact. I would like to thank also Jacques Feiner for making his sublime pictures of the landscapes of Yemen available for publication. A particular thanks goes to Pierre David who allowed us to publish a picture of the Cedron Valley in Jerusalem taken by his late son Simon. I am also very grateful to Johannes Rebsamen who cycled all the way down from Zürich to ascend Mont Ventoux and take a picture. Last but not least I would like to thank all the landscape offices that have graciously made pictures of their projects available for publication.

I am grateful more particularly to Lucas Dietrich, who immediately grasped the significance of this book from our first encounter at Thames & Hudson. I would like to thank all his team, beginning with Sam Wythe who took the entire rough manuscript through a very thorough and thoughtful copy-editing process. My thanks go also to Sarah Vernon-Hunt, for her unrelenting patience, understanding and highly professional editorial support over the past two years, as well as to Maria Ranauro for her incredible resourcefulness with images, and to Paul Hammond for his skilled work on production of the book. I would like to thank particularly Al Rodger at Praline for the constructive critical exchanges we had, his patience and the beautiful comprehensive layout that has resulted.

Finally, I would like to thank my daughters Celeste and Hannah for their enthusiasm, trust and alertness throughout this endless project. May their fascination for creative discovery prevail above all things. Last but not least, I would like to thank my wife Yael for her loving support and endurance through all the ups and downs of the past seven years. May she now discover this book for the first time, as a token of my love and dedication, and as an invitation towards new horizons together.

Sources of Illustrations

Index

Aarhus University 28, 263; 1.25, 10.16
Abarkuh 120; 5.15
absolutism 187, 194–96, 209; 7.60, 7.64
Adams, Ansel 285; 11.4
Agence TER 302
agriculture 17, 46, 48, 52, 55, 56, 69, 71, 73, 76, 117, 129, 136, 138, 140, 145, 173, 178, 327; 2.12, 2.24, 2.26, 7.59, 8.11; birth of in the Fertile Crescent 45; spread by Etruscans 93; decline of in Mesopotamia 55; early development of 50; Egyptian 59; Faiyum 2.28; on Crete 71; pastoral 21, 117; 1.11a, 1.11b; Roman 94; Segesta 4.3
Aire River 326; 12.37
al-Andalus 138, 173; 5.45
Alberti, Leon Battista 202
Alexander the Great 89, 120; 3.45, 3.49, 3.51, 3.52, 5.15
Alexandria 89, 97, 105; 3.55, 4.12
Alhambra 138; 5.43, 5.45, 5.60; Court of Lions 5.52; Court of the Myrtles 5.42, 5.48, 5.49; Garden of the Partal 5.46
al-Idrisi, Muhammad 138; 5.56
Alphand, Adolphe 233, 245, 248, 252; 9.13, 9.22, 9.28, 9.30, 9.31, 9.34, 9.37, 9.39, 9.40, 9.46
AlpTransit see Sigirino Mound
Amazons 76; 3.22, 6.10
Ameratsu-omikami 311; 12.11
Amsterdam 174, 175, 178; 7.8; Schiphol airport 333; 12.47
anamorphism 176, 183; 7.6, 7.23
Andalucia 136; 5.45, 5.60
Andre, Carl 269; 10.30
Anthropocene 6, 13, 283
Antwerp 178; Cargo Hall 329; Park Spoor Noord 329; 12.42
Apollo 69, 76, 79, 83, 219; 3.31, 3.34–3.38, 3.42, 3.43, 3.47, 7.51, 8.50, 8.51
Apollo 8 281; 10.55
Appian Way 4.6, 4.8
aqueducts 53, 59, 94, 97; 2.1, 4.6, 4.8, 4.9, 4.23, 6.43
Arcadia 76; 8.22, 9.12, 11.18; birth of 91
archetypes 10, 19, 125; 1.5a, 1.5b, 5.47; forest clearing 10, 16, 19, 28, 30, 42, 112, 118, 125, 129, 181, 219, 255; 1.1, 1.5a, 1.8, 1.22, 1.23, 1.25, 1.51, 7.26, 7.37, 8.2; walled garden 10, 15, 19, 28–30, 33, 35, 42, 46, 53, 61, 88, 98, 112, 117, 125, 129, 101, 105–12, 138, 181, 266, 306, 335; 1.6, 1.30, 1.31, 1.34–1.37, 1.49, 10.23, 10.26, 11.33
Archimedes: screw 55; 5.45; Cave of 3.48
Arcueil, Vache Noire roof park 302; 11.39
Aristotle 88–89, 141
Artigues, Jaume 299
Ashurbanipal 45; 2.1, 2.10
Asplund, Gunnar 263; 10.15
Assyria 45, 53; 2.1, 2.17
astrolabe 141; 5.19, 5.57
Atelier Descombes Rampini (ADR) 326; 12.37
Atelier Dreiseitl 317; 12.22
Atelier Girot 12.24
Atelier Phusis 308; 12.8
Atget, Eugene 285; 11.3
Athena 83; 3.35, 4.35
Athens 76, 79, 83; 3.33; Charter 260
Atlanta, BeltLine project 329; 12.43
AUA 270
Auckland, Albert Park 9; 0.1
Avebury 15, 21–23, 306; 1.0, 1.10–1.13, 1.15–1.16, 1.18–1.21, 1.24; Ridgeway 23; Silbury Hill 21, 23; 1.11a, 1.11b, 1.16, 1.17, 12.35, 12.36; Swallowhead Spring 23; 1.11a, 1.11b, 1.17; West Kennet Long Barrow 21, 23; 1.11a, 1.11b
avenues 9, 252; 1.16, 1.45, 7.12, 7.59
axis 10.13, 162, 168, 183, 187, 188, 192, 202, 207, 224, 227; 7.23, 7.24, 7.37, 7.38, 7.43, 7.51, 8.65, 10.0, 10.41

Babel, Tower of 2.18
Babur, Emperor 30; 1.26, 12.2
Babylon 42, 53, 55, 88; 2.18; temple of Marduk 42
Bacon, Roger 136
Baden-Baden 97
Badminton 227, 228; 8.63, 8.64
Baghdad 140, 173; 5.45; House of Wisdom 138, 140; 5.55
Bagh-i Fin 33–36; 1.32–1.37, 1.40–1.47; Qajar pavilion 1.47; Suleyman Spring 33; 1.32, 1.34, 1.35, 1.36, 1.37, 1.44
Bagh-i Wafa see Garden of Fertility
Bagnaia 155; 6.21, 6.22, 6.25; see also Villa Lante
Baha' al-Din, Shayk 178; 7.12
Bahr Yusuf 59–65, 66; 2.28, 2.29a, 2.29b, 2.31, 2.32, 2.34, 2.35, 2.36, 2.38, 2.39
barbarians 112, 115, 122, 125; 4.42, 5.17
Barcelona 28, 299; 3.13, 11.27–11.29; Barceloneta 299; 11.28,

11.30; Barrio Gotico 299; Botanical Garden 336; 13.3; Montjuïc 28, 336; 13.3; Parc del Laberint d'Horta 3.13; Plaça del Mar 299; 1.29
Barillet-Deschamps, Jean-Pierre 245
Baroque 18, 28, 35, 42, 168, 176, 178, 192, 202, 273, 330; 4.25, 6.48, 7.1, 7.8, 7.44, 7.45, 7.59, 7.60, 8.15, 8.27a, 8.27b, 8.63, 8.67, 9.11
BASE 12.46
Basel: 'Grün 80' garden show 208; 12.6; Merian Park Brüglingen 308; 12.6; Novartis Campus 302; 11.36
Bath 97; 4.7
baths 219; of Caracalla (Rome) 4.7; Roman 61, 97
Batlle i Roig 319; 12.23
Bauhaus 260, 265, 273; 10.8
Bausch, Pina 302; 11.35
Beemster Polder 174, 197; 7.4, 7.5
Beijing 66, 317; 7.62; Fragrant Hills 248; University campus 311; 2.10; Western Mansions 197; 7.62
Belgrand, Eugène 245
Berlin 13, 15, 238, 245, 252, 262, 286; 9.6, 9.14, 9.18, 10.18; Charlottenburg 238; Hansaviertel 270; Horseshoe Estate 259; 10.4; Invalidenpark 308; 12.8; Marzahn 262, 10.12; Mauer Park 13; 0.9; Schöneberger Südgelände Park 13, 286; 0.6, 11.10; Siemensstadt 260; 10.8; Tiergarten 238, 241, 264; 9.2, 9.13, 9.16–9.19, 9.25; Wall 0.9
Bernini, Gian Lorenzo 7.53
Berthier, Jean-Baptiste 7.11
Beuys, Joseph 286; 11.9
Birkenhead Park 248; 9.42, 9.45
Black Sea 16, 21, 50, 51; see also Deluge
Blaisse, Petra 13.1
Blake, William 201; 8.1
Blenheim 228; 7.60, 8.65–8.67; Woodstock Park 224, 228
Bohigas, Oriol 299
Bohr, Niels 265
Bomarzo 168; 8.35; Sacro Bosco 168; 6.53, 6.54, 6.55
Bordeaux: Botanical Garden 302; 11.37; Parc aux Angéliques 330; 12.44
Boscoreale, Villa Arianna 4.1; 4.14
Boston 9.14; Arnold Arboretum 9.43; Back Bay Fens 252; 9.43; Emerald Necklace 252; 9.43; Franklin Park 252; 9.43
Boyle, Richard (Lord Burlington) 207; 8.12, 8.13, 8.19
Brandenburg 238; Muskauer Park 231; 8.72
Brasília 197, 262; Cultural Centre 10.13; Esplanade of Ministries 262; 10.13
Bridgeman, Charles 207, 209, 213, 227; 8.21, 8.26, 8.27
Broadacre 262; 10.14
Brown, Lancelot 'Capability' 202, 227, 228; 8.4, 8.21, 8.63, 8.64, 8.67, 8.68
Brunier, Yves 335; 13.1
Buddhism 306, 311; 3.51, 6.57, 12.10
Buenos Aires 252, 291; El Rosedal 9.41; Reserva Ecológica Costanera Sur 291; 11.14
Bureau des Paysages 302
Burle Marx, Roberto 269; 10.27, 10.28
Burlington, Lord see Boyle, Richard (Lord Burlington)
Bustamante, Jean-Marc 285; 11.7

Cairo 59, 136
Caldwell, Alfred 270; 10.34
calendar 52, 54, 57; 2.19; astrological 52
Canal: de Bourgogne 194; de l'Eure 194; de l'Ourcq 9.32, 10.40, 10.46, 10.47, 10.52; du Midi 66; 194; 2.41; Great Northern 59; Peripheral 66; 2.43, 10.19
Canaletto 227; 8.63
Canosa, Josep Luis 336; 13.1
Caracas, Parque del Este 269; 10.27
Carson, Rachel 6, 288
Cartesian 202; balance and symmetry 181; dualism 183; rules 219; diagrams 175; see also Descartes, René
Cartier-Bresson, Henri 285; 11.5
cartography 147, 174, 194, 197; 5.21, 6.5, 7.9
Cassini family 194
Castle Howard 204, 213; 8.3; Mausoleum 1.23, 8.23, 8.25, 10.6; Ray Wood 28, 168, 202; 1.23; 8.2, 8.3, 8.7, 8.22; Sea Horse Fountain 8.4; South Lake 8.7; Temple of the Four Winds 209; 8.23
Çatalhöyük 49, 52; 2.8, 2.9
Catalonia 127, 285, 299; 3.13, 5.0, 5.25, 11.7, 11.97; Garraf Waste Landfill project 319; 12.23
Celts/Celtic 19, 120, 125
Central Park 28, 42, 241, 252, 255; 1.51, 9.42, 9.44–9.48
chahar bagh 33, 129; 1.26, 1.26, 1.31, 1.32, 1.48, 5.3, 5.4
Chambers, William 227; 8.60
Chandigarh 197, 262
Charlotte, East Farm 270; 10.33
Chartres Cathedral 118, 120; 5.7, 5.14, 5.62
Chatsworth 168, 202, 228; 5.49, 6.48, 8.4, 9.5

Chemetoff, Alexandre 302; 10.52, 11.38
Cheonggyecheon River 314; 12.17
Chiswick House 28, 207, 209, 213, 219, 224; 1.24, 8.12–8.19
Christianity 35, 115, 117, 122, 125, 127, 129, 136, 143; 1.8, 4.45, 5.3, 5.4, 5.12, 5.13, 5.17, 5.38, 5.50
Chur, Fürstenwald cemetery 308; 12.7
Church, Thomas D. 266; 10.24
CIAM 260, 262, 263, 265, 270; 10.8, 10.10, 10.12, 10.13, 10.84
Ciliwung River 313; 12.14
Cistercians 117, 129; 5.0, 5.8a–c, 5.25, 5.26a, 5.26b, 5.29
Citeaux 127
Clément, Gilles 291; 11.16
climate 118; 1.5a, 1.5b, 5.61, 12.22; change 6, 9, 13, 16, 52, 281, 288, 291, 308, 317, 326; 1.2
Clos de Vougeot 127
Cohen, Preston Scott 338
Colbert, Jean-Baptiste 194; 7.54, 7.56
Cold War 6, 281
Conques 117; 5.2, 5.12; Abbey of St Foy 127; 5.24
Constructivism 10.0, 10.48
Copacabana 269
Copenhagen: green 'finger plan' 270; King's Garden 168; 6.52; Norrebro Park 338; 13.4
Copernicus, Nicolaus 147, 152, 153; 6.17
Corajoud, Claire 270; 10.36
Corajoud, Michel 270; 10.36
Cordoba 125, 136, 138, 140, 141; 5.44, 5.45, 5.58
Corinth 3.48; Gulf of 83; 3.26a, 3.26b, 3.46
Corner, James 288, 329; 12.41
Cor-ten 333, 336; 11.31, 12.49, 13.3
Costa, Lucio 197, 262
courtyards 71, 266; 5.51, 7.16, 10.23 Islamic 5.47; Roman villas 97–99
Crary, Jonathan 237
Crete 16, 17, 55, 69–71, 73, 76; 1.4, 3.1, 3.2–3.7, 3.11, 3.12, 3.14–3.17
Creuse 11.16
crops 21, 46, 49, 53, 55, 56, 57, 66, 125, 129; 2.25; barley 49; cereal 46, 99; grain 125; 'three-field' system 145; wheat 49; 3.10
Ctesiphon 89; 3.49
Cubism 270, 336
cults 51, 76, 120, 122; 3.19, 3.31; Apollo 3.31; chthonic 69, 79, 83; Demeter 73; fertility 17, 56, 71, 73, 83, 88; Gaia 3.31; Gothic forest 115; Hadrian and cult initiation 105; Isis 4.33; Lares 98; Nordic forest 115; tree 5.38
cuneiform script 54; 2.10, 2.21
Cyrus the Great 30; 0.4, 1.27, 1.28, 1.48, 4.41

Daedalus 3.8, 3.13
dance 16, 302; 7.17, 10.18, 11.35
Darwin, Charles 236; 9.8
Dasht-e Kavir see Great Salt Desert
Dasht-e Lut 33, 46, 206; 1.38
Davioud, Gabriel 245; 9.0
Davos 10, 28; 0.5, 1.22
Deconstructivism 273, 280–01; 10.37, 10.40, 10.44, 10.45, 10.54
deforestation 76, 204, 288
Deleuze, Gilles 283
Delphi 69, 76, 79–87, 88; 3.0, 3.25–3.45, 3.43, 3.56; Amphissa Valley 83; 3.26a, 3.26b, 3.35, 3.45, 3.46; Castalian Spring 79, 83; 3.25, 3.27, 3.36, 3.38, 3.40; Oracle (Pythia) 79, 83; 3.27, 3.28, 3.32, 3.38, 3.39, 3.46; gymnasium 3.34; Kerna Spring 79, 83; 3.25, 3.39; omphalos 79; 3.30, 3.31; Phaedriades mountains 79, 306; 3.26a, 3.26b, 3.27, 3.36, 3.40, 3.56; Sacred Way 79; 3.25, 3.27, 3.28, 3.38, 3.42; temenos wall 3.35, 3.42, 3.45, 3.47; temple of Apollo 83, 206; 3.38, 3.39, 3.42, 3.46, 3.47; Tholos of Athena 83; 3.33, 3.35; Treasury of the Athenians 3.28, 3.29
Deluge 16, 30; 1.2, 2.10; Black Sea 21, 45, 50; 1.3, 1.4
De Maria, Walter 269
Demeter 69, 73, 76, 79, 83; 3.10
Derrida, Jacques 273
Descartes, René 174, 175, 192, 197; 7.3
Descombes, Georges 326
desert 19, 33, 35, 46, 48, 53, 55, 56, 59, 61, 120, 206; 1.26, 2.0, 2.23, 2.24, 2.35, 4.46, 5.47; plateau of Iran 1.28
Desvigne, Michael 330; 12.44, 12.45
Detroit, Lafayette park 270; 10, 34
Dézalier d' Argenville 7.10
Domesday Book 118
Dordrecht 326, 327; 12.38
drainage 10, 56, 59, 143, 174, 330; 0.5, 2.23, 2.24, 5.61, 7.5
Duchamp, Marcel 257; 10.1
Duisburg 286; Nord park 302; 11.32, 11.33
Dungeness 30, 283, 293; 11.19; Prospect Cottage 293; 11.0, 11.19–11.26
Dutch Golden Age 173, 197; 7.8

Earth Summit 6
East India Company, Dutch 173, 174
Eckbo, Garrett 270; 10.33
ecology 217, 302, 311, 313, 314, 317, 319, 321, 330, 335, 336;
    12.31, 12.32, 12.41, 13.5
Eden, Garden of 16, 30, 53, 120; 1.30
Ehret, George Dionysus 8.61
Eiffel, Gustave 245; 9.34, 9.35
Einstein, Albert 257, 265
Eleusis 76, 79, 83; 3.10, 3.33; Mysteries 73; 3.20, 3.21
El Lahun 59; 2.29a, 2.29b, 2.31, 2.32
English style 231; 8.21, 9.11
Ensérune 143; Oppidum 5.63
Eridu 52, 55
Ermenonville 233, 238; 9.2
erosion 30, 76; 9.27
Essen 286; Schurenbach slag heap 299; 11.31; see also Ruhr
Etruscans 93, 98, 99
Euclid 88
Euphrates 49, 50, 52, 53, 55, 56; 2.7, 2.13, 2.15, 2.22, 5.22
Europa 71; 3.7

Faiyum Oasis 45, 48, 66, 59–65; 2.0, 2.28–2.31, 2.33–2.37b,
    2.39, 2.40; irrigation project 45
Ferrater, Carlos 336; 13.3
Fertile Crescent 30, 42, 45, 46, 49, 52; 2.7
fertility goddess 49, 51, 69, 71; 2.9, 2.13, 3.1, 3.10
Fibonacci, Leonardo 136, 147
Field Operations 288, 329; 11.13, 12.41
Figueras, Beth 336; 13.3
Fischer, Howard 11.8
Fisker, Kay 263
flood(s) 16, 45, 53, 55, 174; 1.44; Nile 48, 56, 61; 2.29a, 2.29b;
    control 7, 326–27; 12.38; see also Deluge
Florence 28, 148, 151, 153, 266; 6.12, 6.14, 6.15; Boboli
    Gardens 155; 6.56; Palazzo Pitti 6.56
Fontainebleau 168, 188; 7.43; Grand Canal 7.19
forest(s): ancestral 23; clearings 10, 16, 19, 28, 30, 42, 112,
    118, 125, 129, 181, 219, 255; 1.1, 1.5a, 1.8, 1.22, 1.23, 1.25,
    1.51, 7.26, 7.37, 8.2; derivation of word 28; medieval 5.10;
    dieback 6; Nuremberg 5.9; see also deforestation
fountains 129, 131, 148, 155, 157, 162, 194, 204, 219, 269, 306;
    4.17, 5.49, 5.43, 5.49, 5.50, 6.10, 6.26, 6.33, 6.35, 6.36, 6.37,
    6.38, 6.42, 6.45, 6.56, 7.16, 7.30, 7.51, 7.52, 7.58, 7.62, 10.30,
    10.43, 10.50, 11.5, 12.3–12.5; see also water
Fouquet, Nicolas 181, 187, 197; 7.20, 7.29
Fox, Charles 235
Franco, General 299; 11.27
Franquelin, J. B. 7.57
French Revolution 231, 243; 7.10
frescoes 99; 4.1, 4.13, 4.15, 4.20, 4.21; Knossos 73; 3.14, 3.16
Friedrich, Caspar David 235; 9.3

Gaia 79; 3.31
Galileo Galilei 147, 152, 153; 6.18
Gandhara 3.51
garden city 257, 259, 260; 10.2, 10.3, 10.8
Garden of Fidelity 30; 1.26
garden(s): absolutist 8.12; American 266; Anglo-Chinese 339;
    Assyrian 1.28; Babylonian 55; 1.28; Baroque 55, 174, 176,
    183, 187, 197, 201, 204, 209; 7.0, 7.61, 8.12, 8.55; botanical
    252, 302; 11.37; carpet 1.39; Chinese 169, 317; 12.19–12.21;
    cloister 125, 129; Cubist 260, 269; 10.7; derivation of
    word 0.7; Egyptian style 5.46; enclosed 1.51; English 204,
    207, 209; 8.11, 8.2, 8.7, 8.20, 8.28, 9.26; English Garden
    Movement 8.71; formal 178, 207; French 187, 197; 7.10,
    7.29, 8.55; gravel 11.25; hanging 53, 61; 2.1; Isfahan 178;
    Islamic 138; 5.49, 5.60; Italian 207; 6.51; Japanese 224,
    269; 8.59, 9.38, 10.26; Lucullus 99; Mannerist 6.53, 6.54,
    6.55; medicinal 122; 5.6; medieval 122–25; Ming 42, 248;
    1.49, 6.50; Minoan 42; modern geometric 270; Modernist
    266; moss 6.57; Mughal 35, 55, 181; Persian 101; 1.39,
    1.40; Picturesque 202, 207, 248; 8.23, 8.26, 8.55; pleasure
    53, 89, 97–99; Postmodern 11.26; Renaissance 28, 55, 92,
    168–69, 207, 209; 6.51, 6.52; rock 12.21; Roman 55, 94, 101,
    103, 112; 4.21; Taj Mahal 7.18; terraced 168; 'The Garden in
    Movement' 291; 11.16; walled 10, 15, 19, 28–30, 33, 35, 42,
    46, 53, 61, 88, 98, 112, 117 125, 129, 138; 101, 105–12, 181,
    266, 306, 335; 1.6, 1.30, 1.31, 1.34–1.37, 1.49, 10.23, 10.26,
    11.33; Zen 339; see also Kew Gardens; paradise
Gaudí, Antoni 5.31
Geneva 326; 12.37
geographic information system (GIS) 197, 286; 11.8, 12.29
geomancy 169; 5.20
geometry 33, 53, 57, 88, 136, 148, 162, 169; in gardens 35,
    122, 151, 157; 4.16
Ghinucci, Tommaso 155, 157; 6.21
Gibbs, James 8.22

Gilgamesh 45; Epic of 16, 30, 45, 53; 2.10, 2.13, 2.17
Giotto 115, 143; 5.1
Girardin, René Louis de 231, 233, 238; 9.2
Global Landscape Architects 313; 12,16
Goldsworthy, Andy 269, 291; 11.15
Göring, Hermann 263, 264
Gortyn 16, 17, 71; 1.4, 3.7
Gothic 122, 213; 5.17, 5.39
Goths 125; efforts to christianize 5.17
Granada 125, 138; 5.42, 5.43, 5.46, 5.48, 5.60; see also
    Alhambra
Grand Teton Mountains 266; 10.22
Grant Associates 280; 10.53
graphometre 177; 7.9
Gravel, Ryan 329; 12.43
Great Exhibition 9.5
Great Salt Desert 33, 138, 178; 1.32, 1.33a, 1.33b, 1.38, 1.45
Great Wall of China 112; 4.46
Greenaway, Peter 8.24
green belt 257, 259; 5.9, 9.14; Grünzug 238, 252; 9.14;
    Greensward' project 255
Grenoble, Parc Paul Mistral 302; 11.38
grid(s) 94, 174, 273; 0.8, 1.6, 4.5; Jeffersonian 43, 197, 262;
    1.50, 7.5, 7.63; Land Grant 10.14
Grimal, Pierre 98
groma 97, 155; 4.5
Gropius, Walter 260, 270; 10.8
Grotesque 204
grottoes 188, 245; 7.30, 7.34, 9.32
Guevrekian, Gabriel 260; 10.7
Gustafson Porter Landscape Architects 12.3
Gustafson, Kathryn 306; 12.3

Haag, Richard 302; 11.32, 11.34
Hades 73; 3.10, 3.20
Hadhramaut Mountains 46; 2.6
Hadrian, Emperor 105, 112, 219; 2.7, 4.26, 4.27a, 4.27b, 4.39,
    8.50; Hadrian's Wall 112; 4.42
Hadrian's Villa 93, 98, 101, 105–12; 4.0, 4.26–4.35, 6.58;
    Canopus canal 105; 4.0, 4.31–4.35, 4.38; Maritime Theatre
    4.28, 4.36; Piazza d'Oro 4.39, 4.41; Poecile 4.28–4.31, 4.37,
    4.38; Serapeum 105; 4.31–4.33; Thermal Baths 105
Haerle, Christoph 0.8
Hafez of Shiraz 15, 138, 306; 12.2
ha-has 207; 8.20, 8.29, 8.30
Halicarnassus, Mausoleum of 3.22
Hambledon Hill 19; 1.7
Hamburg 28, 259; Stadtpark 28, 259; 10.6
Hamilton Finlay, Ian and Sue 270; 10.35
Hampton Court 168, 197; 7.60
Hanover 265
Harappan civilization 50
Harbaqa Dam 49; 2.7
Hargreaves Associates 313; 12.13
Harvard University 270, 286; 11.8; Tanner Fountain 269; 10.30
harvest 16, 46, 52, 53, 56, 117, 125, 136; 2.5, 5.7, 5.61; cult/
    rituals 51, 76; 2.14, 3.9
Haussmann, Baron 245
Hawara 61; 2.40
Hawksmoor, Nicholas 202, 213; 8.2, 8.7, 8.23, 8.25
hedges 98, 207, 213, 308; 4.17, 4.25, 7.44, 7.45, 8.14, 8.18,
    10.32; box 181, 207; 5.3, 5.4, 7.25–7.27, 10.25; Cubist 270;
    hedgerows 187, 204; 8.11, 8.42; hornbeam 181; 6.48, 6.49,
    6.52, 7.27, 7.35, 7.36; see also topiary
Heidelberg, Hortus Palatinus 168
Heimatschutz 265
Heimatstil 264
Heizer, Michael 269; 10.29
Hellenistic civilization 89, 91, 97, 101, 105; 4.12, 5.57
henges 19, 21–23; 1.10–1.13, 1.15, 1.16, 1.18–1.21; see also
    Stonehenge
Heraclitus 88
Hercules 91; Farnese 188; 7.39, 7.40, 7.43
herms 188; 7.37, 8.13, 8.14
Herning, Geometrical Garden 270; 10.32
Herrenhausen 197
Hesiod 91
High Line 329; 0.6, 11.10, 12.41
Hilberseimer, Ludwig 270; 10.34
Hippodamus 7.63
Hiroshima 265; 10.21, 10.26
HNS 326, 333
Hoare, Henry 224, 248; 8.59
hoes 49, 59; 2.2, 2.37a, 2.37b
Hogarth, William 219, 265
Holbein, Hans 174, 176; 7.6
Homer 91; 3.13
Horn, Rebecca 11.30

hortus conclusus 35, 99, 125, 153
Howard, Ebenezer 257–59, 260, 262; 10.2, 10.3, 10.9
Høyer, Steen 338; 13.4
Huangpu River 317; 12.19
humanism 105, 145, 197, 202; 7.39, 7.40
Humboldt, Alexander von 236; 9.7
hunting 19, 71, 243; 4.12, 6.1, 7.11
Huygens, Christiaan 174; 7.2
Huyghe, Pierre 283; 11.1
Hyères see Villa Noailles
hygiene 97, 235; 9.21
Hypnerotomachia Poliphili 148, 157, 162; 6.11, 6.41, 6.46

IBA Emscher Park 299, 302, 336; 11.32, 11.34
Ida, Mount 71, 73; 3.4, 3.5
illusionism 181, 183, 187; 7.23, 7.31, 7.33, 7.34, 7.38–7.40, 7.46;
    see also trompe l'oeil
Impressionism 237
Indo-European 16; 1.3
industrialization 6, 22, 209, 235
Industrial Revolution 209, 227, 228, 235; 8.69
Indus Valley 46, 49, 50, 55
International Style 262
IPCC report (1990) 291
irrigation 30, 33, 35, 42, 45, 46, 48, 49, 50, 53, 55, 56, 59, 61,
    66, 71; 1.6, 1.33b, 1.34, 1.45, 2.0, 2.1, 2.6, 2.14, 2.15, 2.24,
    2.27, 2.28, 2.34, 2.37a, 2.37b, 2.41, 5.58; drainage 2.23;
    Egyptian 59; Euphrates 52; flood 46; 1.44; Islamic 136, 138;
    leaching 2.23; monastic 127; see also Faiyum Oasis
Irwin, Robert 333; 6.58, 12.49
Ise Naiku shrine 311, 339; 12.11, 13.5
Isfahan 178; 7.12; Ali Qapu palace 7.17; and Europe 178;
    Bazaar 7.14; Chahar Bagh 178, 181; Chehel Sotun 178; 7.13;
    Hasht Bihisht 178; Khajou bridge 178; 7.15; Maidan 178;
    7.14, 7.16; Shah Mosque 7.14, 7.16; Si-o-seh Pol 178; 7.15;
    Friday Mosque 5.59; Ustadh Iwan 5.59
Ishtar 45, 51, 71; 2.13, 2.14
Islam 12, 30, 35, 124, 125, 136–43
Ismantorp ringfort 1.9
Ittingen 117; 5.3, 5.4

Jackson Hole, Resor House 266; 10.22
Jarman, Derek 283, 306; 11.0, 11.19, 11.20, 11.22, 11.23, 11.26
Jarmo 45, 46, 52
Jericho 45, 49, 52
Jerusalem 10, 124; 0.3, 5.22
Joseon kingdom, Korea 336; 13.2
Joseph Canal see Bahr Yusuf
Judaism 35, 173, 174, 178; 5.53

Kabul 30; 1.26
Kamogawa River 214
Kampung Melayu 12.14
Kandinsky, Wassily 273
Karkas mountains 1.32, 1.33a, 1.33b, 1.35, 1.36, 1.37, 1.42
Karlsruhe 197; 7.59
Kashan 33, 35, 56; 1.32, 1.44, 1.45
Kassel 197; Documenta 283; 11.1, 11.9
Kent, William 201, 204, 207, 209, 213, 219, 224, 227, 228;
    8.0, 8.8, 8.9, 8.12, 8.13, 8.19–8.22, 8.26, 8.27a, 8.27b, 8.30,
    8.33–8.37, 8.47, 8.48, 8.63
Kew Gardens 227; Oriental Garden 227; 8.60; Pagoda 227;
    8.60; Palm House 227; 8.62
Khan, Ali Mardan 7.18
Kienast, Dieter 270, 308; 12.6, 12.7
Kiev, Pechrsk Lavra Monastery 311; 12.9
Kiley, Dan 270; 10.33
Knossos 17, 71, 73; 3.8, 3.11–3.14, 3.16
Kyoto 314, 317, 335; 6.57, 8.57, 13.0; Kamogawa 314; 12.18;
    Saiho-ji temple 168; 6.57; Shimogamo Shrine 314

labyrinth 71; 3.8, 3.13
Lady and the Unicorn tapestry 117; 5.5
Lafayette, General 197
Lanci device 155
Land Art 269, 285, 333
Lange, Gustav 0.9
Lange, Willy 10.20
laser scanning 321; 12.28
Latour, Bruce 335
Latz, Peter 302; 11.32
Law of Universal Gravitation (Newton) 201, 204; 8.5, 8.6
Le Brun, Charles 187; 7.20
Le Clézio, J. M. G. 9
Le Corbusier 148, 197, 260; Plan Voisin 260, 10.10; Ville
    Radieuse 260, 262, 263; 10.9, 10.11
Leeghwater, Jan 174; 7.5
Leibnitz, Gottfried Wilhelm 192, 283

L'Enfant, Pierre Charles 197; 7.63
Lenné, Peter Joseph 238, 241, 248, 252; 9.11, 9.13, 9.15, 9.31
Le Nôtre, André 181, 187, 197; 7.20, 7.47, 7.53–7.56, 7.60, 7.63
Lepenski Vir 50; 2.11
Le Roy, Louis 286
Letchworth 259; 10.3, 10.4
Le Vau, Louis 187; 7.20
Lewerentz, Sigurd 263; 10.15
Liébana, Beatus de 5.22
Ligorio, Pirro 148, 157, 168; 6.10, 6.53, 6.54, 6.55
Limmat River 313; 12.15
Lin, Maya 305; 12.1
Linnaeus, Carl 227, 235; 8.61
Lisbon 178; Ribeira das Naus shipyard 313–14; 12.16
Little Sparta 270; 10.35
London 207, 227, 245, 255; 8.14, 9.6; Crystal Palace 235;
    9.5; Diana, Princess of Wales Memorial Fountain 306;
    12.3–12.5; Hampstead 259; Hyde Park 231, 241, 306; 9.5,
    12.3–12.5; Regent's Park 235; 9.4; Serpentine 306;
    12.4; St James's Park 231; 8.71
London, George 7.60, 8.4
Lorenzetti, Ambrogio 147; 6.2
Lorrain, Claude 209, 224; 7.1, 8.10, 8.55, 8.56
Los Angeles 66, 270; 2.43; Getty Center 168, 333; 6.58, 12.49;
    Getty Villa 105; 4.16, 4.25
Louis XIV 66, 187, 194; 7.29, 7.47, 7.51, 7.53, 7.54, 7.57, 7.58,
    12.45
Lucullus 99
Lüneberg Heath 288; 11.12
Luopans 124; 5.20
Lyon, Parc Blandan 330; 12.46

McHarg, Ian 286
Madrid: Rio project 329; 12.40; Salon de los Pinós 329
Malia 73; 3.19
Mannerism 168; 6.53, 6.54, 6.55
Mansart, Jules-Hardouin 7.51
Manzanares River 329; 12.40
maps/mapping 54, 145, 147, 176, 177, 286, 305; 5.21, 7.8, 7.9;
    Cantino map 147; 6.5; Carte des Chasses 177; Delmarva
    Peninsula Project 286; 11.8; La Nouvelle France 197; 7.57;
    mappae mundi 124, 257; 5.22; al-Idrisi's world atlas 5.56;
    prayer 124; SYMAP system 286; 11.8
Marey, Étienne-Jules 10.1
Mari 53; 2.22
'Marly, Machine de' 194; 7.58
Marrakesh 46; Oasis 2.2, 2.3
Marville, Charles 285; 9.25
Massachusetts, Berkshire Boardwalk 311; 12.12
Matala 71; 3.6
mathematics 35, 53, 54, 66, 88, 136, 145, 148, 173, 175, 178,
    202; 2.20, 7.6
Mattern, Hermann 270
'Maunder Minimum' 197
Mauryan Empire 55
meadows 306, 308; 12.7, 12.24, 12.34; alpine 10
measurement 53–55; of time 53; 2.19; see also calendar
Mecca 141; 5.57, 7.14; Ka'ba 124; 5.19
Media 46, 49, 50, 55, 99; 2.11
Medicis 99, 148, 153, 168; 6.12, 6.13, 6.14, 6.15, 6.20;
    Catherine de' 187; Marie de' 168; 6.56
Medina Azahara 138
Melbourne 326
Menzel, Otto 10.6
Mercator, Gerhardus 147, 176
Mesa, Virgin River 269; 10.29
Mesara Plain 71, 73; 3.3, 3.6
Mesolithic 21
Mesopotamia 10, 30, 46, 48, 49, 50, 51, 52, 55, 57, 66, 71,
    99; 2.21, 2.23
Middle Ages 42, 115, 117, 118, 120, 122, 124, 136, 138, 141,
    257; 4.45, 5.9, 5.11, 5.61, 5.62; legacy of 143
Mies van der Rohe, Ludwig 266, 270; 10.22, 10.34
Migge, Leberecht 259, 260; 10.4
Miletus 88–89; 3.50, 7.63
Ming dynasty 42, 169; 1.49, 4.46, 6.50
Minneapolis, General Mills Entry Landscape 288; 11.11
Minoan civilization 17, 51, 55, 69–73, 93; 3.1, 3.2, 3.8,
    3.11–3.14, 3.18, 3.19, 3.23
Modernism 259, 260–66, 270, 280; 10.8, 10.24, 10.28, 10.33
Moeris, Lake 59; 2.28, 2.36
Mohenjo-Daro 55
Moller, C.F. 263
monasteries/monasticism 28, 42, 117, 118, 125–27, 129, 138,
    143; 5.3, 5.4, 5.8a–c, 5.27, 5.29, 5.37
Monreale Cathedral 138, 143; 5.50
Montady, Étang de 5.63
Morales, Ignasi de Solà 283

Mosbach, Catherine 302
Moschino, Simone 6.53, 6.54, 6.55
Moscow 260
Moses, Robert 263, 264
motorways 264, 329; 10.20
MRIO arquitectos 329
Mudéjar architecture 5.59
Mughals 30, 35, 55, 178, 181; 1.26
Munich 28, 241; Englischer Garten 28, 231, 241; 9.16, 9.20
Muñoz, Juan 11.29
Muthesius, Hermann 259
Muybridge, Eadward 10.1
Mycenae/Mycenaeans 59, 71, 73–76; 3.23
mythology 71, 101, 151, 245; 7.37, 7.43, 8.10, 8.15, 9.0, 10.55;
    Egyptian 7.1; Greek 89; 3.4, 3.15, 3.54; and landscape 98,
    148; Norse 120

Nacktkultur 264; 10.18
Naginski, Erika 338
Napa Valley 266; 10.24
Naqsh-e Rustam 3.52
Nash, John 235; 8.71, 9.4
Nasrid dynasty 138; 5.48, 5.60
navigation 141, 145, 147, 174; 5.19, 5.57, 6.5
Nazis 6, 264–65
NEAT 319
Neoclassicism 238
Neolithic 21, 23, 45, 52, 69, 288; 1.10, 1.11a, 1.11b, 1.7–1.9,
    11.12, 11.22
Neo-realism 285
Nevada 269; 10.29
New Orleans 326
New River 8.25
Newton, Isaac 201–02, 204, 208, 219, 227; 8.1, 8.5, 8.6, 8.42;
    Law of Universal Gravitation 201, 204;.8.5, 8.6; Newtonian
    revolution 202–07; 8.69
New York 245, 248, 255, 263; 0.6, 1.51, 9.6, 9.13, 10.17; Fifth
    Avenue 255; Frick Collection 266; 10.23; Manhattan 255,
    329; 9.44, 9.48, 12.41; Meatpacking District 329; 12.40;
    Museum of Modern Art 10.54; National 9/11 Memorial
    222; 12.48; Ocean Flood Barrier 326; 12.39; Prospect Park,
    Brooklyn 243; 9.21, 9.46; Staten Island 326; 12.39; see also
    Central Park and High Line
Niemeyer, Oscar 197, 262
Nile 57, 59, 61, 89, 105; 2.28, 2.35, 2.36, 4.33, 5.22, 7.1;
    Delta 2.30; Valley 61; 2.29a, 2.29b, 2.30, 2.32; flood 48, 56,
    61; 2.29a, 2.29b; mosaic 4.12; see also Faiyum Oasis
Nineveh 45, 53, 61; 2.1, 2.10
Noguchi, Isamu 269; 10.26
Nouvel, Jean 276
Nuremberg 5.9; Zeppelinfeld stadium 264; 10.19

oasis 33, 48; 2.2, 2.3, 2.7, 5.52; see also Faiyum Oasis
Olmsted, Frederick Law 243, 248, 252, 255; 9.13, 9.21,
    9.42–9.46
OMA 13.1
orchards 45, 46, 52, 59, 61, 117, 118, 125, 129, 147; 1.6, 4.13,
    4.26, 4.27b, 5.0, 5.29, 5.35, 6.4, 6.13
Orsini, Francesco 6.53, 6.54, 6.55
Osiris 56; 4.33, 7.1
Ottoman Empire 178
Oudolf, Piet 329
overgrazing 76, 145, 157, 204, 288; 11.12

Page, Russell 266; 10.23
palaestra 101, 103; 3.34, 4.24, 4.38
Palestrina see Praeneste
Palissy, Bernard 168
Pan 91; 3.55, 8.43–8.45
paradise 15, 30, 33, 35; garden 10, 33, 53, 76, 103, 138, 151,
    181, 306; 1.6, 1.28, 1.29, 1.30, 1.33, 1.46, 11.33
Parc de la Villette 257, 273–74, 276; 10.0, 10.38–10.52
Parc des Buttes-Chaumont 28, 233, 243–48, 252; 9.0,
    9.22–9.39
Paris 28, 187, 238, 252, 255, 262, 270, 330; 9.2, 9.6, 9.13,
    9.14, 9.40, 9.41, 10.10, 10.30, 10.36; Bois de Boulogne 231, 236,
    241; 9.9; Bois de Vincennes 241; Boulevard Périphérique
    273, 276; 10.39a, 10.39b, 10.40; Canal St Martin 9.40;
    Exposition des Arts Décoratifs 260; Exposition Universelle
    243; Jardin du Luxembourg 168; 6.56; Plan Voisin 260;
    10.10; Porte d'Italie 11.3; Tuileries gardens 168; UNESCO
    garden 269; 10.26; see also Parc de la Villette and Parc des
    Buttes-Chaumont
parkways 263, 266; 10.17, 10.20
Parnassus, Mount 79; 3.0, 3.26a, 3.26b, 3.27
parterres 155, 162, 207; 1.48, 6.23, 6.26, 6.34, 6.35, 6.51, 6.58,
    7.10, 7.18, 8.4, 10.7; embroidered 181, 192; 7.10
Pasargadae 10, 30, 89; 1.27, 1.28, 1.40, 1.48; River 0.4

Pascal, Blaise 173, 192
Pasolini, Pier Paolo 3.9
Passaic River 285; Fountain Monument 11.5
Pastoral style 243; 8.71
Pataliputra 55
paths 19, 23, 155, 194, 207, 238, 241, 243, 248, 260, 269; 1.31,
    6.31, 6.39, 8.19, 8.58, 9.27, 9.29, 9.44; asphalt 245, 263; 9.17,
    9.28, 9.31; broadwalk 311; 12.12; 'cinematic' 273; 10.38,
    10.44, 10.45; circuit 224; 8.59; cruciform 162; forest 162;
    6.47, 8.51; pilgrim 115, 169; 5.12, 5.62; serpentine/winding
    213, 219, 255, 273; 8.2, 8.9, 9.22, 9.23b; raised/suspended
    280; 10.42
patte d'oie 177, 194, 197, 241; 7.63, 7.64, 8.12, 8.18
pavilions 1.41, 1.43, 1.47, 8.2, 8.57
Paxton, Joseph 235, 248; 9.5, 9.42, 9.45
peristyles 98, 99, 103, 105, 129, 140; 4.17, 4.20, 4.25, 4,29,
    4.37, 4.39, 5.48, 5.50, 7.51
Persephone 69, 73; 3.10, 3.20
Persepolis 3.52
perspective 145–71, 176, 181, 183, 202, 207, 227; 6.6,
    7.21–7.24, 7.29, 7.32–7.34, 7.37, 7.38, 7.41, 7.53, 7.56, 8.56
Peterhof, Monplaisir Palace 197; 7.61
Peter Walker Partners 333; 12.48
Petrarch 143, 145; 5.64
Phaistos 17, 42, 71, 73; 3.3, 3.15, 3.17; Disc 71; 3.18
philosophy 112, 173, 175, 213, 293; 11.4; Greek 88
Picturesque 71, 168, 192, 202, 204, 209, 224, 227, 233, 238,
    241, 243, 248, 336; 7.1, 8.10, 8.15, 8.22, 8.23, 8.24, 8.25,
    8.54, 8.60, 12.19
plants 19, 30, 73, 99, 202, 235, 236, 264, 321; 3.12, 8.60–8.62,
    9.36, 10.28, 11.14, 11.21, 11.25, 11.37, 12.19; bougainvillea
    333; 12.49; fig 7.49, 7.50; iris 3.14; lily 219; 3.16, 4.1; lotus
    46; medicinal 120, 122; 5.6; myrtle 46, 138; oleander 4.14;
    papyrus 61, 89; 3.54, 4.11; roses 30, 46, 138, 306; 3.13, 5.3,
    5.4, 5.60, 6.52; sea kale 11.24; tulips 46
Plato 88
plough 46, 52, 94, 118, 145; 2.12, 4.3, 5.61
Poblet, Santa Maria de 115, 127–35; 5.0, 5.25–5.41; derivation
    of name 5.28; lavabo 129; 5.36, 5.40, 5.41
point clouds 321; 12.29, 12.33
Pompeii 42, 93, 99, 101–03; 4.1, 4.18, 4.22, 4.23, 4.24; House
    of Julia Felix 4.17, 4.19, 4.20
Ponte, Alessandra 336
Pope, Alexander 201, 204, 209, 213; 8.8, 8.9
Porcinai, Pietro 266; 10.25
Postmodernism 270, 280; 10.36
Potsdam 238, 248; Bornstedt church 9.12; Ruinenberg 9.12;
    Sanssouci park 238; 9.11, 9.12; Gardener Academy 238
Poussin, Nicolas 173, 209; 7.1, 8.56
Praeneste (Palestrina) 98, 105; 4.12
Priapus 56, 101; 4.21
Princen, Bas 285, 293; 11.2, 11.18
PROAP 313; 12.16
Pückler-Muskau, Prince Hermann von 231; 8.72
Pythagoras 88, 89

qanats 33, 49, 56, 59, 138; 1.31, 1.33b, 1.36, 1.44, 2.4, 2.27

Reed Hilderbrand 311; 12.12
Reichsautobahn 264–65; 10.20
religion 23, 49, 52, 311; 0.3, 2.12, 3.21, 3.22; at Çatalhöyük 49;
    Zoroastrianism 51; Minoan 71; see also Christianity
Renaissance 28, 35, 42, 105, 141, 145–71, 181, 207, 235, 245;
    4.25, 6.49, 6.57, 8.15, 11.36
renaturalization 12, 317; 12.33, 12.36
Repton, Humphry 228, 231; 8.70a, 8.70b, 8.72
Rhine: Valley 302; River 112; 4.43
Riebicke, Gerhard 264; 10.18
Rio de Janeiro 269; 10.28
Riquet, Pierre-Paul 194; 2.41
rites 23, 52, 105, 120; 1.7, 1.8, 1.15, 3.19, 3.21; Christian 124,
    125; funerary 1.8; Greek 56; harvest 76; 3.9; mortuary 1.7;
    polytheistic 19; purification 3.37; Pythian 83; ritual building
    4.36; ritual gatherings 19; 1.15, 1.18; Roman 56
Rococo 204
Roman: civilization 35, 71, 89, 93–103, 105, 125; 3.54; Empire
    94, 97, 101, 112, 115, 125; 4.5; garden design 94, 101, 103;
    Republic 98, 99; 4.6; roads 94, 97; 4.6
Romanesque 5.16, 5.24
Romanticism 238, 248; English 228; German 9.3
Rome 17, 42, 93, 94, 99, 101, 168, 219, 285; 4.3, 4.7, 4.8, 4.9,
    4.12, 4.15, 4.40, 5.22, 6.51, 7.1, 8.10, 11.5; Campus Martius
    99; Capitoline Hill 4.10; fall of 112, 115; Forum 4.10, 4.18;
    founding of 94; 4.2; Palatine Hill 94; Pantheon 227; 8.17;
    Via Sacra 4.10
Rotterdam: Museum Park 335; 13.1; Schouwburgplein 273,
    280; 10.37, 10.54
Rotzler Krebs Partner 313

Rousham 201, 213, 219, 224; 8.0, 8.26–8.43; Apollo's Glade 8.27a, 8.27b; Bowling Green 213, 219; 8.27a, 8.27b, 8.29, 8.31, 8.32, 8.35, 8.36, 8.42, 8.44, 8.46; Cold Bath 219; 8.51, 8.52; Concave Slope 8.34, 8.37, 8.38, 8.42; Eyecatcher 213; 8.29, 8.35; Gothic Seat 8.30, 8.42; Octagon Pond 8.41, 8.43, 8.45; Palladian Doorway 8.30; Praeneste Terrace 219; 8.39, 8.40, 8.41, 8.43, 8.46, 8.50, 8.51; Pyramid Meadow 219; 8.27a, 8.27b, 8.36, 8.37; Temple of Echo 219; 8.49, 8.52, 8.53; Venus's Vale 168, 219; 8.27a, 8.27b, 8.40, 8.41, 8.43, 8.44, 8.46, 8.48
Rousseau, Jean-Jacques 219, 231, 233, 235, 238, 241, 326; 9.2, 9.3; Rousseau Island, Tiergarten 238; 9.15, 9.19, 9.25
ruderal movement 286; 11.10
Rudofsky, Bernard 7
Ruhr 299, 302, 336; 11.31, 11.35
Ruisdael, Jacob von 174; 7.7

Saarinen, Eero 10.33
Saclay, Plateau 330; 12.45
sacro bosco ('sacred wood') 28
Sadi Carnot, Nicolas Léonard 236
Safavids 178; 1.32, 7.12, 7.13
Saiho-ji, Kyoto 168, 6.57
St: Augustine 115, 117; Benedict 115; Francis 115, 117; 5.1
St Gall plan 122; 5.23
St Petersburg 197; 7.61
Saint-Hilaire, Geoffroy 236
salinity/salt 52, 55, 56, 66; 2.23, 2.24, 2.36
Samarra 140; 5.54, 5.55
San Francisco: Bay 313; 10.24; Crissy Field 313; 12.13
Santiago de Compostela 5.2, 5.12, 5.24
Scapestudio 326
Sceaux 192, 194; 7.54–7.56
scenography 181, 194, 213, 219, 224; 8.33, 13.3
Scharoun, Hans 270; 10.8
Scheemakers, Peter 8.33
Schinkel, Karl Friedrich 238
Schmitthener, Paul 264
Schreber, Moritz 259
Schumacher, Fritz 259; 10.6
Schweingrüber Zulauf 13; 0.8
Sckell, Freidrich Ludwig von 241; 9.20
Seattle 11.32; Gas Works Park 302; 11.34
Segesta 79, 91; 3.24, 4.4; Doric Greek temple 3.53
Seifert, Alwin 264–65; 10.20
Sennacherib, King 53
Seoul: Cheonggyecheon River Park 314; 12.17; Seonyudo Island Park 336; 13.2
Serra, Richard 299; 11.31
Sesklo 50
sexagesimal system 53–54; 2.19
shaduf 56, 61; 2.26
Shah Abbas 33, 143, 178; 1.32, 1.33a, 1.33b, 7.12, 7.17
shakkei principle 224; 8.57
shamans/shamanism 69, 71, 120, 127
Shanghai: Expo 2010 317; Houtan Park 317; 12.19
Shibam 46, 59; 2.4, 2.27
Shintoism 311
Shiraz 15, 138; Musalla Gardens 306; 12.2
Shugaku-in 224, 227; 8.57
Sialk, Tepe 33, 51, 56; 1.32, 1.44, 2.14
Sigirino Mound, Ticino 319–21, 305; 12.0, 12.24–12.27, 12.29–12.34
Silbury Hill see Avebury
Silk Road 42, 147, 178
Singapore: Bishan-Ang Mo Kio Park 317; 12.22; Future Cities Laboratory 313; Gardens by the Bay 280; 10.53
Sitio 269; 10.28
slaves/slavery 48, 89, 94 98, 187, 228
Smith, Adam 228
Smithson, Robert 269, 285; 11.6
Socrates 101
Sonoma, Donnell House 266; 10.24
Sørensen, Carl Theodor 168, 263, 270; 1.25, 6.52, 10.16, 10.32
South–North transfer 66, 2.42
Speer, Albert 264; 10.19
Stegmann, Povl 263
Steinitz, Carl 286; 11.8
Stockholm 270; Skogskyrkogården cemetery 263; 10.15
Stonehenge 19, 21; 1.8
Stourhead 224, 227, 248; 8.54–8.59; and English landscape style 224, 227; Pantheon 224; 8.54; temple of Apollo 8.56, 8.57
Stowe House 207, 209, 224, 228; 7.60, 8.20–8.22; Elysian Fields 224; Temple of British Worthies 168
Studio Associato Secchi 329; 12.42
Stürmer, Johann Heinrich 9.18
Sualem, Rennequin 194; 7.58

Sumerian civilization 53, 55, 66; 2.10
surveying 54, 55, 59, 61, 94, 174, 177, 194, 197, 245; 2.15, 4.5, 7.57; advanced 319, 321; devices 187; 7.48; see also graphometre; groma; Lanci device and laser scanning
Suzhou 169, 248; 1.49, 6.50
Sylvestre, Israel 7.24, 7.29, 7.34
Syracuse 89, 97; 3.48, 3.55; Arethusa Spring 4.11

Tacitus 112, 140; 4.44
Taj Mahal 178; 7.18
Tarrasó, Olga 299; 11.28
Tati, Jacques 270; 10.31
Taut, Bruno 259; 10.4
terraces 9, 46, 93, 118, 129, 168, 181, 183; 0.2, 1.48, 5.25, 5.27, 5.29, 5.32, 6.12, 6.39, 6.51, 7.0, 7.25–7.28, 7.30, 7.32, 7.41, 7.44, 7.45, 8.27a, 8.27b; 12.0; Delphi 83; Egypt 56, 59, 61; irrigated 45, 49, 55; Villa Lante 155, 157; 6.34, 6.39, 6.43
Terragni, Giuseppe 266
terrain vague 283–302, 306; 0.9, 11.1–11.3, 11.5, 11.7, 11.13, 11.18, 11.19, 11.23, 1.27, 11.31, 11.35; definition of term 283
Tessenow, Heinrich 259, 264
Thays, Carlos 252; 9.41
Thebes, Egypt 15, 30; 1.1, 1.29
theme parks 8.59; Disneyland 248
Thompson, Benjamin 241
Thoreau, Henry David 311
Thurgau, Hochäcker fields 5.61
Tianjin, Qiaoyuan Westland Park 317; 12.20, 12.21
Tigris, River 52, 53, 55; 2.13, 3.49, 5.22
Titian 145; 6.1
Tivoli 148; 6.10; see also Hadrian's Villa
Toledo 138, 178; 5.51
tombs 56, 129, 263, 306; 0.3, 12.2; of Cyrus the Great 30, 1.27; of Meketre 30, 1.29; of Nebamun 15; 1.1; 'tholos' 71
topiary 98, 151, 181, 294; 0.2, 4.16, 4.19, 4.20, 4.25, 6.48
topography 15, 16, 23, 35, 46, 97, 174–78, 207, 219, 224, 248, 283, 319; 1.25, 3.11, 3.25, 4.32, 5.61, 7.54, 9.22, 9.30, 12.7, 12.46, 13.1
Toronto 291; Tommy Thompson Park 288; 11.13
trade 7, 46, 49, 76, 140, 178; 6.19; routes 30, 42, 46, 99, 138, 147, 148; triangular slave 153, 187; see also Silk Road
tree(s): almond 46; 5.0, 5.29; apple 46; apricot 46; ash 120; 5.11; beech 15, 21; 8.68; birch 120, 194, 288; cedar of Lebanon 252; 8.16, 9.36; chenar 1.41; cherry 329; chestnut 12.0; citron 99; citrus 46, 138; 4.15, 7.49, 7.50; cypress 30, 33, 99, 129, 266, 306; 0.3, 1.28, 1.41, 1.47, 3.45, 4.13, 5.15, 5.31, 8.16, 8.19, 9.12, 10.25; date palm 1.1, 2.25, 2.38; destruction of 53; fig 46; fruit : 93, 98; ginkgo 252, 308, 311; 2.10, 9.36, 12.10; hazel 120; 5.35; healing properties 120; hinoki cypress 311; 12.11; holly 5.5; lilac 311; 12.9; lime/linden 21, 120, 308; 5.14, 8.4, 8.66; Lombardy poplar 7.55, 9.12; lotus 311; 12.10; Moreton Bay fig 9; 0.1; nut 93; oak 21, 120, 227, 263, 266, 308, 311, 333; 1.10, 1.25, 5.13, 8.64, 9.12, 10.24, 11.9, 11.37, 12.48; olive 46, 83, 93, 99, 101; 0.2, 0.3, 2.2, 3.11, 3.35, 4.13, 4.40, 9.12; orange 66, 306; 5.46, 5.58, 5.60, 7.30, 12.2; palm 46, 59; 4.14; Parkinsonia 11.28; peach 46, 99; pear 46; pine 329; 4.15, 10.15; plane 35, 71, 99, 252; 3.7; plum 46; pomegranate 30, 46; 1.1, 1.30, 2.3, 3.20; sacred 19, 120; sequioia 8.46; sycamore fig 1.1, 1.29; yew 181; 7.25, 7.27, 8.32; Yggdrasil 120
triangulation 53, 147, 151, 174, 177, 187, 194, 197; 2.15, 2.19, 6.5, 7.9, 7.11, 7.48, 7.63
tribes 53; barbarian 122; Cheruschi 112; Dorian 76; Germanic 4.43; Indo-European 1.3; Medes 546; nomadic 21, 45, 52; Scythia 76; Semitic 1.3; tribal forest cultures 125; Turkic 1.3
Tribolo, Niccolò 153; 6.15, 6.20, 8.33
trigonometry 88, 141
trompe l'oeil 207, 213; 8.30; see also illusionism
Tschumi, Bernard 273, 276; 10.39a, 10.39b, 10.49
Turenscape 317; 12.19, 12.20
Turner, J.M.W. 233, 236, 237; 9.1, 9.10
Turrell, James 269
Tyre 71; 3.6

Ubaid culture 52, 55
Umayyads 136, 138
Unwin, Raymond 259; 10.3
Ur 52, 53, 55; 2.23; Standard of 2.16; ziggurat 52
Urban Renewal 10.34
Uruk 45, 52, 53, 55

Vanbrugh, John 202, 204, 209, 213, 228, 312; 8.2, 8.7, 8.23, 8.66, 8.67
Van Valkenburgh, Michael 288; 11.11
Vatican, Belvedere 6.51, 12.7
Vaux, Calvert 243; 9.21, 9.44

Vaux-le-Vicomte 28, 42, 173, 181–92, 194, 197, 204, 227; 1.48, 6.58, 7.0, 7.20–7.46 , 8.38; Grand Canal 7.43
veduta 151
Venetian school 145
Venice 147, 148, 151, 178
Ventoux, Mont 143, 145; 5.64
Venus 219; 8.43, 8.45
Vera, Paul 260
Verrazzano, Giovanni da 7.57
Versailles 192, 194–97, 330; 7.11, 7.18, 7.30, 7.37, 7.47–7.53, 7.58; Fountain of Apollo 7.51; Grand Cascade 7.61; Latona Fountain 194; 7.52; Orangerie 194; 7.49, 7.50, 7.53; Parterre du Midi 194; 7.53; Pièce d'Eau des Suisses 7.53
Viganò 329; 12.42
Vignola, Jacopo 153, 155; 6.21, 6.22
Villa: Castello 28, 151, 153, 168; 6.15, 6.16, 6.44; d'Este 148, 153; 6.10; I Collazzi 266; 10.25; La Petraia 151; 6.14; Medici, Fiesole 151, 168; 6.12; Poggia a Caiano 151; 6.13
Villa Lante 28, 145, 168, 181, 188; 6.0, 6.58, 7.37, 8.3, 8.38; il conservone 8.3; Deluge grotto 6.0
Villa Noailles: Grasse 9, 0.2; Hyéres 260; 10.7
Villandry 168, 192; 6.51
villas 42, 93–113, 168, 207; 8.19, 9.4; Roman 4.25,.26, 4.39
Villepinte, Parc du Sausset 270; 10.36
vineyards 117, 118, 125, 127, 129; 5.25, 5.34, 12.0
Virgil 91, 93, 94, 98; 3.53
Visigoths 127; 5.26a, 5.26b
vistas 207, 224, 241, 276; 8.57, 9.2
Vogt Landscape Architects 302; 11.36
Volksparks 259, 260

Walker, Peter 269, 333; 10.30, 12.48
walls 46, 101; 0.9, 5.27; adobe 33; 0.4, 1.28, 1.6, 1.31, 1.46, 1.47, 2.4; crenellated 5.35; cyclopean 76; defensive 129; fortification 3.23; temenos 69–91, 306; 3.35, 3.42, 3.45, 3.47, 5.35, 8.20, 12.7
Washington, D.C. 197; 7.63, 7.64
water: Albolafia water wheel 136; 5.44; basins 181, 219; 1.40, 3.39, 3.40, 4.22, 4.25 4.29, 7.23, 7.28; canals 49, 52, 53, 59–65, 105, 173, 174, 183, 188, 194; 2.28, 2.29a, 2.29b, 2.31, 2.32, 2.34–2.36, 2.38, 2.39, 2.43, 4.0, 7.8, 7.30, 7.32, 7.41, 7.47, 7.51, 7.61, 9.32, 9.40, 10.38, 10.40; cascades 183, 245; 7.54, 7.61, 8.48, 9.32, 10.26; cisterns 49, 56; 0.2, 4.20, 5.25, 5.27, 5.30, 5.32–5.34; dams 9, 49, 59, 61, 227; 2.6, 2.7; ditches 9, 19, 21, 23, 317; 1.12, 1.17, 1.18, 1.19; divider 2.5; drainage 59, 174, 317; 0.5, 2.24, 4.20, 5.61; dykes 59, 174; 7.7; -elevating methods 45; hydrology 94, 97; levees 49, 52, 53, 173, 241, 326; moats 7.42; polders 174, 175, 326; 7.8; ponds 188, 245, 311; 1.1, 1.24, 1.29, 6.57, 7.33, 13.0; pools 33, 79, 83, 219; 1.35, 1.36, 1.37, 1.43, 4.7, 4.25, 4.29, 4.37, 5.42, 5.49, 6.48, 6.50, 7.0, 7.13, 7.33, 7.35, 7.36, 12.22; pumps 173, 174; 7.58; reflecting qualities 5.42, 5.49; reservoirs 8.3; rills 30, 35, 49, 53, 219; 0.5, 1.28, 1.40, 8.53; sound of 5.46, 9.32; storm- 317; 12.22; troughs 30, 46, 52; watermills 140; wells 46, 49, 120, 124
Wenders, Wim 302; 11.35
West 8 280, 329; 10.37, 10.54, 12.40
wheel 52; potters' 52; water 136; 5.44
windmills 173, 174; 7.7
Wise, Henry 227; 7.60, 8.4
Wittfogel, Karl 46
Wordsworth, William 228, 235
World War: I 259; 10.5; II 6, 262, 264; 11.10
Wright, Frank Lloyd 262; 10.14
Wright, Thomas 202; 8.6
writing 53, 54, 66, 120; 2.22

Xinjiang 140

Yangzte River 59
Yazd, Iran 19, 33; 1.6, 1.31, 1.50
Yellow River 66; 2.42
Yggdrasil 120
Yosemite National Park 91; 11.4; El Capitan 3.56
Yu, Kongjian 317

Zeus 71; 3.4, 3.5, 3.7, 3.30
ziggurats 52; 2.18, 2.23
Zoroastrianism 51
Zurich: Hardtum stadium 291; 11.17; Letten 313, 314; 12.15; Oerliker Park 13; 0.8